VMware Horizon Suite

Building End-User Services

VMware Press is the official publisher of VMware books and training materials, which provide guidance on the critical topics facing today's technology professionals and students. Enterprises, as well as small- and medium-sized organizations, adopt virtualization as a more agile way of scaling IT to meet business needs. VMware Press provides proven, technically accurate information that will help them meet their goals for customizing, building, and maintaining their virtual environment.

With books, certification and study guides, video training, and learning tools produced by world-class architects and IT experts, VMware Press helps IT professionals master a diverse range of topics on virtualization and cloud computing. It is the official source of reference materials for preparing for the VMware Certified Professional Examination.

VMware Press is also pleased to have localization partners that can publish its products into more than 42 languages, including Chinese (Simplified), Chinese (Traditional), French, German, Greek, Hindi, Japanese, Korean, Polish, Russian, and Spanish.

For more information about VMware Press, please visit **vmwarepress.com**.

vmware PRESS
Official Cert Guide
VCAP5-DCA
Essential Virtual SAN
Networking for VMware Administrators
Official Cert Guide
VCP5-DCV

VMware Horizon Suite

Building End-User Services

Stephane Asselin
Paul O'Doherty

vmware® PRESS

Upper Saddle River, NJ • Boston • Indianapolis • San Francisco
New York • Toronto • Montreal • London • Munich • Paris • Madrid
Capetown • Sydney • Tokyo • Singapore • Mexico City

VMware Horizon Suite

Published by Pearson Education, Inc.

Publishing as VMware Press

ISBN-10: 0-13-347908-0

ISBN-13: 978-0-13-347908-9

Library of Congress Control Number: 2014907775

Printed in the United States of America

First Printing: June 2014

Warning and Disclaimer

Every effort has been made to make this book as complete and as accurate as possible, but no warranty or fitness is implied. The information provided is on an "as is" basis. The authors, VMware Press, VMware, and the publisher shall have neither liability nor responsibility to any person or entity with respect to any loss or damages arising from the information contained in this book or from the use of the CD or programs accompanying it.

The opinions expressed in this book belong to the author and are not necessarily those of VMware.

Special Sales

For information about buying this title in bulk quantities, or for special sales opportunities (which may include electronic versions; custom cover designs; and content particular to your business, training goals, marketing focus, or branding interests), please contact our corporate sales department at corpsales@pearsoned.com or (800) 382-3419.

For government sales inquiries, please contact governmentsales@pearsoned.com.

For questions about sales outside the U.S., please contact international@pearsoned.com.

ASSOCIATE PUBLISHER
David Dusthimer

ACQUISITION EDITOR
Joan Murray

VMWARE PRESS PROGRAM MANAGER
David Nelson

DEVELOPMENT EDITOR
Ellie Bru

MANAGING EDITOR
Sandra Schroeder

SENIOR PROJECT EDITOR
Tonya Simpson

COPY EDITOR
Keith Cline

PROOFREADER
Paula Lowell

INDEXER
Lisa Stumpf

EDITORIAL ASSISTANT
Vanessa Evans

COVER DESIGNER
Chuti Prasertsith

COMPOSITOR
Trina Wurst

Dedication

Stephane and Paul worked many long hours to bring together their thoughts, ideas, and experience to collaborate on this project. They would like to dedicate this book to the readers who have provided feedback, support, and insight to their work, thus enabling them to develop and deliver great content.

Contents

Introduction

Writing this book has been a challenge because of the speed of change in the VMware end-user computing software products. When we first talked about the idea of writing about Horizon Suite, Mirage had just been acquired, Workspace was a 1.0 product, and the current release of View was 5.1. It is hard to believe that the evolution of the product line has happened so quickly in a little over a year. With the release of Horizon Suite 6, the need for a book that covers VMware View, Mirage, and Workspace has never been greater, so the effort was worth it.

Much greater than our challenge is the challenge for you, the reader, who is facing a world in which desktop management has become the management of stateless, mobile, streamed desktop or mobility tablet and smartphone workspace management. One might wonder whether in this age of readily available content, along with a plethora of how-to videos, a book dedicated to understanding these technologies has value.

We asked ourselves the same question, and when we reflected, we considered all the times that we really learned something. In reflecting, we realized that we learned the most when we got information that was relevant to what we were doing and was easy to understand and that stepped us through what we really needed to know and allowed us to understand 80% of what was important while leaving the 20% for us to look up. It is with this attitude that we approached our topics to save you some time and ease the learning process.

In approaching each topic, we have considered architecture, deployment, and operations, which represent the key understanding that you need to deploy each product within the Horizon Suite comfortably. We have also considered the important integration points between the products, such as delivering View or ThinApp through Workspace. Based on feedback, we have also looked at some critical areas of interest to our readers such as VMware View and Microsoft Lync integration and PC over IP (PCoIP) offloading technologies.

VMware has done much innovation at the infrastructure level that delivers key competitive advantages. Topics such as virtual software-area networking (SAN) and other performance accelerators are considered in addition to vSphere features such as View Storage Accelerator. Although we have covered much, some topics will have to wait until the next release, such as vCenter Automation Center for Desktops. As always, your feedback and support is key in determining what topics make it into the next release.

Motivation for Writing This Book

As fast as *VMware View: Building a Successful Desktop* was completed, the market evolved from virtual desktop infrastructure to end-user computing. The difference is that end-user computing takes into account all end-user services and not just desktop requirements. Addressing all end-user computing requirements cannot be done with a single product and requires a suite of products. Horizon is that answer. There was, however, no comprehensive guide to the suite, so we have pulled together expertise, experience, and resources to develop *VMware Horizon Suite: Building End-User Services.*

It is our hope that after reading this book you will be equipped with a more thorough understanding of how to deploy the components of Horizon Suite. We also hope that in reviewing each product you will understand how to match up the solution with the requirement. Each component of Horizon is targeted toward a user requirement; a better understanding of the features and capabilities ensures that they are deployed to meet the right use case. For example, VMware Mirage is designed to address the complexities in managing a distributed desktop environment, whereas Workspace is designed for user mobility and device independence. In bringing together this information under a single publication, we hope to simplify the learning process and shorten your timeframe. Stephan and I polled our subscribers and learned that there was strong interest in certain areas. We have addressed those explicitly, such as in our chapters reviewing View and Lync integration as well as multimedia options. By stepping you through the architectural and design considerations for View, Workspace, and Mirage, we also hope we can save you some time by avoiding common missteps or pitfalls by sharing our own experience with these products.

Who Should Read This Book

This book is targeted at IT professionals who are involved in delivery of end-user services from an enterprise, managed service, or provider perspective. Those individuals who might already be comfortable with VMware View should read this book to understand the other products of Horizon Suite, such as Mirage or Workspace.

How to Use This Book

If you are looking for knowledge on a particular product (View, Workspace or Mirage), you can read just the relevant chapters. We have approached the topics starting with the familiar View, and then the closely related Workspace, and then Mirage to help you develop an understanding of Horizon Suite. This book is split into 12 chapters, as follows:

- **Chapter 1, "The New End-User Model":** The chapter covers the evolution of the end user and an introduction to Horizon Suite.
- **Chapter 2, "VMware View Architecture":** This chapter covers the architecture of VMware View 6.
- **Chapter 3, "VMware Workspace Architecture":** This chapter covers the architecture of VMware Workspace 1.8.

- **Chapter 4, "VMware View Implementation":** This chapter covers the installation of VMware View 6.
- **Chapter 5, "VMware Workspace Implementation":** This chapter covers the installation of VMware Workspace 1.8.
- **Chapter 6, "Integrating VMware View and Workspace":** This chapter covers the integration of VMware View and Workspace.
- **Chapter 7, "View Operations and Management":** This chapter covers the most common VMware View operations.
- **Chapter 8, "VMware Workspace Operations":** This chapter covers the most common VMware Workspace operations.
- **Chapter 9, "VMware Horizon Mirage":** This chapter covers VMware Mirage architecture and installation.
- **Chapter 10, "Multimedia":** This chapter covers how to deliver multimedia within a View desktop environment.
- **Chapter 11, "Integrating Lync and VMware View":** This chapter covers the integration of Microsoft Lync and VMware View.
- **Chapter 12, "Performance and Monitoring of VMware Horizon":** This chapter covers performance monitoring of VMware View.
- **Appendix A, "A Design Questionnaire Worksheet":** This is a comprehensive design checklist for end-user computing.
- **Appendix B, "VMware View Network Ports":** Network diagrams showing the configuration for VMware View for an internal deployment and one that has components in the DMZ and clients connecting from the Internet.

Bonus e-Chapter

Technology is ever changing, at a pace where it's not easy to keep up with all the changes. This couldn't be truer at VMware. Just take a look at the releases of VMware View within the past 12 months: three minor releases and one major release, which was just recently announced publicly. VMware View 6 is a game-changer. It has multiple new functionalities and major improvements in the end-user experience and the delivery of high-end graphics. VMware added a major component that delivers full integration of Microsoft Windows Remote Desktop Services Hosts (RDSH) in this release, which at the time of this writing was not yet public.

For this reason, we decided to dedicate an electronic chapter on application virtualization. In this chapter, we cover various aspects of AppVirt, including how to deliver hosted applications using View 6. This feature delivers fully integrated applications and server-based desktops running on Microsoft RDSH. In addition, it will also provide Windows applications seamless window access from Windows or OS X clients. View with hosted applications will give full-screen access to Windows apps from iOS and Android devices to enable mobility in this critical era of cloud computing. The simplicity of this solution is that it leverages existing technology using standard Horizon clients (Windows, OS X, iOS, and Android) with PCoIP.

We firmly believe that even though we were not able to provide this chapter within the book at the time of release, it is important enough to provide electronically. With the purchase of *VMware Horizon Suite: Building End-User Services*, you receive access to the electronic chapter "Application Virtualization: How to Configure and Integrate Application Virtualization and VMware Hosted Applications," available for download at www.informit.com/store/vmware-horizon-suite-building-end-user-services-9780133479089.

About the Authors

Stephane Asselin, with his 22 years of experience in IT, is an architect in the End-User Computing business unit at VMware. In his recent role, he had national responsibility for Canada for EUC planning, designing, and implementing virtual infrastructure solutions and all processes involved. At VMware, Stephane has worked on EUC presales activities, internal IP, and he has worked as a technical specialist lead on beta programs. He has also done work as a subject matter expert for Horizon Workspace, View, Mirage, vCenter Operations Manager, and ThinApp projects. Previously, he was with Computer Associates as a senior systems engineer, where he worked on enterprise monitoring presales activities and as a technical specialist. As a senior consultant at Microsoft, he was responsible for the plan, design, and implementation of Microsoft solutions within major provincial and federal government, financial, education, and telcos.

In his current role in the EUC business unit at VMware, he's one of the resources developing enablement materials for all products of the Horizon Suite and technical documentation for training. Knowledge transfer to customers is a key element of his current role. Stephane has co-produced whitepapers such as "VMware Horizon Mirage Branch Office Reference Architecture" and "Horizon Workspace Reference Architecture." In addition, he runs the popular website myeuc.net.

Paul O'Doherty works for the CTO office of OnX enterprise solutions as a cloud solutions and EUC specialist, specializing in the architecture and delivery of cloud-based infrastructure and end-user services. Paul has written several books, including *VMware View 5: Building a Successful Virtual Desktop*, released by VMware Press. Prior to that, Paul spent 10 years as the managing principal consultant at Gibraltar Solutions architecting and delivering end-user computer and virtualization environments in Fortune 500 companies involving VMware, VMware View, Citrix XenApp, and XenDesktop technologies. Paul has a broad range of infrastructure experience and has achieved numerous industry certifications, such as VCP, CCEA, MCITP, and RCSP, and is recognized as a VMware vExpert. In addition, Paul maintains a popular blog at http://virtualguru.org and has contributed to sites such as http://virtualization.info and is reoccurring speaker at VMUG sessions and other technical conferences.

Acknowledgments

This is my third project where I have had the opportunity to publish, but it is the first where I'm co-author with a good friend. In the past, I have contributed chapters, but sharing the full writing responsibility has been a whole different ball game.

When Paul and I spoke, I knew that this was the right project for us to bring our experience together to create a good reference for others. This, of course, could not have been possible without the contributions and review of our own tech editors, Justin Venezia and Mike Barnett. Technical review is a critical piece in developing a project like this. In addition to the direct support of our technical editors, I want to thank a number of people for their support and guidance, including Simon Long, a colleague and avid blogger (www.simonlong.co.uk), Michael Burnett at Nutanix, and Todd Methven, an HP end-user client expert who has contributed to our lab and enabled us to test all the ideas and concepts we had. In addition, I would not have been able to dedicate the time without the support and understanding of my manager at VMware, Andrew Johnson.

I also want to thank my supporting team for providing the opportunity and effort to get this book done: Joan Murray, Ellie Bru, as well as my friend and co-author Paul O'Doherty.

My biggest support group is my family, who continue to support all of daddy's crazy projects. I would like to thank my wife, Marie-Josée, for her incredible patience and understanding, and finally, my three, not "so little anymore" kids: Vincent, Raphaelle, and Guillaume.

—Stephane Asselin

After writing my first publication, *VMware View: Building a Successful Desktop*, I was elated by the response and support I received from the people who invested in it. I was equally excited about the changes in the VMware product line that transformed a virtual desktop product into an entire end-user computing suite. Trying to cover the entire Horizon Suite would not have been possible if I had not been able to engage my good friend Stephane as co-author. I was also relieved when my original editing team, Joan Murray and Ellie Bru, offered their continued support. (Why they do not run in the opposite direction whenever I come up with a new idea still puzzles me.) I also want to thank Tonya Simpson and Seth Kerney, who worked hard to put this book together. In addition to this great team, we were lucky to work with two knowledgeable and experienced technical editors, Justin Venezia and Mike Barnett. My thanks goes out to them for keeping us both focused and honest. Writing a book can be challenging, but I found the experience of writing with this group a real pleasure, which is a measure of their professionalism.

My greatest appreciation goes to my wife, Heather, and family, who even after the time asked on the first book were willing to provide unwavering support on the second. My two wonderful girls, Briar and Hannah, never complained about the time spent writing and kept me motivated with their enthusiasm and encouragement for this project.

I hope that our efforts translate to a greater level of understanding of Horizon Suite for those of you reading this book. I would also like that if in reading this we save you a little time or help in your success so that you can pursue the things you are passionate about.

—Paul O'Doherty

Technical Reviewers

Justin Venezia is a consulting architect with VMware's End-User Computing Professional Services Engineering group. In this role, he actively participates in real-world delivery of EUC solutions to VMware customers, he supports VMware's EUC PSO organization with technical content development and enablement, and is involved in EUC engagement delivery. Prior to his role at VMware, Justin was a field architect with Citrix Consulting Services. He has also worked as an architect and IT manager in the healthcare and banking/financial verticals.

Mike Barnett is a systems engineer at VMware specializing in end-user computing. He has worked in IT for 11 years and has been working with VMware technology since 2008. Mike has presented at local VMware user groups as well as VMworld in 2011. He worked in the VMware Global Support Services organization supporting end-user products before moving into the field.

We Want to Hear from You!

As the reader of this book, *you* are our most important critic and commentator. We value your opinion and want to know what we're doing right, what we could do better, what areas you'd like to see us publish in, and any other words of wisdom you're willing to pass our way.

We welcome your comments. You can email or write us directly to let us know what you did or didn't like about this book—as well as what we can do to make our books better.

Please note that we cannot help you with technical problems related to the topic of this book.

When you write, please be sure to include this book's title and author as well as your name, email address, and phone number. We will carefully review your comments and share them with the author and editors who worked on the book.

Email: VMwarePress@vmware.com

Mail: VMware Press
ATTN: Reader Feedback
800 East 96th Street
Indianapolis, IN 46240 USA

Reader Services

Visit our website at www.informit.com/title/9780133479089 and register this book for convenient access to any updates, downloads, or errata that might be available for this book.

Chapter 1

The New End-User Model

The Evolution of the End User

VMware's product line has rapidly evolved to become a more complete end-user suite. VMware acquired Wanova and its flagship product Mirage. The founders of Wanova had extensive experience in wide-area networking (WAN) and had already developed and sold a WAN services company, Actona, which was acquired by Cisco. The experience in WAN optimization was the basis of the company name Wanova.

Mirage was designed to centralize and optimize desktops by providing layered image management over both local-area network (LAN) and WAN links. Endpoints are synced to a centralized virtual desktop (CVD) in the datacenter. The CVD is built using OS and application layers, in addition to a driver library that can be managed and changed. Any changes are synchronized back to the endpoint, enabling centralized management without sacrificing the decentralized execution of a traditional desktop environment.

VMware View, VMware's vSphere-based virtual desktop solution, provides online and offline access to desktops in the datacenter. Users can connect to virtual desktops running in the datacenter from various types of View clients. If the virtual desktop needs to be run in a disconnected/offline mode, users running Windows clients can check out the virtual machine (VM) so that it runs as a local mode desktop; changes to the desktop are synchronized to the datacenter when they reconnect. Unlike local mode desktops, Mirage does not make use of a hypervisor as it runs as an agent on a traditional XP or Windows 7 operating system. VMware announced that View would be part of the Horizon Suite, which thus consists of VMware View, VMware Mirage, and VMware Workspace.

VMware Workspace is targeted to delivering services in a way that is more tablet, mobile, and Cloud friendly. It was included in Horizon Suite to deliver a virtual workspace that provides a single portal for the user to access enterprise and Cloud-based applications, data services, and View desktops.

If you are currently considering deploying end-user computing (EUC), it is likely you will have requirements for all three: a virtual desktop delivered with View, mobile and tablet-based users accessing Workspace, and traditional desktops delivered through Mirage.

You'll see several terms in this book used interchangeably. When describing a virtual desktop, the text may refer to a virtual instance, View desktop, or (as previously mentioned) virtual desktop. When the text describes the larger View environment, you might see View infrastructure, virtual desktop infrastructure (VDI), or the abbreviation View. For VMware Mirage and Workspace, both Mirage and Workspace are used to reference the products. This book focuses on the core products and their related architecture. It is assumed that you have an understanding of vSphere and its related components, so this book does not cover these items.

This book covers VMware View, Mirage, and Workspace: their architectures, planning considerations, and how to properly install and configure each environment.

An End-User Service Catalog

Inevitably, the understanding of Cloud technology will become as fundamental as the understanding of virtualization is in IT today. One of the key concepts behind Cloud computing is the idea of a service catalog. A service catalog is not a VM or a collection of VMs, but rather a complete solution that the end user can consume. In making the transition from supplying virtual desktops to delivering services to end users, this is an important concept to understand.

How can you deploy virtual desktops, provide end-user-driven storage repositories, and integrate software-as-a-service (SaaS) applications and traditional Windows applications in a service? This is the value message of Workspace, which integrates all of these services.

You will see the idea of a service catalog used heavily in VMware Workspace, where a View desktop is one of the services you can offer. *Entitlement* is the term used across the end-user product line to enable a service for a user. In View, you entitle desktops to Active Directory users or groups. In Workspace, you entitle users to access different services to build a service catalog, as shown in Figure 1.1.

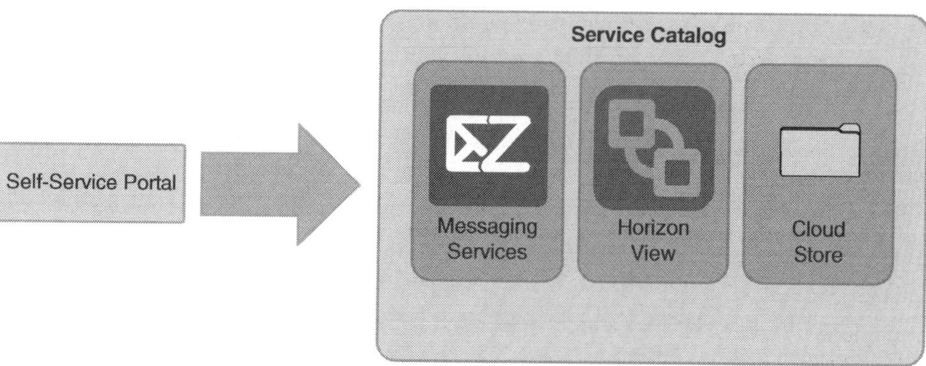

Figure 1.1 Service catalog

The post-PC era refers to the replacing of traditional desktops with mobile devices such as tablets and smartphones. Although businesses still largely use Windows-installed computers, tablets are now out-shipping desktops and laptops, even though they have been around for only three years. To make the transition to the post-PC era, you must consider entitling users to service catalogs, of which a View desktop is an important component.

By focusing on a service catalog, you can ensure that the planning you are doing now will enable you to service any type of end-user device without reengineering the entire environment. Even though a lot of Cloud-based apps are being developed, desktops will be around for some time because a large percentage of our day-to-day applications use traditional enterprise-based client-server applications. The goal of this book is to enable you to deploy a single framework that leverages VMware View, Workspace, and Mirage to deal with a multitude of end-user requirements.

How Do View, Mirage, and Horizon Workspace Deliver a Service Catalog?

Delivering a service catalog involves understanding what is delivered by each of the products within the Horizon Suite. When it was View, it was pretty straightforward. With Horizon Suite, you have View, Mirage, and Workspace.

VMware View

Each component of the Horizon Suite delivers different business value and meets different end-user requirements. View delivers virtual desktops running in the datacenter from a centralized vSphere environment. It provides several technologies designed to manage key components of the end-user experience: Persona for end-user data management, Composer for deployment and image management, and ThinApp to enable application delivery without interoperability problems. These technology components are managed through the View Connection Server to deliver a consistent and robust end-user experience, enabling the desktop to be delivered as a service.

VMware Mirage

Mirage provides centralized image management, and so is similar to Composer-created View desktops. However, it is installed as software in the operating system of the endpoint. Mirage runs an agent that synchronizes changes made to CVD, essentially providing uniformity to a distributed desktop environment. This enables desktop services to manage the CVD in the datacenter while the agent ensures consistency on all endpoints. Mirage enables you to extend your service catalog to deliver centralized management to a decentralized desktop environment. Mirage can support online desktops and laptops that might be offline or online as a full operating system runs on the endpoint. In addition, VMware now supports running Mirage in a virtual desktop environment.

VMware Workspace

Workspace provides an integration with View to enable you to present desktop-as-a-service (DaaS). In addition to presentation, it integrates other Cloud-like services, such as unifying web and Cloud and traditional Windows applications using ThinApp through a single portal. It also provides users an easy way to exchange files and documents by integrating data services. The integration of Workspace enables you to provide a complete suite of services with the flexibility to deliver to any device form factor. If the ideal end-user experience is a View desktop, you integrate and deliver it through Workspace. If the ideal end-user experience is direct access to web or Cloud applications, you can entitle these services in Workspace.

Considerations for Deploying View, Mirage, and Workspace

Each component of the suite is deployed very differently. Workspace comes as a vApp made up of five virtual appliances, whereas View and Mirage are more traditional installations. It is important to understand some of the considerations when deploying each.

VMware View

When deploying View, you have many things to consider. One of the first things to understand before getting into the design is what the business strategy is for the virtual desktops, as shown in Figure 1.2. Is it to replace physical desktops? Is it part of a bring-your-own-device (BYOD) initiative? Understanding the intended use enables you to properly plan the integration of virtual desktops in your environment. When you understand the use case, it is important to understand what services end users require; this factor will significantly influence your design.

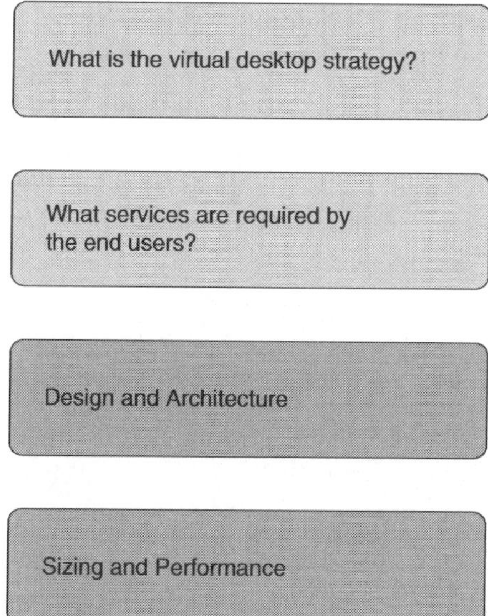

Figure 1.2 Considerations

How the use case can influence design is perhaps best illustrated with an example. In the first example, company XYZ runs several manufacturing plants in which computers are deployed throughout the shop floor and are used by various personnel throughout the day in 24-hour shifts. The primary application is used for text input to control various aspects of the manufacturing process. No information is stored on the computer.

The company has decided to use tablets to remove the need for fixed computer stations and to enable the operators to inspect the adjustments they are making within the computer program against what is happening on the line. A VMware View environment will be used to centralized the desktop and enable access through the tablets.

In the second example, company ABC is an engineering design company that designs large industrial flow and control pump replacement parts. The company would like to use VMware View to provide more flexibility for its engineers to design, regardless of where they are located. In addition, it wants to enable access to the engineer's desktops while they are consulting and reviewing aspects of the design with ABC's customers.

You can see clearly in these examples why knowing the use case upfront can have a large impact on the architecture and the design. For company XYZ, the end user would likely be classified as a light user, so resources might not be my primary concern, but View compatibility with the tablet device likely would be. For company ABC, 3D rendering can often pose problems if not considered carefully in the design. In addition, engineers are likely to require a significant amount of CPU and memory allocated to their View desktops.

VMware has significantly improved graphics capabilities in the platform and now offers three distinct types of video support:

- **Soft 3D and SVGA:** Software 3D Renderer and Super Video Graphics Array (SVGA) are provided through the VMware display driver. The Soft 3D and SVGA support is installed when you install the VMware Tools within the VM. Because it has no hardware dependencies, services such as VMotion and Distributed Resource Services (DRS) and the automation of VMotion are fully supported.
- **vDGA:** Virtual Direct Graphics Acceleration (vDGA) is a PCI pass-through to an underlying graphics card. It enables you to pass through the graphics processing of a VM to an underlying physical graphics card and dedicates a graphics processing unit (GPU) to the VM. The relationship between the VM and GPU is one to one. Because it is a one-to-one relationship, VMotion and DRS are not supported. It is a property of the VM, however, so to VMotion a VM, you can disable vDGA temporarily.
- **vSGA:** Virtual Shared Graphics Acceleration (vSGA) enables you to pass through the graphics processing of a VM to an underlying physical graphics card that has multiple GPUs or CPUs shared among VMs. The amount of video memory that can be assigned is restricted to 512 MB, but it does enable you to address the engineering requirements of ABC from within a virtual desktop. The configuration of vSGA is very flexible and can be set to Software, Hardware, or Automatic. The Software setting only uses vSphere software 3D rendering, even if physical GPUs are available in the host. VMotion and DRS are supported using this setting. Hardware is the opposite and forces the requirement of a GPU in the vSphere host. If one is not present, a VMotion will be restricted, and the VM may not be able to be powered on. Automatic is the option in the middle and enables you to switch from vSphere software 3D rendering to physical GPUs based on availability.

When you know the business strategy, it is easier to deduce which features are required for the end users. As alluded to in the preceding paragraph, the business case drives the use case, and the use case determines which features of View will be most critical to the users. An understanding of the features required also helps influence the design. For example, in company XYZ, stateless desktops (a desktop in which customizations or writes are not preserved between user logons) are likely ideal, which means that View Composer will likely be a key component of the architecture. View Composer enables a single image to be represented to many different users without requiring a full clone of the parent image for each virtual desktop. Through the use of a linked clone tree, a single 20-GB desktop image can be shared to multiple VMs while appearing to be an independent desktop OS to each user.

In addition, it is likely that View Blast would meet the requirement. View Blast is the integration of HTML5 support that was added in View 5.2 SP1. It enables the desktop to be delivered over a web browser that supports HTML5 without requiring the installation of a client. VMware recommends it for users who do not spend a significant amount of time interacting with the View desktop. For users who do spend hours working on their desktop, PCoIP (PC over IP) will provide the most robust high-fidelity experience.

For company ABC, if each engineer and designer has a specific set of tools, a dedicated full-clone desktop (the relationship between the end user and assigned View desktop is preserved along with any user changes between logons) that is associated with each individual user is more appropriate. Having a large number of stateful desktops also heavily influences the design and architecture.

Design and architecture is influenced by the business case, end-user requirements, and by the scale of the environment. If you are designing an environment that will scale to deliver thousands of View instances, how you structure the View environment is very important.

When scaling the environment, should you just create a single vSphere environment with one large cluster and just keep adding capacity? Should you intermix the View management and infrastructure servers with the virtual desktops? Should you extend your server virtualization to add View desktops? There is a way of scaling a View environment recommended by VMware, and it focuses on a modular approach versus a single vSphere, single cluster, as shown in Figure 1.3.

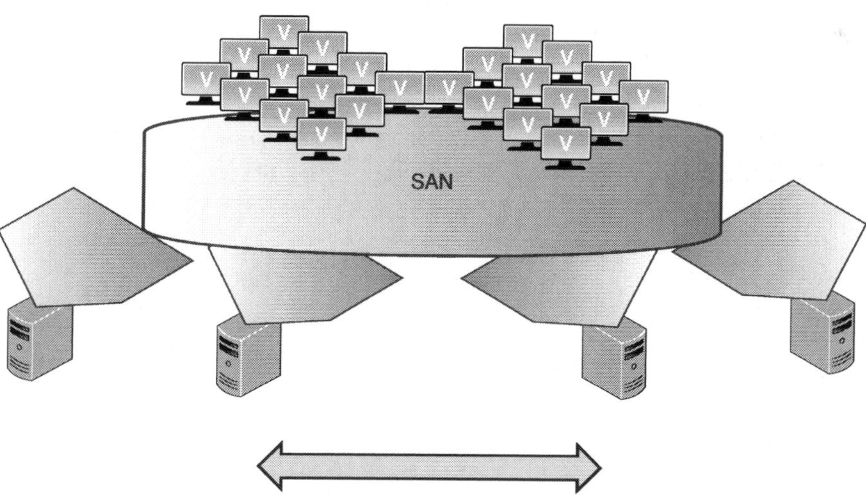

Figure 1.3 Scale out

VMware does not recommend this approach, of course, but instead recommends separating management and compute clusters. A management cluster is recommended to have a minimum of three vSphere hosts to provide N+N redundancy versus N+1 or single-cluster failover. The management cluster is referred to by VMware as the management block and provides an environment where the View and vSphere management servers run. This may include Connection and Replica Servers, as well as View Security, Composer, and Transfer Servers. It may also run vCenter, VMware Update Manager, and perhaps vCenter Operations Manager for monitoring the View environment.

View Connection servers replicate metadata through the Active Directory Lightweight Directory Service (AD LDS). Each Connection Server must be connected by a LAN. Seven is the maximum number of Connection Servers that you can deploy together. Seven allows for five active Connection Servers running, with two possible failures. This collection of Connection and Replica Servers is referred to as a *pod*. A maximum of seven Connection Servers is supported within a cluster or pod. Each View Connection Server supports 2000 concurrent connections for a theoretical maximum of 14,000; however, it is recommended that you do not exceed 10,000 concurrent connections per pod. The operational maximum set by VMware is 10,000 desktops managed by a single pod.

In addition to a management block and Connection Server pod, you will also have a compute cluster. A compute cluster is a cluster for running View desktops. The compute clusters for running virtual desktops are known as View blocks. View blocks are controlled by management blocks. VMware recommends that no more than 2500 View desktops be deployed in a View block. This means that you will have a single management block running a pod of Connection Servers to manage several View blocks, as shown logically in Figure 1.4.

This modular approach enables you to scale in a predictive fashion. Each management block is designed to control 10,000 concurrent connections. So, if each View block is designed to support 2500 users, you know that you will need one management block for every four View blocks.

When scaling to 10,000 View desktops, multiple vCenter servers are recommended. Using multiple vCenters enables you to redistribute operations that can be resource intensive, such as redeploying the View desktop system drives to bring the OS back to a clean state. (Operationally this is known as a View refresh; for additional details, see Chapter 7, "View Operations and Management.")

Sizing and performance go hand in hand with your design and architecture. There are several aspects of sizing and performance from the CPU and memory required per View desktop to the calculation of disk and network I/O. Assuming users are migrating from physical desktops, there is no better way to calculate resource requirements for a virtual desktop than running a proper performance and capacity assessment tool against the current physical desktops. This is critical if you are designing an environment that will scale to thousands of View desktops.

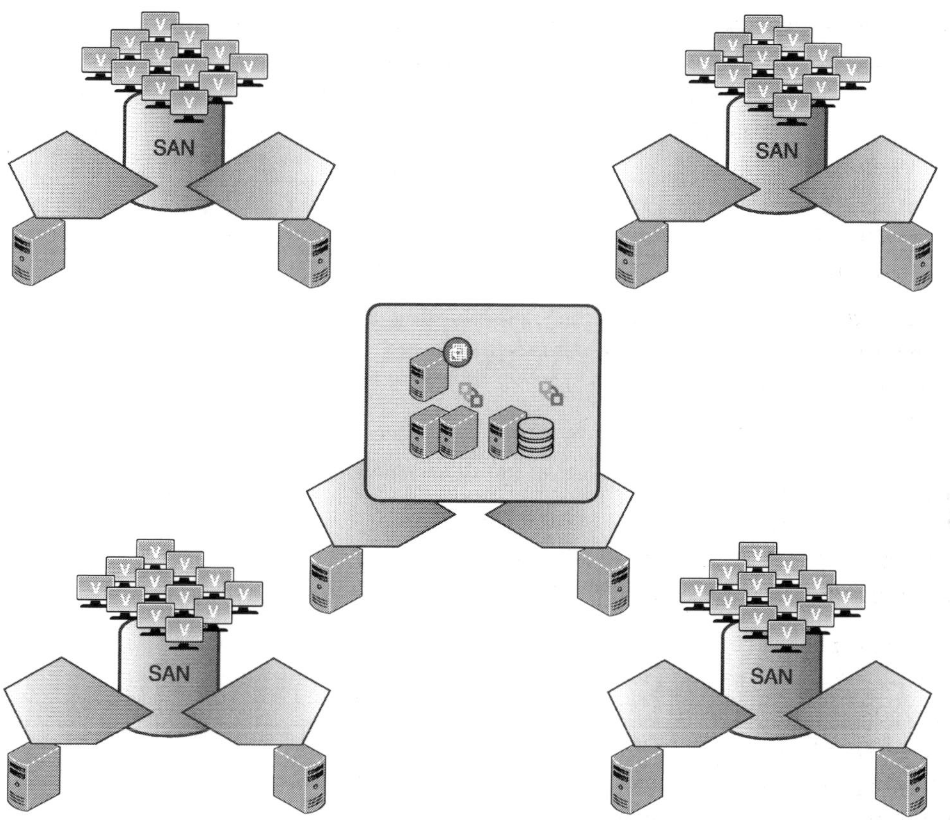

Figure 1.4 A Management block controlling View blocks

You can apply some general guidelines in sizing View desktops. Several common considerations are how many vCPUs should be assigned, how much memory, and whether you should use a 32-bit or 64-bit OS? Multiple vCPUs only benefit multithreaded applications. The reality is, however, that most modern Windows desktop operating systems and applications support multithreading. For example, multithreading is supported in Microsoft Office 2010. As multiple vCPUs add overhead, you generally should not add more than one unless utilization is over 60% of a single vCPU.

Unlike in physical environments, if you overallocate CPUs by configuring a View desktop with multiple vCPUs, you are not just wasting CPU cycles, but you might be forcing delays. Assigning multiple CPUs means that the hypervisor must wait for two physical cores to become available to schedule execution. If you have mixed single vCPUs with multiple vCPUs, you can be forcing a wait state that is not required. Although this is less common now that you have CPUs with many cores, it can be a factor because a virtual desktop environment typically has a much higher VM-to-core ratio. This is where understanding your target workload through proper analysis using tools like SysTrack from Lakeside Software can ensure you properly allocate resources instead of over- or underallocate them.

The question of whether to deploy an x86 versus 64-bit desktop OS is tied to the memory allocation. If your View desktop does not require more than 4 GB of memory, a 32-bit desktop is likely to meet your requirement. If it requires more than 4 GB, a 64-bit desktop OS is required. For example, according to Microsoft, the Windows 7 64-bit OS has a memory limitation of 192 GB. The other consideration is whether the application itself is only 64-bit. If this case, you will need to deploy the 64-bit OS and adjust your memory requirements accordingly.

Network requirements vary considerably depending on what services are enabled within the View desktop. It is therefore important to understand the user requirements so that you can estimate your bandwidth requirements. For example, the basic PCoIP protocol requirements are approximately 250 Kbps per session. Offering high-resolution video can require an additional 4096 Kbps per session. Table 1.1 lists a sampling of the PCoIP bandwidth requirements.

Table 1.1 Sample PCoIP Bandwidth Requirements

PCoIP base requirements	250 Kbps
Multimedia video	1024 Kbps
3D graphics	10,240 Kbps
480p video	1024 Kbps
1080p video	4096 Kbps
Bidirectional audio	500 Kbps
USB peripherals	500 Kbps
Stereo audio	500 Kbps
CD-quality audio	2048 Kbps

NOTE

This table is for reference only as base requirements, USB peripherals and bidirectional audio will vary considerably between customer environments and depend largely on implementation and the properties of the environment.

Storage sizing is a bit of a science in virtual desktop environments. This is because virtual desktop environments have different I/O characteristics depending on the operational activity or state of the desktop. For example, if 100 virtual desktops are simultaneously powering on, a burst of I/O activity is occurring. If the virtual desktops are powered on and users are logged in, this is considered normal or operational I/O activity. To properly size the environment from a storage perspective, you need to understand both these I/O properties (burst and operational) and also the capacity and size of storage required. Although this might seem straightforward, size and I/O requirements can be in stark contrast to one another. For example, View Composer thinly provisions storage requirements, so from a capacity perspective, it requires less storage. Because View Composer uses a linked clone tree, the storage I/O requirements can be very high.

Storage vendors treat burst I/O and capacity and operational requirements distinctly from a sizing perspective because they are typically pinned to different storage tiers. Burst I/O requirements are often placed on solid-state drive (SSDs) or flash drives because these technologies can deliver a tremendous amount of input/output operations per second (IOPS). Because they tend to cost more, general storage or capacity requirements are usually placed on SATA or SAS disks. To determine the burst I/O, it is common to follow some general guidelines:

- Determine the high-water mark for IOPS per View desktop.
- Take the total IOPS and separate them as a percentage of reads versus writes.
- Factor the performance penalty based on the RAID configuration, as shown in Table 1.2.

Table 1.2 RAID Penalties

RAID Type	IOPS Write Penalty
RAID 1	2×
RAID 5	4×
RAID 6	6×
RAID 10 (1+0)	2×

NOTE

You can aggregate these further. For example, I have seen I/O calculators that consider different states of the virtual desktop (powering on, idle, low utilization, and so on) to factor a more accurate I/O number.

For example, consider Figure 1.5. We have estimated 25 IOPS per View desktop, with 60% reads and 40% writes. We have 100 View desktops to deploy. We calculate the reads at 15 × 100 (25 × 60%) to give us 1500 IOPS. We then add the write IOPS with the penalty, (10 × 1000) × 4 due to RAID 5), to give us 4000 IOPS. The expected burst I/O is estimated to be 5500 IOPS.

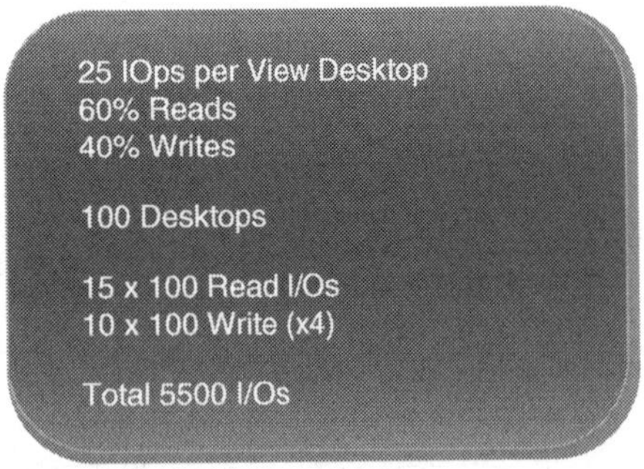

25 IOps per View Desktop
60% Reads
40% Writes

100 Desktops

15 x 100 Read I/Os
10 x 100 Write (x4)

Total 5500 I/Os

Figure 1.5 IOPS example

Virtual desktops are expensive to deploy from a storage perspective. With the advancements in deduplication technology, the footprint of a desktop deployment on storage has been dramatically reduced. The issue is no longer the cost of "space" alone. Deduplication removes the "like" blocks and stores just one copy and provides references to dependent data. In a virtual desktop environment that consists of hundreds if not thousands of copies of a Windows desktop OS, the possible consolidation of storage is very high. However, the I/O required for a single VM can also be high; in production, VMs have been observed to require 25 to 100 IOPs per virtual desktop. Although the storage footprint is small, the performance requirement is extremely high, as shown in the example in Figure 1.5. The performance footprint of a virtual desktop environment can vastly exceed the performance demanded of all but a very few high-performance, high-demand enterprise software solutions such as Oracle, SQL, and large Microsoft Exchange environments.

Virtual Storage Accelerator

VMware has introduced several technologies that increase performance while reducing cost. VMware implemented virtual storage acceleration (VSA), which is a form of local host caching. When a VM is deployed, a digest file is created that references the most common blocks of the VM's OS. In operation, the digest file is used to pull the requested blocks into memory on the ESXi host. This reduces the read requests that are serviced by the storage system by introducing a host-based cache.

View Composer, Stateless Desktops, and Storage Reclaim

VMware View enables the deployment of a stateless desktop. A stateless desktop essentially redirects the writes so that the majority of the desktop is read-only. A stateless desktop is a much cheaper desktop to deliver and manage operationally because it is not customized to an individual user and makes use of View Composer linked clone technology. This enables a large number of desktops to use very little space. The decoupling between the user and desktop and the use of Composer allows more flexible deployment options. Stateless desktops can make use of local SSDs on the ESXi host to deploy the OS disk of the VM. The benefits have been somewhat difficult to realize, though, because operationally the OS disk must be re-created to reclaim unused space and reduce the size of the tree.

VMware View 5.3 introduced a reclaim process that enables this to be done automatically and to take place outside production times. This enables a linked clone tree to be deployed for an extensive period of time and reduces the manual operational process of reclaiming space.

vSphere Flash Read Cache

vSphere 5.5 introduced the capability of pooling locally installed SSDs on the vSphere hosts to a logical cache accelerator that all read-intensive VMs can benefit from. The vSphere Flash Read Cache aggregates all read requests so that they are cached locally on an SSD drive versus in memory (as is the case with VSA). This creates a separate caching layer across all hosts (provided they have local SSDs installed) to accelerate performance. Although not specifically designed for virtual desktop environments, it will enhance any read activity across the virtual desktop compute cluster.

Virtual SAN

VMware has entered the storage virtualization market with the release of VMware Virtual SAN. A Virtual SAN enables the customer to completely segregate the virtual desktop environment onto a storage-area network (SAN) that is built using local SSD and host hard drives (HHDs) that are collected and presented logically as a single, shared storage environment. Segregation or separation of the virtual desktop environment provides the benefit of isolating the View requirements on a distinct set of physical resources so that there is no overlap at the hypervisor or storage levels between View desktops and production enterprise workloads. The benefits of Virtual SAN are many:

- Predictive hardware performance
- No risk of virtual desktop performance impacting general storage performance
- Scalable, building block approach to deployment
- Centralized storage through logical SAN presentation

- Native support for vSphere High Availability (HA), VMotion, and DRS
- Reducing the cost of storage while still providing all the benefits of a SAN

The solution is based on micro converged infrastructure in which a physical server with local SSDs and HHDs runs the vSphere ESXi and a storage controller, as shown in Figure 1.6. For storage controllers that support passthrough, complete control of the SSDs and HHDs attach to the storage controller. For storage controllers that do not support passthrough, RAID0 mode is used. This essentially creates a single-drive RAID0 set using the storage controller, which requires you to manually mark the SSDs within vSphere.

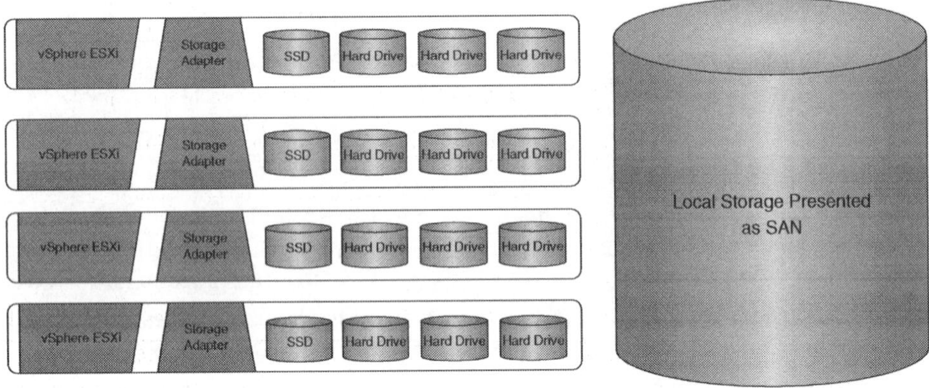

Figure 1.6 Virtual SAN logical diagram

VMware Mirage

VMware Mirage is based on a Distributed Desktop Virtualization (DDV) architecture that makes use of physical endpoints and a Mirage agent. Although it was initially designed to address a physical desktop environment and remote and mobile workers, it now works with VMware View. In a simple architecture as shown in Figure 1.7, the desktop image is stored in the datacenter on a Mirage Server. This desktop image is referred to as a CVD. The endpoint runs the Mirage agent, which synchronizes changes made to the endpoint OS.

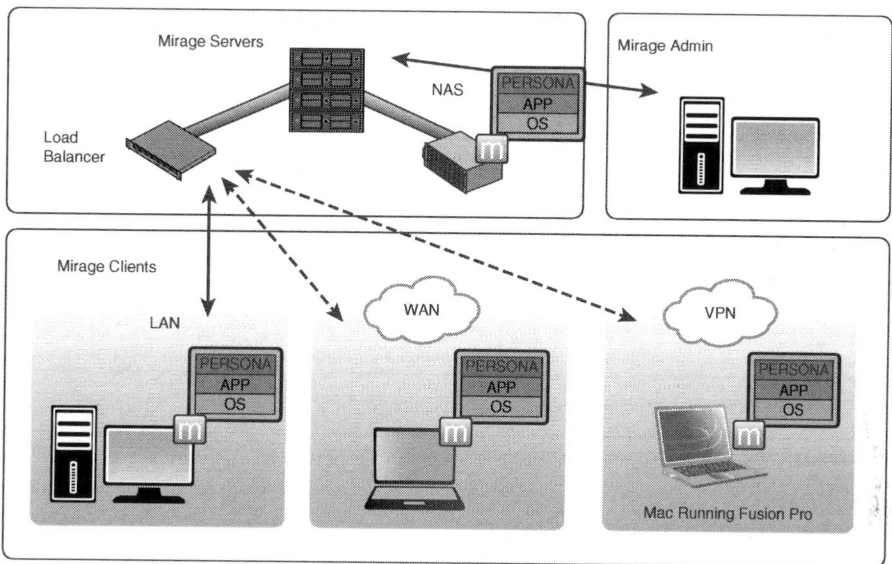

Figure 1.7 Simple Mirage architecture

A Mirage desktop is not a single layer, but is actually made up of five layers that are treated distinctly. What makes Mirage so powerful is that it will only synchronize the changes to the datacenter made within a layer, not the entire image, thus making it extremely efficient on the network. In addition, it is possible to update individual layers centrally and have those changes pushed down to the endpoint, making it also a great migration tool. When you change a layer, it does require a reboot. In upcoming releases, however, VMware is looking at which layers can be dynamically changed without rebooting. Currently, Mirage supports migrations between Windows XP and Windows 7 only, although Windows 8 is on the roadmap.

The use cases for Mirage are diverse and include the following:

1. Centralized image management
2. Centralized desktop data backup
3. Migration from Windows XP to Windows 7
4. As an enhancement to disaster recovery to provide endpoints
5. System provisioning of desktops

When deploying Mirage, you want to consider several things. Mirage supports upload and download operations of the base and application layers. Unlike View, which streams the display of the desktop using PCoIP, Mirage delivers layer changes over the network. Although designed to be highly efficient on the network, there are some key considerations when deploying Mirage in large environments. To avoid each endpoint downloading the CVD, you can make use of a branch reflector, as shown in Figure 1.8. A branch reflector acts as a proxy for the downloading and synchronization of CVDs and endpoints. A branch reflector is deployed on the remote side of the WAN to reduce network transmission. A branch reflector downloads image changes locally, enabling Mirage agents to download from the branch reflector. Using a branch reflector can reduce the bandwidth requirements during mass deployments.

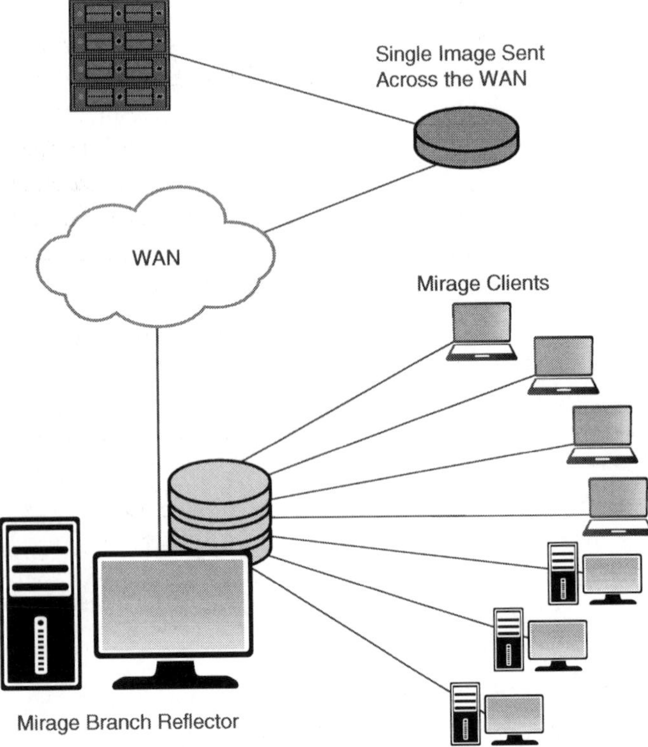

Figure 1.8 Branch reflector

Another key consideration is the availability of your Mirage Servers. It is recommended that Mirage Servers be load balanced to ensure that one is always available to service the environment.

The deployment considerations for Mirage require a proper understanding of how much bandwidth is required for downloading and uploading between the Mirage clients and servers. You can mitigate the download requirements by properly understanding the environment and placing branch reflectors to reduce the number of direct downloads by Mirage agents.

VMware Workspace

Workspace is like a universal aggregator for a variety of end-user services. The 1.0 release of Workspace was released on March 4, 2013. VMware acquired a virtualization technology for Android and iOS-based phones from Trango in October 2008. Trango developed a Mobile Virtual Platform (MVP) for phones and that was eventually released by VMware as Horizon Mobile. Horizon Mobile is designed to deliver Mobile Access Management (MAM) for business applications to smartphones.

In actual fact, MVP is only used for Android phones, and app wrapping was removed from Workspace 1.5 as Apple provided native abilities in iOS. VMware Workspace 1.5 and 1.8 consolidate Workspace 1.0 and Horizon Mobile into a single universal broker for delivering applications to PCs, tablets, and smartphones. In addition, the Horizon Mobile API is likely to take advantage of new Mobile Device Management features of Apple iOS 7. Workspace's Mobile Device Management is likely to change again with VMware's recent acquisition of a leading software provider in this space, AirWatch. Because a lot of changes are taking place around this particular feature set, it is not something we will focus on in this book.

You'll learn more about VMware Workspace deployment in Chapter 6, "Integrating VMware View and Workspace," but for now, one of the key considerations is what services you will aggregate initially. With Workspace, you can integrate View. You can also deploy Data Service, which was formerly known as Project Octopus and is similar to Dropbox or Box.net, only designed from the start for enterprise customers. Data Service runs entirely on premise, which makes it unique from other solutions on the market. You can also provide access to any number of third-party web or Cloud-based applications and access to smartphones. In addition, for Windows clients, you can stream application virtualization packages using VMware ThinApp. All these options are available as different modules in Workspace, as shown in Figure 1.9.

To deploy modules that will meet a specific business requirement, an important consideration is understanding your end-user requirements. Also, you must verify with the phone manufacturer whether the smartphone model is VMware enabled for the MAM component of Horizon; this is applicable only if it is based on Android. VMware has several agreements in place with Verizon and Samsung in the United States, but you should verify that the make and model of the Android phone is on the hardware compatibility list (HCL) as part of your deployment planning.

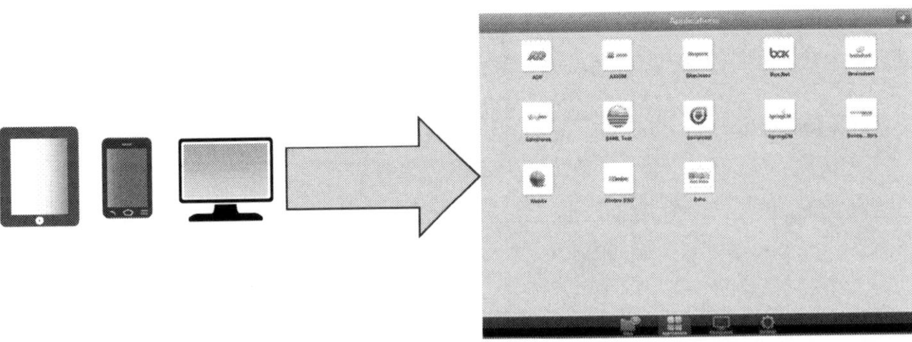

Figure 1.9 VMware Workspace modules

Each module within VMware Workspace has its own deployment and architecture considerations. For example, with data services, you must understand how much storage you will provide for each user to determine how much is allocated to data services.

It is better to have a short list of modules that you plan on enabling initially and then to bring additional modules or service online as required. This actually is generally true of VMware View, too. Many virtual desktop projects have floundered because too much emphasis was put on deploying features versus deploying aspects of the technology that address core business requirements. The nice thing about View and Workspace is it is easy to extend the architecture as additional business requirements are identified.

An Introduction to VMware View, Mirage, and Workspace

So far, this chapter has discussed each product at a high level and reviewed some deployment considerations, but you have not yet read about the basic building blocks of each. This section covers each product and its base-level components.

VMware View

VMware View is made up four major server roles: View Connection Server, View Replica Server, View Security Server, and View Transfer Server, as shown in Figure 1.10.

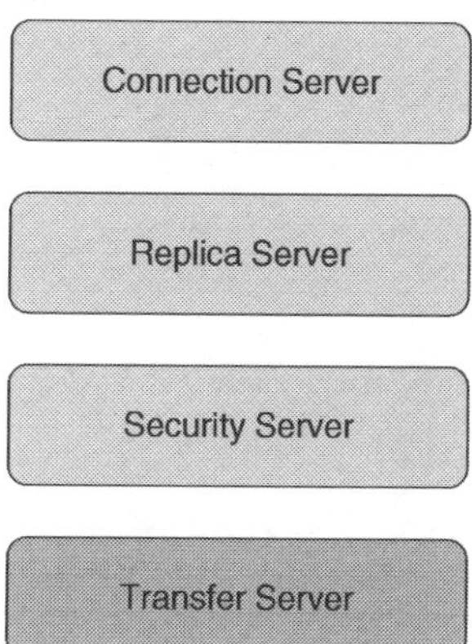

Figure 1.10 View servers

The View Connection Server fulfills the role of the traditional connection broker, which is a core piece of all virtual desktop environments. The Connection Server is to a View environment what vCenter is to a vSphere environment. In other words, it is the one-stop shop for management, maintenance, configuration, and administration of the environment. Because it plays such a key role, it is a good idea to install not one but two Connections Servers. The second Connection Server is referred to as a Replica because it shares the metadata that is stored in the AD LDS. AD LDS provides Active Directory (AD) services for AD-aware applications without the overhead of AD domains and forests. It is designed purely to replicate application information between servers. Both the primary Connection Server and Replica leverage AD LDS to ensure that they are in sync from a configuration perspective. What is unique with View is that neither the Connection nor Replica Server requires a database to synchronize information between them. Database services are used for other services such as the Event and Composer database.

The View Security Server provides a secure gateway service and is typically deployed within a demilitarized zone (DMZ), as shown in Figure 1.11. It enables the entire View environment to be presented securely through PCoIP, HTTPS, or Remote Desktop Protocol (RDP), reducing the number of ports that are opened in the forward-facing firewall. It thus acts as a client proxy.

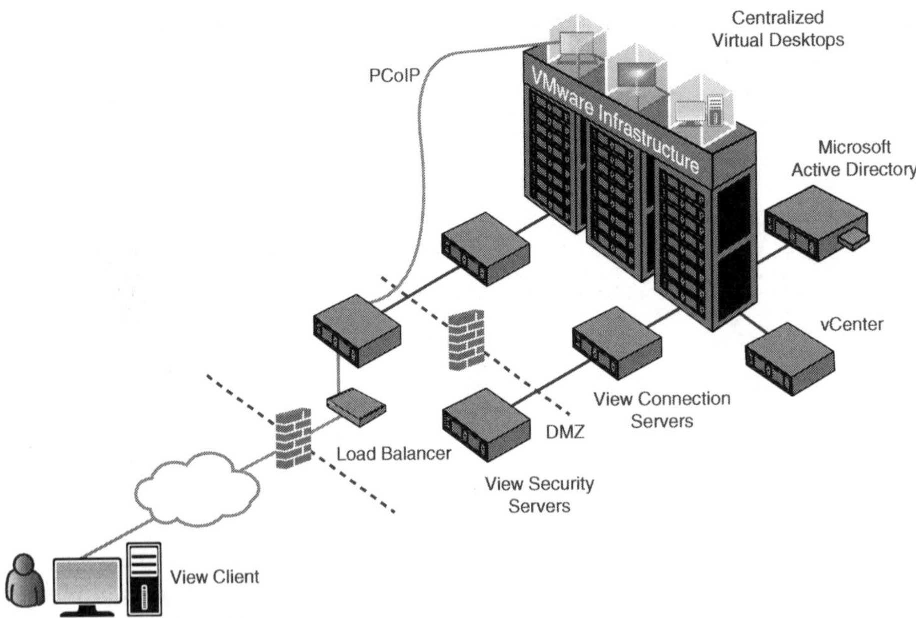

Figure 1.11 Security Server

The View Transfer Server enables the local mode client and offloads the checking out or copy of the View desktop and synchronization of the changes from the Connection Server to a dedicated server in the environment, as shown in Figure 1.12.

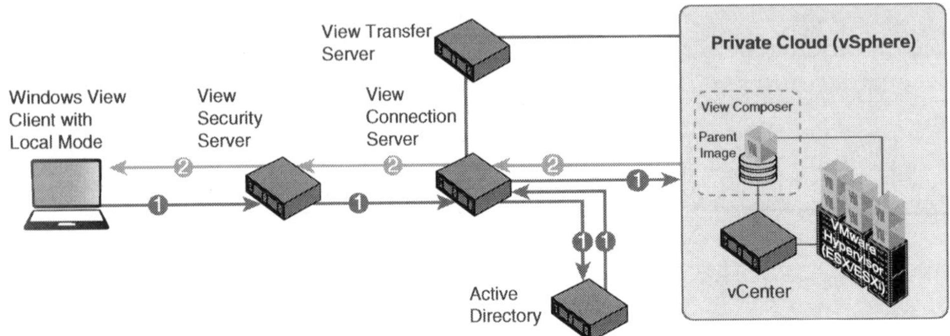

Figure 1.12 Transfer Server

View Composer enables the deployment of linked clones within a View environment. It does require a database to keep track of the connections and components of the service. Because View 5.1 Composer can be a dedicated server versus a service that runs on vCenter, as shown in Figure 1.13, this enables Composer to scale much better than earlier releases.

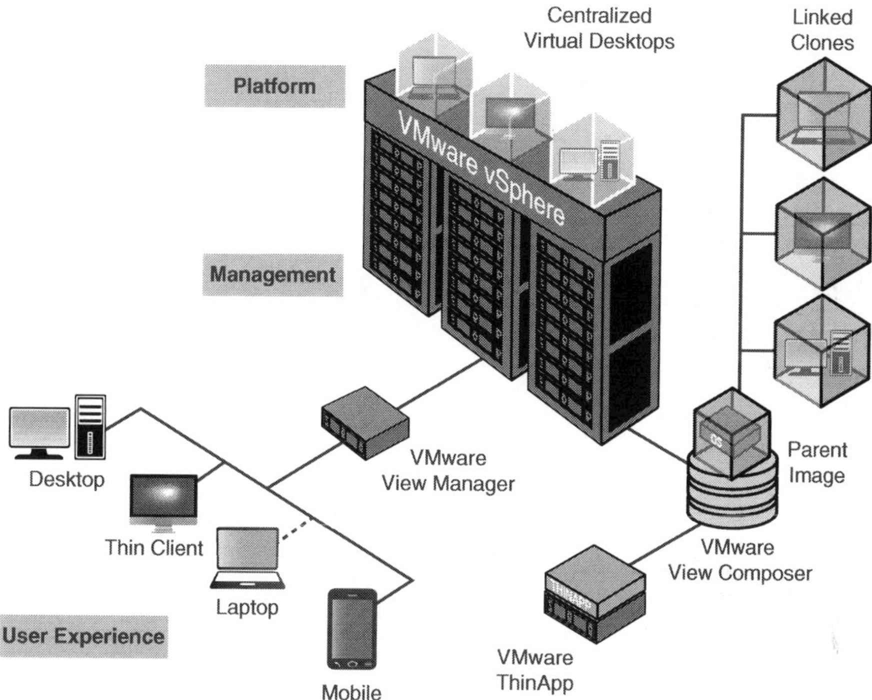

Figure 1.13 Composer can be a dedicated server

Chapter 2, "VMware View Architecture," provides a more detailed overview of the key pieces of View architecture and related components, such as View Persona.

VMware Mirage

VMware Mirage is designed to take advantage of resources on the endpoint and distributes and manages an image through layered technology, as shown in Figure 1.14.

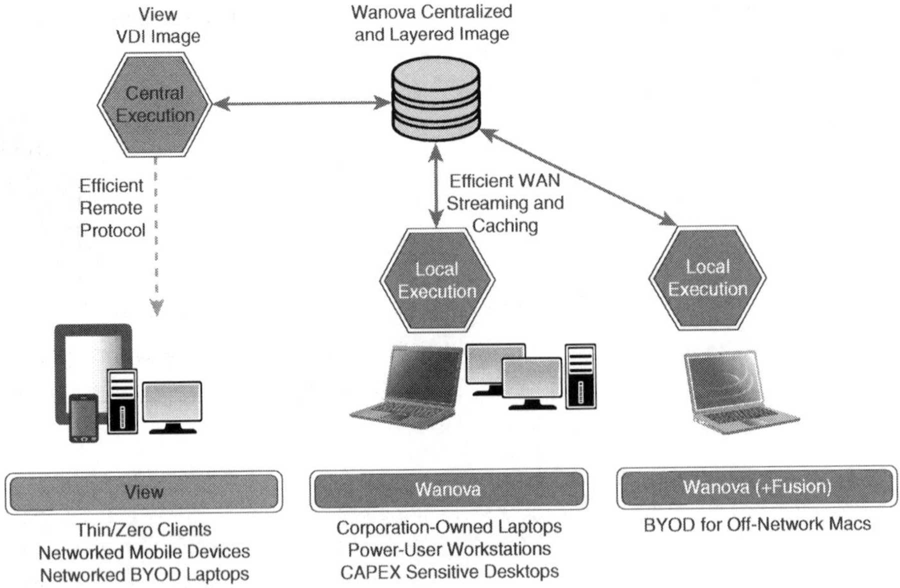

Figure 1.14 VMware Mirage

Several key pieces of the architecture are required to make this work efficiently. At a high level, they are the Mirage Server, Management Server, the CVD, the Mirage client, and the branch reflector, as shown in Figure 1.15.

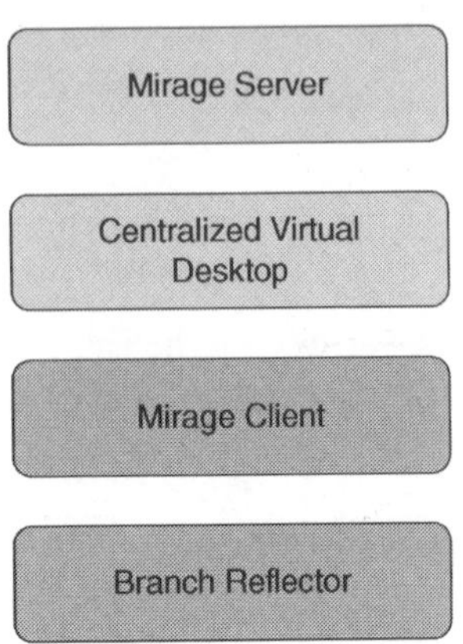

Figure 1.15 VMware Mirage components

The Mirage Server resides in the datacenter. It provides storage and management of the CVDs. Multiple Mirage Servers can be clustered together to ensure availability of the service. It is important that the Mirage Server be dedicated to this role, and it is not recommended that it provide any other services.

The CVD is a layered desktop image that includes five layers. A base layer generally includes the OS and core applications such as antivirus software. It is possible for a CVD to exist without a base layer. In addition, there is an app layer, which is a department- or user group-specific application. A driver profile is a repository of drivers designed to be used with specific hardware platforms, and a customized layer includes machine state information such as the hostname and unique identifier for the desktop. There is also a user settings and data layer, which encompasses any changes made by the end user.

The Mirage agent is installed on the endpoint device and enables the execution of a CVD. In addition to running a CVD, it can also convert an existing desktop image to a CVD, so it is used to migrate images to the datacenter as well.

The branch reflector optimizes downloads of base layers, the driver library, and app layers to avoid each Mirage client downloading the CVD directly or synchronizing all the changes directly. The branch reflector proxies the download requests to reduce the number of client connections. In a remote site, the Mirage clients connect to the branch reflector on the local LAN, and the branch reflector connects to the Mirage Servers, as shown in Figure 1.16.

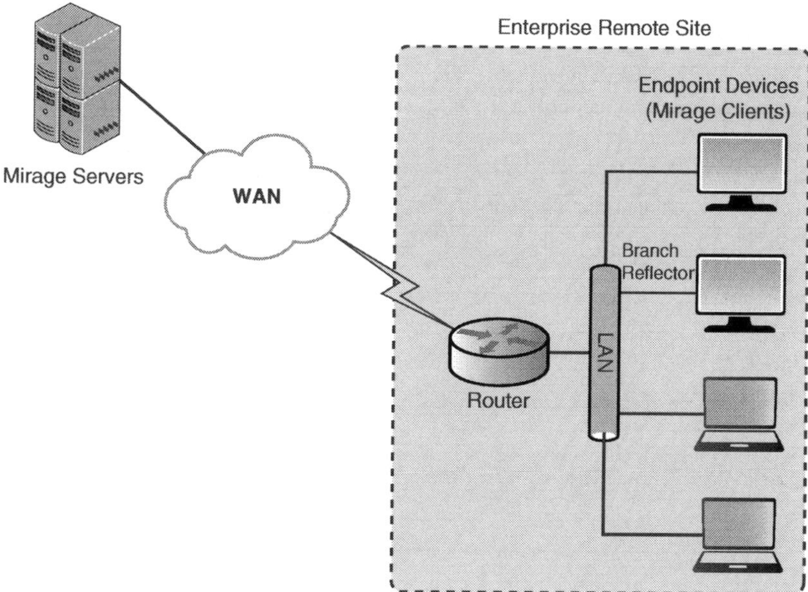

Figure 1.16 Branch reflector

You'll learn more about these high-level components in Chapter 9, "VMware Horizon Mirage."

VMware Workspace

VMware Workspace architecture is made up of a series of virtual appliances that provide various services to the Workspace environment, as shown in Figure 1.17.

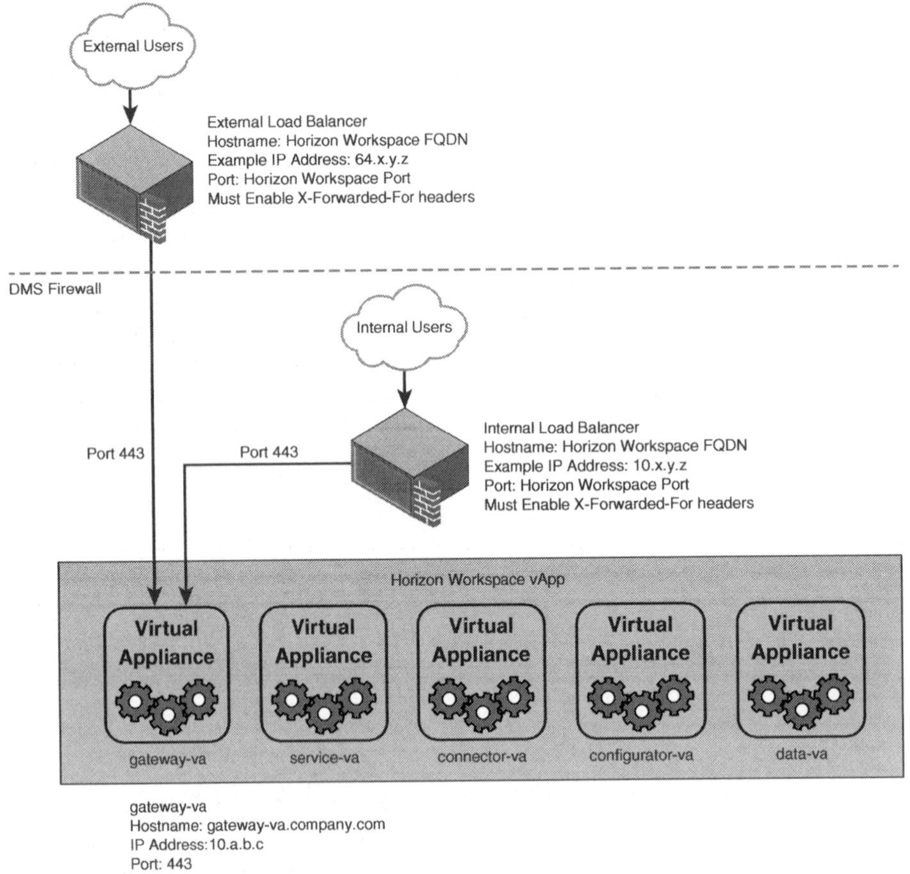

Figure 1.17 Horizon Workspace

The six virtual appliances (VAs) provide the services listed in Table 1.3.

> **NOTE**
>
> A virtual appliance, the Horizon Mobile Manager, was added when Horizon Mobile was integrated in 1.5.

Table 1.3 VMware Workspace vApp Virtual Appliances

Virtual Appliance	Description
Configurator VA	The configurator VA is used to set and configure and push the configurations to the other VAs.
Service VA	The service VA provides ThinApp synchronization and user and group management through a web interface.
Connector VA	The connector VA provides synchronization of directories, View pools, and ThinApp catalogs along with user authentication.
Data VA	The data VA controls the file storage and sharing service (formerly Project Octopus).
Gateway VA	The gateway VA routes end-user connections to the appropriate back-end Workspace virtual appliance.
Horizon Mobile Management	HMM controls, manages, and enables you to configure corporate workspace on a user's smartphone. Rather than an enforced management model like in a Mobile Device Management (MDM) platform, access is managed, enabling the user to self-select the corporate applications. This is generally referred to as Mobile Access Management (MAM).

To access VMware Workspace, you need a Workspace web client. VMware makes a Windows, Android, iOS, and OS X client. In addition to these standard clients, there is also a web client for agentless installations.

Summary

This chapter introduced the core pieces of the Horizon Suite: View, Mirage, and Workspace. In addition, it covered some high-level predeployment considerations and the base-level components of each solution. The following chapter drills down into the architecture and outlines how each is installed and configured. In addition, the next chapter discusses operational aspects of each technology. This chapter also discussed the importance of looking at your next EUC project as an opportunity to build proper services for your end users that are designed around a service catalog. A service catalog enables users to consume these services as required without the need for IT to deploy each individually. Instead, IT can simply entitle the user to access the service.

Because VMware Mirage is a new acquisition to the VMware Horizon product line, this chapter outlined the high-level differences and use cases in which Mirage might be more appropriate than centralized View desktops. By the time you finish reading this book, you will feel comfortable architecting, deploying, and managing the solutions in the Horizon Suite in concert with each other.

Horizon Suite, in combination with View, Mirage, and Workspace, enables you to manage virtual, physical, and mobile platforms, allowing you to address a wide variety of end-user requirements. More importantly, you can provide a wide variety of business services that are easy for the users to consume and simple for you to manage.

Chapter 2

VMware View Architecture

Introduction

It seems that the complexity of a virtual desktop environment has increased exponentially since the technology was first introduced. This has been driven by the demand to scale the solution to meet the needs of environments with thousands and tens of thousands of desktops. As the scale increased, problems that were manageable with a 100 virtual desktops became acute problems. The complexity has come from pressure to continually improve the capabilities of a virtual desktop and also to address load by offloading it to different layers of the architecture such as caching on the host versus storage infrastructure.

This chapter starts with the common server rolls found in a View environment. Then we discuss the client components, and then review how to architect so that scale can be achieved without redesigning the solution. Of course, one of the fundamental questions that is asked even before design is how to get started understanding the scope of the environment you need to architect.

Approaching the Design and Architecture

When customers begin the deployment of a large VMware View implementation, they often have a target number of seats and a notion that it is going to be a large undertaking, but struggle to find an approach. Let's first begin with a discussion on approach, and then discuss architecture.

Phase I: Requirements Gathering and Assessment

For a large virtual desktop infrastructure (VDI) project, you should begin with gathering the requirements and an assessment. Gathering the business and technical requirements rationalizes which features of VMware View or Horizon Suite you need to deploy. For example, if you have a large number of laptop users, you might decide that VMware Mirage will be a key part of the overall solution.

The purpose of an assessment is to capture information from the physical desktop environment so that you can move to the second step in the process, analyze, as shown in Figure 2.1.

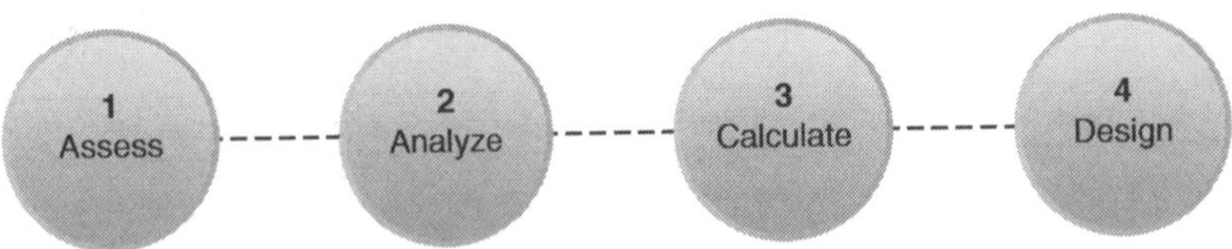

Figure 2.1 Stages in developing a View design

If you are deploying anything more than a few hundred seats, you should use a proper assessment tool. A proper assessment tool ensures that you have accurate numbers to begin your analysis.

In addition to analysis, a controlled proof of concept (PoC) is extremely valuable in gathering feedback to ensure you have good planning information. For example, if a desktop OS upgrade is part of the virtual desktop deployment, it is a good idea to run a PoC to understand how the known operating system impacts your planning and capacity requirements. A number of great assessment tools are available to help you determine virtual desktop suitability, look at application usage, and evaluate which applications can be virtualized through ThinApp. One great tool for assessing is Liquidware Labs SysTrack software, shown in Figure 2.2.

You can see that this assessment tool provides detailed key performance metrics, such as disk I/Os, as well as an indication of whether the desktop is a good candidate for desktop virtualization. In addition, it will indicate the average and peak performance requirements, making it easy to factor in a large number of desktops.

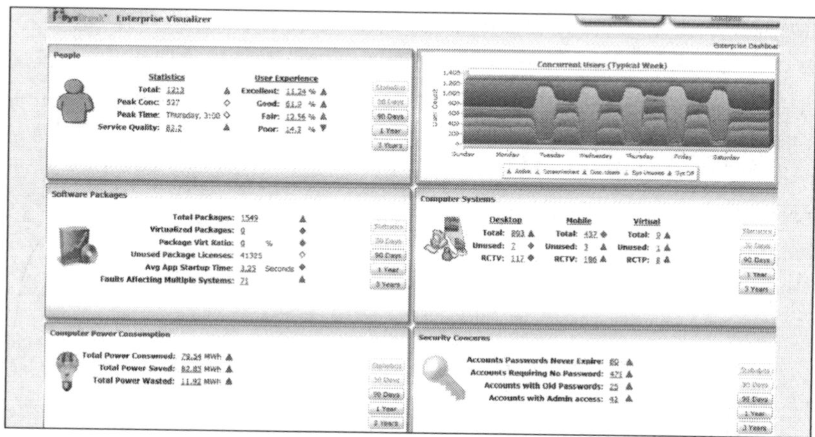

Figure 2.2 Lakeside SysTrack

Phase II: Analysis

Even with the best underlying measurements, you should always factor in the usage type or segmentation of users consuming the virtual desktop environment. Generally, user segmentation type falls into three broad categories: light, medium, and heavy users. The point in planning for these broad categories of users is to make allowances in the hardware specifications. For example, suppose that from your lab or PoC environment, you identify that most virtual desktop sessions are using about 2 GB of memory and a single vCPU with a 30-GB OS image. Rather than plan on the average, you should adjust the average with the usage types mentioned.

For example, say that the production environment will service 5000 desktops. As the IT architect for the company, you know that a large percentage of these desktops will go to engineers and designers. So, out of the 5000 seats, you expect that 40% of those will be heavy-usage users. The next largest portion of users has an average usage requirement and makes up another 40% of the population. If you break this out, the planning starts to look like Table 2.1.

Table 2.1 User Segmentation

User Type	Seats	Percentage
Heavy users (engineers and designers)	2000	40%
Medium users (day-to-day use)	2000	40%
Light users (light clerical work)	1000	20%
Total number of seats on VMware View	5000	

This step is necessary because both capacity planning and PoC environments tend to provide a snapshot of usage versus actual usage. It is very difficult to ensure that you have captured data that represents exactly what you will see in production. There is really no single tool to do this, so you must combine what you know about the environment and your metrics to develop your hardware requirements.

In addition to the hardware required for the virtual computer, also consider network bandwidth. For example, if your heavy users are consuming a lot of memory and CPU to do 3D rendering, they might also be leveraging a large amount of network for PC over IP (PCoIP).

Phase III: Calculate

Now that we have our assessment numbers and have done some analysis to determine how these numbers adjust for our specific environment, we can run our calculations. In the example, we defined about 2000 users that will be high-end users. If we combine what we learned using the assessment tool, we can calculate numbers that represent our production requirements.

You can use user segmentation and the analysis to guide your hardware estimates. For example, if you know that the configuration of the desktop required by the heavy-usage users is two vCPUs and 6 GB of memory, you can calculate the amount of memory and CPU that you need to provide from a host perspective to service this workload and user type.

It is important to have a reasonable virtual machine (VM)-to-core ratio, which for desktops is typically around 8 to 10 VMs per core. Using an assessment tool, you can verify these general numbers with actual numbers from your environment. If you have a dual CPU 6-core VM, then you have the potential to run 96 to 120 VMs. Keep in mind, though, that because you will want to allow for host failures, you should ensure that a percentage of surplus capacity exists for failures. For example, if you are deploying 1000 desktops and each host is capable of running 100 VMs, deploying 10 meets your normal operational load. However, if you lose a host, and the VMs are restarted on the remaining 9 servers, it will impact performance.

Do the same calculations to determine the ideal memory per host. For example, if each VM requires 2 GB of memory and you configure 256 GB of memory per host, you will need approximately 10 hosts running the full operational workload. Again, you must factor in the potential for host failures to ensure that the remaining hosts can absorb any performance impact.

If we go back to the example of disk input/output operations per second (IOPS), we can see that whereas most desktops average between 8 and 10 disk I/Os, a few of the heavily utilized ones are running at 50 to 60 disk I/Os. If we determine that our 2000 engineers run a lot of I/O-intensive software, we can use the assessment average of 50 I/Os to describe the I/O of our high-end users; our average might be 10 I/Os and light 8.

Typically, the other important consideration is the percentage of reads versus writes when we talk about disk I/Os because writes are usually factored based on the RAID configuration and associated penalty (as shown in Table 1.2 in Chapter 1, "The New End-User Model") to allow for the performance difference between a read versus a write on a storage subsystem.

Taking all this into consideration, we can prepare our final calculations and determine our total requirement for I/O, which defines our performance specifications. In addition, we must analyze our storage requirements. To do this, we categorize our desktops between stateful and stateless. Stateful desktops are usually deployed if desktops are customized so they are unique to a particular user (in contrast to stateless, which are not).

To determine how much storage is required for stateful desktops, we take the total image size and add the space required for the swap, log, and some additional overage for growth. Suppose, for example, that we determine that we will have 64 VMs per datastore and that each OS VM disk (VMDK) is 37 GB. In addition, let's say that our swap file size is 2 GB and our log file size is 100 MB and that we will allow 10% for growth. If we plan on deploying 64 VMs per datastore and 500 VMs in total, we require 20.8 TB of storage (see Table 2.2).

Table 2.2 Stateful Desktop Example

Feature	Requirement	Reasoning
VMs per datastore	64 VMFS (Virtual Machine File System)	Recommended limit of full clones per datastore
VM datastore size		Size based on the following calculations: Raw file size = 37,000 MB Log file size = 100 MB Swap file size = 2048 MB Free space allocation = 10% overhead Minimum allocated datastore size = (VMs * (Raw + swap + Log) + Overhead) = (64 * (37,000 MB + 2048 MB + 100 MB) + 244 GB) = 2.6 TB
Number of datastores	1 per 32 virtual desktops	Number of VMs / VMs per datastore = 500 / 64 = 8
Total storage		Number of datastores * Datastore size = 8 * 2.6 TB = 20.8 TB

Stateless desktops do not require as much space as you are deploying a parent VMDK and a number of delta files. If you use the vSphere Storage APIs – Array Integration (VAAI), you can have 100 stateless VMs per datastore. (Note that if you place the parent VMs or Replica disks on separate datastores, you cannot makes use of the VAAI primitives.)

We take the size of the delta, log, and swap and add 10% overhead for growth, and then multiply that times the total number of VMs to get a size per datastore based on 100 VMs.

Allowing for both the Replica and delta files on the same datastore, and if we deploy the same number of VMs as in our Table 2.1 example, 500, we get 3.5 TB of storage capacity required for stateless desktops (see Table 2.3).

Table 2.3 Stateless Desktop Example

Feature	Requirement	Reasoning
VMs per datastore	64 VMFS	Recommended limit of full clones per datastore
VM datastore size		Size based on the following calculations: Raw file size = 4096 MB Log file size = 100 MB Swap file size = 2048 MB Free space allocation = 10% Overhead Replica = VM 37,000 MB Minimum allocated datastore size = (VMs * (Raw + Swap + Log) + Overhead) = (100 * (4096 MB + 2048 MB + 100 MB) + 61 GB) + 36 GB Replica VM = 707 GB
Number of datastores	1 per 100 virtual desktop	Number of VMs / VMs per datastore = 500 / 100 = 5
Total storage		Number of datastores * Datastore size = 5 * 707 GB = 3.5 TB

Phase IV: Design

After our assessment, analysis, and calculations, we have numbers that can be used to influence our design. One of the major design decisions involves storage. It usually comes down to three high-level decisions that you need to make from an architecture perspective: Do I segregate the virtual desktop environment using a dedicated storage hypervisor platform like VMware Virtual SAN or Nutanix? Do I aggregate the performance of my current SAN solution using local SSDs in the hosts leveraging technology like FusionIO? Or do I expand my current enterprise storage system to handle the performance requirements demanded by the VDI environment? In general, I find the right decision tends to be very customer specific. Virtual SAN and Nutanix can be great solutions that separate virtual desktops from enterprise server workloads, thus ensuring the demands of one do not impact the demands of the other. If you have already standardized with a particular hardware vendor, introducing another storage of converged infrastructure might not be reasonable. In this case, as FusionIO and companies like them OEM their cards to hardware providers, this can be a more acceptable approach. If the storage has been designed with mixed workloads and virtualization in mind, extending the existing storage solution might be the best approach. The most important thing is to plan to address the service and performance requirements over the lifespan of the solution. If you know that your virtual desktops are going to require 50,000 IOPS, make sure that you can deliver it not only on day one but also over the next 3 years as well.

VMware View Server Architecture

In a View environment, several server roles can be deployed. Each provides a specific capability or function. Not all roles are required; certain technologies should be deployed only if you intend to use them. For example, if you are not going to deploy local mode desktops, it is unlikely that you would deploy a View Transfer Server. All the primary server roles are installed from the same executable, and the type of server is determined by the selected role, as shown in Figure 2.3.

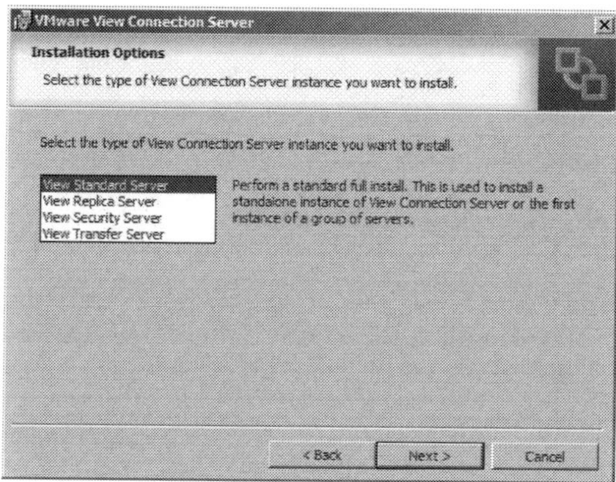

Figure 2.3 All Primary Server Roles are installed from the same executable

VMware View Connection Server

The View Connection Server is a required server role within the View architecture. It connects a user request to an available View desktop within the virtual desktop environment. It is installed on a Windows Server OS and serves as the connection broker to the virtual desktop infrastructure. A View Connection Server does not require a database to store the configuration information. Instead, it stores the configuration in the Active Directory Lightweight Directory Services (AD LDS), which is deployed during the installation.

AD LDS supplies directory services for applications without the overhead of an entire Active Directory Domain Services (AD DS) implementation. The application does need to be directory aware so that it can store its metadata in AD LDS. View stores information about entitlements, View desktops, and system parameters.

VMware View Replica Server

The Replica Server enables you to install a second instance of the Connection Server in the View environment to ensure redundancy. Like the Connection Server, it runs as software on a Windows server.

The metadata is shared between the Connection Server and the Replica Server using AD LDS. Even though you have installed a second connection broker to provide redundancy, you still must have a solution that enables you to seamlessly redirect end-user connection requests to certain Connection Servers so that you can complete maintenance tasks such as patching. To do this, consider deploying a load-balancing service in front of Connection and Replica Servers. Many software- and hardware-based load balancers can be deployed in front of a View Connection or Security Server. Figure 2.4 shows a load-balancing service connected with a Connection and Replica Server.

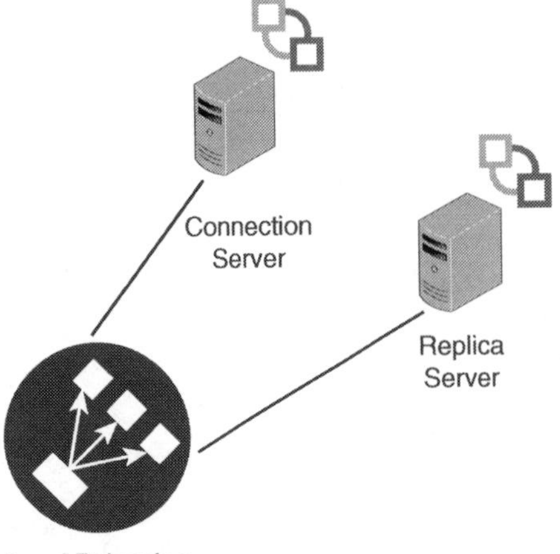

Figure 2.4 Load balancing Connection Servers

VMware View Security Server

A View Security Server acts as a client proxy to the View environment and reduces the amount of access and open ports required to make a connection to a View desktop. Like the other View Server types, it is installed on a Windows Server operating system. It is usually deployed in a demilitarized zone (DMZ), as shown in Figure 2.5. If you deploy a load-balancing solution in front of the Security Servers, ensure that you do not load balance the connection between the Security Servers and their configured Connection Server. This is because there is a 1:1 relationship between a Security Server and a Connection Server (although you can have many Security Servers point to a single Connection Server).

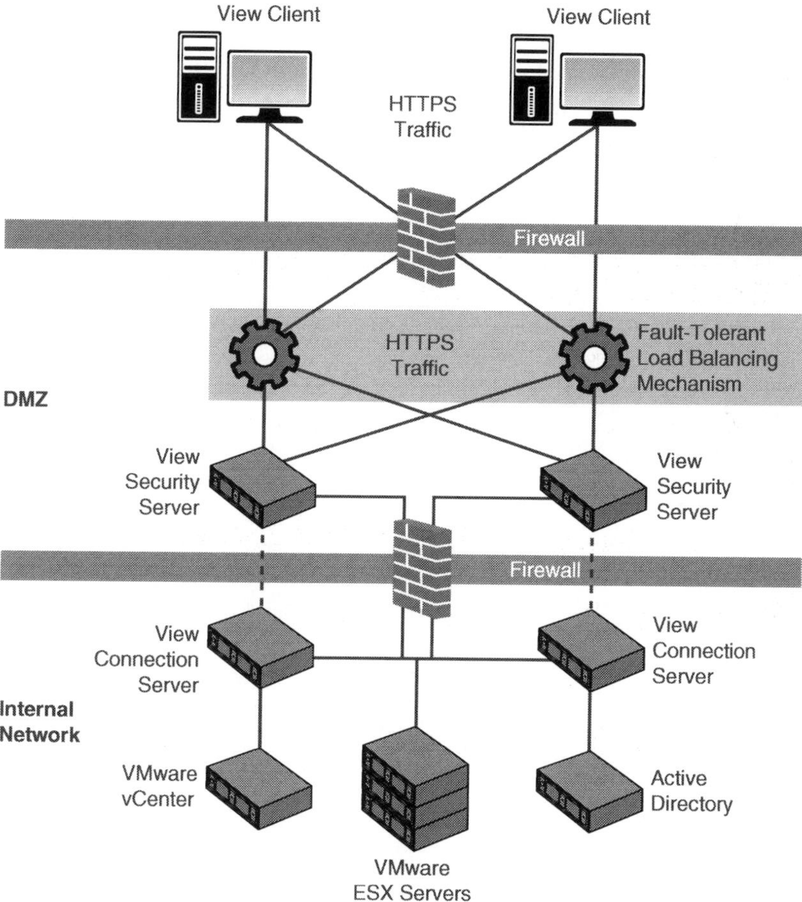

Figure 2.5 VMware View Security Servers

Because it is installed in the DMZ, it is important that the underlying Windows OS be hardened. You can find complete details on hardening the Security Server in the *VMware View Security Hardening Guide* available on VMware's website. In general, follow these steps:

1. Avoid joining the Security Server to the Windows Active Directory.
2. Keep the server properly patched with all recommended security hotfixes.
3. Create specific administrator accounts and add them to the local Administrators group.
4. Disable any Windows Services not required. For example, the following should be disabled on Windows 2008 Server:
   - Application Experience
   - Application Management
   - Certificate Propagation
   - Com+ Event System
   - DHCP Client
   - Distributed Link Tracking Client
   - Distributed Transaction Coordinator
   - Diagnostic Policy Service
   - IPsec Policy Agent
   - Print Spooler
   - System Event Notification
5. Replace the existing self-signed certificates with ones signed by an official certificate authority such as Symantec, Comodo, GoDaddy, or GlobalSign.

The port requirements for a Security Server vary depending on what services you are enabling; for example, if you are going to use RDP and PCoIP, you must ensure that the Security Server can reach the View desktop network segment through the internal firewall over ports 3389 (RDP) and 4172 (PCoIP). In addition to the services you enable, there is also a dependency on which components of the View architecture you deploy. If you deploy a Transfer Server (which the next section covers), you also need to open ports from the Security Server to the Transfer Server to allow the exchange of configuration and synchronization traffic. Generally, you must open ports from the external clients to the Security Server, from the Security Server to the Connection Server, from the Security

Server to the Transfer Server, and from the Security Server to the network segment on which the View desktops are deployed, as shown in Figure 2.6.

Table 2.4 provides the protocols, port, and source and destination information for the ports used for communication between the View Client, Security Server, Connection Server, and View desktop segment. Although it is possible to configure a Security Server to work on port 80, it is not recommended (as specified in the table) because of the inherent security risks; VMware recommends this because usernames and passwords would be set in clear text. The only real-world example of this would be if the Secure Sockets Layer (SSL) certificate management is offloaded to a load-balancer network appliance.

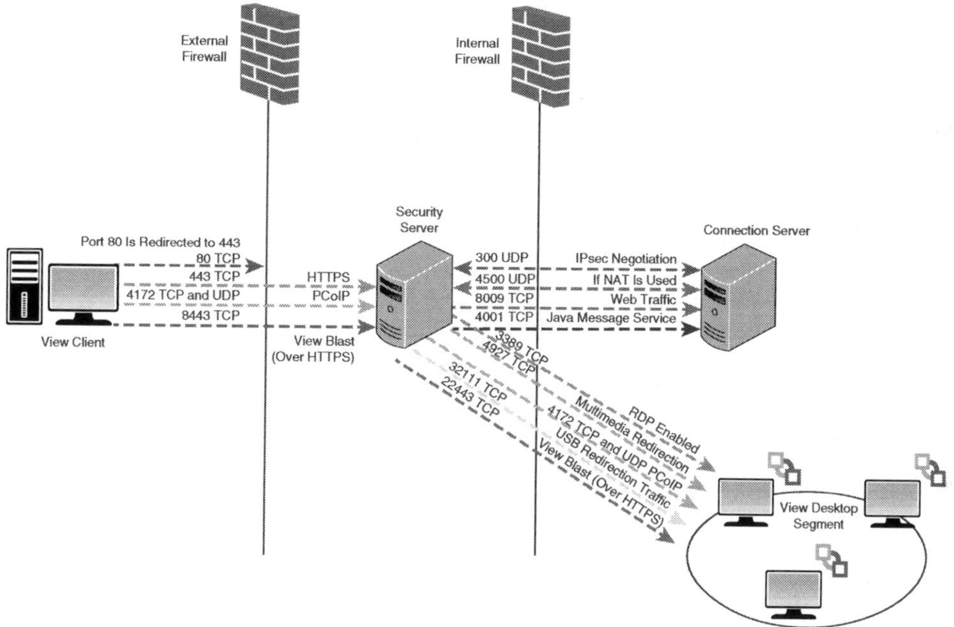

Figure 2.6 Security Server traffic flow

Table 2.4 Security Server Port Requirements

Source	Destination	Port	Protocol
View Client	Security Server	443	HTTPS
View Client	Security Server	80	HTTP (not recommended)
View Client	Security Server	4172	PCoIP (TCP and UDP)
Security Server	View desktop subnet	4172	PCoIP (TCP and UDP)

Source	Destination	Port	Protocol
Security Server	View desktop subnet	3389	RDP
Security Server	View desktop	9427	MMR (multimedia redirection)
Security Server	Connection Server	8009	AJP13 (Apache JServ protocol)
Security Server	Connection Server	4001	JMS (Java Messaging Service)
Security Server	Connection Server	500	IPsec and ESP (UDP)
Security Server	Connection Server	4500	NAT Traversing (UDP)
Connection Server	Security Server	500	IPSec and ESP (UDP)
Connection Server	Security Server	4500	NAT Traversing (UDP)

Local Mode VMs

Local mode VMs are enabled through policy on the VMware View Server and are supported by Transfer Servers and View Clients running the local mode plug-in. Essentially, the local mode plug-in is similar to VMware Player, which enables you to run the VM on the local client using desktop resources. The View Client with local mode works only for Windows.

Keep in mind that when using local mode you are running the VM locally. This means that the local desktop should meet the Microsoft hardware specifications of the OS you have checked out. For example, you cannot check out a Windows 7 VM through local mode on a Pentium 233-MHz machine.

You also must ensure that the local client has enough space to run the virtual desktop. Only the used space within the virtual desktop is transferred. Suppose, for example, that your virtual desktop is 20 GB, but only 15 GB is being used. In this case, when you check out the desktop, only 15 GBs are downloaded to the local client. It is important when planning space for local mode that you allow for the requirements of the local OS, the used space in the VM, and any snapshots required for synchronizing or capturing any deltas in local mode.

VMware View Transfer Server

The VMware View Transfer Server enables you to separate the file copy of a local mode transfer to a separate server within the View environment. Like other software components of View, the Transfer Server installs and runs on a Windows server. The Transfer Server must also be a Windows VM. When the software is installed, the Distributed Resource Scheduling (DRS) rules are created for the VM so that DRS is set to manual. This has the effect of turning off Automatic VMotions for the VM.

The Transfer Server is essentially a large storage repository for the virtual desktop images so that the overhead of copying the VM does not have to run on the Connection Server and can run on a specific server. The Transfer Server runs on Windows Server 2003 or 2008. When the pieces are installed, users can check out a VM provided they have permissions to do so. You can halt transfers by putting the Transfer Server in maintenance mode.

From an architecture perspective, you can have a single View Transfer Server or multiple. The decision of whether to add additional Transfer Servers is based on the number of check-in/out requests. Each transfer server can support a maximum of 20 concurrent check-in/out requests.

If you have multiple Transfer Servers, you must be careful how you configure the repository of the storage location of the View desktop images that can be used for local mode desktops. If you have a single Transfer Server, you can configure a local path location when you add the Transfer Server (for example, T:\View_Repository). If you have multiple Transfer Servers, however, you must use a file share to ensure that each server has access. When you use a file share, you need to specify an account to be used for connectivity reasons. From a security perspective, you should add only the minimal permissions necessary. The Active Directory account requires Read, Write, and Modify permissions on the repository.

When the repository is configured, you must publish a base image or Replica to the Transfer Server. Publishing it copies the Replica to the Transfer Server repository and stores it in an encrypted form, as shown in Figure 2.7. This figure shows that a View desktop is not usually made up of a single disk or virtual disk (VMDK) file. A View desktop will separate out swap onto a temp disk. You also have the option of separating out the local profile onto a user disk and an OS disk that runs the operating system. The Replica or base disk gets copied to the Transfer Server.

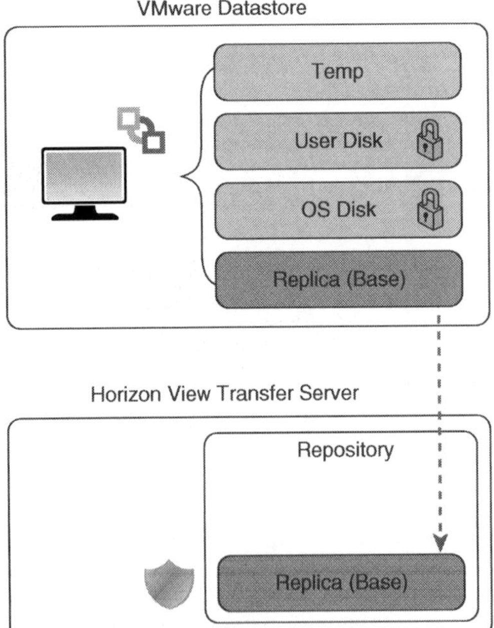

Figure 2.7 Publish desktop process

When planning the deployment of View Transfer Servers, you want to consider four major operations, as discussed in the following subsections.

Check-Out

During the check-out process, the entire virtual desktop image is copied to the VMware Client running local mode. As a Composer desktop derives from four disks (Disposable Data Disk, User Data, the OS Disk, and the Replica), the process copies the Replica from the Transfer Server and the User and OS Disk from the VMware datastore. A lock is placed on the VM so that it cannot be used while the VM is checked out, as shown in Figure 2.8.

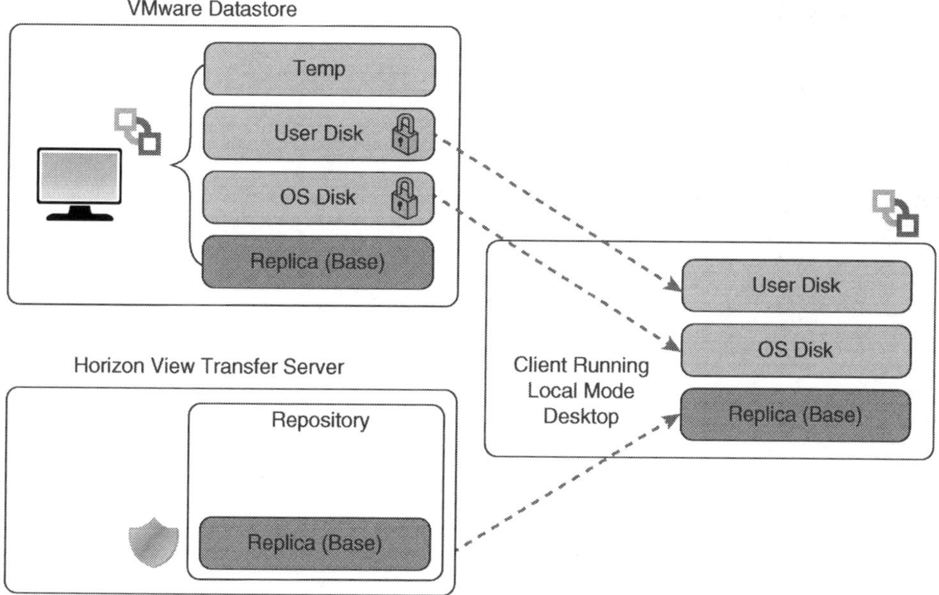

Figure 2.8 The check-out process

Check-In

The check-in process is similar to the check-out process, only the files that contain the local changes are copied back up to the virtualization environment. This is the user data and OS disk. The Replica or base image has not changed, so it is not copied up. After the files are copied up, the locks are removed, and connections are again directed to the View desktop within the virtual infrastructure. From a user perspective, the virtual desktop in the datacenter resumes being their primary device.

Replication

Replication copies the User and OS disk back to the virtualization environment for the purpose of keeping the files in sync. The locks are maintained, but the primary View desktop remains the local mode desktop, as shown in Figure 2.9. The frequency of replication is controlled by policy and determines whether the user has an element of control over the process.

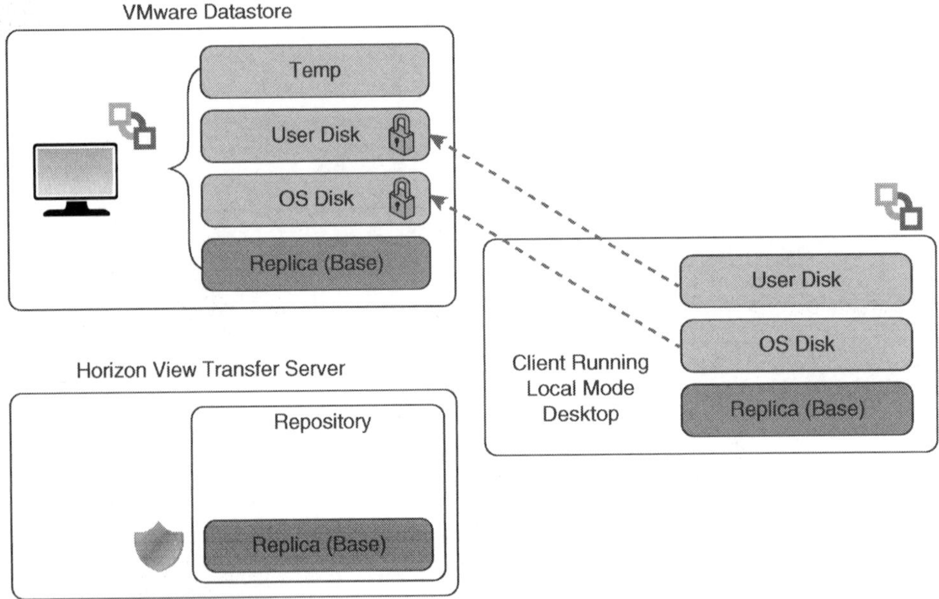

Figure 2.9 Replication

Rollback

A rollback enables you to remove local mode access or recover from a lost, stolen, or corrupt local image. A rollback discards the local files, unlocks the files on the View desktop stored centrally, and redirects all subsequent connections there. It is possible to allow an end user to perform a rollback by setting a View policy that enables this. If a rollback is performed while the local mode desktop is in use, the session is ended, and when the user reconnects, she is directed to the centrally located View desktop. It is really a two-step process after the local files have been discarded, as shown in Figure 2.10.

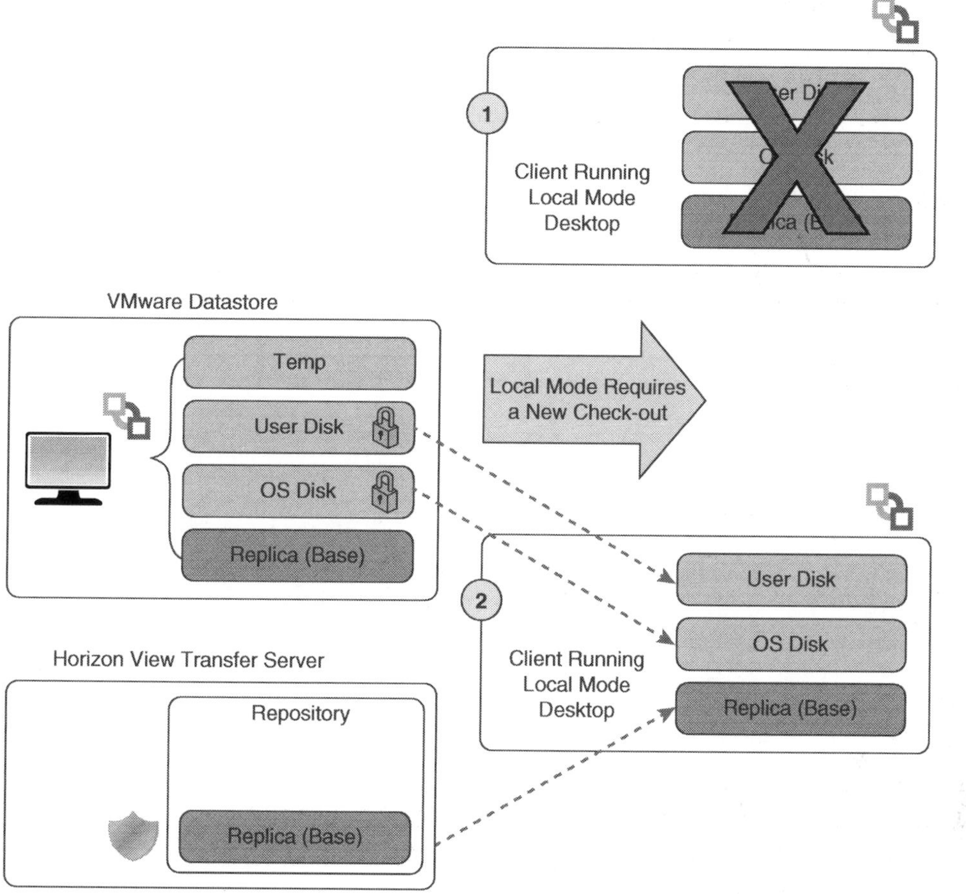

Figure 2.10 Rollback

Desktop Pools

Within VMware View, virtual desktops are configured in pools. *Pools* are logical groups of virtual desktops that are configured in the VMware View Administrator console and have certain configurations and settings applied to them. For example, you could have a pool of desktops configured to use PCoIP, to be autoprovisioned, or to be deployed in a certain OU in the active directory.

When planning a VMware View environment, you should predetermine what pools you need and what configurations are required within those pools. The critical component is whether the desktop is floating or persistent. Floating desktops tend to be stateless in nature and can take advantage of a View Composer to reduce the storage requirement to deploy them. Persistent desktops require the user to preserve data between desktop reboots.

View Composer

View Composer is a service that enables you to thinly provision View desktops by using the concept of linked clones. It is installed on a Windows OS and requires its own database. It can be installed either on the vCenter Server or a dedicated View Windows Server 2008 R2 VM as a standalone Composer instance.

It is a little more complex than the linked clone technology used in VMware workstation (although based on a similar concept). To use View Composer, you create a VM that is going to be your master View desktop image or parent image. Once created, you power it down and take a snapshot. When you create a pool of View desktops using this parent and snapshot, a Replica is created. The Replica is always thinly provisioned and is used to create the remaining virtual desktops in the pool, as shown in Figure 2.11.

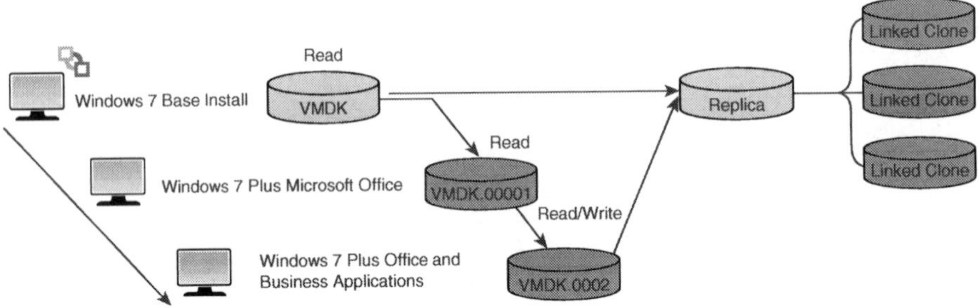

Figure 2.11 View Composer

The logic behind creating a Replica first is that you can create different snapshots associated with the parent image and use them to update existing Replicas or combine them to create new Replicas. This separation between the parent and Replica provides more flexibility in the operational management of the desktop pool because a single parent with multiple snapshots can be the foundation for all the desktop pools. In addition, this separation allows operational activities to take place on the parent without impacting the pools already deployed.

By default, Replicas are stored on the same datastore as the linked clone tree, but you have the option of specifying the datastore on which it is created. This provides the flexibility of storing Replicas, which generally experience heavy read activity during deployment and operational maintenance activities, on a higher service tier of read-optimized storage such as SSDs.

When you use View Composer, a View desktop is made up of a similar combination of disks, with the exception of the secondary OS disk. The separation of the OS of the VM into an OS and secondary OS disk enables you to update the OS disk without destroying the relationship of the VM to other IT services, such as the Active Directory and network.

This becomes important when you perform operational activities that refresh or change the OS disk. The secondary disk contains the MAC, the globally unique identifier of the OS, and other items that identify the uniqueness of the OS.

The separation of the unique factors of the OS from the OS disk becomes important if you want to roll the View desktops in the pool back to a clean state. This is called a refresh and involves discarding the OS disk that is currently in use by the View desktop and re-creating it from the original Replica. By having a secondary OS disk, things such as the trust relationship between the OS and the AD are maintained, thus minimizing the disruption of this activity, as shown in Figure 2.12.

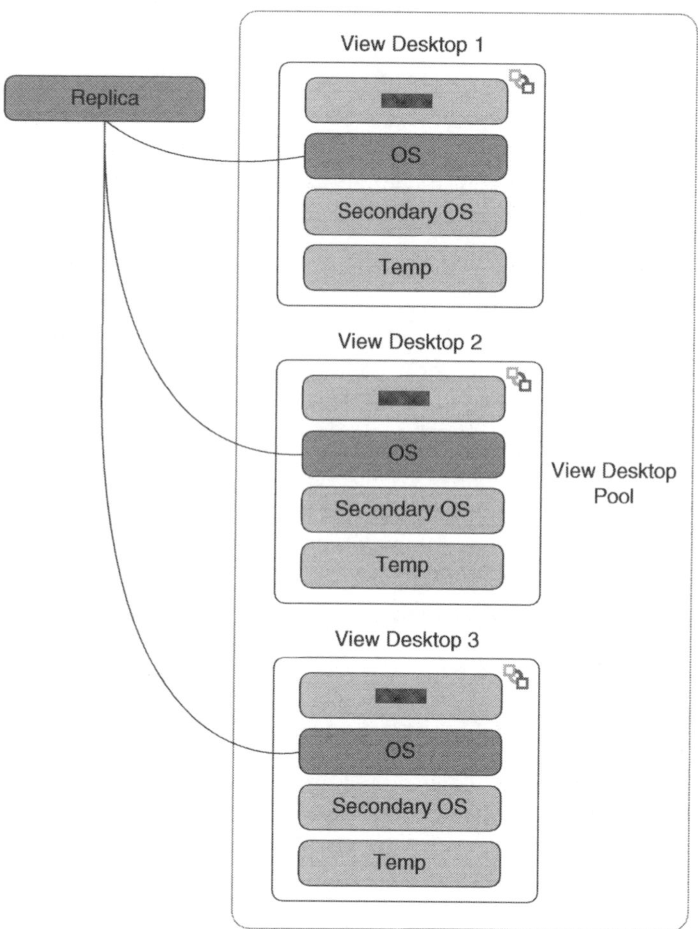

Figure 2.12 A refresh replaces the OS disk.

In addition, you can perform a rebalance, which enables you to redistribute the View Composer desktops across different datastores. You can also use it to migrate View Composer desktops to different datastores. The underlying operation actually performs a refresh and then redeploys the View desktops evenly across the given datastores.

The other option that you have is a recompose, which involves replacing the associated Replica with a different one. Because there are operational considerations when applying each of these operational procedures to a View desktop pool, see Chapter 7, "View Operations and Management," for additional details.

You should also consider pool size if using View Composer. View Composer enables you to take advantage of linked clones. Because linked clones are essentially differential or snapshot files linked to a master or parent VM, you can make changes to the parent and propagate the files. If you update the parent VM with patches, for example, and want to push them to the associated linked clones, you perform recompose. This essentially re-creates the OS disk to reflect the changes in the new Replica. If you have created pools of more than 500 virtual desktops, recomposing can take substantially more time than if you had used pools of 50 virtual desktops. Therefore, be careful when sizing your View desktops per pool.

The effect of re-creating the OS disk is that any changes made since the last refresh are lost. This can represent a risk if you are not using things such as a stateless-friendly antivirus solution because your definition files might need to be downloaded again. You can mitigate this risk by using sound operational processes such as patching the OS disk and performing a recompose (which replaces the OS disk with the updated one) or using stateless-friendly software. In the case of the stateless-friendly antivirus software, the agent usually points to a location that stores the definitions (instead of storing them locally) so that the refresh does not require an update. In addition, you must combine stateless with the user of Persona so that user configurations are stored outside the View desktop so that they are retained between refresh and recompose operations.

This contrasts with what happens in stateful desktops, in which the writes are applied directly to the View desktops disk and so are not lost between reboots.

All the linkage and metadata information is stored by View Composer using its associated database. This database can be installed locally or on a dedicated Microsoft SQL or Oracle server. For details on the installation requirements, see Chapter 4, "VMware View Implementation."

Persona Management

Persona Management is important because it separates the user-specific information from the View desktop. The ability to do this has been around for some time in traditional server-based computing environments using technologies such as Windows Roaming Profiles. Separating the user data into a profile enables you to store it centrally but cache it locally when the user is logged in. If an OS failure occurs and you lose the OS, you can allow users to log in to a second instance and redownload all their configuration and user-specific settings from the central location.

The ability to do this becomes critical when leveraging certain technology such as nonpersistent or floating View desktops. Floating desktops are a pool of View desktops that are not explicitly assigned on login to the user requesting a connection. In this case, the user might not log in to the same desktop every time because the association between the user and View desktop is nonpersistent, as shown in Figure 2.13.

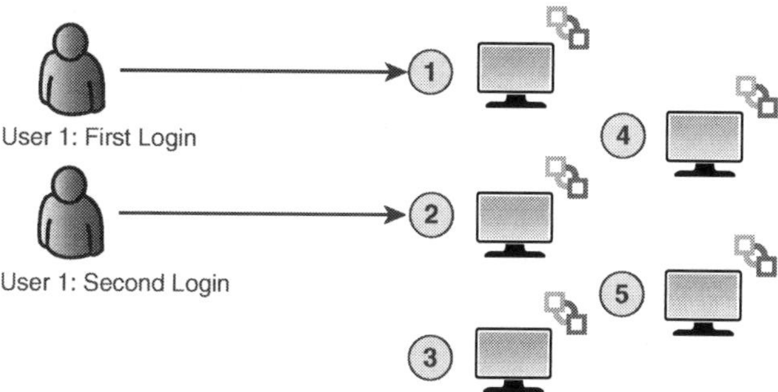

Figure 2.13 Floating desktops

Because a user might log in to a different View desktop, you need to centralize the user persona. View Persona is provided with VMware View to offer an alternative to Windows Roaming Profiles. This is in addition to redirecting the local profile to a separate User disk or VMDK. We mentioned the capability to redirect the local profile to a User disk when we looked at the architecture of the Transfer Server. Although it might seem redundant to redirect the local profile to a User disk and then replace the local profile with View Persona, they are not exclusive and can be used with each other. The User disk provides a dedicated drive to allow the View Persona to be cached, but still enables the changes to trickle up to the central location. The dedicated drive for caching View Persona improves the login times, but ensuring that all information is synchronized with a centrally stored View Persona directory ensures that any information can be recovered, as shown in Figure 2.14.

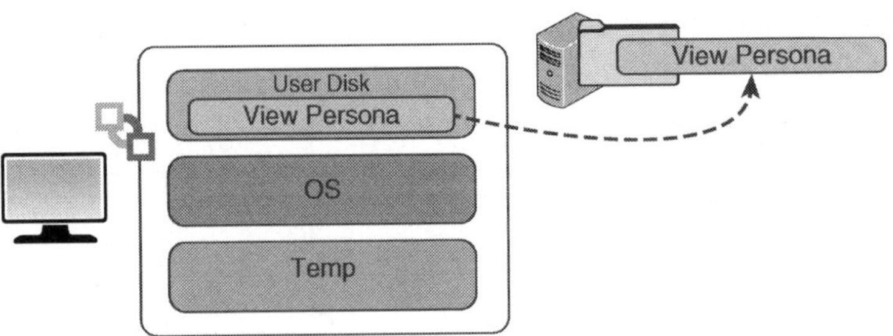

Figure 2.14 User disk and View Persona

PCoIP

PC over IP (PCoIP) is the principal display protocol for VMware View environments. The traffic is made up of TCP control plane traffic and User Datagram Protocol (UDP)–based data or user traffic. As of VMware View 4.6, PCoIP uses port 4172 for TCP and UDP traffic. PCoIP has reserved port numbers with the Internet Assigned Numbers Authority (IANA). You can find a complete list of port requirements on VMware's site at http://kb.vmware.com/kb/1027217.

PCoIP continually checks the network for available bandwidth and to determine round-trip latency. In a LAN environment, the default settings are configured to provide the best end-user experience. If you are going to be providing virtual desktops for remote access, you should create a testing environment where you can simulate latency and bandwidth scenarios to ensure that you can properly tweak PCoIP and the VMs.

Much work has been done in VMware View 6 to enable you to optimize the traffic. In addition, many new capabilities were added. VMware View 5 enabled you to proxy PCoIP through a View Security Server. Refer to Figure 2.6, earlier in this chapter, to see the traffic flows that occur when View Security Servers are deployed.

You can add a PCoIP offload card or APEX 2800 to the ESXi host. By doing so, you can push some of the resource requirements to an accelerator card. The offload cards are designed to run up to 64 high-resolution screen sessions and enable you to increase the virtual desktop density by 30% to 40%. You can find additional information on the APEX 2800 at www.teradici.com/pcoip/pcoip-products/teradici-apex-2800.php. View desktops that do a lot of graphic-intensive operations that require heavy encoding and decoding of PCoIP are good candidates for these cards.

According to Teradici's internal testing, PCoIP has been designed to run up to 250 ms of latency; the company has tested it beyond but generally finds the user experience degrades over this limit. Teradici offers a VDI university on its support site (http://techsupport.teradici.com/ics/support/default.asp?deptID=15164) that is a great reference.

It goes through each possible tuning parameter in depth, but you must sign up for a free support account.

You can tweak a number of settings to adjust the protocol for WAN and bandwidth. These settings are adjusted on the virtual desktop within the registry or using a Group Policy Object (GPO) template on the OU of the virtual desktops:

- **Maximum Bandwidth:** This setting enables you to set the peak available bandwidth (BW) for each VM. The average bandwidth should fall well below this setting.
- **Bandwidth Floor:** This setting sets the threshold below which PCoIP will not limit itself if there is contention on the network.
- **Maximum Initial Image Quality:** This option sets the initial BW when the PCoIP is rendering an image.
- **Minimum Image Quality:** This setting controls the minimum quality for video performance.
- **MTU size:** If you adjust the maximum transmission unit (MTU), you also should adjust everything else along the path.
- **PCoIP Encryption Setting:** This setting enables you to adjust the type of encryption to improve performance of the session.
- **Frame Rate Limit:** This setting is the most important adjustment that you can make. PCoIP is set to 30 frames per second (fps) out of the box. You can adjust this down to 10 to 15 fps and still get reasonable video performance.

Teradici provides the general reference guidelines shown in Table 2.5 to help you adjust these settings.

Table 2.5 PCoIP Adjustments

Maximum Frames per Second	Desktop Workload (Estimate)	Notes
60	PCoIP Host Card Default, which is appropriate for 3D CAD and 3D video games	Extreme graphic
30	VMware View PCoIP Default for HD video	
24	Film frame rate	
16	Better video	
10 to 12	Video	

In addition, you can adjust the performance of PCoIP in certain types of scenarios. You can disable the build-to-lossless (BTL) capability of PCoIP. *Lossless* describes a class of data compression that essentially ensures that the exact original image is reconstructed. *Lossy* is a separate class that allows for some but not all the data to be reconstructed. As it relates to PCoIP, you can halt the rendering of the graphics at the lossy stage. Typically, when PCoIP renders an image, it goes from lossy to lossless as the graphic is constructed. Setting the display protocol to stop at lossy can save up to 30% of the total bandwidth consumption (see http://blogs.vmware.com/performance/2011/09/vmware-view-pcoip-build-to-lossless-.html).

You can configure these optimizations by importing the Group policy administrator template, which is installed when you install VMware View on the server. You can find it in the following location:

> <install_directory>\VMware\VMware View\Server\extras\GroupPolicyFiles\pcoip.adm

This template can be imported in the OU where the virtual desktops are installed or into the local policy of the virtual desktop.

QoS and PCoIP

One other key design consideration that often gets overlooked is preparing the network for PCoIP. When introducing a new service that is going to be critical, most organizations comprehensively review the network and introduce the new class of traffic in a proper way. Take, for example, Voice over IP (VoIP). Most organizations have only two classes of traffic on their network: VoIP and everything else. When designing your VMware View environment, treat PCoIP in a similar fashion to VoIP and prioritize it. To prevent LAN congestion, implement quality of service (QoS) for your PCoIP traffic. Although QoS deals with prioritization when traffic is constrained, PCoIP should be prioritized on your network. You should prioritize both the TCP and UDP traffic on 4172. Teradichi provides an excellent checklist to help you check your current network configurations against the settings ideal for PCoIP (http://communities.vmware.com/servlet/JiveServlet/downloadBody/16186-102-1-20133/PCoIP_ Protocol_Virtual_Desktop_Network_Design_Checklist%20r2.pdf). In addition, VMware considers it a best practice to tag PCoIP using QoS.

One common problem is the default configuration for dealing with congestion when QoS is configured on Cisco routers. QoS enables you to configure a series of queues so that you can prioritize traffic. When congestion occurs, a router uses whatever congestion-avoidance mechanism is configured. By default, an interface drops newly arrived packets when the queue is full, leading to data loss. This congestion-avoidance mechanism is known as *tail drop* because essentially the tail end of the data stream is dropped to deal with congestion. The default should be changed to Cisco's weighted random early detection (WRED). WRED uses the IP precedence, which determines the importance or priority of the packet and randomly drops packets before the queue is full to maintain consistency. This allows WRED to differentiate between streams to be able to apply the random drops. To ensure good performance of UDP and in turn PCoIP, you should update the default congestion avoidance mechanism to WRED.

Summary

A well-architected virtual desktop environment offers management, energy savings, and a higher level of security, and it delivers a good user experience. To ensure you can implement the solution properly, you must understand what your bandwidth and storage requirements are going to be. You should also ensure that user profile information is properly delivered and centrally stored using View Persona. In addition, you should understand how to use application virtualization in your View environment.

Although we have not talked about application virtualization, ThinApp is a great technology. It enables you to associate applications to users (versus integrating them into the OS image). Take the stateless desktops that were described earlier in this chapter. If every time we needed to deploy a new application we had to create a new image and then reintroduce the revised image into our desktop pool, we would quickly have a large number of images to manage. By using application virtualization, we can store the applications outside the OS disk and integrate them using shortcuts stored in Persona. This gives us the best of both worlds: providing users the applications they need while easing management and deployment by using stateless desktops.

Because a virtual desktop environment involves a multitude of technology, you should ensure that you have a well-documented architecture and design document. Taking the time to complete this step will assist you greatly when you start talking to your storage and networking teams. The time spent in calculating your I/O requirements from a network and storage perspective will ensure that each team understands what you need to deliver a View desktop to your end users and avoid problems down the road. Be cautious and ensure that you have a complete picture and that anything you are unsure of is properly vetted so that you know how the deployment of VMware View will look in your environment.

Now that you understand the basic architecture of a VMware View environment, you are ready to look at installation, which Chapter 4 covers. When moving from architecture to implementation, make certain to note any additional training and transitioning that might be required to move from delivery to operations.

The best technology solutions work because support and operation have been integral parts of the rollout of the solution. The same holds true when you are moving a large number of users from physical to virtual desktops. Although it is still desktop support, a number of capabilities will be new to the desktop support team and can change the way they provide support in some cases. Consider, for example, the ability to refresh a desktop or application in a matter of minutes from View's Administrator console. To take advantage of these capabilities, the desktop support team must also understand them. Chapter 7 covers operational best practices when looking after a large VMware View environment.

Chapter 3

VMware Workspace Architecture

Introduction

VMware Workspace enables you to deliver a broader range of services to your end users. A production implementation of Workspace is different, however, from importing the Open Virtual Appliance (OVA) file and configuring the default components. You must consider additional requirements, such as Secure Sockets Layer (SSL) offloading and load balancing. In addition, Workspace is very sensitive to name resolution and time synchronization to ensure that each virtual appliance can communicate and authenticate users properly. Some of these considerations are just deploying additional virtual appliances while others require third-party services. This chapter reviews what you need to consider upfront and how you deploy a highly available production implementation of VMware Workspace.

Approaching the Design and Architecture

To understand when additional virtual appliances are warranted, you must understand how much capacity each virtual appliance is designed to support. For example, VMware Workspace requires one gateway virtual appliance for every 2000 users. Table 3.1 lists the design or capacity specifications of each component of VMware Workspace. (Note that only Workspace virtual appliances are listed; refer to your vendor documentation for connection limitations on any third-party appliances such as load balancers.)

Table 3.1 Virtual Appliance Limits

Virtual Appliance	Description	Limit
Configurator	Use to configure the remaining virtual appliances.	Only one configurator virtual appliance is allowed.
Connector	Used to support different authentication methods within Workspace. For high availability, multiple connectors should be load balanced.	One connector can support 30,000 users.
Manager	Enterprise deployments require two or more manager virtual appliances.	Each manager virtual appliance can support 100,000 users.
Gateway	Provides access and the namespace for VMware Workspace. For high availability, multiple gateways should be load balanced.	One gateway is required for every 2000 users. In addition, one gateway is required for each data VA; so, if you have 2000 data users, you will need 2 gateway VAs.
Data	The data virtual appliance provides the file-sharing capabilities for VMware View.	Each data virtual appliance can support 1000 users. A minimum of 3 data virtual appliances is required in production: 1 manager and 2 user data appliances.

Planning Considerations

In planning and architecting VMware Workspace, you need to understand not only the Workspace vApp components and how they are implemented but also what services that Workspace depends on. For example, the virtual appliances rely heavily on the fully qualified domain name to find and communicate with each other. This makes them reliant on Domain Name System (DNS). Therefore, you must ensure that forward and reverse name lookups are correct for each of the appliances. During the installation, this name resolution is verified as part of the prerequisite checking that is done. In addition to DNS, Workspace is dependent on several other external services. This section covers some of the required supporting services to ensure that your VMware Workspace environment is deployed properly.

IP Pools

VMware Workspace deploys from an OVA software package into a vApp consisting of five virtual appliances. During the deployment, the vApp looks for an IP pool configured from within the vSphere environment to understand what DNS servers should be used to verify forward and reverse name lookups. IP pools are network configurations that are assigned to a virtual machine (VM) network and used by vApps. This information ensures that the verification checks can be completed and the installation can proceed. To configure the IP pool, complete the following steps:

> **NOTE**
>
> Configuration of IP pools happens from within vCenter.

1. Open the vSphere Client and log in using the appropriate credentials.
2. When connected to vCenter, select **Home** and **Networking**.
3. Select the **IP Pools** and click **Add**.
4. Provide the IP pool a name, and configure IP and DNS information. (Note that VMware Workspace requires the DNS settings but does not need the IP pool to be enabled.)
5. After you have configured your setting, select the **Associations** tab and select the virtual network on which this IP pool should be enabled, and click **OK**.

Network Services

The dependency on name resolution was mentioned earlier in this section, but VMware Workspace is dependent on several other network services. When Workspace is installed, you specify the URL that users will browse to in order to log in to the service. If you intend to allow external access to the URL, it is recommended that you install a reverse proxy that supports SSL offload. A reverse proxy would sit in the demilitarized zone (DMZ) and take Workspace client requests originating outside the corporate network and forward them to the gateway server on the internal network, as shown in Figure 3.1.

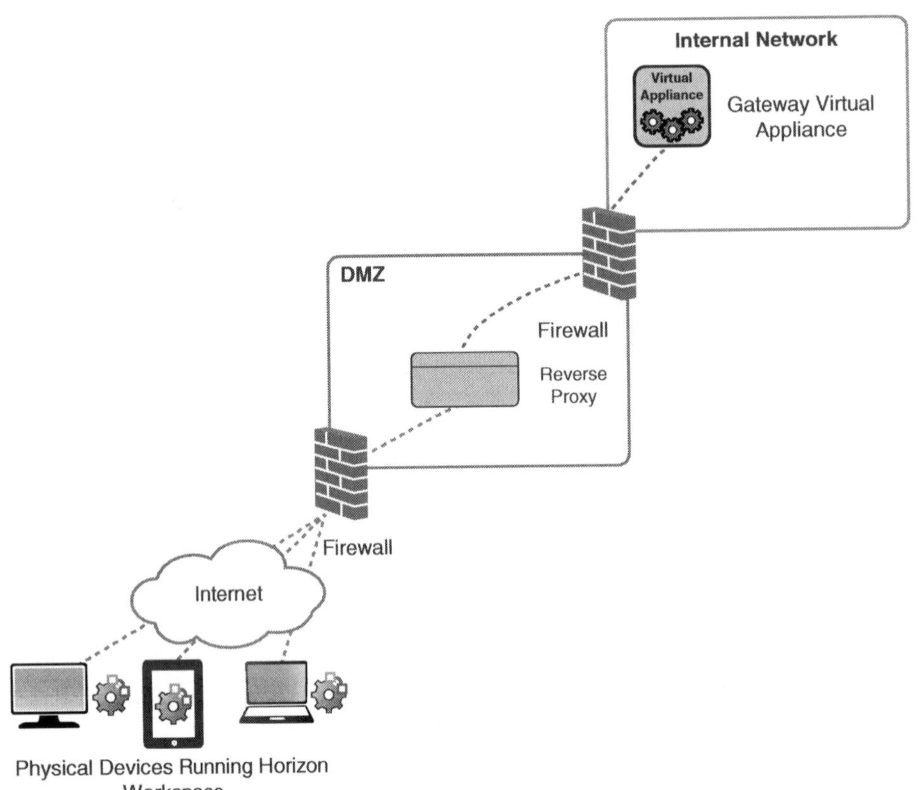

Figure 3.1 Reverse proxy and VMware Workspace

The load balancer is used to ensure high availability (HA) of the gateway virtual appliance, which provides the client access point for VMware Workspace. In Figure 3.2, we have inserted the load balancing and the second gateway virtual appliance, so we have a logical configuration more closely resembling production.

Most network appliances that provide reverse proxy and SSL offload functionality often come with an HA option that provides a cluster configuration to ensure that when one appliance fails the other takes over. This means that, in addition to the load-balancing service for the gateways, you might have a second appliance deployed in the DMZ to ensure availability of the reverse proxy and SSL offload functions.

SSL offload is the capability of the appliance to support certificates and the encryption and decryption of traffic as required while forwarding or responding to client requests.

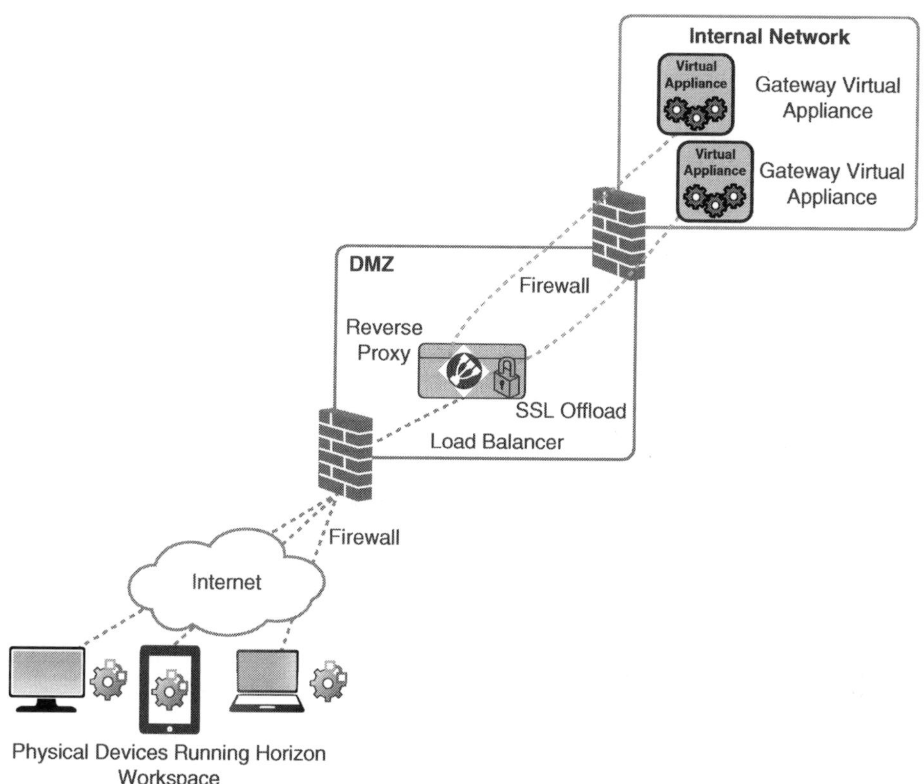

Figure 3.2 Reverse proxy and load balancing

NTP

All the virtual appliances make use of Network Time Protocol (NTP) to ensure time accuracy. Within VMware Workspace, many synchronization activities take place, such as synching Workspace and View so that changes and availability of View pools are accurately reflected. In addition, Workspace has the option of using native Kerberos authentication by deploying a dedicated connector appliance. Kerberos tokens are time sensitive, and time accuracy is critical to ensuring that synchronization takes place. It is important that the NTP server specified for Workspace, vCenter, and the Active Directory be the same to avoid problems.

Authentication

VMware Workspace supports a single Active Directory (AD) or a multidomain AD forest. However, as of 1.8., multiforest AD deployments are supported. Multiforest enables you to deploy multitenant configurations. *Multitenant* refers to the ability to have segregation for authentication and Workspace portal so that you can support multiple customers or companies. You can, however, integrate RSA SecurID tokens to add additional layers of security for remote access. In addition, although the default is AD authentication, you can use native Kerberos, but both RSA and native Kerberos will require a separate, dedicated connector virtual appliance.

A single AD requires Lightweight Directory Access Protocol (LDAP) queries, whereas a multidomain AD requires queries to the Global Catalog. The Global Catalog contains information about all the domains within the AD, and therefore it enables you to query any of the underlying groups. Chapter 6, "Integrating VMware View and Workspace," covers the slight differences in configuration.

AD accounts and groups are first synced using LDAP connectors to import user and group information into Workspace. Once imported, the AD group and account information is used to map to Workspace groups. Once mapped, the synchronized groups and users are entitled or associated to resources within VMware Workspace, as shown in Figure 3.3.

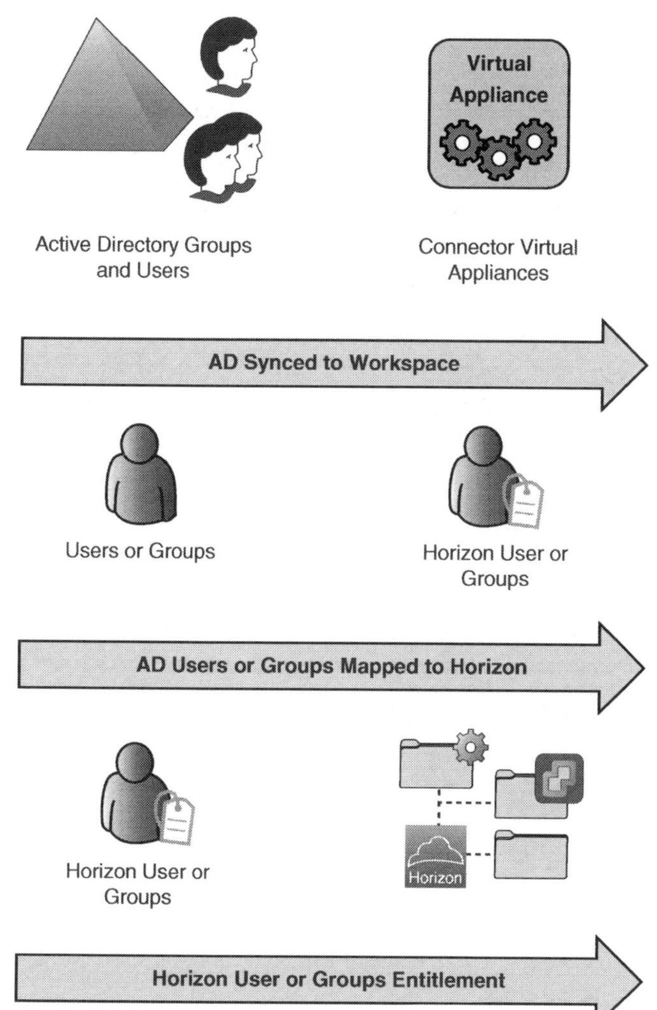

Figure 3.3 VMware Workspace account entitlement

Certificates

During the installation, the configurator creates a self-signed root certificate authority (CA). A certificate is generated for each virtual appliance based on this root CA as part of the installation process. The certificate is associated with the fully qualified domain name (FQDN) for each appliance, with the exception of the gateway appliance. Because the gateway is the access point for all clients, the certificate is generated based on the FQDN of Horizon Workspace that you specify as part of the installation, as shown in Figure 3.4.

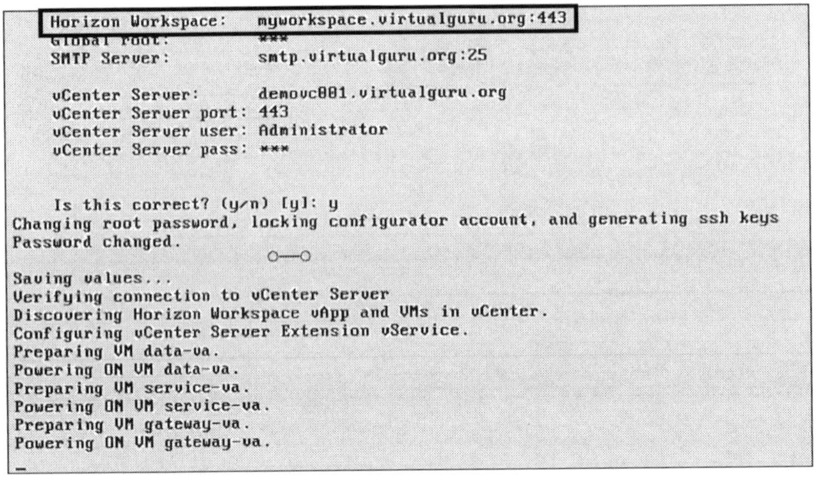

```
    Horizon Workspace:      myworkspace.virtualguru.org:443
    Global root:            ***
    SMTP Server:            smtp.virtualguru.org:25

    vCenter Server:         demovc001.virtualguru.org
    vCenter Server port:    443
    vCenter Server user:    Administrator
    vCenter Server pass:    ***

    Is this correct? (y/n) [y]: y
Changing root password, locking configurator account, and generating ssh keys
Password changed.

Saving values...
Verifying connection to vCenter Server
Discovering Horizon Workspace vApp and VMs in vCenter.
Configuring vCenter Server Extension vService.
Preparing VM data-va.
Powering ON VM data-va.
Preparing VM service-va.
Powering ON VM service-va.
Preparing VM gateway-va.
Powering ON VM gateway-va.
_
```

Figure 3.4 VMware Workspace FQDN

The VMware Workspace FQDN is used for the gateway because the gateway is used to connect all client sessions to Workspace. Using a more user-friendly name, such as myworkspace.virtualguru.org for users in the virtualguru.org domain, makes it easier and less ambiguous than gateway-va.virtualguru.org.

Because the self-signed root CA generated by the configurator obviously is not part of a public CA, the root CA must be pushed to each of the virtual appliances within Workspace to ensure that there is trust and enable communications.

If you choose to use the self-signed certificates, you must make an adjustment to each client to ensure that it recognizes it is a valid root certificate provider. The process will vary from device to device, but to ensure that it is clear, the following example based on a Windows 7 desktop running Internet Explorer 9 is provided here. (For information on using public and internal CAs, please refer to Chapter 5, "VMware Workspace Implementation.")

Using the Self-Signed CA Example

1. Download the self-signed root CA from the gateway virtual appliance at the following location:

   http://<gateway hostname>/horizon_workspace_rootca.pem

2. When prompted, select **Save As** and specify a location locally to save the file.
3. After downloading, select the certificate, right-click, and click **Install certificate**.
4. When the Welcome to the Certificate Import Wizard starts, click **Next**.
5. Change the default on the next screen to **Place all certificates in the following store**, and click the **Browse** button.
6. Select the **Trusted Root Certificate Authorities**, and click **OK**.
7. Once selected, click **Next** and **Finish** on the final screen.
8. When prompted with the security warning about the root CA, click **Yes**.
9. On the Certificate Import Wizard Confirmation successful import confirmation dialog box, click **OK**.
10. Close Internet Explorer and, along the taskbar of the desktop, right-click the VMware Workspace agent and select the **Open Workspace Web Page** option. Verify that you are not prompted with a security warning about the site.

The other two options you have for certificates for your environment is to use trusted public or third-party CAs or internal CAs. The use of public CAs is perhaps the easiest because the appliances are preconfigured to trust a list of common third-party CAs as part of the default configuration. Using third-party CAs is also the recommended certificate method.

The configurator virtual appliance is used to push any updated configuration information to the virtual appliances that make up VMware Workspace. To replace your existing CAs with third-party certificates, simply log in to your configurator appliance and, on the SSL Certificate page, cut and paste your SSL certificate and private key. The configurator then pushes the updated certificates to the remaining virtual appliances.

If you have installed additional connectors to authenticate using native Kerberos or RSA SecurID versus using the default AD username and password, you need to update these certificates manually by browsing directly to the connector under the SSL certificate page. For more information about this process, see Chapter 8, "VMware Workspace Operations."

To use a private CA, you must overwrite the existing certificates within the file system of the configurator virtual appliance and rerun the certificate wizard to update the configuration and push the changes to the other virtual appliances. Additional connector virtual appliances should be completed manually.

If you are using a load balancer that supports SSL offload, the process is more straightforward because the certificate exchange is done before the Workspace environment. This can simplify the process, but because every network appliance differs between vendors, refer to the vendor's documentation for configuration details. (F5, for example, lists many of its deployment guides online at www.f5.com/products/documentation/deployment-guides.)

SMTP

Simple Mail Transfer Protocol (SMTP) is required by VMware Workspace to enable the data virtual appliance or the appliance that provides Cloud file storage and collaboration capabilities (similar to Dropbox) called data services to send messages and alerts.

Because most enterprise customers use Exchange, this section includes the details to set up an SMTP relay for the data virtual appliance as an example. This example applies to Exchange 2007 and 2010.

To set up the relay for VMware Workspace on Exchange, complete the following steps:

1. Create a new receive connector, name it Horizon, and then select **Custom** for the receive connector.
2. Leave the Local Network Settings as is because it will listen to all local IPs on port 25.
3. On the Remote Network Settings, clear 0.0.0.0–255.255.255.255, and then add the IP address of the data virtual appliance.
4. When the new custom receive connector is created, go into the properties of this connector, go to the **Permission Groups** tab, and add **Anonymous Users**.

Although you have created the receive connector, it is not yet activated. To activate the connector, issue the following cmdlet using PowerShell:

```
Get-ReceiveConnector "Horizon" | Add-ADPermission -User "NT AUTHORITY\
ANONYMOUS LOGON" -ExtendedRights "Ms-Exch-SMTP-Accept-Any-Recipient"
```

This cmdlet retrieves the receive connector that was created, adds a permission to AD for the Anonymous Logon group, and assigns that group the Ms-Exch-SMTP-Accept-Any-Recipient permission for the group.

External Storage

The data services component of VMware Workspace requires storage for user files. By default, when the data virtual appliance is deployed, it has several virtual hard drives (VMDKs) with a combined total of 175 GB of storage, as shown in Figure 3.5. (Note: Only 10 GB are allocated for user data storage.)

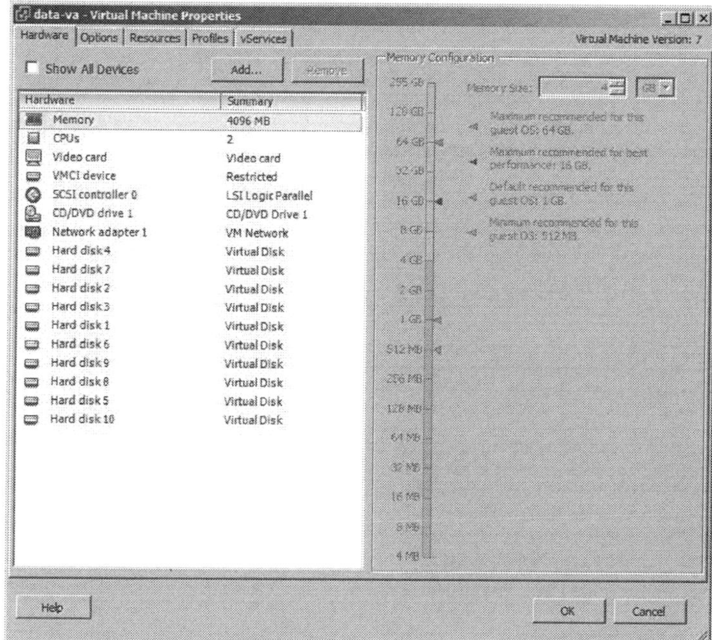

Figure 3.5 Data virtual appliance

Adding additional VMDKs is fine for smaller environments with less than 6 terrabytes of storage, but larger environments should use a true network-attached storage (NAS) appliance delivering native Network Filesystem Storage (NFS). NFS Version 3 or higher is required. (For the steps to integrate NFS and additional VMDKs, refer to Chapter 5.)

To estimate the amount of size required for data services, VMware recommends 2.5 times the total of each user's quota. For example, if you have set a quota of 10 GB/user and have 50 users, you need 1250 GB of storage space.

It is recommended that you have more than one data virtual appliance in your environment to ensure reliability. As part of VMware Workspace, a data-va template is provided to enable you to deploy additional appliances (Note that if you upgrade from 1.0 to 1.5 you will need to re-create the template. See Chapter 8 for additional details.)

To add an additional data virtual appliance, follow these steps:

1. Get an IP address that has been preregistered in DNS (forward and reverse lookups).
2. Go to the configurator-va VM console, log in, and run the `addvm` command:

   ```
   hznAdminTool addvm -type-DATA -ip=[New IP]
   ```

   Note that the new data virtual appliance is deployed in maintenance mode.

After the new data virtual appliance is deloyed, you must properly configure it; complete the following steps to ensure that it is properly deployed in the environment:

1. Log in as root.
2. If required, set the proxy information using the following command:

   ```
   export http_proxy="proxy url:port"
   ```

3. If you use LibreOffice, download and install it using the installer:

   ```
   ie. /opt/zimbra/libexcec/libreofficeinstaller.sh
   ```

4. If you use a Microsoft Windows Preview Server, run the `zmlocalconfig` command to point the data virtual appliance at the Preview Server.

Configure the existing data virtual appliances to recognize the new server:

1. Reboot each to ensure that they are aware of the new data virtual appliance.
2. Populate the SSH keys on each machine using the zimbra account.
3. Log in to each data VM:

   ```
   su -zimbra (to switch to the zimbra user)
   ```

4. Run the `zmupdateauthkeys` command:

   ```
   /opt/zimbra/shh/authorized_keys/zmupdateauthkeys
   ```

5. su back to root.
6. Restart the memory cache as root:

   ```
   /etc/rc.d/memcached restart
   ```

Take the data VM out of maintenance mode:

1. Log in to the configurator web interface https://<configurator-va>.
2. Open the System information page and select the data VM and click **Exit maintenance mode.**

To add additional VMDKs, you simply power off the data VM appliance and add them as you would any normal VM. Once they are added, power up the virtual appliance and log in as root. For the additional VMDKs to be recognized by Data Service, you need to run the following script:

```
/opt/vmware-hdva-installer/bin/zca-expand-lv
```

If you are doing a large installation and plan on using native NFS, you mount the NFS store to the data virtual appliance. To do this, log in to the console as root and run the following command:

```
/opt/vmware-hdva-installer/bin # ./mount-nfs-store.pl -nfs[SERVER NAME]:/
[DIRECTORY]
```

PostgreSQL

VMware Workspace comes with an internal PostgreSQL 9.1 database or support for running an external PostgreSQL 9.1 database. The lack of support for other database platforms can be a drawback for VMware Workspace because it is typically a new requirement from a customer perspective. This section covers a number of benefits with PostgreSQL so that you can plan your environment accordingly.

PostgreSQL is an open source object-relational database system known for reliability and scalability. In addition to the open source version of PostgreSQL, VMware offers vFabric Postgres, or vPostgres. vPostgres is a PostgreSQL virtual appliance that has been tuned for virtual environments. For example, vPostgres supports Elastic Database Memory, which enables the VM to support Memory Resource Management on a vSphere host. vSphere Memory Resource Management is a combination of capabilities that enables the host to optimize and control the use of memory by the VM under a variety of circumstances. Some of these features are native to vSphere, whereas others require installation of the VMware Tools. These capabilities include the following:

- **Transparent page sharing (TPS):** Removes redundant pages with the same content.
- **Ballooning:** Artificially forces the VM to leverage memory paging to release memory when resources are constrained.
- **Memory compression:** Compresses pages that are swapping out.
- **Hypervisor swapping:** ESXi directly swaps out the virtual machine's memory.
- **Swap to host cache:** Reclaims memory by storing the swapped-out pages in the host cache on solid-state drives.

While the internal PostgreSQL database runs on the service virtual appliance, vFabric vPostgres is not included under Horizon Suite or VMware Workspace licensing. The internal Postgres database is intended to simplify the installation for proof-of-concept deployments, but VMware strongly recommends that you use an external Postgres database in production.

To protect your external Postgres database, you can take advantage of VMware vSphere HA, which would protect against host failure, as shown in Figure 3.6.

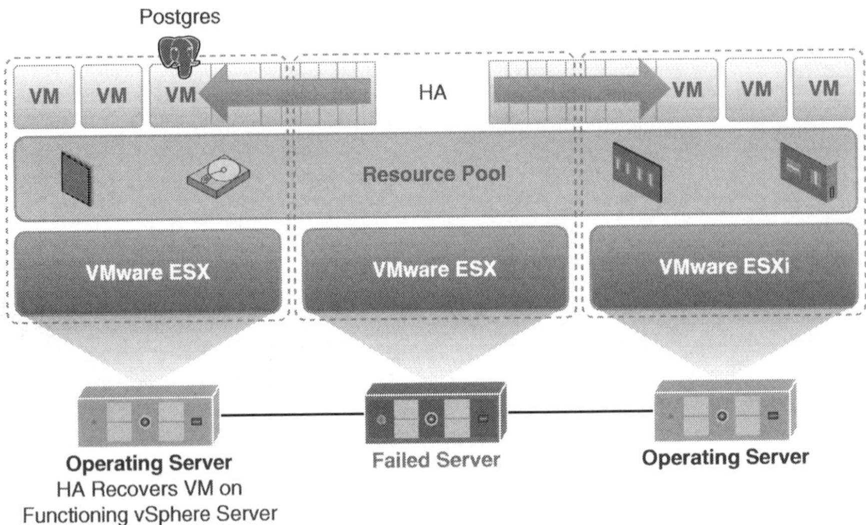

Figure 3.6 vSphere HA and Postgres

VMware HA is set as a property of a virtual cluster and is typically configured based on vSphere host monitoring or heartbeats between hosts. You have additional fine-tuning that can be done by adjusting the Admission Control and the Admission Control Policy. The Admission Control determines whether performance or the availability of the VMs is respected when a failure occurs. By enabling the Admission Control Policy, you are allowing VMs to power on until the point at which resources would start to be constrained. By disabling Admission Control, you allow VMs to power on even if performance is degraded due to a lack of available resources.

The Admission Control Policy enables you to set and specify how many host failures are tolerated and whether you are designating specific hosts to power on the VMs. In addition, you can set how much capacity as a percentage to reserve in the advent of a failure. For additional information about Admission Control and Admission Control Policy, refer to VMware's website.

In addition to host monitoring, you can tune VM monitoring, which monitors heartbeats from the VMs and I/O to determine whether the VM is still responding. If it is not, it restarts the VM. Application monitoring allows for the creation and customization of an application monitor by using the VMware software development kit (SDK) and requires additional configuration. By default, both VM and application monitoring are enabled.

vSphere HA also uses at least two datastores to communicate with hosts in the cluster to ensure that if a VM management network fails, hosts can determine the appropriate response even if network communication is interrupted.

Postgres Availability

In addition to using VMware's HA, Postgres supports a master and slave model. There can only be one master, but there can be multiple slaves. Changes can be moved between master and slave by shipping logs using a Write Ahead Log (WAL), as shown in Figure 3.7.

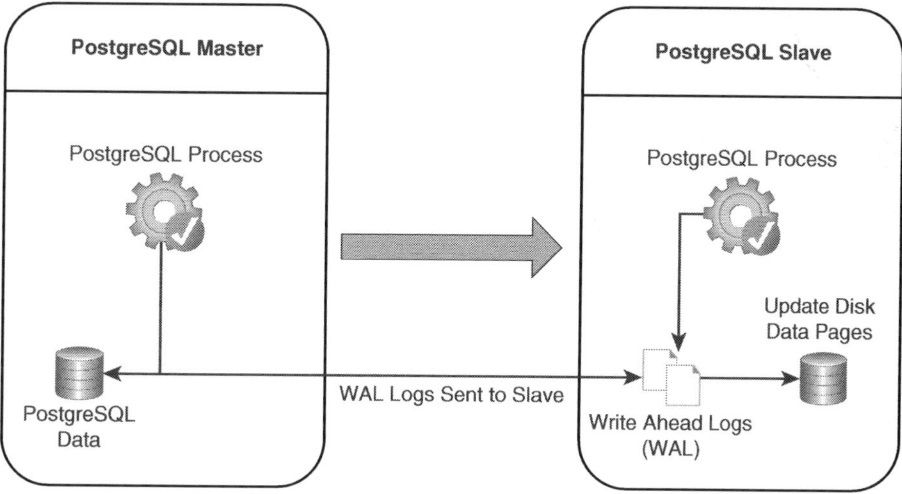

Figure 3.7 Postgres master and slave

For details on how to set up a Postgres cluster based on open source software, refer to the www.postgresql.org/ website. The example provided in this section uses vPostgres to give you a high-level understanding of how to configure a Postgres cluster.

The vPostgres virtual appliance ships as an OVA and is based on SUSE Linux Enterprise Server 11 SP1. To deploy it, simply import the OVA and agree to the license prompt. When the virtual appliance boots, it attempts to find an IP address and boot:

1. As part of the console boot process, you must agree to an additional license prompt. To allow the boot loader to continue, type **yes**.
2. The virtual appliance will boot and set a default password, which will be displayed on the login screen along with the utility to update it.
3. Log in as root with the default password, and run the following command to update the password: `/opt/aurora/sbin/set_password`. (It is important that you use this utility to ensure that Postgres is configured properly and the service starts.)
4. Complete the same process once again to deploy a second virtual appliance, which will become the slave.

Now that you have a primary and slave vPostgres virtual appliance, you are ready to tune the appliance based on the number of expected connections. VMware provides reference architecture for a VMware Workspace environment supporting 30,000 connections. For ease of reference, this example uses these specifications. You can download the document "VMware Horizon Workspace Reference Architecture" from their site and use it to adjust your hardware requirements accordingly.

For simple reference, Table 3.2 lists the specifications to support 30,000 connections; you can also find these within the Reference Architecture document as well.

Table 3.2 Resource Requirements for 30,000 Connections

Resource	Value
vCPU	4 vCPUs
RAM	8 GB
Root disk	2 GB
Data disk	32 GB
SWAP disk	16 GB
Diagnostic disk	2 GB

To configure vPostgres properly after the deployment of the master and slave virtual appliances, you need to configure the virtual appliance with the appropriate hardware configuration, create a new user and database for storing the VMware Workspace data, and then set up the cluster. To update the configuration of the vPostgres appliance, simply power it off and change the properties of the VM so that it has sufficient resources and space and power it back on.

To verify whether SUSE has recognized the hardware changes, you can verify the CPU using `cat` to dump the /proc/cpuinfo file and use `grep` to search for the number of processors and amount of memory, as shown in Figure 3.8.

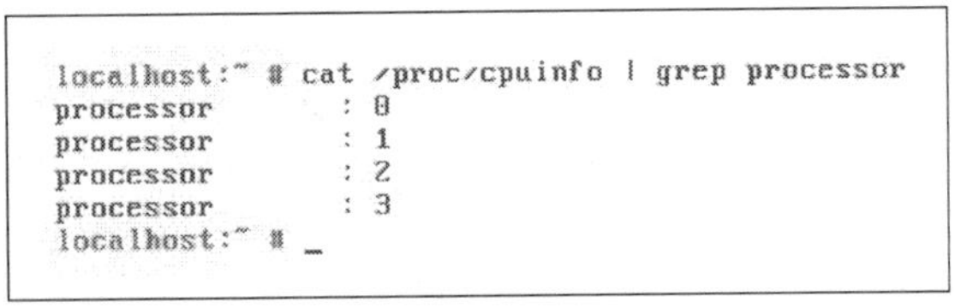

```
localhost:~ # cat /proc/cpuinfo | grep processor
processor       : 0
processor       : 1
processor       : 2
processor       : 3
localhost:~ # _
```

Figure 3.8 grep cpuinfo

It is also possible to check the memory using the same method to `grep` the /proc/meminfo file to see whether SUSE has recognized the change in memory, as shown in Figure 3.9.

```
localhost:~ # cat /proc/meminfo | grep MemTotal
MemTotal:          8195968 kB
localhost:~ # _
```

Figure 3.9 grep meminfo

If you have adjusted the size of the virtual hard drives attached to the VM, you can verify this using the `df-h` command, as shown in Figure 3.10. Verify virtual disk changes to verify this.

```
localhost:~ # df -h
Filesystem           Size  Used Avail Use% Mounted on
/dev/sda2            1.9G  749M  1.1G  42% /
devtmpfs             4.8G   92K  4.8G   1% /dev
tmpfs                4.8G   68K  4.8G   1% /dev/shm
/dev/sdb              32G  187M   30G   1% /var/vmware/vpostgres/9.1
/dev/sdd             2.0G   34M  1.9G   2% /opt/aurora/dbg
localhost:~ # _
```

Figure 3.10 Verify volume sizes

Because you will want to ensure that both the master and slave have sufficient capacity to run the entire environment, both should be configured with the same hardware resources and volume sizes. When that is completed, you are ready to create a database to be used by VMware Workspace.

The configuration file for Postgres is called postgresql.conf. Within the file, you can adjust a variety of settings that affect how Postgres runs, such as the maximum number of connections that are accepted. You should verify that the default of 100 connections is sufficient for your environment. To adjust any of the settings in this file, use your favorite editor to adjust the values, and then save the file. The file is read on startup, so you must reboot or restart Postgres to apply the changes.

After you have checked your configuration settings, you must create a Postgres user and database for VMware Workspace. Although you can enter the commands one at a time, the `psql` command supports a file input. Listing 3.1 shows an example of the input file, which creates a Postgres user named workspace and a database named workspace_db and assigns the appropriate permissions and access.

Listing 3.1 Sample Input File

```
CREATE ROLE workspace LOGIN
# creates the workspace user
PASSWORD 'Password'
#specifies a password
NOSUPERUSER INHERIT NOCREATEDB NOCREATEROLE NOREPLICATION;
ALTER ROLE workspace;
#adds appropriate permissions
CREATE DATABASE workspace_db
#creates the workpace_db database
WITH OWNER = postgres
#sets the owner
ENCODING = 'UTF8'
TABLESPACE = pg_default
CONNECTION LIMIT = -1;
GRANT CONNECT, TEMPORARY ON DATABASE workspace_db TO public;
GRANT ALL ON DATABASE workspace_db TO postgres;
GRANT ALL ON DATABASE workspace_db TO workspace;
\connect workspace_db;
CREATE SCHEMA workspace_db AUTHORIZATION workspace;
SET search_path = workspace_db;
# adds the workspace_db database to the search path
CREATE EXTENSION citext SCHEMA workspace_db;
```

If you have created the file first and then intend to copy it to the vPostgres appliance, keep in mind that the default permissions do not allow root to use `scp` or `ssh`. You can temporarily adjust this by editing the /etc/ssh/sshd_config and revising the PermitRoot-Login from **no** to **yes** and resaving the file. After enabling access, restart the service using `service sshd restart`. Do not forget to disable it again, because the recommended approach is to use a user account for file transfers, not root. Also ensure that you update the permissions on the file so that the Postgres user can read and execute the file.

Administration and creation of databases is done using the Postgres user ID, so you need to change to the Postgres user using `su postgres`. You can find the Postgres commands in the /var/vmware/vpostgres/current/bin directory location. If you want to avoid typing full paths, either add the directory to your path variable or switch to the directory. To add the path statements, simply edit the bashrc file located in `$HOME/.bashrc` and add the following lines:

```
export PATH=$PATH:/opt/vmware/vpostgres/current/bin
export PGDATA=/var/vmware/vpostgres/current/pgdata
```

The first statement adds the Postgres binaries to the path, and the second defines where the server data is located for Postgres.

When you are in the directory, you can just pass psql the file using this command:

```
/opt/vmware/vpostgres/current/bin/psql -f /tmp/create_workspace_db.do
```

After you have created the database, you have to point VMware Workspace at the database instance. The database configuration can be changed from the configurator virtual appliance either during the initial installation using the wizard or by logging in and clicking the **Database Connection** link. Once selected, simply change from the default to the Database Type to **External** and point the JDBC URL to the database and enter the user ID and password, as shown in Figure 3.11.

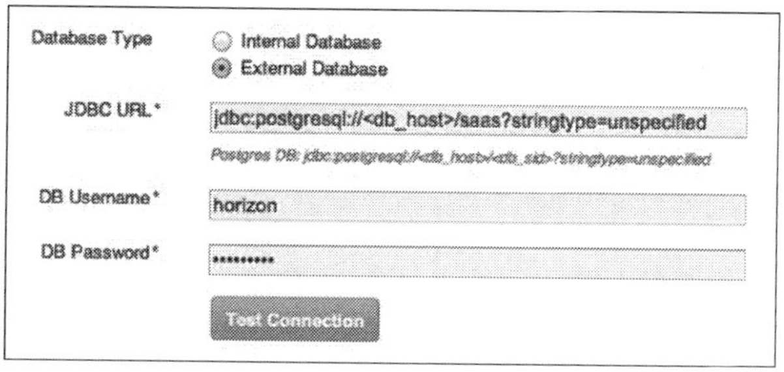

Figure 3.11 Change database type

In addition, you must open the Postgres port on the service virtual appliance. To do this, log in as root on the service virtual appliance from the console. Adjust the firewall and run the following command:

```
iptables -A INPUT -p tcp --dport 5432 -j ACCEPT
```

Postgres Clusters

Setting up a Postgres cluster is a two-step process. First you set up the master server, and then you set up the slave. The settings that control Postgres and the cluster are in postgressql.conf. To configure a cluster, you need to edit this file and add information so that the Postgres cluster is properly configured. In addition, you configure an archive in which the WALs are stored. Access to this archive enables the slave to connect and access the WAL files to ensure that it keeps in sync with the databases and configurations on the master.

You should create an archive location and change the owner and permissions so that the proper user has access. For example, if you complete these steps as root and want to do the replication under the Postgres account, change the owner and permissions for this user. After you have a directory permissioned and assigned to the correct user, edit the postgressql.conf to turn on archive mode. In addition, specify the location of the archive directory under the Archiving of the postgressql.conf section, as shown in Figure 3.12.

```
192.168.91.129 - PuTTY
#checkpoint_completion_target = 0.9      # checkpoint target duration, 0.0 - 1.0
#checkpoint_warning = 30s                # 0 disables
#checkpoint_segments_max = 300   # Maximum dynamic value of checkpoint_segments,
0 disables

# - Archiving -

archive_mode = on                # allows archiving to be done
                                 # (change requires restart)
archive_command = 'cp -i %p /var/vmware/vpostgres/current/pgdata/archive/%f'
        # command to use to archive a logfile segment
#archive_timeout = 0             # force a logfile segment switch after this
                                 # number of seconds; 0 disables

#------------------------------------------------------------------------------
# REPLICATION
#------------------------------------------------------------------------------

# - Master Server -

# These settings are ignored on a standby server

max_wal_senders = 3              # max number of walsender processes
                                 # (change requires restart)
```

Figure 3.12 Archive settings

To enable the slave to connect to the master virtual appliance, you also need to configure the master to listen for the slave. This is done in the cluster configuration file, which is pg_hba.conf and is located in the pgdata directory as well. Simply add the following line to the configuration file specifying the IP of the slave virtual appliance. (Note that in this case we are doing the replication using the Postgres account; if you have created a different account, ensure that you specify it.)

```
host replication postgres [IP Address]/32 trust.
```

To apply these changes, restart the Postgres HA service by issuing the following commands:

```
service aurora_mon stop
service aurora_mon start
```

After completing the configuration of the master VM, you are ready to set up the slave virtual appliance. Log in as root and edit the `$HOME/.bashrc` file so that the path includes the vPostgres executables and pgdata variable. Stop the HA service by typing the following:

```
service aurora_mon stop
```

Because your slave will contain a copy of the pgdata directory on the master, you need to delete the existing one and complete a backup recovery to restore the master pgdata directory to the slave server. Make sure that you are not in the pgdata directory, and then run the following command:

```
rm -fr $PGDATA
```

Once you have cleared out the directory on the slave, ensure that the directory is empty and run the following command, which restores the pgdata directory from the master server to the slave:

```
pg_basebackup -h [Master IP] -D $PGDATA -U [USERID i.e. postgres]
```

Now if you do a list of the directory, you should see the recovered contents from the master server, as shown in Figure 3.13.

```
login as: root
root@192.168.91.130's password:
Last login: Mon Mar 17 22:09:56 2014 from 192.168.91.129
Slave:~ # pushd /var/vmware/vpostgres/current/pgdata/
/var/vmware/vpostgres/current/pgdata ~
Slave:/var/vmware/vpostgres/current/pgdata # ls
archive        pg_hba.conf     pg_subtrans           recovery.conf
backup_label   pg_ident.conf   pg_tblspc             root.crt
base           pg_log          pg_twophase           server.crt
global         pg_multixact    pg_xlog               server.key
id_dsa         pg_notify       pgstartup.log
id_dsa.pub     pg_serial       postgresql.conf
pg_clog        pg_stat_tmp     postgresql.conf.auto
Slave:/var/vmware/vpostgres/current/pgdata #
```

Figure 3.13 Directory contents

On the slave server, you will notice that rather than a postgresql.conf file you have a postgresql.conf.auto file. To ensure that there are no problems in the event of a failover, create a soft link from postgresql.conf to the postgresql.conf.auto file using the following command:

```
cd $PGDATA && ln -s postgresql.conf.auto postgresql.conf
```

You must create a recovery.conf file on the slave server, which provides the steps required during a recovery. The configuration of the file is as follows:

```
restore_command = 'scp [MASTER IP]:/archive/%f %p'
standby_mode = on
recovery_target_timeline = 'latest'
primary_conninfo = 'host=[MASTER IP]application_name=slave'
```

When the recovery file is set, you can exchange certificates with the master vPostgres appliance to ensure the Postgres account can log in from the slave server and complete the replication. To exchange keys, type the following commands:

```
ssh-keygen -t dsa
```

> **NOTE**
> You will be prompted to store the key in a specific location, but the defaults are fine.

```
ssh-copy-id -i ~/.ssh/id_dsa.pub postgres@[MASTER IP]
```

Once this is done, restart the Postgres HA server on the slave server, and your cluster is complete using the following command:

```
service aurora_mon start
```

For additional details on how to configure and create clusters using vPostgres, refer to VMware's knowledge base.

Summary

Moving to VMware Workspace adds considerable complexity from an architecture perspective, but it simplifies the consumption of services from an end-user perspective. Rather than just a desktop, the user can select applications, share files, and collaborate with other users. To ensure these services are stable, you need to plan carefully. This chapter covered the supporting services required for VMware Workspace and how to plan the architecture, and provided examples of configuring dependent services and ensuring availability.

To assist you, VMware provides reference architecture guides for scaling VMware Workspace. In addition, some third-party vendors are starting to provide reference architectures based on deploying on their hardware platform. For example, Nutanix provides a reference architecture for scaling VMware Workspace on its converged infrastructure. Nutanix provides a server and storage tier in a single physical appliance, which is clustered to ensure availability. In addition to this chapter, refer to VMware's website or third parties for additional information on building a resilient Workspace service. Another excellent source of information for Postgres backup and recovery is the www.postgresql.org website. Although VMware has added additional value to Postgres through vPostgres, many of the underlying utilities and commands remain the same.

Chapter 4

VMware View Implementation

This chapter describes how to get the components of a VMware View environment up and running. We assume that you have properly completed a full installation of vCenter and SQL Server; we just want to remind you that a proper installation for these two solutions must be done before starting the View installation. Some components can be installed in parallel (for example, installing the View Composer software or the View Agent on the virtual desktop). This chapter covers the required steps to deploy the following components:

- VMware View
- VMware View Connection Server
- VMware View Composer
- VMware View Security Server
- VMware View Agent
- VMware View Client

This chapter also covers the navigation of the VMware View Admin UI, both the basics and customization options. In addition, you will learn about a non-VMware tool that enables you to personalize the web administration interface of View.

VMware View Deployment and Design Considerations

A couple colleagues of mine who focus on delivery use this phrase often: "Plan the work, work the plan." The saying is not from them; the common saying goes back to church sermons in the 1800s (which kind of makes sense for the people at the time, day-to-day laborers and such). When planning a View deployment, proper planning is key to a successful deployment. Too often people skip some or most of the very necessary steps of a virtual desktop infrastructure (VDI) deployment, regardless of the solution they use.

Most virtual desktop deployment projects come down to how well you have prepared yourself to succeed. Have you involved the right players? Have you thought about involving all the possible players that might have an impact on the success of your deployment? Have you made sure to obtain sign-off from the corporate stakeholders of each of the line of business that will be impacted by such a project? Did you make sure to find an executive sponsor and keep him appraised of all your progress along the way? These are just a sampling of the questions you should ask yourself when undertaking a project like this. Always keep in mind that virtual desktops are very disruptive; they provide benefits in a million different ways, but they will also spotlight any flaw that might have been overlooked or forgotten. The better your planning is, the more chance you have in achieving success; that's just the nature of the beast.

VMware has produced a lot of good collateral on planning for a successful View deployment. You can search by vertical sectors (healthcare, finance, government, and so on), or you can use one of their "vanilla" designs and tailor it to fit your needs. One of the good foundation documents for your planning process is the *VMware Horizon View Architecture Planning Guide* (https://www.vmware.com/support/pubs/view_pubs.html). On its own, this guide is not enough, but it's a solid foundation and covers the basics of a deployment, will make you think about sizing the environment appropriately, and contains hardware and software recommendation.

Entering a virtual desktop design project by first looking at hardware and software is a mistake I see often in the field. One of the major selling points for VMware View is that it's simple to install and set up. Well, one of the flaws of the product is that exact same point: It's simple to install and set up. I've seen a lot of deployments where a customer sets up a proof-of-concept or test/lab environment in just a few hours. Everything gets done, all the pieces fit together, and they obtain their virtual desktop. Seems like magic, right?

That's hardly the case. This is usually where these types of deployment will fall short. It will work fine for the immediate future, and it might even hold steady for the first couple of users. But then, it hits them, all the use-case scenarios that they forgot to think about:

- What about the remote users?
- What about the task worker with specific application requirements?

- What about the power users who need that horsepower to do their jobs?
- What about the call center users working 24/7 who cannot entertain the idea of downtime in their environment?
- Have you planned for any or all of these?

In your eagerness to try out the solution, perhaps you skipped the planning process. Even though you might have hit a single homerun and gave a few desktops to your users, you might have lost the game in the first couple of innings, without even realizing it.

Small steps will get you where you're trying to go. In a virtual desktops project, even though you're planning for all the possible scenarios, getting quick hits is the key to get traction for the project. Be careful, though; small, quick hits do not equal skipping the planning process. You should determine all the possible use cases that you need to cover in your deployment. What service-level agreements (SLAs) do you need to meet? Providing a virtual desktop for a task worker doing Word editing will usually not entail the same network and storage requirements as providing a virtual desktop for a doctor who needs to be able to log on in less than 6 seconds, for example. After you have gone through your list, prioritize it, double-check it, have the proper players review it, and make sure that your sponsor agrees with your list. We wanted to provide you with an extensive list of questions that would help you build your planning document, would make you ask the right questions, and would cover as many possible scenarios as you might encounter. See Appendix A, "A Design Questionnaire Worksheet," for a more exhaustive list of questions.

In the planning process, it is recommended to cover the following:

- What are the business requirements?
- What are the technical requirements?
- What will your endpoints look like (regular PCs versus multiple flavors of mobile clients)?
- What operating system (OS) do you need to support or will you need to support in the future?
- Where will your server be located?
- How many users will you support (concurrent at a minimum)?
- What applications will you need to support?
- Is there an application deployment solution already in place? If so, does it support virtual desktops?
- What type of network will you need to support (multilocation versus single site)?

- Are there any security/compliance regulations that you need to follow?
- What's your user authoritative directory source?
- How do you manage user data today? How will it be managed in the virtual desktop?
- How will your user access their desktop (third-party virtual private network [VPN] solution in the mix)?

Those are just a few examples of the questions you should ask during the planning stage of your virtual desktop deployment project.

When you're confident that you have covered all the bases, it's time to jump in. Whenever possible, you should always start with a controlled environment. Cover the use case you're confident will work, and build from there. It comes back to the 80-20 rule: You can spend most of your effort trying to include the most difficult scenario up front, consume all your resources, and possibly fail; or you can start with a simple use case. Look for a local site test deployment where you will give controlled and monitored access to task workers using the Office productivity suite, for example; this is usually a use case that will win you credibility up front and help you build a strong foundation for the other use cases.

The following section covers the installation process for each of the VMware View components, detailing them in a logical order of installation and explaining why each component exists and its role in the whole equation. It is assumed here that all the prerequisites have been met.

As discussed earlier in this chapter, you can approach the installation of VMware View in a number of ways. Some of the steps can be done in parallel; it's not necessarily a linear process. When required, we explain why it is important to complete certain steps before or after the component installation. Figure 4.1 will help as a visual reference to follow throughout your deployment process. Keep this as a reference point. You can come back to it any time during your deployment. And finally, make sure that you do not skip any steps.

This diagram serves as a quick reminder of various components you can install and how they tie in to each other.

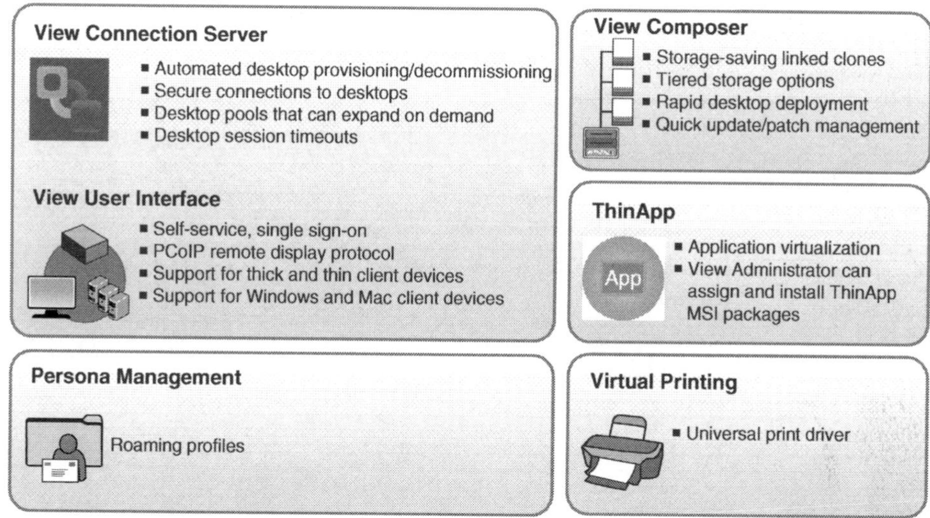

Figure 4.1 View components

Table 4.1 provides a quick reminder of the components you should make sure that you have ready before starting an installation of VMware View.

Table 4.1 General Preparation Checklist

Item	Description
Virtual machine or physical system to serve as a View Manager system	The *VMware View Installation Guide* provides lists of supported operating systems for all View components. The system must be joined to the Active Directory domain before installing View.
VMware View installation files	VMware View Connection Server installation binaries. VMware View Composer binaries. VMware View Manager Agent installation binaries. VMware View Client installation binaries.
Static IP address	It is strongly recommended that you assign your View Manager system a static IP address and create an associated DNS A record entry (Domain Name System Address) record. View Manager security servers require an externally accessible fully qualified domain name (FQDN).

Item	Description
External clock source configured	Maintaining accurate time is necessary for the operation of the View Manager components, so a Network Time Protocol (NTP) clock source or equivalent must be configured for the View Manager system.
VMware View license files	VMware View license files.
VMware vCenter Server hostname	The name of the VMware vCenter Server to use for deploying virtual desktops.
Microsoft Sysprep tools installed on your vCenter Server system	If you are using guest customization, Sysprep must be loaded on your vCenter Server system.
VMware virtual machine to be used as the virtual desktop template or parent virtual machine	This virtual machine must be currently registered in your vCenter Server inventory.

Installing VMware View

If you are running VMware View as a virtual machine (VM) on Windows 2008 R2, much of the performance tuning is complete. The vCPUs and memory sizing should follow the guidelines mentioned in the sizing guidelines; having proper resources to handle the user connecting to your environment will ensure that your users stay happy and that you keep your job.

One piece of advice we recommend you do, on top of the initial performance tuning from Windows 2008, is to adjust the pagefile based on the memory you've allocated to the VM.

Validate where the pagefile is located. If you haven't changed the default location, it will be under the C: drive, and it will be system managed. Manually set the pagefile for the system based on 1.5 times the memory assigned to the VM. You can complete this process as follows:

1. Open Server Manager on the VM.
2. Select **Change System Properties**.
3. Display the Advanced tab and select **Settings**.
4. On the Advanced tab, and under Virtual Memory, select **Change**, as shown in Figure 4.2.

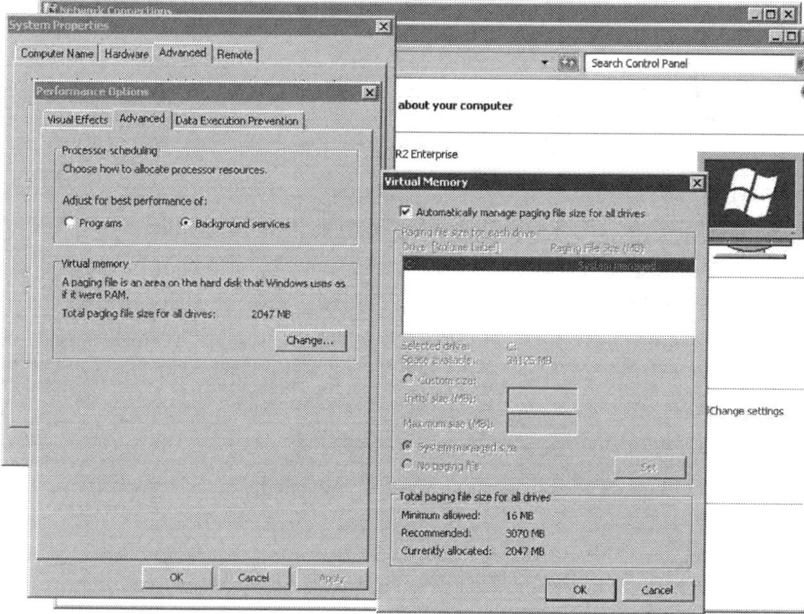

Figure 4.2 Pagefile location

5. Select **Custom Size** and set the minimum and maximum value to 1.5 times the memory allocated.
6. Click **Set**, and click **OK** and **OK** again.
7. When prompted, reboot the VM.

The first server you should install is a standard View Connection Server. As mentioned, you can install four kinds of View Connection Servers: View Standard (or the first Connection Server in the environment), View Replica (or all servers after the initial Connection Server is installed), and Security Server.

Before starting the installation process, be sure you have reviewed all the pre-requisites for the installation of your first View Server:

- Your VM is domain joined.
- You have a fixed IP address.
- Proper name resolution (forward and reverse).
- The windows firewall should stay turned on during install *traffic*. (The installer will automatically configure the firewall upon install.)

- Proper Active Directory access permission (local administrator of the server VM at minimum).
- Active Directory access to create appropriate OUs or OUs precreated before installation by AD admin. (In almost all the cases, this is done outside of the installation process, by AD admins.)

Note that the Active Directory domain must be a 2003 domain functional level, at a minimum. It is also critical that you validate the lifecycle of the OS on which you will install the View Connection Server. We strongly recommend checking with Microsoft; they have a detailed lifecycle policy for their OS. Depending on the type of support you have with your licenses, you will have different dates for end of life of the OS. It varies from mid-2015 to 2020 in some cases. Check here for more information: http://support.microsoft.com/lifeselect.

It is also important to note that installing VMware View Connection Server on a domain controller is not supported.

Also note that VMware does not support installation of the View Connection Server alongside any other applications. It should be installed on its own purpose-built server.

To install the first Connection Server, follow these steps:

1. Launch the VMware View Installer (right-click the executable and choose **Run as Administrator**), and click **Next** on the Welcome screen.
2. Accept the license agreement and click **Next**.
3. Accept the default location (C:\Program Files\VMware\VMware View\Server\) and click **Next**.
4. Because this is the first server, select **View Standard Server**, as shown in Figure 4.3, and click **Next**. (Leave HTML Access checked, we will configure it later in the book.)
5. Here is something new in the 5.x releases and above of VMware View: You now have to enter a data recovery password. This password is required to restore backup from the View Connection Server. Enter the password information, confirm it, enter an optional reminder, as shown in Figure 4.4, and click **Next**.
6. Have the installer automatically configure the Windows firewall, and click **Next**. Note that the installer does not check the firewall state during the installation; it simply prompts you to configure it automatically or not to. If you choose to configure the firewall on your own, be sure to note all the required ports for View communication.

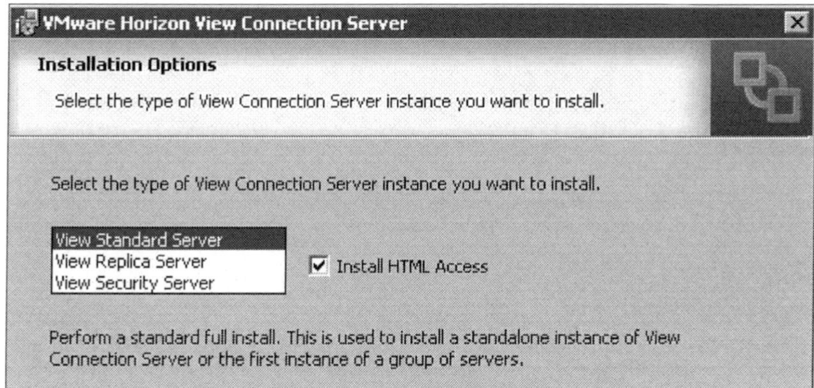

Figure 4.3 Choose View Standard Server.

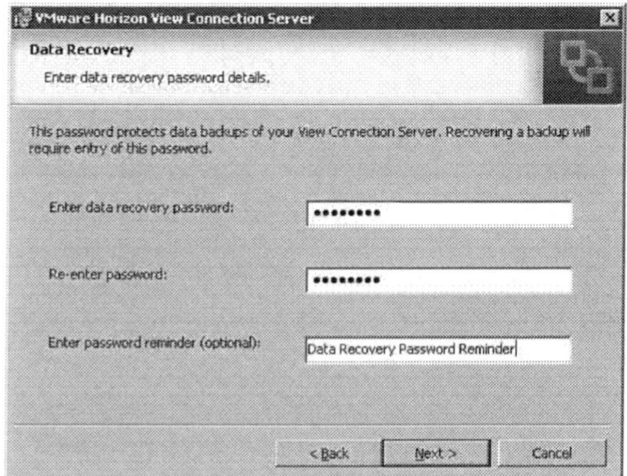

Figure 4.4 Data recovery password

7. Also something new in the 5.x releases and above of VMware View, for security purposes, is that you must authorize a user or a group of users to be able to access the View Administrator interface. We recommend that you authorize the local Administrators group and manage access through that group, as shown in Figure 4.5, and click **Next**.

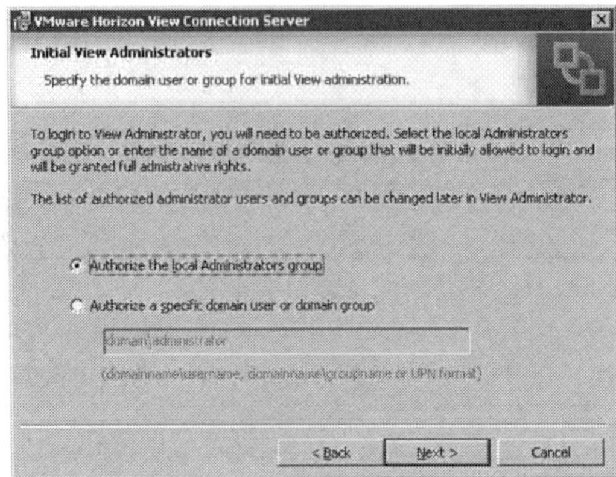

Figure 4.5 Administrator authorization

8. The next screen is optional. It asks you whether you want to participate in the anonymous user experience improvement program. If you participate in the program, we suggest that you review the information VMware collects. Even though everything is anonymized, you should make sure that you will not break any security or compliance policy of your organization if you leave the option checked (Anonymous User Experience Improvement Program). Click **Next** after you make a choice.
9. Click **Install**, and then click **Finish**.

During this process, the installer adds the AD LDS Server role. You will see the step flow-through during the install. The AD LDS Server role is necessary for View Connection Server.

The installer installs nine services on the Windows Server:

- **VMware Horizon View Blast Secure Gateway:** Provides secure HTML access to View desktops
- **VMware Horizon View Connection Server:** Provides connection broker services
- **VMware Horizon View Framework Component:** Provides event logging, security, and COM+ framework services for View Manager
- **VMware Horizon View Message Bus Component:** Provides messaging services between View components
- **VMware Horizon View PCoIP Secure Gateway:** Provides secure tunneling for the PC over IP (PCoIP) protocol

- **VMware Horizon View Script Host:** Disabled by default, but provides support for third-party scripts
- **VMware Horizon View Security Gateway Component:** Provides secure tunneling services for View
- **VMware Horizon View Web Component:** Provides View web services
- **VMwareVDMDS:** Provides the View LDAP directory services

After VMware View is installed, you can connect to it by launching the shortcut on the desktop or by opening a web browser and going to https://[Connection Server]/admin. You can note that even though you have not set up any certificate or configured a secured connection, the View Connection server is listening on 443, by default, and not port 80. We cover changing the certificate to a well-known certificate later in the chapter.

Be aware that the *admin* is case sensitive, and the IP address can be used in place of the server name, which is not case sensitive. If you omit the /admin, you are redirected to the client installation page, which now points you to the VMware site (https://my.vmware.com/web/vmware/info/slug/desktop_end_user_computing/vmware_horizon_view_clients/1_0#win). Earlier installations used to redirect you to a client installation page that was local. When the VMware model for client release changed, and they separated the release timeline of View clients to View Server, they decided to point the client installation page directly to the VMware website, ensuring that any client connecting would be redirected to the latest software for the product. It is also possible to manually configure an alternative location. This might be required if you have to do something specific like maintain a different version of the client. When you connect to the console for the first time, you are prompted to install Adobe Flash Player (if it's not already installed). The Administrator console requires Adobe Flash 10 or later. After you have logged in, you need to configure the environment so that everything is running properly.

Configuring the View Connection Server

There are three versions of VMware Horizon: Standard, Advanced, and Enterprise. All versions of Horizon include View, and the Enterprise version also includes more advanced features, such as Hosted Applications and vSAN. After logging in, you need to add the license. Click **Edit License**, as shown in Figure 4.6.

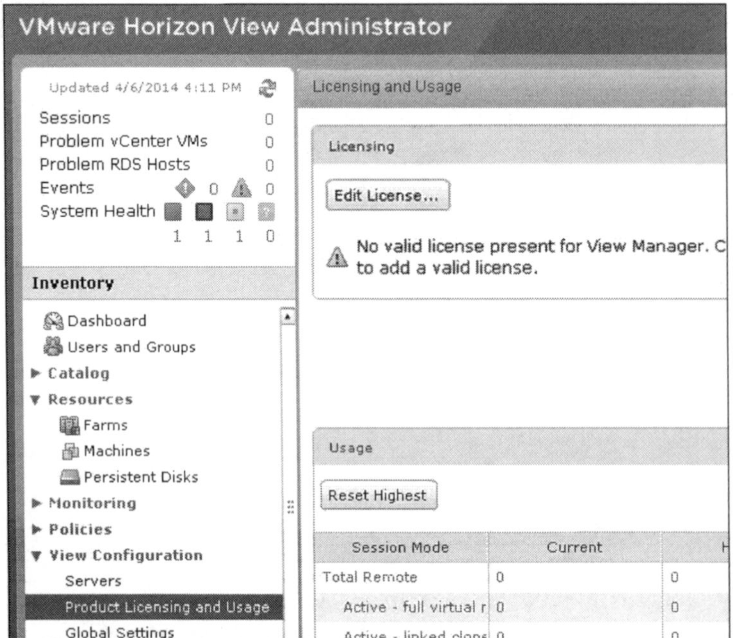

Figure 4.6 Adding the license

Enter the VMware View serial number in the provided field.

The full license enables Desktop connectivity, View Composer, and Application Remoting, as shown in the Figure 4.7.

You now have to add vCenter Server, but you should ensure that the View Composer service is running first (optional installation component). View Composer supports both 32-bit and 64-bit versions of SQL and Oracle. In addition, VMware View can be installed on a separate server or with vCenter. In View, View Composer creates a self-signed certificate during installation, so a certificate exchange is done when configuring View to communicate with View Composer. It is also a good idea to ensure that you can resolve the vCenter hostname from the Connection Server. You should do a forward-and-reverse lookup using the hostname and then IP. This can easily be done by running `nslookup` from the command prompt.

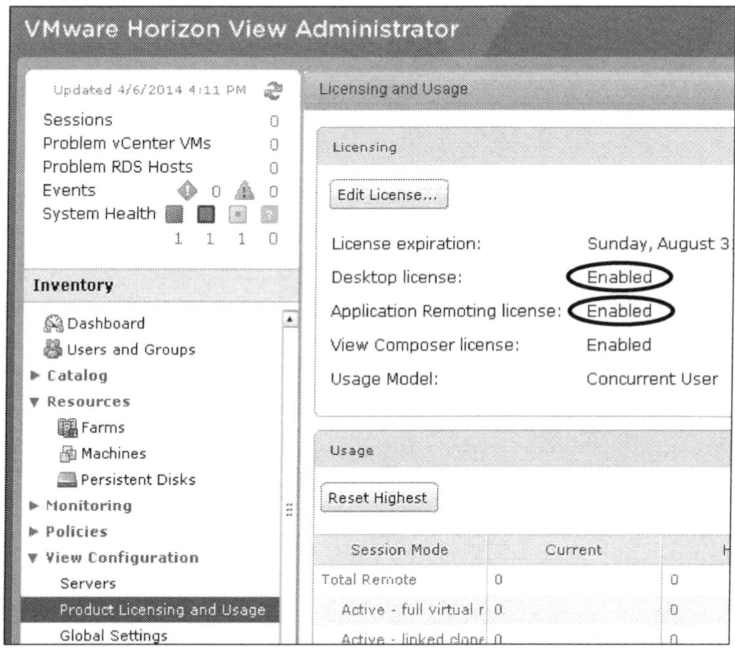

Figure 4.7 Full license enables View Composer and App Remoting

Your vCenter server installation should be on a Windows 2008 R2 server similar to the View Connection Server. We recommend the same as for the previous installation: When launching the initial installation of Composer, you should right-click on the EXE file and choose to **Run as Administrator**.

To install View Composer on vCenter, follow these steps:

1. Click **Next** on the installation wizard screen.
2. Accept the license agreement and click **Next**.
3. Accept the default path for the installation and click **Next**.
4. Type in the name of the ODBC connection you created, as shown in Figure 4.8. You must enter a username and password. Make sure that the username exists before doing this step. As good measure, the password used for this should be a complex password that very few people would know.

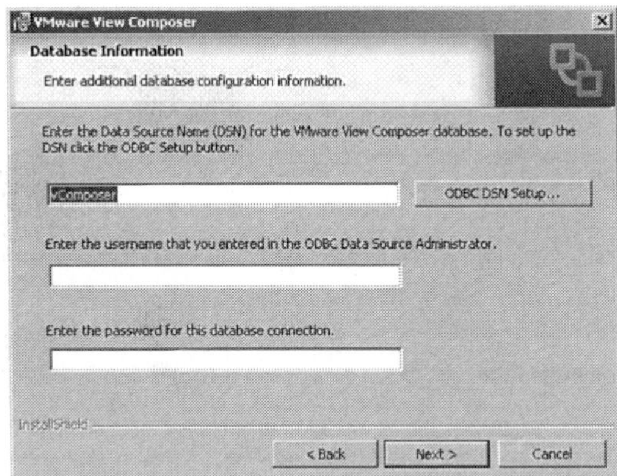

Figure 4.8 Specifying the DSN connection

5. Accept the default port (18443) and have the installer create a Secure Sockets Layer (SSL) certificate, as shown in Figure 4.9.

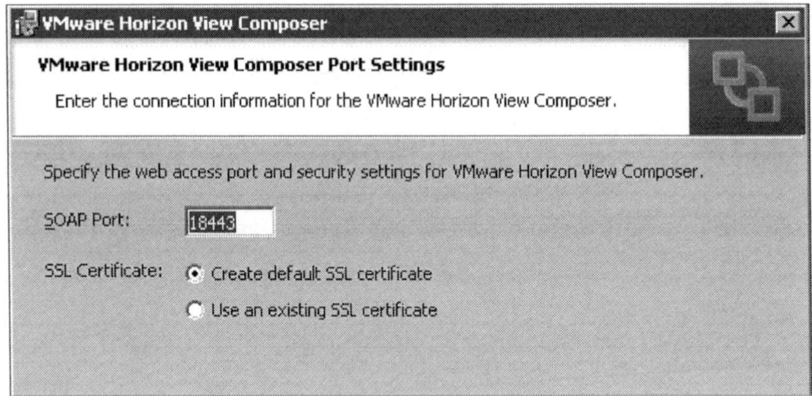

Figure 4.9 SOAP port

6. Click **Install** to install the View Composer service, and click **Finish** when it is complete.

At this point, a reboot is required. Because we just went through the steps of installing View Composer on vCenter server, you should make sure that rebooting the vCenter Server will not impact your environment, in case any other solutions are also depending on vCenter.

Adding vCenter Server

You are now ready to add vCenter Server to the View Connection Server. Under View Configuration and Servers in the right pane, click the **Add** button to configure your vCenter Server connection (see Figure 4.10).

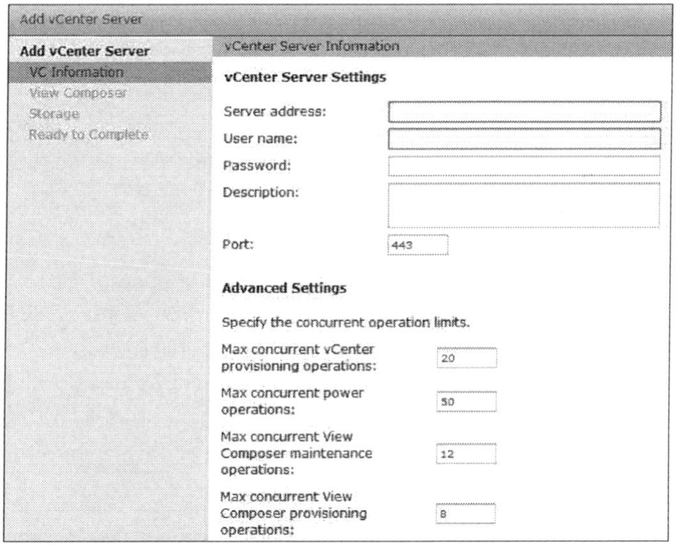

Figure 4.10 Adding vCenter Server

Specify the FQDN of your vCenter Server and the VMware View service account name created in earlier.

On the setup screen, you must also specify four advanced options settings. The first one is the maximum concurrent vCenter provisioning operations: the maximum number of concurrent VM cloning and deletion operations on this vCenter server (full clones). It is important to use a number that will work for your environment. If you have deployed a small environment, 5 to 10 might be your maximum number of concurrent operations, to make sure that you don't render the vCenter Server unstable. If it's a bigger deployment and you have sized your vCenter Server accordingly, you might want to put a bigger number of concurrent operations, perhaps 20 to 25. It would be wise to look at this number, verify whether the default value of 20 is good for you, and adjust the number after the deployment has been running for a few days and you've had a chance to run provisioning operations. It will basically come down to how much time the provisioning operation will take for users to be able to reach their desktop when a pool is created.

The second advanced setting is the maximum power operations: the maximum number of concurrent VM power-on, power-off, reset, and configuration operations (full clones and linked clones). Here again, this value will vary per environment. The default value of 50 might work for you. You might need to adjust it, after a few days running your environment, and you'll find a number that works well for you.

The third advanced setting is the maximum View Composer maintenance operations: the maximum number of concurrent View Composer recompose, refresh, and rebalance operations (linked clones). View Composer operations are I/O intensive. You must set this value carefully to avoid problems with your environment. The default value of 12 is a fair number. If you find that 12 concurrent recompose operations puts too much workload on your vCenter Server, you can bring that value down (remembering that in previous pages we deployed View Composer on the vCenter Server).

The fourth advanced setting is the maximum View Composer provisioning operations: the maximum number of concurrent View Composer creation and deletion operations (linked clones). This number is usually a little lower than the number you have set for the concurrent vCenter operations. The default value of 8 works well with properly sized vCenter Server. As with the other settings, we recommend that you test your environment, validate the workload that vCenter will receive during a Composer provisioning operation, and adjust if necessary.

After you confirm all the advanced settings, click **Next**. At this point, View tests connectivity to the vCenter Server with the supplied credentials. If you entered the wrong information, you will be notified to correct before proceeding.

One common mistake is to forget to use the right account or forget to put the domain information before the account information.

If your user account information is correct, because this is the default installation and you haven't deployed any public certificates yet, you will get a warning that an invalid certificate was detected. VMware recommends the use of certificates signed by a trusted certification authority (CA). Click **View Certificates**, and then click **Accept**.

You will now configure the View Composer information.

Here again, VMware recommends that before you add View Composer to a View deployment to install a valid SSL certificate signed by a trusted CA. In a test environment, you can use the default, self-signed certificate installed with View Composer, but you must accept the certificate thumbprint. Installing the certificate can be done at a later stage; it doesn't have to be done during installation.

You have verified that the Composer service is running on the vCenter Server. In the View Composer configuration page, three choices present themselves to you, if you have the proper View Premier license. You want to choose the second choice, View Composer co-installer with vCenter Server. The default port for communication between both components is 18443. When you click **Next**, View will establish a connection with the Composer service and, similar to the previous step, will notify you that an invalid certificate was detected. *Invalid* might be the wrong terminology; it simply saw a nonpublic, untrusted private certificate, which during the initial installation is not a problem. Click **View Certificates**, and then click **Accept**.

It is important for View Composer connectivity that you use the format [domain\username], but the vCenter connectivity accepts username only. For consistency, it is best to use the same format in both.

Click **Add** under Domains in the View Composer Settings. Then add the domain information in the Add Domain box, as shown in Figure 4.11. This enables the management of computer accounts in the Active Directory. Click **OK** and **OK** again to save the configuration.

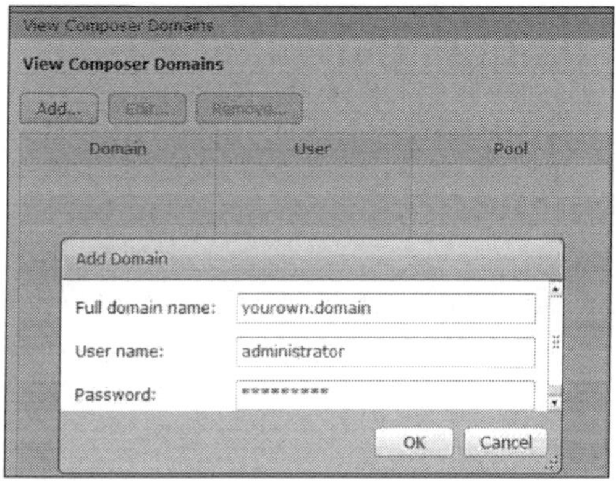

Figure 4.11 Entering domain information

You should now see the vCenter Server and your first Connection Server as part of the configuration.

The next page in the wizard is to configure storage settings. You want to enable the View Storage Accelerator (VSA) whenever possible. This feature was added starting with View 5.2 and is important to leverage in a production deployment. ESXi hosts can be configured to cache VM disk data, which improves performance during I/O storms, such as when many desktops power on and run antivirus scans simultaneously. Hosts read common data blocks from RAM-based cache instead of reading the OS from disk. By reducing input/output operations per second (IOPS) during boot storms, VSA lowers the demand on the storage array and uses less storage I/O bandwidth.

Keeping in mind that this memory reservation is done at the ESXi host level, if your physical host can be sized to put the memory aside for this specific feature, it is strongly recommended to turn on this feature. Also keep in mind that this feature is turned on at a cluster level, meaning that if you have four physical hosts in your cluster, for example, when you turn on this feature, ESXi will reserve the amount of memory you indicated on every host. The values range from 100 MB to 2048 MB. From experience, we've seen good use of this feature when set between 1024 MB and 2048 MB.

Memory oversubscription in a virtual desktop deployment is never recommended, when using VSA or not. You should plan your deployment accordingly and avoid memory oversubscription whenever possible.

Configuring View Replica Server

To ensure reliability, install a second View Server. VMware recommends that two vCPUs be used for a View Connection Server for a small deployment. We would recommend to size it to four vCPUs for larger deployments. For production, you want at least two View Servers that use an appliance-based load balancer such as F5. The process to install the second View Server is identical to the first, except that the second server is a Replica Server. The second Replica Server points to the first View Connection Server, as you can see in Figure 4.12.

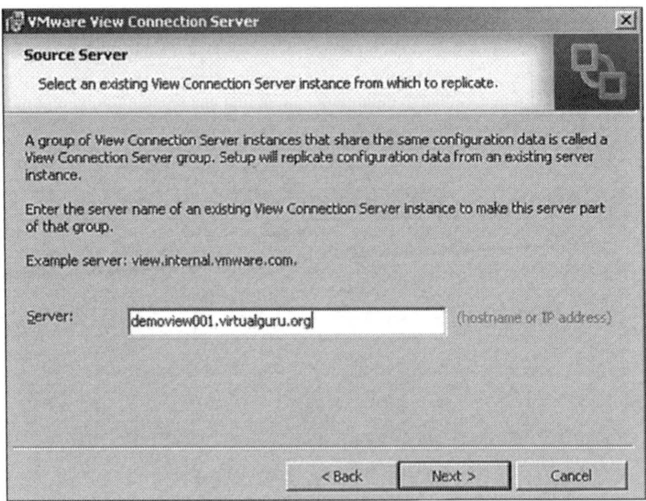

Figure 4.12 Adding a second View Connection Server

The Event Database

The Event Database was introduced in VMware View 4.5 to enable you to store any event that occurs in the View environment to an external database. Adding an Event Database is optional but highly recommended. It is difficult to manage the Connection Server without the Event Database, which can be a key source of information when you are troubleshooting issues. The database is supported on Microsoft SQL Server or the Oracle database. You can create an Event Database by first creating the database in SQL and then configuring the connection within VMware View. With the Event Database, unlike other database configurations, you don't need to create an ODBC connection. You simply add the connection information to View. The Event Database requires local SQL authentication, so the first step is to create a local SQL account and ensure that it has the appropriate access to the Event Database. You can create a local SQL account as follows:

1. Open SQL Management Studio and connect to your database instance.
2. Open the Security and then the Logins modules.
3. Right-click **Login** and select **New Login**.
4. Under the General Settings, ensure SQL Server authentication.
5. Provide a login name, such as **svc_Events**, and provide a password. Note that SQL 2008 requires this to be a complex password, so stay away from any dictionary words.
6. Retype the password to confirm it.
7. Because this is a service account, deselect the following:
   - Enforce Password Policy
   - Enforce Password Expiration
   - User Must Change Password at the Next Login
8. Under the default database, select your Event Database, such as **vEvents**.
9. Select the **User Mapping** page.
10. Select **db_owner** in addition to the default public access and click **OK**.

After creating the local SQL account, you can then add the Event Database from the View Administrator console. Under View Configuration, select **Event Configuration**.

Provide the name of your database server, the type, and a user ID in the fields shown in Figure 4.13 to connect. The table prefix ensures that the Event Database can be unique to this collection of VMware View Servers. If you have another site, both can use the same database service because the table prefix is unique. You have to provide a prefix, however, if you have only a single site for VMware View Servers.

Figure 4.13 Adding an Event Database

After you connect the Event Database, you can set the period in which events appear in the console and the duration in which events are considered new, as shown in Figure 4.14. After you have the settings configured, click **OK**.

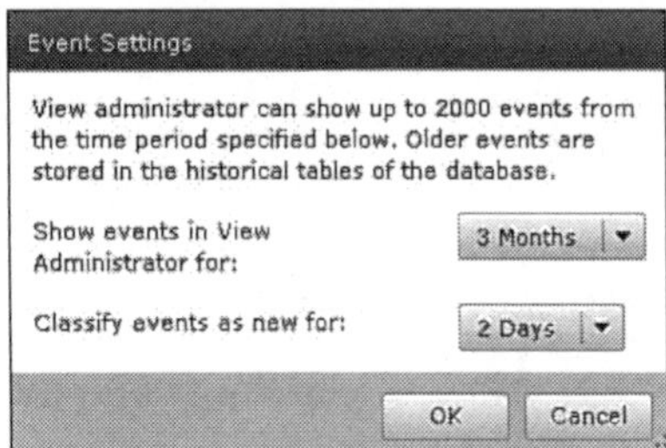

Figure 4.14 Setting the event display options

A feature that was added starting with View 5.2 was to have the possibility to forward View events to a syslog server. Although not used that much, if there is a syslog server already present in the organization, it might be wise to leverage that existing server. This will usually be handled by the security team; make sure that you work with them and obtain proper file and port access, as shown in Figure 4.15.

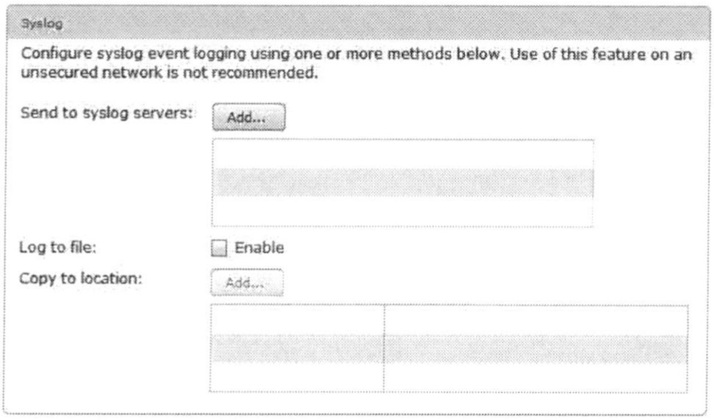

Figure 4.15 Syslogging events

Security Servers

Security Servers are another type of View Server but designed to be deployed to simplify remote access. Because they are usually deployed in a demilitarized zone (DMZ) situation, they are not required to be part of the Active Directory. They reduce the number of connections that are required to be open on the forward-facing firewall of a DMZ and corporate or internal firewall. Each Security Server is paired with a specific Connection Server. So, if you are load balancing two Security Servers in the DMZ, you require two View Servers deployed internally.

New in VMware View 5 is the capability to proxy PCoIP. Prior to version 5, only the Remote Desktop Protocol (RDP) was available through a Security Server. To work, the connections must be tunneled through the Security Servers. Typically, the Security Servers are deployed in a DMZ and should be load balanced behind an appliance-based firewall such as F5, as shown in Figure 4.16. If you are load balancing the Security Servers, you should not load balance the connectivity from the Security Servers to the Connection Servers because a one-to-one relationship exists between Security Servers and Connection Servers.

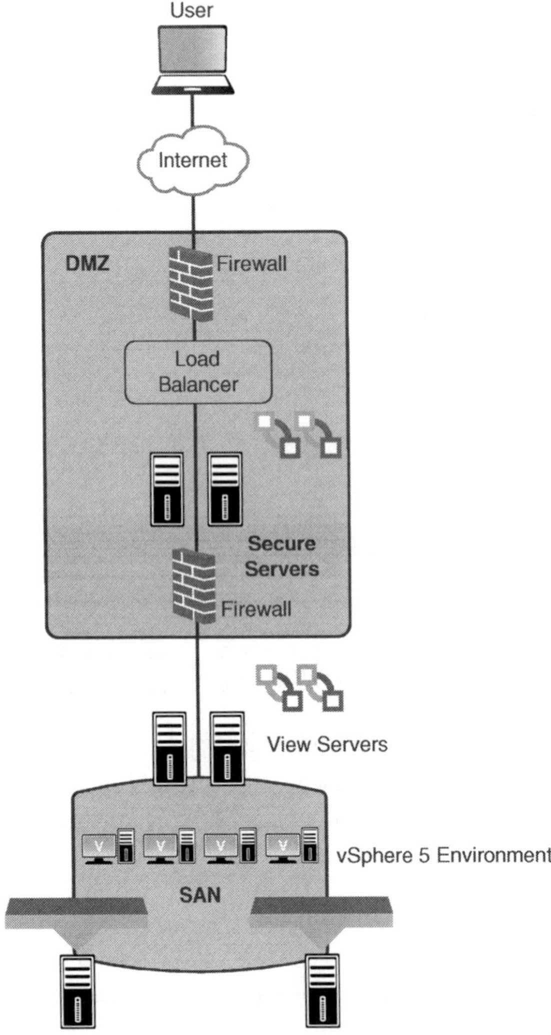

Figure 4.16 Security Servers are deployed in the DMZ.

Firewall Rules

To allow the traffic to pass through the external firewall to your Security Server, you should translate the external IP to the internal IP and ensure the required ports are open using Network Address Translation (NAT). You can find a detailed network flow diagram in the Appendix B, "Network Ports (Internal and External)." The following ports must be open:

1. PCoIP traffic between the View Client and Security Server (external)
    a. TCP 443 for the website
    b. TCP 4172 from client to Security Server
    c. UDP 4172 between client and Security Server in both directions
    d. TCP 8443 between client and Security Server in both directions (Blast access, optional)

    To allow the traffic to pass, you must set the following rules on the internal firewall.

2. PCoIP traffic between the View Security Server and virtual desktop (internal)
    a. TCP 4172 from Security Server to virtual desktop
    b. UDP 4172 from Security Server to virtual desktop in both directions
    c. TCP 32111 from Security Server to virtual desktop in both directions

You must set up several things for the Security Server to work properly. The first consideration is the external URL. If you are going to provide access to a View environment remotely, you must register a public-facing IP address and register it in DNS. Let's use the example of access.virtualguru.org. The DNS name is important because during the configuration of the Security Server, you configure it to respond to this external URL versus its own hostname. Although we discuss straight installation in this chapter, it is not typical that remote access is offered with single-factor authentication. It should always be combined with a two-factor authentication method such as RSA or RADIUS.

Adding the Security Servers

The first thing you should do is define a pairing password, which you do from the View Connection Server, not the Security Server.

First, log in to the View Connection Server. Then, under View Connection Servers, click the **More Commands** button, as shown in Figure 4.17.

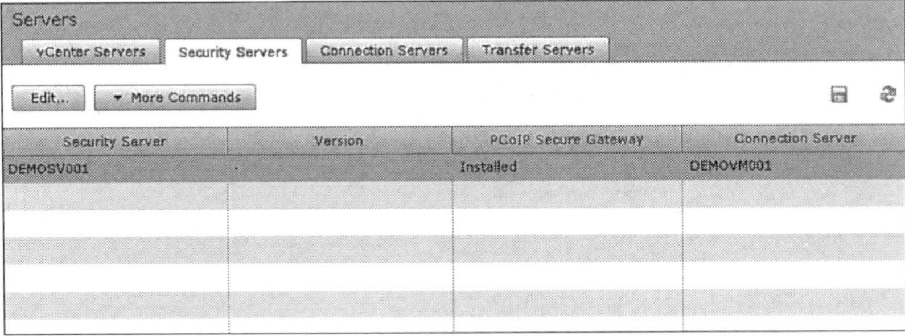

Figure 4.17 Adding the Security Server

Specify the Security Server pairing password, confirm the password, and set the password timeout. You should specify a short amount of time for security reasons and also ensure that the Security Server pairing is done before the expiry.

Now you can install your Security Server using the following steps:

1. Launch the Connection Server Installer and click **Next**.
2. Click **Next** on the patent agreement screen.
3. Accept the license agreement and click **Next**.
4. Accept the default location and click **Next**.
5. Select **View Security Server** and click **Next**.
6. Provide the IP or hostname of the Connection Server to which this Security Server will be associated, and click **Next**.
7. Provide the pairing password you configured in the View Server and click **Next**.
8. Specify the external URL to which this Security Server should respond (for example, access.virtualguru.org) and also the IP address to which this DNS name is registered for PCoIP connections. Then click **Next**.
9. Allow the installer to automatically configure the firewall. I recommend that you definitely leave the firewall intact when deploying the Security Server Security Server in the DMZ. Then click **Next**.
10. Click **Install**, and then click **Finish**.

If you are going to tunnel PCoIP, you must tell the View Server paired with the Security Server to use PCoIP Secure Gateway for PCoIP to desktop. Under the View Server, select **Edit** and ensure that **User PCoIP Secure Gateway for PCoIP Connections to Desktop** is selected. The **Use Secure Tunnel Connection to Desktop** setting is the default and should be left as is, as shown in Figure 4.18. The External URL and PCoIP External URL point to themselves for the internal View Server, which is fine. Only the Security Server needs to respond to the external IP addresses.

Edit Security Server - DEMOSV001

Server name: DEMOSV001

HTTP(S) Secure Tunnel

External URL: https://daas.virtualguru.org:443

Example: https://myserver.com:443

PCoIP Secure Gateway

PCoIP External URL: 63.251.179.17:4172

Example: 10.0.0.1:4172

OK Cancel

Figure 4.18 Enabling the PCoIP Secure Gateway

After the gateway is properly installed, if you refresh the View Administrator console under Security Servers, you should see your server there, as shown in Figure 4.19.

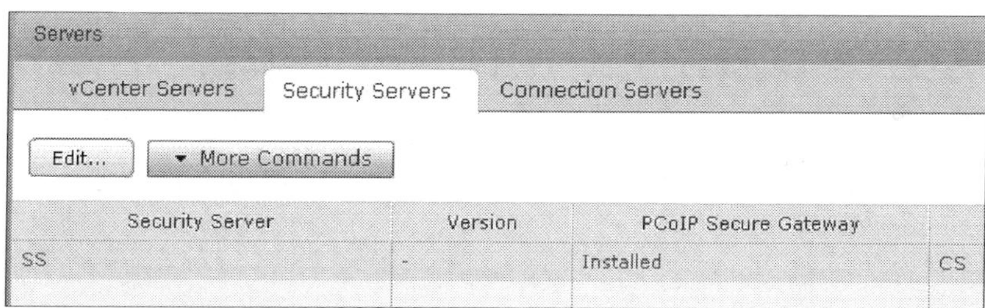

Figure 4.19 Viewing your Security Servers

If you need to change the External URL or IP for tunneling PCoIP, click **Edit** on the Security Server.

Installing the View Agent

When accessing a virtual desktop through the View solution, you require a listener on the virtual desktop, a component that will interact between the guest OS and the View Server to supply the user with a connection.

1. Launch the View Agent Installer and click **Next**.
2. Click **Next** on the patent agreement screen.

3. Accept the license agreement and click **Next**.
4. Leave the default option enabled, **Accept the default location**, and click **Next**.
5. After your choices are done, click **Install**.
6. Once the installer has completed the install, you must reboot the virtual desktop.

View Agent Custom Setup Options

When you install View Agent on a virtual machine, you can select custom setup options. Table 4.2 describes options for the client.

Table 4.2 View Agent Custom Setup Options

Option	Description
USB Redirection	Gives desktops access to locally connected USB devices on their desktops. Windows 2003 and Windows 2008 do not support USB Redirection. **NOTE** You can use group policy settings to disable USB Redirection for specific users.
View Composer Agent	Lets View Agent run on the linked-clone desktops that are deployed from this VM.
Virtual Printing	Lets users print to any printer available on their Windows client computers. Users do not have to install additional drivers on their desktops.
PCoIP Server	Lets users connect to the View desktop using the PCoIP display protocol. Installing the PCoIP Server feature disables sleep mode on Windows 8, Windows 7, and Windows Vista desktops and standby mode on Windows XP desktops. When a user navigates to the Power Options or Shut Down menu, sleep mode or standby mode is inactive. Desktops do not go into sleep or standby mode after a default period of inactivity. Desktops remain in active mode. **NOTE** If you install the PCoIP Server feature on Windows Vista, the Windows group policyDisable or enable software Secure Attention Sequence is enabled and set to Services and Ease of Access applications. If you change this setting, single sign on does not work correctly.
vCenter Operations Manager	Enable desktop network information to be forwarded to a vCenter Operations Manager Server.

Option	Description
PCoIP Smartcard	Lets users authenticate with smartcards when they use the PCoIP display protocol.
View Persona Management	Synchronizes the user profile on the local desktop with a remote profile repository, so that users have access to their profiles whenever they log in to a desktop.

The next step after the reboot is to log in to the virtual desktop and validate that everything installed properly. Look at the installed service and make sure that the View Client is in a running stated. (When the client is installed, it's set to automatically start.)

When you are satisfied that everything is running smoothly, that you haven't received any error message upon login, the next step would be to release the IP information of the virtual desktop.

This is the final step before you shut down the virtual desktop to take a snapshot of the environment.

This is done mainly to avoid any IP addressing conflict that might happen when you build a new View automated linked-clone pool. Because Composer spins up the desktop automatically, if you keep the IP address before shutting down the virtual desktop, when View Composer builds the pool, the first time, there will be an IP conflict because all machines are built from the same Gold master image.

Once the virtual desktop is shut down, all that is left to do is take a snapshot to make it ready for View; you are now ready to build automated desktop pools.

Installing the View Client

There are multiple flavors of the View Client. VMware has worked very hard over the past few years to cover the broadest addressable client devices. They have native clients for the iOS, Android, Linux, OS X, and Windows devices.

For mobile devices, it is recommended to look up the respective application catalog and download the latest client from there (for example, the Apple App Store or Google Play Store).

For the Linux, OS X, and Windows platforms, you can download the client from the VMware website or you can simply point your browser your View Connection Server (https://<ServerFQDN>); the server will redirect you to the proper download link on the VMware website.

Installing the View Client on any platform is very straightforward. The only configuration options are to decide whether you want to allow USB Redirection (Windows version) and to enter the View Connection Server information. Figure 4.20 shows you those two options when installing the client.

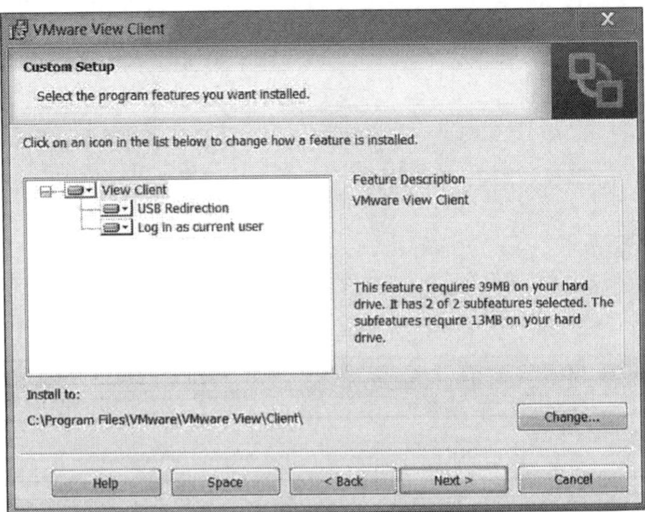

Figure 4.20 View Client installation options

Once the View Client is installed, you can customize the login to pre-populate some of the connection information. To do so, all you have to do is create a shortcut (for example, on the user desktop) with the file WSWC.exe. This is the executable used to launch the VMware View Client. If you left the default installation directory, this file is located under C:\Program File\VMware\VMware View Client\. Figure 4.21 shows all the possible options for this executable.

One of the lesser-known features that you might find useful as an administrator is the capability to run multiple View Clients simultaneously. Although not officially supported by VMware, a lot of people in the field who have to do admin work in View environments or that have to connect to multiple environments at the same time find this feature something they could not live without.

Note that running multiple View Clients simultaneously is not the same as connecting to multiple desktops in different pools from the same View Connection Server.

```
C:\Program Files\VMware\VMware Horizon View Client>vmware-view.exe /?

C:\Program Files\VMware\VMware Horizon View Client>Usage:
  vmware-view.exe [OPTION...]

Help Options:
  -h, --help                    Show help options

Application Options:
  --languageId                  LCID of language to use (if available), e.g. 0x409
for English
  --nonInteractive              Suppress error message boxes for fully scripted sta
rtup
  --unattended                  Start in unattended mode. Connects to the entitled
desktop without user interaction
  --printEnvironmentInfo        Prints information about the system
  --shutdown                    Shutdown all desktops and relevant UI components
  --serverURL                   URL for the View Connection Server
  --userName                    User name for server login
  --password                    Password for server login
  --domainName                  Domain for server login
  --smartCardPIN                PIN for smart card login
  --desktopName                 Desktop to autostart
  --desktopProtocol             Desktop display protocol to use (if available)
  --desktopLayout               Specify desktop screen size (e.g. fullscreen, multi
monitor, windowLarge, windowSmall, or 800x600)
  --file                        File with additional command line parameters
  --connectUSBOnStartup         Connect all USB devices to a desktop when it is lau
nched (true or false)
  --connectUSBOnInsert          Connect a USB device to the foreground desktop when
 the device is plugged in (true or false)
  --noVMwareAddins              Prevents loading of VMware-specific virtual channel
s (e.g. ThinPrint)
  --supportText                 Support information file for the client
  --standalone                  Support it for backwards compatibility, and the def
ault behavior is standalone now
  --loginAsCurrentUser          Log in as current user (true or false)
  --appName                     Application to autostart
  --singleAutoConnect           Automatically connect if only one launch item is en
titled
```

Figure 4.21 View Client command-line options

On the Windows platform, you can run the vmware-view.EXE command and use the `-standalone` switch at the end. You can create a shortcut that has the switch embedded in the command window or you can open a command prompt and run the command from there. This will allow you to execute the View Client more than once. The Windows command is `C:\Program File\VMware\VMware Horizon View Client\vmware-view.exe -standalone`.

You can also combine this switch with other options such as the connection server information, the username, and so forth.

On the OS X platform, you run a different command from Terminal to achieve the same result. OS X command: `open -n /Applications/VMware\ Horizon\ View\ Client.app`.

Working with Certificates in View

Earlier in the chapter, we discussed how to deploy VMware View with the default options, which meant that View deployed with the preconfigured self-signed certificates. This is usually okay for small proof-of-concept environments and lab/dev environments, but it is strongly discouraged for use in a production environment. We cover here the high-level deployment of a CA in Active Directory and how to change your certificates in View to use the CA from Active Directory.

One of the first steps is to use an existing CA (third party or internal) or create an internal Active Directory CA. If one does not exist in your environment, here are the steps to configure one that will work with AD.

First, go on an existing Windows server. To simplify the process, create a folder on that machine called C:\Certificates; we will use that folder later. Then you should share this folder out. Make sure that you add a generic group, like the Everyone group or Domain Members group and that you give the folder permissions of at least read.

Then, you want to add the role. Here again, keep in mind that in most production deployments this will already exist within your organization and that you should use the environment already deployed. If someone in your organization has already done this, you can skip ahead to the next section that covers the creation of certificate templates. The following steps are only if you do not already have a CA within your environment:

1. Open Server Manager, **Expand Roles**, right-click **Roles** and choose **Add Role**, and then click **Next**.
2. On the Select Server Roles screen, check the box next to **Active Directory Certificate Services**, as shown in Figure 4.22.

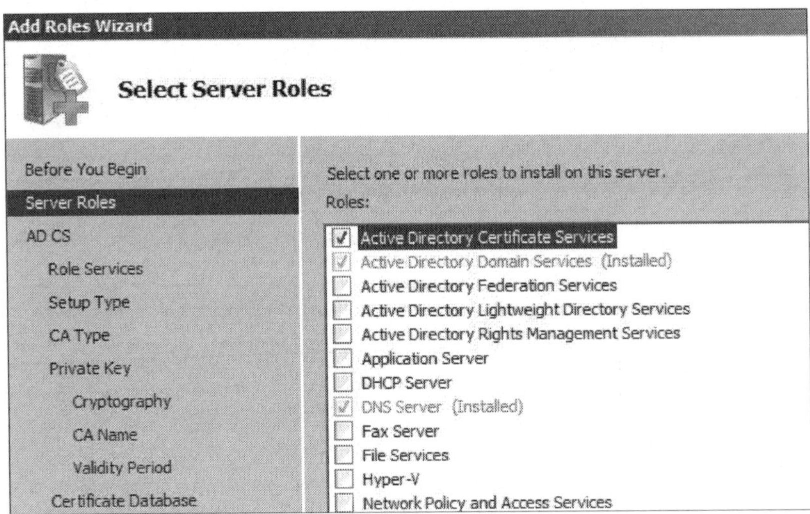

Figure 4.22 Active Directory Certificate Services

3. Click **Next** and **Next**.
4. On the Role Services screen, ensure that **Certification Authority** is checked. Do not check any other boxes.

5. You want to make sure that you choose **Enterprise** in the Setup Type.
6. For the Specify CA Type, select **Root CA** and click **Next**.
7. On the Set Up Private Key screen, leave the defaults and click **Next**.
8. Leave the defaults for **Configure Cryptography for CA** and click **Next**.
9. For Configure CA Name, leave the defaults and click **Next**.
10. On the Set Validity Period screen, change the 5 to a value that works for your organization and leave the years. Then click **Next**.
11. Leave the defaults for Configure Certificate Database and click **Next**.
12. On the Confirm Installation Selections screen, confirm the values, and then click **Install** (Confirm choices on the Confirm Installation page).
13. The install process will take a minute or two. Once done, click the **Close** button.

Creating Certificate Templates

A certificate template allows an AD administrator to create a premade list of certificate options that users and computers can use when enrolling for certificates without having to create complex certificate requests. This can help streamline the process of adding View Clients, desktops, and so on in the environment without having to create and configure individual certificates.

You want to open the Certificate Templates Microsoft Management Console (MMC) snaps-ins from the Management Console. Look at Figure 4.23 for an example of what your Management Console should look like after you've added the snap-in.

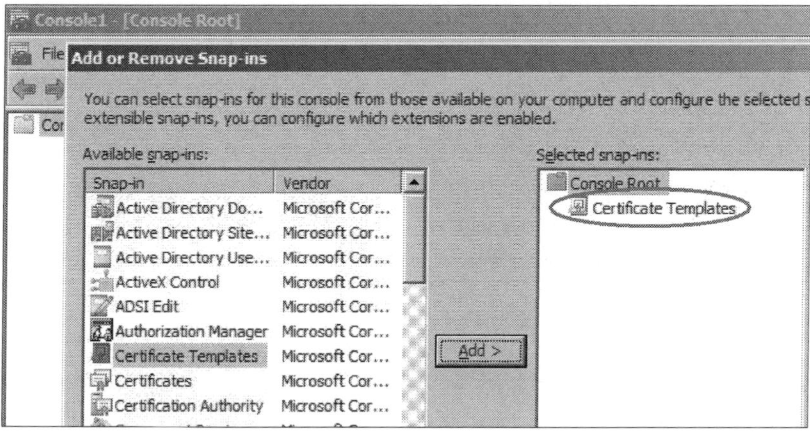

Figure 4.23 Certificate Templates snap-in

1. When you're in the Microsoft Management Console, click **Certificate Templates**. You will see the templates show up on the right side.
2. Select **Web Server Template** (second from the bottom) and right-click it.
3. Choose **Properties**.
4. On the Web Server Properties dialog, display the Security tab.
5. Click the **Add** button, and then click the **Object Types** button.
6. Ensure that all the boxes are checked, as shown in Figure 4.24, and click **OK**.

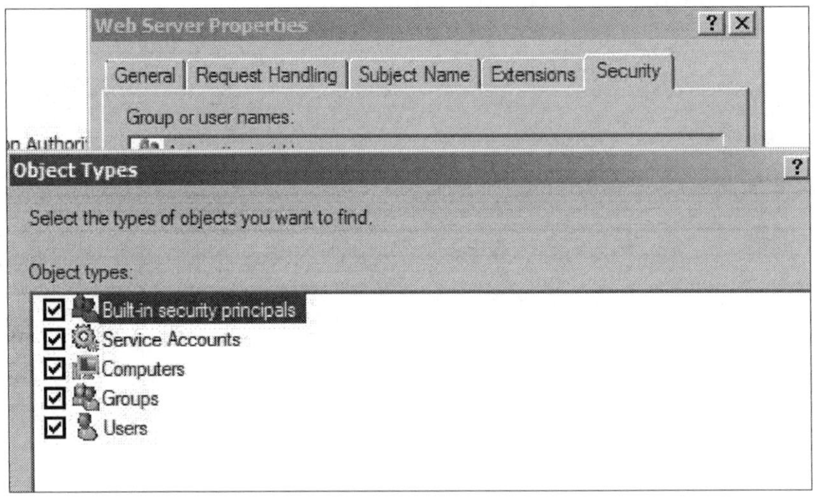

Figure 4.24 Certificate object types

7. In the Object Names box, enter in the short names of all the computers that this certificate will be used for. Short names are things like ConnectionServer01. Long names, or FQDNs, are like ConnectionServer01.company.com.cert-account-names.
8. Click the **Check Names** box, and then click the **OK** button.

   Figure 4.25 shows an example where we have added two Connection Server short names and one Security Server short name.

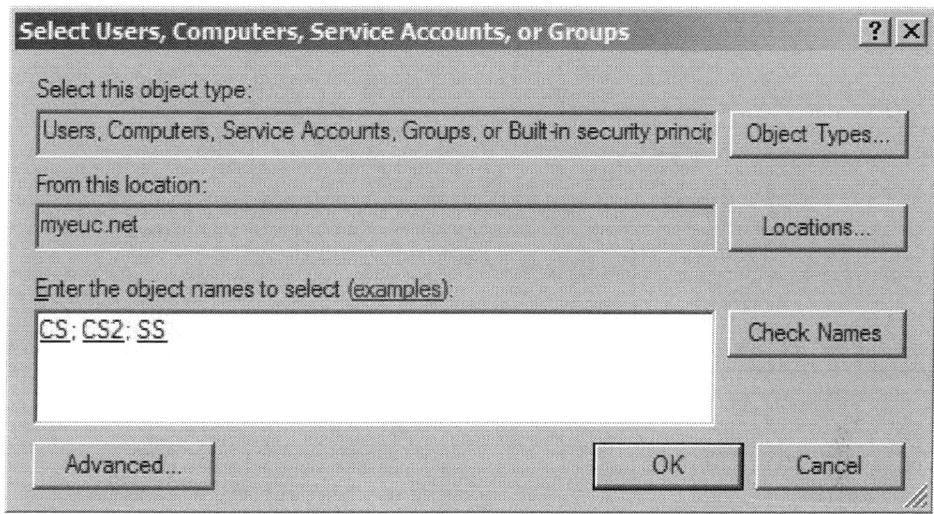

Figure 4.25 Computer objects

9. For each computer object, ensure that it has **Read**, **Write**, and **Enroll** permissions checked, and then Click **OK**.

We will now configure the View Server side of the environment:

1. Go to your Connection Server and log in as the domain administrator.
2. Open an MMC, and from the menu, select **File**, and then select **Add or Remove Snap-Ins**.
3. From the Available snap-ins (on the left), select **Certificate** and click the **Add** button. The Certificates Snap-In dialog box will pop up.
4. Change the Manage location from **My User Account** to **Computer Account**.

   Figure 4.26 shows an example of what this should look like on your View Connection Server.

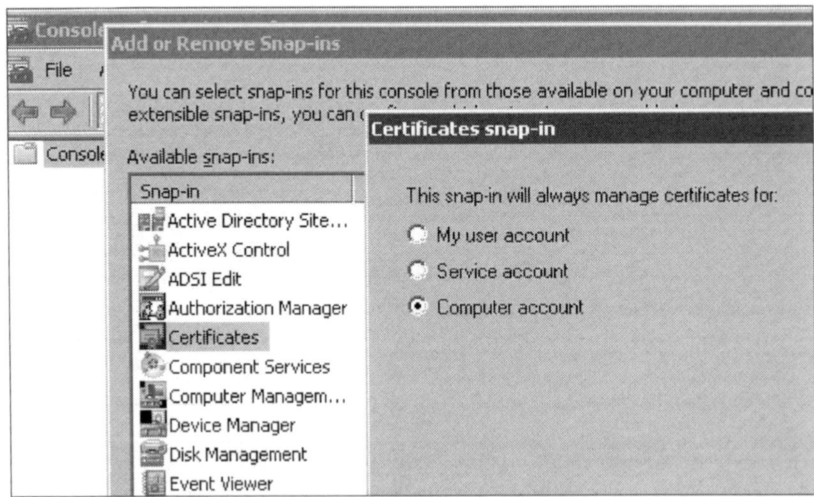

Figure 4.26 View computer certificates

5. You can leave all the defaults options for Select Computer and click **Finish**.
6. In the Console Root column (left), click the plus sign (+) to expand the certificates.
7. You should now select **Personal** and select the **Certificates** folder in there.

We will now request a new certificate for this server:

1. Right-click **Certificates**, and then choose **All Tasks**, and then choose **Request New Certificate**, as shown in Figure 4.27.

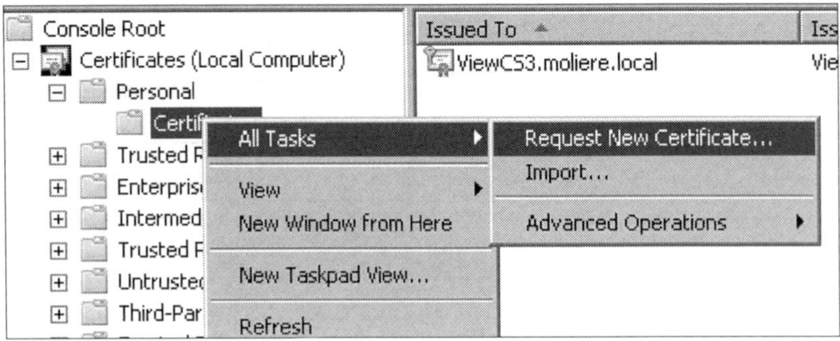

Figure 4.27 View computer certificates

2. Click **Next** and ensure that **Active Directory Enrollment Policy** is selected.
3. Click **Next**, check the box beside **Web Server**, and then click the blue **More Information** link.
4. For the subject name, enter and add appropriate information about the servers that will use these certificates. These items are likely to be Common Name (CN), Country (C), Organization (O), Organization Unit (OU), State (S), and Locality (L).

   For things such as the CN, use both the short name (for example, CS01) and the long name (for example, CS01.company.com). For the alternative name, choose **DNS** and enter and add the appropriate FQDN for each server that will use the certificate.
5. Display the Private Key tab, click the double down arrows on Key Options, and check the **Make Private Key Exportable** box.
6. Click **OK**, and then click the **Enroll** button. Click the **Finish** button.

The last step in the process is to remove the old self-signed certificate from the initial installation. Ensure that the MMC is maximized to its largest size and find the old certificate. It should have vdm in the Friendly Name column. Then complete the following steps:

1. Right-click the old certificate and select **Properties**.
2. On the General tab, in the Friendly Name box, change the vdm to **vdm.old**, and then click **OK.**
3. In the Issued By column, look for View Root CA, and select that certificate. Right-click it and go to Properties.
4. On the General tab, in the Friendly Name box, enter **vdm** and click **OK**.

The final part is to add certificates to View, as follows:

1. Go back to the Active Directory server in the MMC. Select **Certificates** and choose **Computer Account** from the Certificates Snap-In dialog.
2. Expand the **Trusted Root Certificates** folder, find the **<name>-CA** certificates. (They should match the name of the one your created.) Find the one with the little key on it. Right-click the certificate (the one with the key) and go to **All Tasks**, then **Export**.
3. Click **Next** on the Welcome to the Certificate Export Wizard.
4. On the Export File Format page, leave the defaults of **DER** and click **Next**.

5. For the file name, click the **Browse** button and put the file in the directory we created earlier in the chapter (should be something like (C:\Certificates\root_cer.cer).
6. Click **Next** and **Finish**.
7. Click **OK** on the Export Successful dialog box.

Now you need to copy that certificate export to your View Connection Server:

1. Log in to your View Connection Server and access your Active Directory folder where the CER file was saved. Copy the file to C:\Program Files\VMware\VMware View\Server\sslgateway\conf.
2. The next step is to open a command prompt and type the following command:

   ```
   PATH=%PATH%;"c:\Program Files\VMware\VMware View\Server\jre\bin
   ```

   This temporarily adds the jre\bin directory to the path of the View Connection Server (until the next reboot).
3. Go to the C:\Program Files\VMware\VMware View\Server\sslgateway\conf\ directory and type the following command:

   ```
   keytool -import -alias Horizon -file root_cer.cer -keystore trustedkey.key
   ```

4. Enter the administrator password for the keystore password.
5. Enter it a second time to verify.
6. For the Trust This Certificate question, enter **Yes**.
7. Switch to a Windows Explorer window and navigate to C:\Program Files\VMware\VMware View\Server\sslgateway\conf. You're looking for the file trustedkey.key, which you need to rename to **locked.properties**.
8. Open the file with Notepad, and within the file enter the following text (making sure that there are no extra characters or lines after the last line):

   ```
   trustKeyfile=trustedkey.key
   trustStoretype=JKS
   useCertAuth=true
   ```

   The preceding lines are just here to show you where the text starts or ends. If you use this text, only use the three lines of text, not the lines above or below the text.

You have finished configuring the View Connection Server to use the trusted certificate. Now all you have to do is restart the service or reboot the server. It may take a minute or two for the Dashboard to release the "red square" beside the Connection Server. Be patient and refresh the Dashboard after a minute or two. This can be done without the Connection Server being licensed. (For those environments that may be turnkey or waiting for licensing, this can be done in advance.) You can also repeat these same steps for the View Security Server.

Summary

It is important to ensure that each component of the VMware View environment is functioning properly. Check the Event Viewer on the Windows server for error messages related to the installation. In addition, make sure that the services start properly.

At this point, you have all the major infrastructure pieces of the VMware View environment up and running. You need to create VMs and tune them for optimal performance. Before you do, though, look at one other important piece of the VMware View platform: application virtualization. When you understand the benefit of application virtualization, you can integrate it into your View desktops.

Chapter 5

VMware Workspace Implementation

This chapter describes the recommended approach to prepare for a deployment of all the components of VMware Workspace. You learned about the installation of VMware View 5 in Chapter 4, "VMware View Implementation." Remember that a proper installation for View as well as vCenter must be done before starting the Workspace installation. Although the View components are not absolutely necessary, we strongly encourage the deployment of the combined solutions, which showcases the strength of both products working together. Some components can be installed in parallel (for example, installing the View Composer software or the View Agent on the virtual desktop).

VMware Workspace Deployment and Design Considerations

Building a solid Workspace environment, like the other solutions previously discussed, requires strong planning and focus. One of the main strengths of Workspace is that it's easy to install, which is also one of its main weaknesses. The solution comes in the form of a vApp. If you're an existing VMware user/administrator and you have some basic knowledge of vSphere and vCenter, deploying this solution is very easy, which in turn might make you think you can skip some of the planning steps.

To avoid getting lost in the details of the deployment, we concentrate here on three areas you must configure when deploying Workspace:

- Main environment (gateway, configurator, connector, and service virtual appliances [VAs])
- Data environment (installing and configuring Workspace Data to work with Network File System [NFS])
- Applications (ThinApp, software-as-a-service [SaaS])

We cover each of these in detail in the following pages.

Workspace is delivered as a SUSE Linux-based vApp, an Open Virtual Appliance (OVA) file consisting of multiple VAs deployed through VMware vCenter. This solution uses the Workspace VAs described here, plus VMware View and VMware ThinApp:

- **Workspace Configurator (configurator VA):** Provides an administrative console and a web-based user interface to configure the network, gateway, vCenter, and SMTP settings of all the appliances in the Workspace vApp.

  The configurator VA also enables an administrator to manage security certificates centrally and add and remove active modules in Workspace.

- **Workspace Connector (connector VA):** Provides local user authentication as well as Active Directory binding and synchronization services. An administrator can define the directory replication schedule and synchronize View and ThinApp pools and repositories for provisioning to end users.

- **Workspace Manager (service VA):** Provides the web-based Workspace administrative interface, enabling an administrator to configure the application catalog, manage user entitlements, and configure groups and reporting for all the systems in the Workspace vApp.

- **Workspace Data (data VA):** Provides the datastore for user files, controls file sharing policy for internal and external users, provides file preview functionality, and serves the end-user web interface for Workspace.

- **Workspace Gateway (gateway VA):** Enables a single user-facing domain for access to Workspace. As the central aggregation point for all user connections, the gateway routes requests to the appropriate destination and proxies requests on behalf of user connections.

Figure 5.1 shows all the components that are part of a VMware Workspace production deployment.

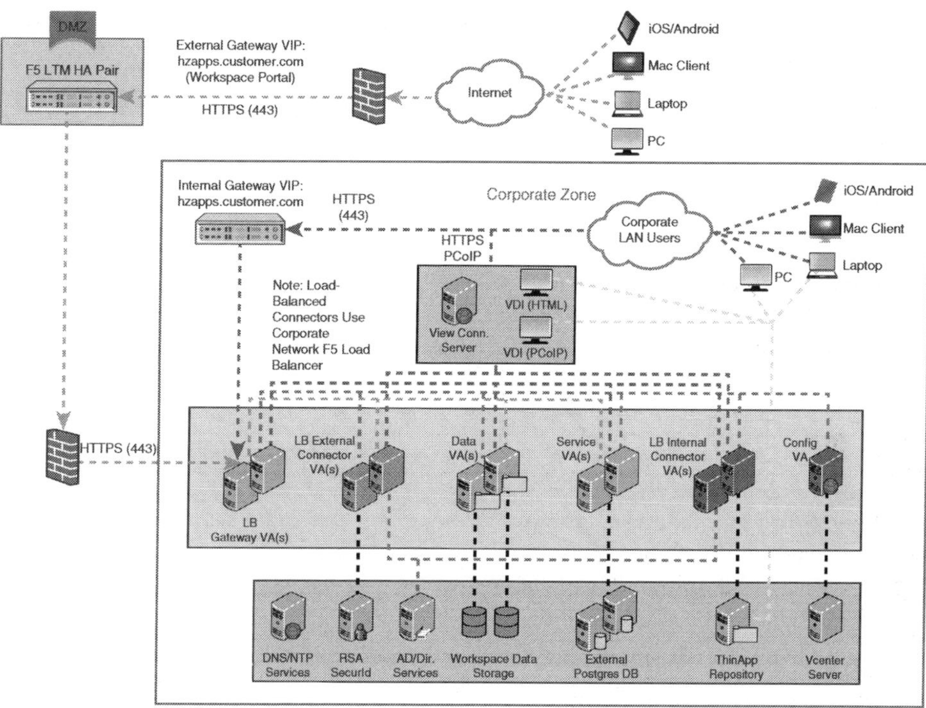

Figure 5.1 Workspace conceptual diagram

You can use Workspace deployment checklists located in the Workspace installation guide to gather the necessary information to install Workspace. You need some or all of the network information for your virtual machines when you create the static IP addresses in the Domain Name System (DNS) before the installation and during a Workspace installation. It is also good practice to validate that your environment meets the requirements of Workspace before deploying it. Refer to the release notes of the solution to validate these (www.vmware.com/support/horizon_workspace/doc/hw_release_notes_18.html#compat).

Workspace Implementation: Initial Setup

This section outlines the detailed implementation procedures of the Workspace environment.

Workspace vApp Appliances

Workspace is a multiple virtual machine (VM) vApp, distributed as an OVA file. You can deploy the vApp to vCenter. The vApp includes several virtual appliances.

Workspace Configurator VA

You start configuring Workspace with this virtual appliance, using both the configurator virtual appliance interface and the configurator web interface. The configurations you make with the configurator are distributed to the other virtual appliances in the vApp.

Workspace Service VA

Workspace Manager (service VA) handles ThinApp package synchronization and gives you access to the Administrator web interface, from which you can manage users, groups, and resources.

Workspace Connector

The connector provides the following services: user authentication (identity provider), directory synchronization, ThinApp-catalog loading, and View pool synchronization.

Workspace Data VA

The data VA controls the file storage and sharing service, stores user data (files), and synchronizes user data across multiple devices.

Workspace Gateway VA

The gateway VA is the single endpoint for all end-user communication. User requests come to the gateway VA, which then routes the request to the appropriate VA. Figure 5.2 shows an example of the vApp after it is deployed in vSphere.

Figure 5.2 Workspace vApp

vApp features include the following:

- Provided as a VA vApp with an installation and configuration wizard
- Easy update and patching
- Operator and Administrator web interfaces to manage your Workspace deployment
- Clustering for scalability and reliability
- Debugging tools
- Internationalization support (UTF-8)

One of the first key prerequisites for a successful installation of Workspace is to make sure that you have the IP and DNS information for all five appliances before the start of the installation process. To deploy the Workspace vApp, you need an IP address and DNS name for each of these five components. (Forward and reverse lookup need to work.) This installation guide does not elaborate on this subject. It's a good idea to document this process, and you can refer to the Workspace deployment checklist in the installation guide for a list of the information you should gather and keep well documented.

Before starting the deployment of your environment, make sure that you have an IP pool available for your environment on the cluster where your Workspace appliances will reside. The IP pool configuration should look similar to that shown in Figure 5.3.

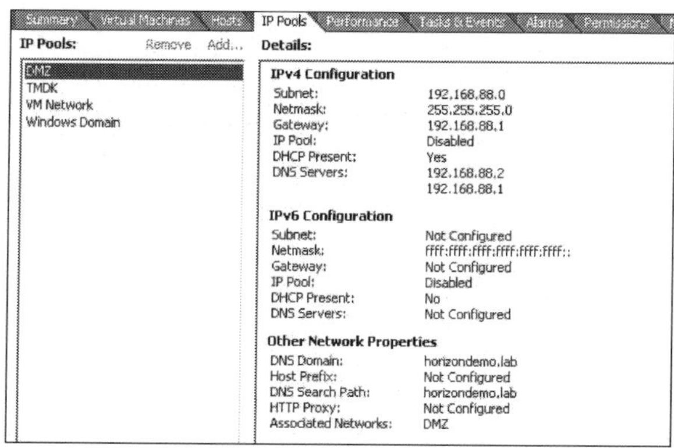

Figure 5.3 IP pools

If you don't know how to set up an IP pool, refer to Chapter 3, "VMware Workspace Architecture," for the steps.

Deploying the Workspace vApp

From vCenter, under Hosts and Clusters, choose the ESXi host or cluster you want to use for the Workspace environment, and from the File menu choose Deploy OVF Template. This will start the OVF Template Wizard.

The first page (Figure 5.4) is where you will select the OVA file that you previously downloaded to a local drive.

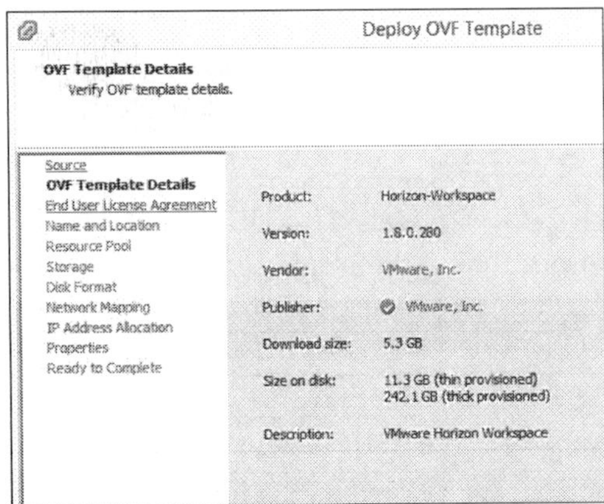

Figure 5.4 OVA deployment

It should always be the case, but make sure that the publisher is recognized and listing VMware, Inc.

The next screen will ask you to name the deployed template. Good practice is to use the name and version number of the template; we recommend using Horizon-Workspace for the name.

Then choose the location. If you are using a vSphere environment that has a folder structure, you would usually obtain this from the vSphere administrator.

The next screen asks you to choose a resource pool. There are no guidelines or recommendations to use a resource pool for Workspace; follow the existing guidelines from your vSphere administrator.

You will have to select the datastore location for the entire vApp. Make sure that you have enough space to handle the entire vApp in the datastore you select. You will be able to add additional Workspace Data drives later and on an additional datastore, so you don't need to account for all the data space you will need.

Now you will be asked for the disk format of the vApp. For purposes of a production Workspace deployment, it is recommended to use Thick Provisioned Lazy Zeroed. Workspace works well in thin provision mode as well, but because this is a production deployment, we strongly recommend allocating the drive space upfront to avoid performance bottlenecks related to storage in the future.

You should now be at the Network Mapping screen. Each VA must have a network selected, as shown in Figure 5.5. This will be for the local vNIC on each appliance, and they should all reside on the same network. Because most of the deployments will require support for external user access, you might think that you would put the gateway VA in your demilitarized zone (DMZ), but this is not a supported scenario. If you need to support web-facing access, you should have a load balancer or reverse proxy in front of your Workspace deployment, as previously shown in Figure 5.1.

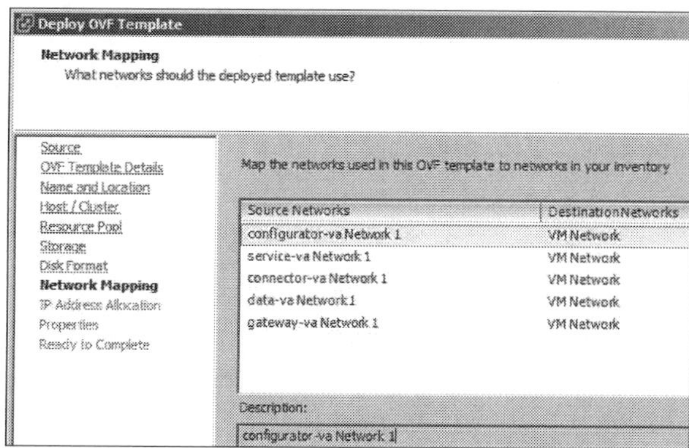

Figure 5.5 Network mapping

Now select the IP address allocation: Fixed, Transient, or DHCP. We recommend going with fixed IP addresses, but if you really need to, Dynamic Host Control Protocol (DHCP) could also be used; we would then strongly recommend that you use IP Reservation in your DHCP server to avoid the changing of the IP addresses on the vApp. (As mentioned earlier, DNS with reverse lookup must be set up before deployment, upon first boot. The configurator VA will look up all the names of the appliances; if it cannot resolve the reverse lookup of each appliance, the deployment will fail.)

Here again, DHCP will work, combining IP reservation and preconfigured DNS for each VA, but it will make your deployment a lot easier if you can use fixed IP addresses (and the latter is the preferred method), as shown in Figure 5.6.

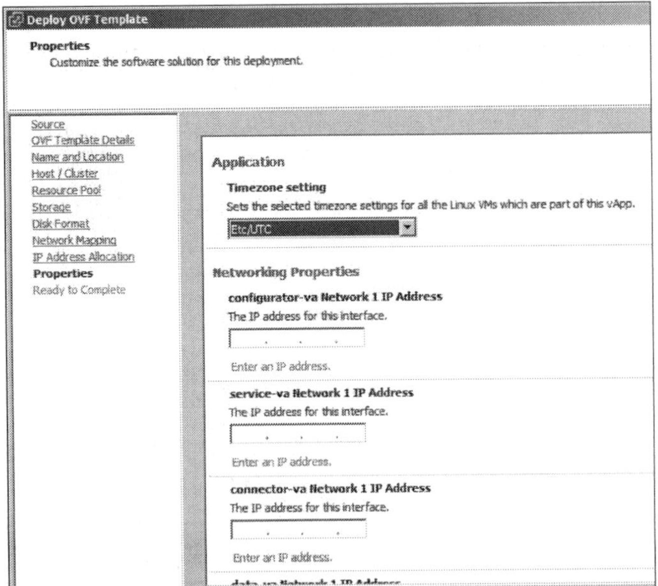

Figure 5.6 IP addresses

VMware Workspace is very time sensitive. Synchronization of each vApp is done upon initial deployment. If you open the configurator console, you can actually see this process being done when the first configurator completes. We recommend that you have a strong Network Time Protocol (NTP) source (low latency and internal to your deployment), and you should have your vApp in the same time zone as your main domain controller and time server (not an absolute requirement, just a strong recommendation).

Now you can review the entire configuration of the vApp to be deployed. Ensure that all settings are correct, and then click the **Finish** button.

At this point, the vApp will deploy; the deployment might take more than an hour depending on the performance of your vSphere hosts and storage.

Workspace Initial Configuration

Use the Workspace VA interface to make initial configurations to Workspace, such as the network, Secure Sockets Layer (SSL), and vCenter extension configuration.

The configurator VA interface leads you through the basic configuration. When you complete the wizard, you must run the web-based Workspace Setup Wizard. You can return to the configurator VA interface at any time to update these settings or to perform other configurations.

IMPORTANT During deployment, leave the VAs, except the configurator VA, powered off. Do not attempt to manually power on any VAs besides the configurator. The Setup Wizard will automatically power on VAs as needed.

After the vApp is fully deployed, you will need to power on the Workspace vApp. Do not directly power on any of the VAs; the vApp will manage all necessary power operations.

After the configurator VA is powered on, you must open the console (or Console tab) to continue the Workspace configuration.

Once inside the console, press Enter to continue.

Respond to the wizard prompts with information specific to your deployment.

The first step in the configuration process is that the configurator VA does a reverse DNS lookup to the DNS server and looks for the IP information and DNS name for each vApp, remembering that you entered that information when you initially deployed the vApp.

One common mistake is for people to create the DNS records for the individual VAs but forget to create the pointer (PTR) records that are associated with the VAs. If you make that mistake, you will be notified of the error on the initial startup, you will be asked to correct this, the vApp will shut down, and you will have to start over. This is a really good validation step that VMware added to the product a little while back. Table 5.1 details the information relevant to the configurator VA.

Table 5.1 Configurator Virtual Appliance Information

Option	Action
Global root password	Type and confirm the global root password you want to use for all five VAs in Workspace.
SMTP server name	Type the SMTP server name. See "Configure an SMTP Server to Work with Horizon Workspace," in the Workspace documentation center. If you want to change your SMTP settings after you install Workspace, see the *CLI Commands for Horizon Workspace Data Guide*.
SMTP port number	Type the SMTP port number.
Workspace FQDN	Type the Workspace fully qualified domain name (FQDN). This domain will be the entry point for end users.
Workspace port number	Type the Workspace port number. The default port number is 443.
vCenter IP address	Type the vCenter IP address or FQDN. **NOTE** Configurator VA registers a vCenter extension and queries the vCenter server periodically to check on the status of the other VMs in the vApp.

Option	Action
vCenter port number	Type the vCenter port number.
vCenter admin username	Type the vCenter administrator's username. The vCenter administrator needs privileges only to Workspace vApp or the resource pool that contains Workspace vApp.
vCenter admin password	Type and confirm the vCenter administrator's password.
Is this correct?	Type **y** if all the information is correct.

The configurator VA processes your information. Depending on your network speed, this process can take up to 20 minutes or more. After it successfully runs, you must run Workspace Setup Wizard.

At this point, the vApp is completely deployed and configured as well as the initial Workspace configuration. Now the Workspace environment is up and running, ready for configuration.

Workspace Setup Wizard

The Workspace Setup Wizard runs in your browser using the configurator VA hostname (for example, https://configurator-va.company.com).

If you're unsure about the URL, just open a session in vCenter in the configurator VA and look at the information listed there. Figure 5.7 is the screen you should see when you start the wizard in your web browser, the first time you access the environment.

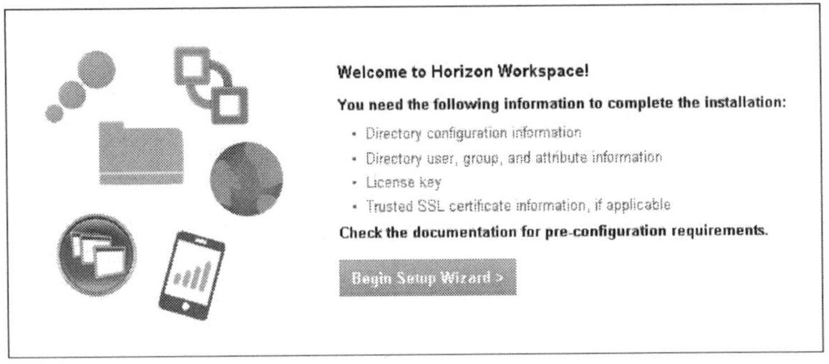
Welcome to Horizon Workspace!
You need the following information to complete the installation:
• Directory configuration information
• Directory user, group, and attribute information
• License key
• Trusted SSL certificate information, if applicable
Check the documentation for pre-configuration requirements.
Begin Setup Wizard >

Figure 5.7 Workspace Setup Wizard

Security Exception

You must set a security exception when you see this message: This Connection Is Untrusted. See the instructions for your browser on setting security exceptions. Figure 5.8 shows the first setup screen of the Workspace Setup Wizard. Keep in mind that the license key is required and that you will not be able to proceed unless you have it.

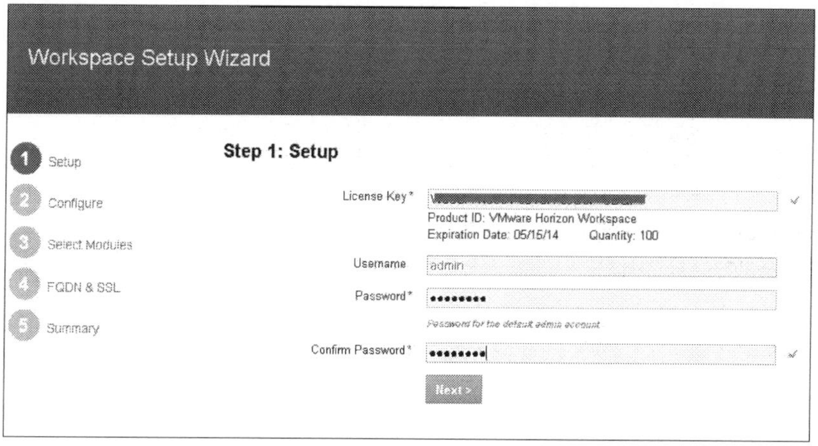

Figure 5.8 License key and admin information

After you enter the license key obtained from VMware (usually from your my.vmware.com portal in the licensing section), you create an administrator password. This administrator account is a special account outside of your enterprise directory. If your connection to Active Directory is unavailable, you can use this account. You will also use this username and password to access the Workspace Administrator, configurator, and connector web interfaces directly.

After you have performed the initial configuration of Workspace, you can use the configurator web interface to perform advanced configuration tasks, such as to change the administrator password.

The next step is to configure the database option. In very small environments (200 users or less), you can use the internal database option (see Figure 5.9). This is useful typically in proof-of-concept, development, or lab environments. In a production environment, VMware recommends using an external database. Workspace provides you two formats of supported databases: vPostgres, (which you can obtain from the VMware site) and Oracle.

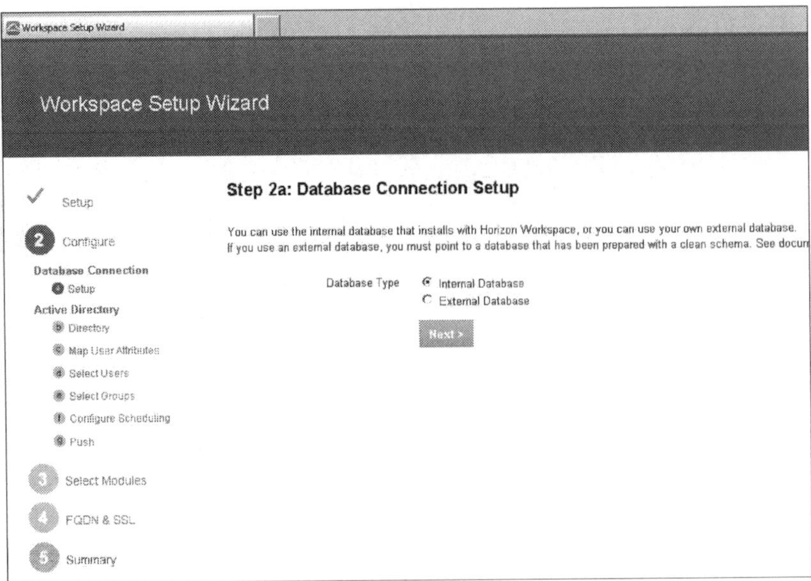

Figure 5.9 Database setup

For the initial installation, we recommend that you use the internal database, complete your setup, ensure that everything is working properly, and then if you are going with a production deployment, switch to external database. Figure 5.10 shows you the Directory page, and Table 5.2 explains the fields you fill out on this web page.

You enter your configuration information on the Directory page to establish a connection to Active Directory, which is used to verify a user's credentials when the user attempts to log in to Workspace.

After you select the correct directory type in the Workspace Setup Wizard, you must enter the correct directory information for your environment. Workspace includes the directory types, Active Directory, and Demo User Store (for evaluation only).

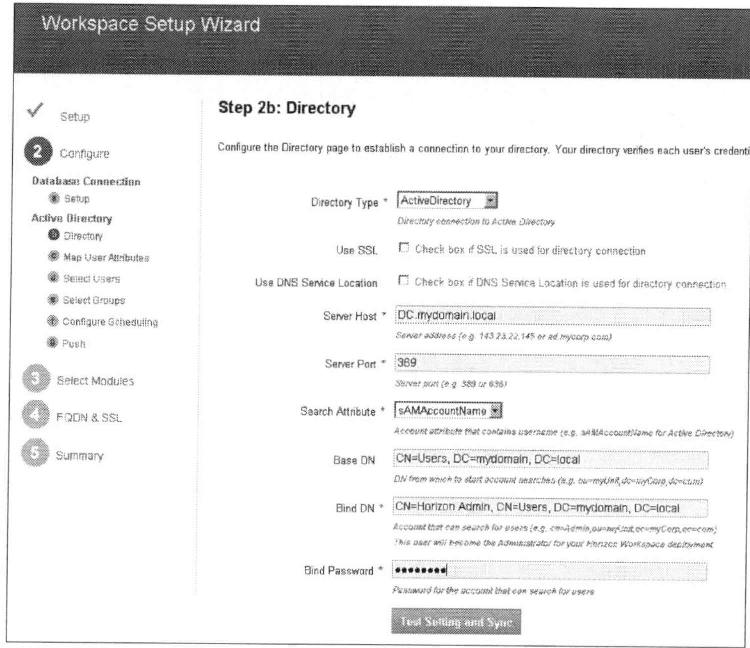

Figure 5.10 User directory configuration

Table 5.2 Active Directory Information

Directory Information	Description
Server host	The text box for the Active Directory host address.
Server port	The text box for the port number for the Active Directory host. For a single-domain Active Directory domain service, the default port for Lightweight Directory Access Protocol (LDAP) is 389; the default port for LDAP over SSL is 636.
Use SSL	You can select the Use SSL check box if that's what you use for your directory connection.
DNS Service Location	You select this if the DNS service location is used for the directory connection.
Search attribute	The drop-down menu for the Active Directory attribute that contains the username. For a single-domain Active Directory domain service, the appropriate selection is sAMAccountName.

Directory Information	Description
Base distinguished name (DN)	The text box for the Base DN, which is the starting point for directory server searches. You can use either Active Directory or Demo User Store (for evaluation only) directory types. See the following examples for best practices when selecting the base DN and bind DN: Base DN: dc=example, dc=com (It is recommended that you use the topmost level for base DN so that you include all users and groups.) Bind DN: cn=admin user, ou=users, dc=example, dc=com (Ensure that Bind DN is below the base DN you select in your Active Directory structure.) You can promote other Active Directory users to the administrator role using the Workspace Administrator web interface. For a single-domain Active Directory domain service, this is the text box for the DN of the starting point for directory server searches (for example, DC=mycompany,DC=com). The connector starts from this DN to create master lists from which you can later filter out individual users and groups.
Bind DN	The text box for the bind DN, including common name (CN), of an Active Directory user account that has privileges to search for users. You can use either Active Directory or Demo User Store (for evaluation only) directory types. The Bind DN account becomes the first administrative account for Workspace that supports Active Directory. The bind DN account user record in Active Directory must include a username, first name, last name, email address, any required extended attributes, and a distinguishedName attribute defined in Active Directory. See the following examples for best practices when selecting the base DN and bind DN: Base DN: dc=example, dc=com (It is recommended that you use the topmost level for base DN so that you include all users and groups.) Bind DN: cn=admin user, ou=users, dc=example, dc=com (Ensure that bind DN is included in the base DN you select.) You can promote other Active Directory users to the administrator role using Workspace Administrator web interface. For a single-domain Active Directory domain service, the bind DN entry must be located in the same branch and below the base DN.
Bind password	The text box for the Active Directory password for the bind DN account.

The next step, displayed in Figure 5.11, is to map the user attributes from your Authoritative user directory to Workspace.

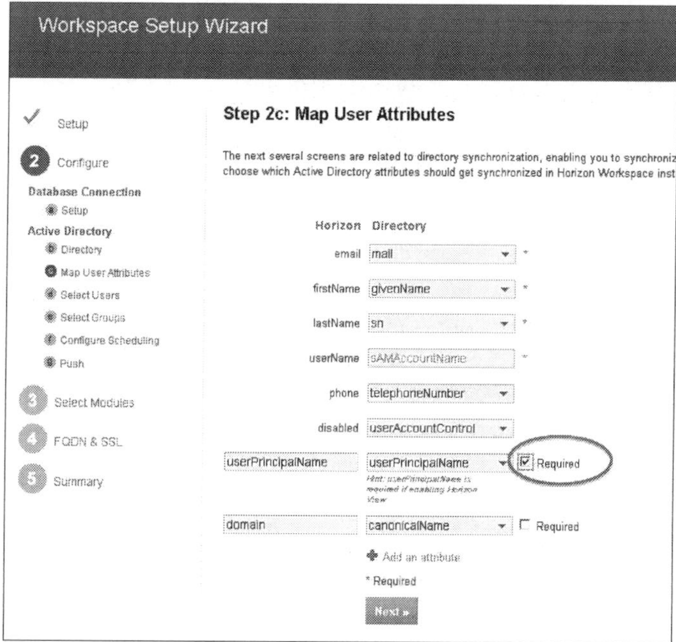

Figure 5.11 User attributes mapping

If you plan to integrate VMware View in the future, check the **UserPrincipalName** check box (UPN). Then, you will be at the step where you need to select users to synchronize with Workspace. On this page, you can put mutliple OUs to scan, but keep in mind that the more OUs and the deeper the tree structure you need to sync, the longer the initial push will take.

Enter the DN where the users are located. For example, if you want to include all the users in the base DN for Company A's Active Directory, use the following query: ou=Users,DC =testDC,DC=acme,DC=com.

Create filters to exclude users you don't want to sync to Workspace (for example, name contains John Smith).

It's good practice to start with a small synchronization, make sure that it is successful, and then add additional OUs.

In Figure 5.12, you can see that we have only three user results in our initial set of results.

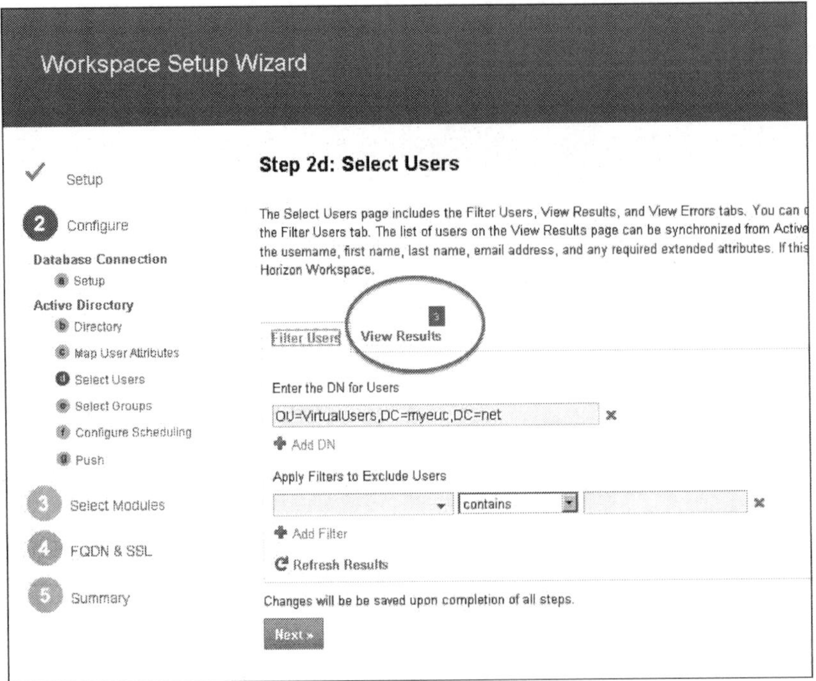

Figure 5.12 User selection

One mistake we sometimes see is that the DN you have selected did not include the administrative user that was previously selected in the Setup Wizard. If you make that mistake, you will lock out the deployment and will have to redeploy. Make sure that if you add multiple OUs that you have at least the one where the Workspace administrator user resides.

Please take the time to go on the View Results screen and double-check that your Workspace administrator is listed in the results.

Then, we move on to group selection. Here you add the group information from your directory type that you want to import to Workspace during the synchronization. You can assign a new name to your directory group in Workspace.

NOTE When you select a group, all members of the group are synced to Workspace. You can sync users from multiple DNs. However, only users under the base DN that you defined in the directory step can be authenticated.

One of the last steps is to configure how often the Workspace environment will poll the Authoritative user directory that you have configured and look for changes in groups or users, as shown in Figure 5.13.

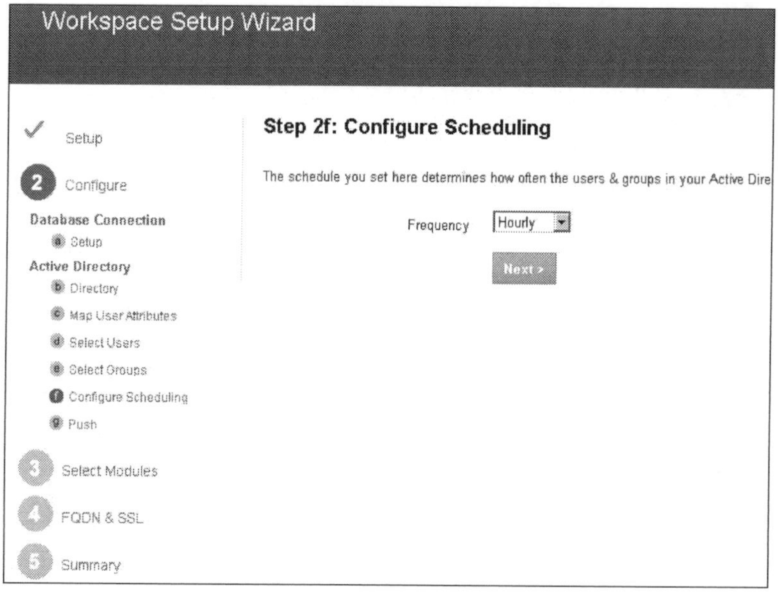

Figure 5.13 User and group synchronization

Best practice here is to choose an interval that will reflect your service-level agreements, up to a degree. For example, if you put an interval that's too short and you have a big Active Directory infrastructure, it will cause a lot of chatter between your Workspace environment and the domain controller you previously configured. If you put an interval of time that's too long, it will take a lot longer for changes to reflect to the Workspace solution, and as a result, your users won't be able to log in until their user accounts are actually synced over. You can always do manual user sync; this is just the interval for the automatic synchronization.

We recommend starting with a small interval; let a few synchronizations happen successfully, and then put in a longer interval. The rate of changes to your Active Directory environment will always be the deciding factor.

We advise against choosing a manual synchronization for this page. It's a common mistake to set this as manual (out of concern for the large amount of synchronization that might happen) and then forget to change it back. The net effect of this is that no users are appearing in Workspace. This is one of those set-it-and-forget-it pages; it's rare that the administrator will think to come back to that setting when the deployment is complete.

The push to Workspace, as displayed in Figure 5.14, might take a while, depending on the number of items to sync.

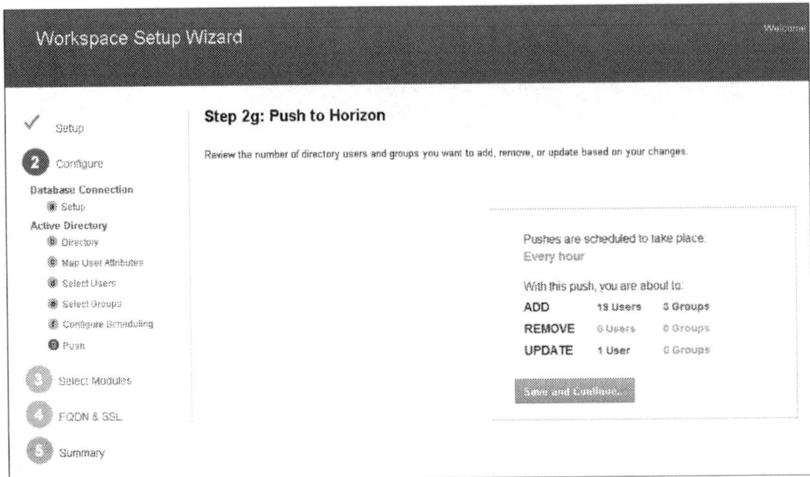

Figure 5.14 User and group synchronization

Review the number of directory users and groups to add, remove, or update based on any changes.

> **IMPORTANT** Do not log in to Workspace until after the push operation is complete. If you add a large number of users, the synchronization process can take a long time. Verify that the users and groups are under the base DN for successful authentication.

On the Select Modules page, do not change any of the states. (That is, leave the module disabled for now.) Next, we cover the SSL certificate, as shown in Figure 5.15.

In a production deployment, you would definitely use a load balancer; Workspace does not provide its own load balancing. We recommend you use a hardware load balancer like an F5 Big-IP solution (www.f5.com) or use a software load-balancer like VMware vShield Edge.

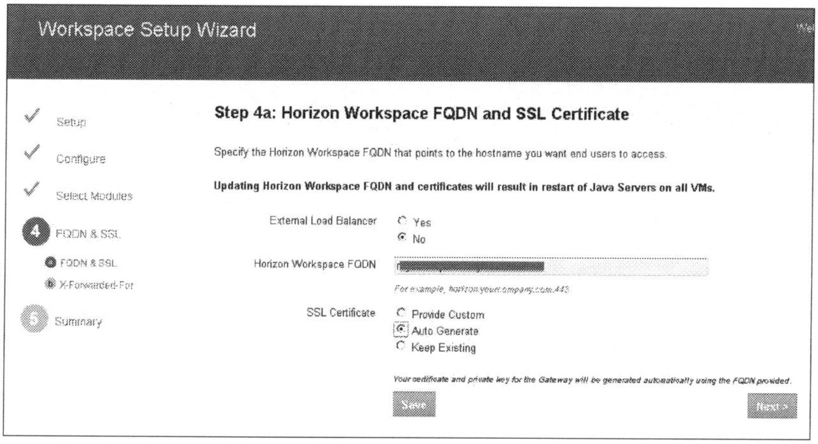

Figure 5.15 SSL setup

For the SSL configuration aspect, three choices are presented to you. Avoid Keep Existing unless this is for a proof-of-concept or small lab scenario. The main reason for this is that the Workspace solution is software that is released by VMware and everybody downloads the same bits. Therefore, the existing SSL certificate that comes bundled with the solution is similar for everyone, meaning that it would be child's play for a hacker to download the VMware Workspace vApp and extract the certificate from the console, and then use it in your environment to impersonate the server connection.

We recommend instead to use a publicly recognized and trusted certificate by choosing the **Provide Custom** option.

The entire certificate chain must be included in the SSL certificate section. A trusted certificate can be uploaded later because Workspace includes a self-signed certificate.

Keep in mind that changing the information in this page will restart the Java servers on all VMs, making the Workspace environment unavailable for a few seconds, maybe minutes, as shown in Figure 5.16. That's why it is best practice to do this properly the first time you set up the environment (so that you do not have to bring the environment down in the future when it's in production and running at full steam).

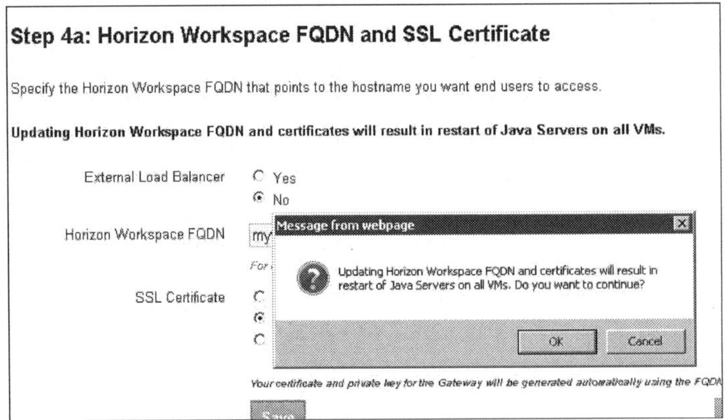

Figure 5.16 Java server restart

In the last step, 4b, you must enter the IP addresses for any load balancers or gateways between the Workspace gateway and the end user. These are the IP addresses that the gateway uses for client identification on the X-Forwarded-For page. The Workspace gateway uses the X-Forwarded-For header to identify source IP addresses from the browser client and determines which connector to log in to based on this IP address. The IP addresses you add here are populated to all the gateways in your environment.

You've completed initial setup and now you are ready to log in to your Workspace Admin web management site.

If you have used Workspace in the past, you will notice that VMware revamped the web interface to have a more up-to-date look (see Figure 5.17). We're happy with this update; it was time for a change.

Because this is the first time you're logging in, you have the option (starting with version 1.8 of Workspace) to do a guided tour of the environment. Feel free to use it. We are detailing in the following pages what each module does and how to configure it.

To bring up the administrative dashboard, as shown in Figure 5.18, click your name in the upper-right corner and choose Administration Console. If you've followed all the steps so far, you should now see all the modules and be ready to configure any or all of them.

Figure 5.17 New sign-in user interface

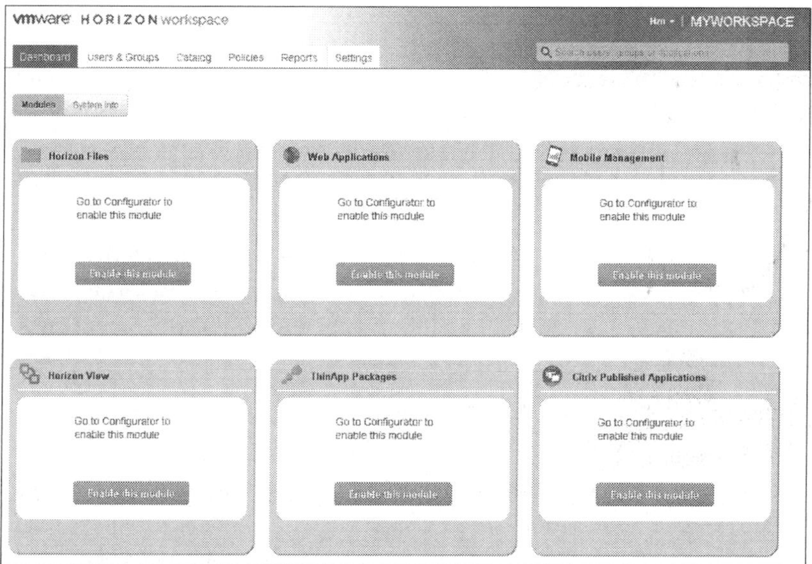

Figure 5.18 New Admin user interface

Notice that you can now switch between the user portal view and the administrative view just by clicking your name and switching context (a very useful improvement).

Table 5.3 describes the various modules.

Table 5.3 Module Information

Module	Description
Data module	The data module is available in the Catalog services section. After it is enabled, the administrator can entitle users or groups to upload and share files with enterprise and nonenterprise users.
Web apps and mobile apps	You can add or import Security Assertion Markup Language (SAML)-enabled Web apps or referred mobile apps from a published Global Catalog (hosted by VMware) from Google Play and iTunes applications stores. Then the administrator can grant users and groups access to these applications. Users can use single sign on to access the SAML-based web applications or install referred mobile applications on their mobile devices.
ThinApp packages	You can import and enable ThinApp packages from a Windows network share. You must log in to the connector and load the ThinApp packages. The administrator can enable/entitle applications to users and groups from the Administrator web interface, and end users can launch these applications using the Workspace Client for Windows.
View pools	While enabling the module, the administrator can sync information about the available View pools and entitlements from the View Connection Server. Once enabled, end users can launch the View desktops they have access to from the Workspace web interface. If you want to enable the View module, you must join the Active Directory domain, sync the View Connection Server with it, and enable SAML authentication.
Mobile management	When this module is enabled, the administrator can provide mobile apps for use on mobile devices. For managed mobile apps, the administrator can import the mobile apps to the catalog, set policies to control their behavior, and grant users and groups access to install the mobile apps on their mobile devices. For referred mobile apps, the administrator can refer mobile apps for installation from a published Global Catalog hosted by VMware or from Google Play or the Apple App Store. After adding referred mobile apps to the catalog, the administrator can specify which users and groups should be referred to those mobile apps.
XenApp	When this module is enabled, Workspace uses the Workspace Integration Broker component and the Citrix software development kit (SDK) to handle single sign on between Workspace and Citrix server farms and Citrix-based applications

Navigating the Administrative Console

Welcome to the Workspace Administrator console login. To go directly to this page, use the address https://*WorkspaceFQDN*/admin. This page requires an Active Directory login that has been granted access to Workspace. If the configuration was successful, logging in here will be available. If the login on this page does not work, logging in to https://*WorkspaceFQDN*/SAAS/login/0 will be necessary with the admin user ID and the password that was set during configuration.

The administrative interface for Workspace has six tabs:

- Dashboard (Modules and System info)
- Users & Groups
- Catalog
- Policies
- Reports
- Settings

The following subsections cover each tab in detail, but let's first configure the various modules.

Enable Workspace Data Module

The Data module gives you the full on-premise file and data-collaboration tools, fully integrated into your workspace.

To continue the Data setup, log in to the Workspace Admin console at https://*WorkspaceFQDN*/admin.

Click **Enable This Module**. You will then be redirected to the configurator web UI. Keep in mind that changes made to the modules are done through the configurator; it's the appliance that keeps all the information for each module and each VA.

After you've enabled the module, you can start using the data portion right away. Workspace sets up a default class of service, so you don't have to change anything if you don't want to. A class of service is a set of rules linked to how the data is used, how much data users associated with that class can use, and other various settings.

Let's take a look at the default installed class of service. Log back in to your Workspace gateway UI (https://*WorkspaceFQDN*/admin), display the Catalog tab, and then click **Horizon Files**, as shown in Figure 5.19.

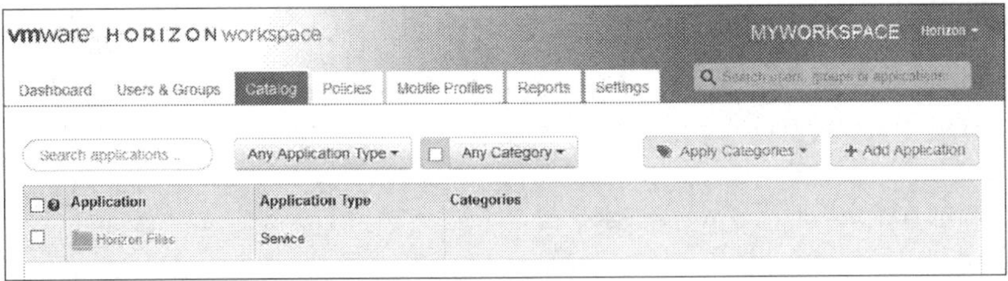

Figure 5.19 Default class of service (CoS)

Take the time to look at every rule in place and adjust to follow your organization policy. For example, the default quota for users who will be associated with that CoS is unlimited. You definitely don't want to leave an unlimited quota for your users; you will get yourself in trouble quickly if you do this. Set a reasonable quota to start. We recommend something small, like 5 GB, and then grow it as necessary. Best practice is to create CoS for the types of user within your organization. We've noticed that most users will have more than enough with 5 GB, but you will have some users within your environment who will require more. That is when you should create another CoS and set different rules for those users.

The data module is straightforward and easy to set up. However, we strongly caution you to do proper planning when enabling this module. It will be the module that will take the most amount of hard drive space, the most quickly, within your datacenter.

As a rule of thumb, at least do the following:

1. Take the number of users you will have deployed within your environment.
2. Classify them by CoS.
3. Define a quota for each CoS.
4. Estimate the percentage of use of those different classes of service.
5. Plan room for growth for each CoS.

Building a matrix of these five points will quickly give you an estimate for the required amount of storage for the data module. Table 5.4 shows a couple of examples of what this could represent from a storage standpoint. It might be harder to grow capacity after deployment, but nothing would stop you from adjusting the quota per user if tight on space. (Keep in mind that a user who reaches or exceeds the quota will potentially lose data.)

Table 5.4 Data Calculation Example

Number of Users	CoS Name	Quota	% of Use	% of Growth for 1 Year	Total
100	IT Admin	25 GB	50%	25%	1.56 TB
1000	Office Worker	5 GB	75%	25%	4.69 TB
100	HR	10 GB	50%	25%	0.625 TB
250	Power User	25 GB	75%	50%	7.03 TB

This would give you a first estimate at 13.9 TB and would at least help you plan for your deployment of Workspace Data module. Understanding your use case will make or break your deployment; you should always remember that user segmentation is key. If you plan on deploying Workspace at scale, make sure that you take the time to architect the Data portion properly; it will often be the most complicated and most demanding piece of the solution.

We did not cover in the example mentioned in Table 5.4 the sharing portion or the file revisions of Workspace Data module. You should account for these as well, but that's a more complex scenario, which we do not cover here.

Another important rule that you will find in the CoS is the maximum file size. Even though it looks like a pretty obvious setting, it is often forgotten or left as default. The default size is 2 GB, which we find a little too high. This solution is not a media file-sharing solution; it's meant to be a store for your corporate users to exchange files and have easy access to all their files from any device. You might have one, possibly two, CoS exceptions where you will need bigger files, but the default CoS should not have a maximum file size that big.

We will now cover a couple of more useful and unique policies that you should configure: external folder sharing and public file sharing.

The public file sharing is pretty straightforward; within the CoS, the Workspace Administrator enables users to share files externally. When this setting is enabled, a user can right-click any of his files, and there will be a public share option.

To enable this, you must ensure that the CoS has the external file sharing enabled. Then, go into the Users & Groups tab and entitle either users or groups to use the Workspace Files Services. Then, you can log in with an authorized user account, click the Files application, and upload a file. (Because this is the first time you're logging in, you won't have any files uploaded.) Right-click the file or click the down arrow next to the file when you're hovering over it and choose to share publicly. This will bring up a pop-up message box with a long URL containing the full address to share this file externally with anyone. Figure 5.20 shows this workflow.

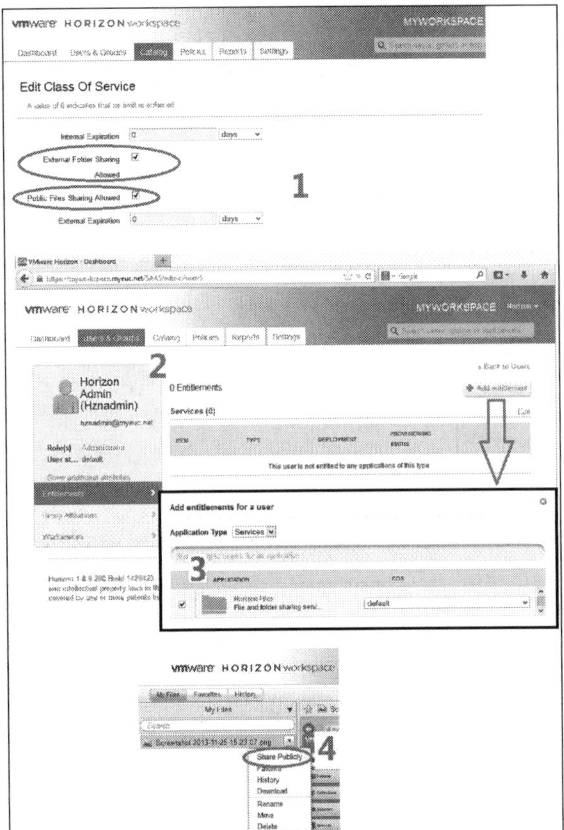

Figure 5.20 External file-sharing workflow

User Entitlement

You can entitle users for any given module (such as Workspace Data) in two ways: using the Catalog tab or using the Users & Groups tab. (For more information on creating Workspace Groups and user entitlement, see Chapter 8, "VMware Workspace Operations.") The following steps detail each. Let's first consider user entitlement from the Catalog tab (see Figure 5.21).

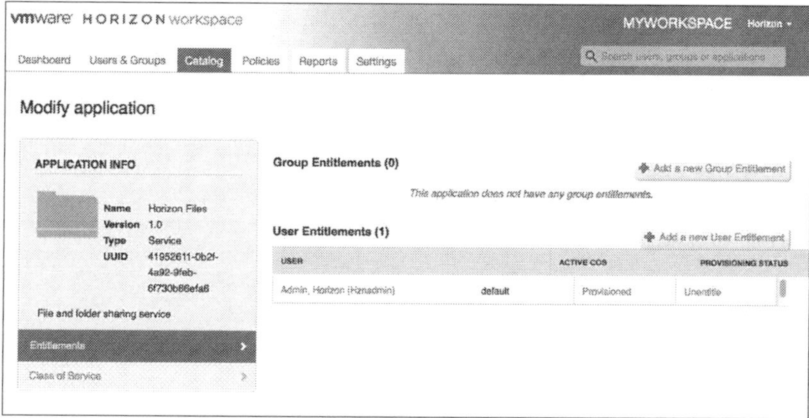

Figure 5.21 User entitlement from the Catalog tab

Clicking each enabled module will enable you to entitle either groups or users, as follows:

1. Click **Add a New Group Entitlement** to add an Active Directory group. If individual users are selected, click **Add a New User Entitlement**.
2. Either type the group name in the search box or use the browse feature to select the correct group.
3. After all appropriate groups have been added, click the **Save** button at the bottom.

Now let's take a look at user entitlement from the Users & Groups tab:

1. Display the Users & Groups tab at the top of the Admin page.
2. Click **Users**, and then click the user entry to be entitled. In our example shown in Figure 5.22, we're using the Workspace Admin user (HznAdmin).

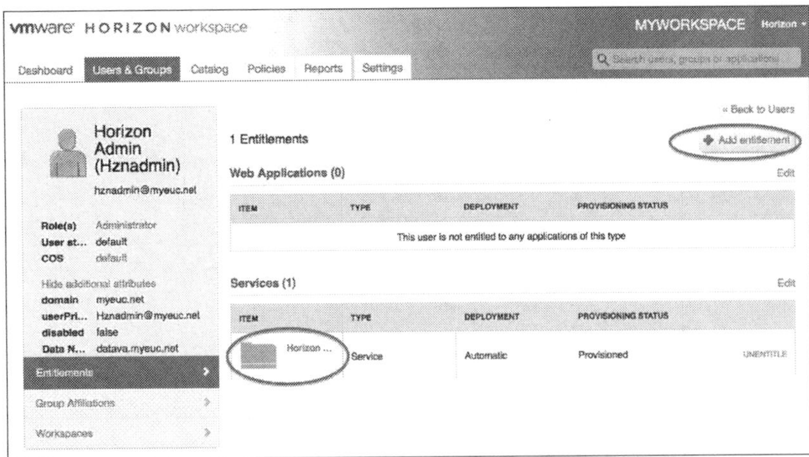

Figure 5.22 User entitlement from the Users & Groups tab

3. Click the **+ Add Entitlement** button.
4. Check the box to enable Data for this user, leave the Active CoS as default, and then click the green **Save** button.

Note that until the Save button is clicked, the actual change is not effective in the environment. If you leave this page by clicking a different tab or just logging out, the user change will not have been committed to the database.

The configured user should now have Data listed under entitlements. From here it is possible to edit entitlements.

Click **Data** to go to the Edit Application page.

For now, if you haven't done anything else, only one CoS is configured, the only choice you will see appear in the drop-down list. We will now configure an additional CoS for your environment. As a reminder, this is especially useful if you have more than one type of user in your environment, because you will then have more than one CoS to reflect the type of user you support (Power User, Task Worker, HR, IT, and so on).

Configuring CoS in Data

Figure 5.23 shows that the users are entitled to use the Data module of Workspace. Adding more users and groups on this screen can be done at this time. It is also appropriate to edit the default CoS for Workspace Data at this time.

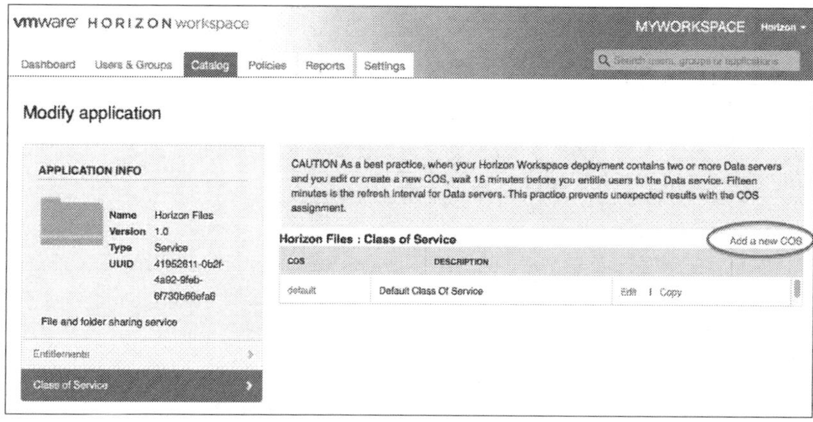

Figure 5.23 Adding a CoS

Click **Class of Service**. You can then modify Data configuration items such as quotas, warning messages, and others.

You can also modify file size limits, the % threshold when users start to receive warnings, and whether users are allowed to share files or folders externally; you can also add expiry dates to those shared items. Another important attribute is which file types can be restricted. A CoS can be created for many different use cases, and therefore multiple different versions can exist and be applied to users based on their requirements and specific use cases.

For your deployment, we strongly recommend not to leave the default unlimited quota on any of the CoS you create. The account quota should be set based on the amount of available Workspace Data storage in the environment (and remember to leave yourself room for growth). Take the time to calculate the amount of storage you will require based on the type of user you will have, the number of users you will have, and the percentage of use. Refer to Table 5.4 to see how to calculate the total amount of storage required. Note that this item is set in megabytes (MB).

After changes here are complete, save your changes and close this window; Workspace Data enablement is now complete.

The Dashboard tab, shown in Figure 5.24, will now show all enabled services configured in this Workspace.

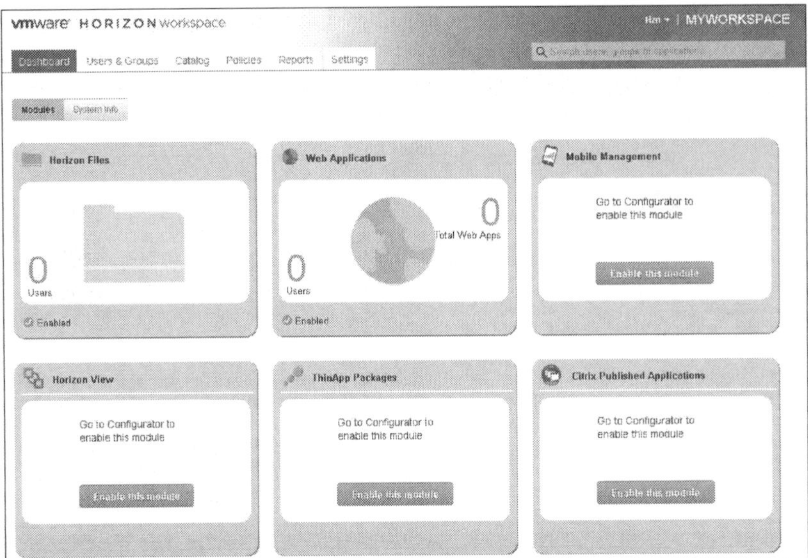

Figure 5.24 Modules in Workspace

From the Workspace Administrator web console, the dashboard will show which modules are enabled and how many users have access. To enable any additional modules, a return to the configurator web console is necessary.

To review the steps required to integrate ThinApp, please refer to Chapter 8.

Enable Integration with View

A very powerful feature of the Workspace solution set is to integrate VMware View with Workspace. The following list provides a quick summary of what is required to achieve this. Chapter 6, "Integrating VMware View and Workspace," covers this subject in more detail.

Prerequisites:

- Use VMware View 5.2 or later.
- Deploy and configure View to use the default port, 443. Workspace does not support other ports for View integration.
- Deploy and configure View pools and desktops with entitlements set for Active Directory users and groups.

- Create the View pools as a user with administrator permissions on the root folder in View. If the user administrator permissions are on a folder other than the root folder, Workspace will not recognize the SAML Authenticator configured in View, and the Workspace pool configuration will not work.
- Enable the user principal name (UPN) attribute on Workspace.
- Verify that DNS entries and IP addresses use reverse lookup for each View Connection Server in the View setup. Workspace requires reverse lookup for View Connection Servers, the View Security Server, and the load balancer. If reverse lookup is not properly configured, the Workspace integration with View fails.
- Sync Active Directory users and groups with View pool entitlements to Workspace.

Return to the configurator web console (https://*ConfiguratorHostname*/cfg) to enable the View module. Go to the Module Configuration page and click **Enable This Module for View**. With the ThinApp configuration complete, the Join Domain section should be unnecessary. Fill out the View portion on the bottom half of this screen and click **Sync**.

Figure 5.25 shows what the wizard looks like after you click the **Enable View Pools** check box, and Table 5.5 describes the information from each field.

View Pools

Enable View Pools ☑

Connection Server* myViewonnectionSvr.mydomain.local

Fully qualified domain name of the initial View Connection Server instance to sync with

Username* mydomain\administrator

Choose an account that was given the Administrators or Administrators (Read Only) role in View Administrator

Password* ●●●●●●●●●●●

The password associated with the above username

FQDN for Client Access* myViewonnectionSvr.mydomain.local

Fully qualified domain name (FQDN) of the server or intermediate device that allows users to connect to View desktops

FQDN port number* 443

Port number of the server or intermediate device that allows users to connect to View Desktops

Enable SSO ☐ Check this box to enable Single Sign-On to View desktops, which allows the Connector to send encrypted user passwords

Choose Frequency Every hour

Save

Figure 5.25 Enable View pool sync

Table 5.5 View Information

View	Description
Initial Connection Server	Type the FQDN of the View Connection Server instance with which you want to sync.
FQDN for Client Access	Type the FQDN of the server or intermediate device, such as Security Server or load balancer that connects users to View desktops.
Username	Choose an account that has the Administrators or Administrators (Read Only) role in View Administrator.
Password	Type the password associated with the Active Directory username.

Launch a View Pool

Now users can launch a View pool from Workspace. Users can also switch the display protocol between Open with View Client (PCoIP or RDP) and Open with Browser (Blast requiring a browser supporting HTML 5).

Prerequisites:

- Install View Client 1.6 or later if View Administrator uses PC over IP (PCoIP) or Remote Desktop Protocol (RDP) as the display protocol. You must install View Client on the machine that launches Workspace. To find out more about the right version of the client to install, visit VMware: https://my.vmware.com/web/vmware/info/slug/desktop_end_user_computing/vmware_horizon_view_clients/2_0.

  Procedure:

  1. Log in to your Workspace instance.
  2. Right-click the selected View pool and choose a protocol to launch the View desktop, as shown in Figure 5.26.

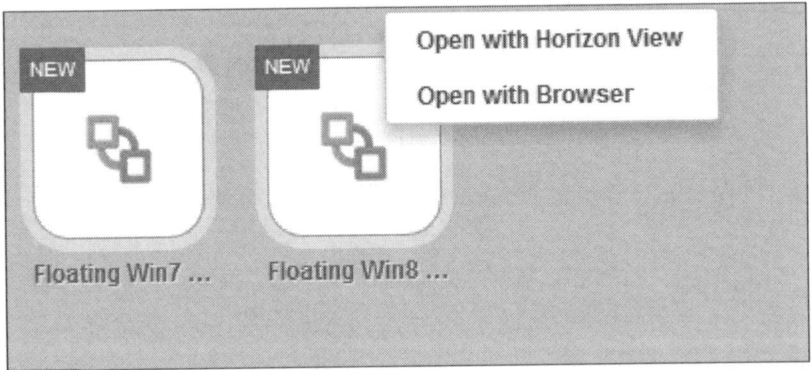

Figure 5.26 View desktop access

You can also be presented with a different view where you will see all the pools entitled to the user directly in the web interface; it depends on how many pools are assigned to that user and whether he has any pool entitled to him at all.

Figure 5.27 shows an example of a user who has two different View pools entitled to him.

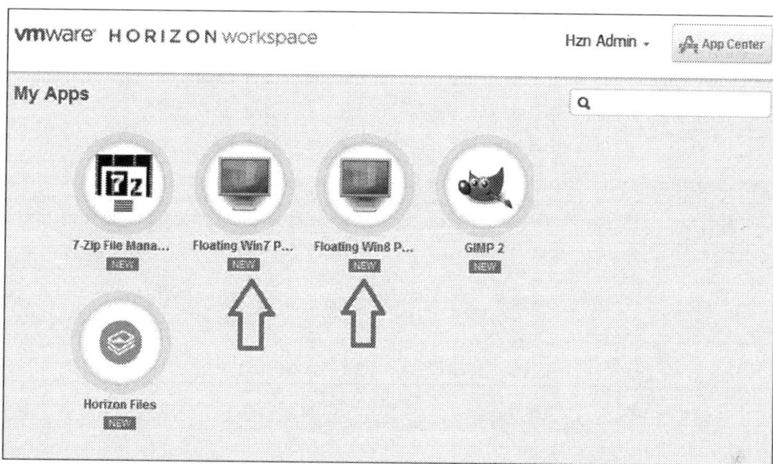

Figure 5.27 Workspace user dashboard

Keep in mind that synchronization of the View desktop pools will follow whatever time interval you have chosen, and if you did not initially click Sync Now and just saved, your changes might not appear until your next synchronization; as a result, your users might think that they have no desktop pool entitled because they are not seeing the update. Make sure to sync and test with an administrator account that you know has at least one desktop pool entitled to him.

Web Applications: SaaS

The last module to enable is Web Applications. Click **Enable This Module**, and now the first four modules are enabled. There is nothing more to configure on this part; as soon as you enable Web Applications, the Global Catalog can be searched for those apps. You have three different options in the Application section, as shown in Figure 5.28: You can add an application from the VMware Global Catalog, you can create your own custom application, or you can import a ZIP or JAR file.

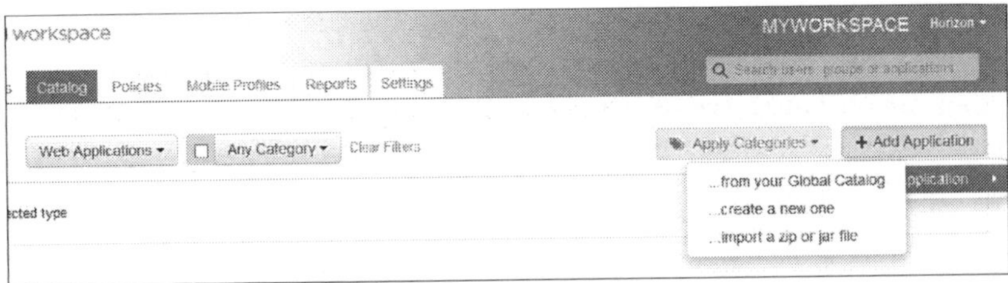

Figure 5.28 Adding an application

We want to focus on an enterprise-wide application. We chose for this example a company that is recognized worldwide and that also has a developer/test account we can use to test the deployment without impacting the production environment. If you already have an SaaS application and you want to use that, go for it. The main reason why we wanted to give an example of a nonimpacting test application is that we did not want someone without experience with SaaS integration going with a production application on the first try.

The first step you should take is to go to www.developerforce.com and create an account with them. This free account will permit you to test SaaS integration into your environment without the risk of bringing down another system in your environment.

In your catalog, choose **Global Catalog**, then find **Salesforce**, as shown in Figure 5.29, in the list and select it.

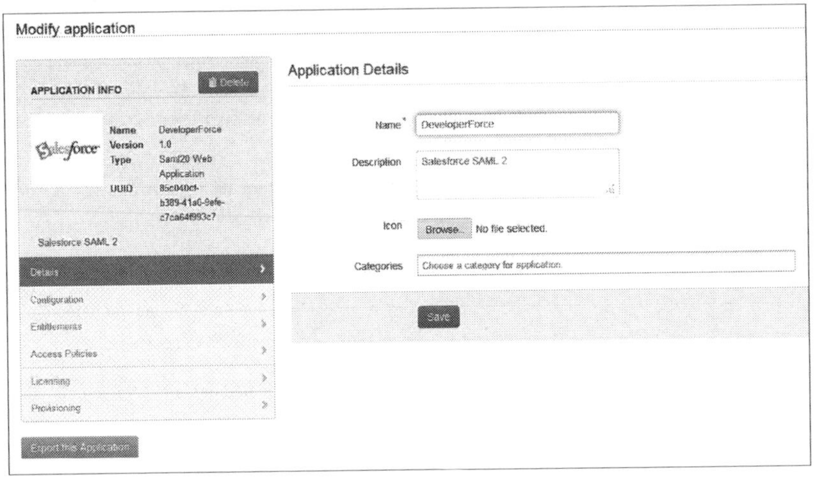

Figure 5.29 Adding an SAML application

The next step is to add your Workspace signing certificate to the SaaS app side (in this case, the DevelopForce environment). To do this, display the Settings tab, select **SAML Certificate**, copy the content of the whole signing certificate section (shown in Figure 5.30), and save it to a CER file.

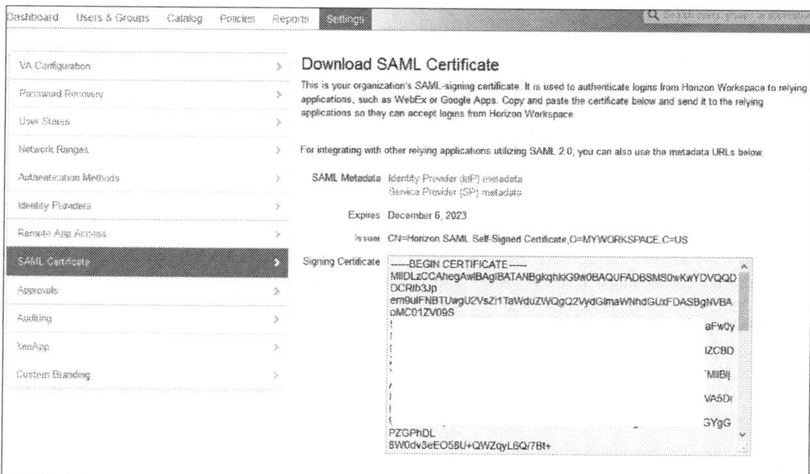

Figure 5.30 SAML certificate

Then, you must tell the SaaS side how to consume this certificate. Log in to your DeveloperForce account with the administrator credentials you previously created.

Go into the Security Controls section and choose **Single Sign-On Settings**. Enable the SAML authentication, and then configure the proper fields (see Figure 5.31).

In the Issuer field, enter the URL for the service VA (that you previously made sure was reachable from the Internet). The text would look like this:

https://<GatewayVA_URL>/SAAS/API/1.0/GET/metadata/idp.xml

The next step is to choose the certificate you previously saved in a CER file by using the **Browse** button next to Identity Provider Certificate.

The last step is to configure the identity provider login URL. It should look something like this:

https://<ServiceVA_URL>/SAAS/API/1.0/POST/sso

The last step before you can try it is to make sure that you have users in DeveloperForce that match your Active Directory environment that is configured in Workspace. The required fields that should match are first name, last name, and email address. Create an account that meets those specifications on the DeveloperForce side.

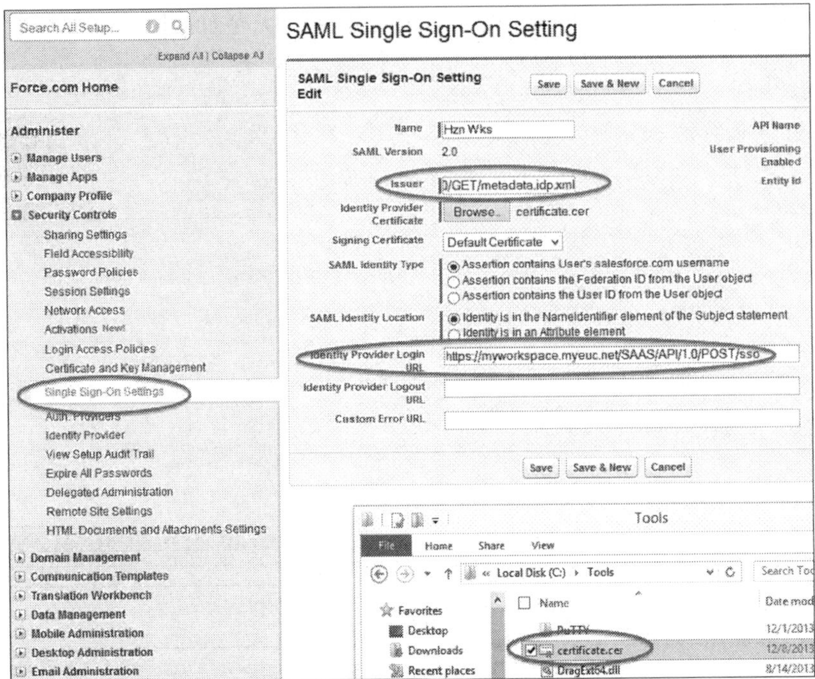

Figure 5.31 DeveloperForce SAML authentication

The last step is to entitle your users to DeveloperForce, going either under the Catalog section and choosing **Application**, **Add User Entitlement**, or by going under the Users & Groups tab and choosing **User Entitlements**.

You have now configured both sides and can test by simply logging in as a user and clicking the DeveloperForce icon. If you've configured everything properly, you will be automatically redirected to DeveloperForce and logged in without having to enter any additional credentials.

Keep in mind that every SaaS application might behave differently. Be sure to check with the web application company as to how they handle SAML authentication and any regulatory compliance you might need to follow to enable this functionality within Workspace.

Modifying Workspace Data Module Storage

When the Workspace Data VA is configured, several default VM disks (VMDKs) are configured. The combined size of all configured VMDK storage is 175 GB. One of these is configured to store Data blobs and by default is only 10 GB. You must add additional disk storage to manage your Data storage resources. You can either add additional VMDKs for Data blob storage or you can use shared network-attached storage (NAS) configured with the Network File System (NFS) protocol.

The storage option you choose depends on your storage requirements. For example, small deployments that require less than 6 terabytes for storage can be configured using VMDKs. For large deployments, however, VMware recommends that you use NFS storage to store your Workspace Data files.

Add Additional VMDKs for Storage

Adding additional VMDKs for storage is done via the normal vSphere mechanism.

Prerequisites:

- Verify that the data VA is running.
- The recommended storage requirement is 2.5 times the user's quota per account, which provides sufficient space for multiple file revisions.
- Use vSphere to add VMDKs for storage.

In vCenter, locate the data VA and right-click on it. You can then edit the data VA settings, as shown in Figure 5.32.

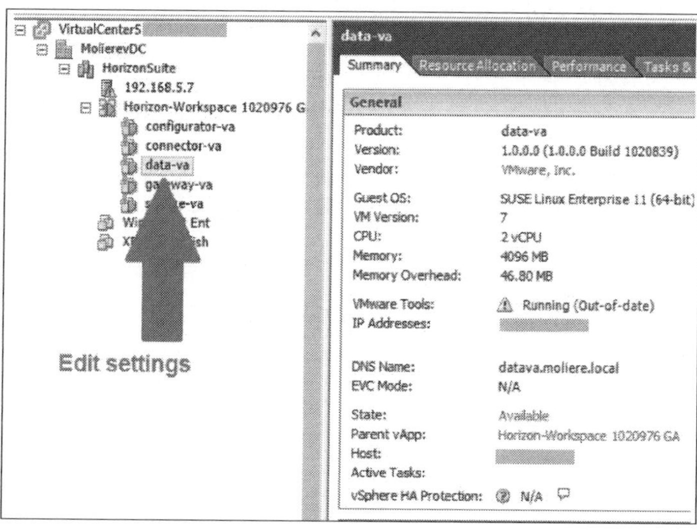

Figure 5.32 Data VA vSphere information

Figure 5.33 shows what the data VA looks like before the disk is added.

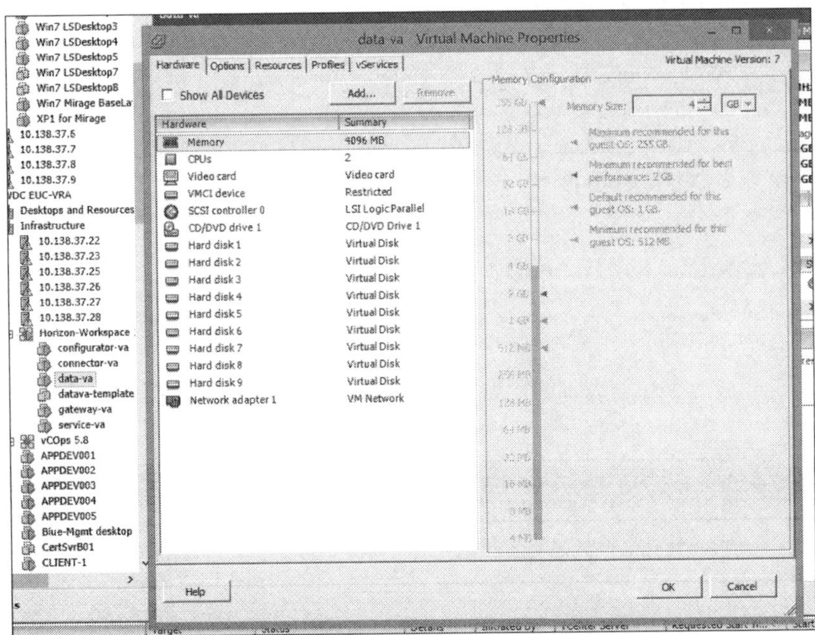

Figure 5.33 Data VA hard disk properties

As you can see, nine hard disks are configured by default.

Figure 5.34 shows what data VA looks like after the disk is added.

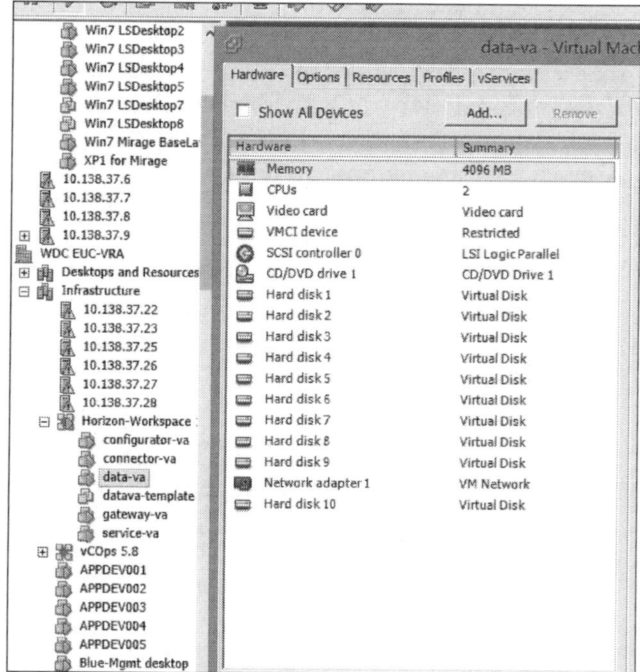

Figure 5.34 Data VA disk added

The next step is to get that disk recognized in the data VA.

Procedure:

1. Log in to the vSphere Client and select the Data Server.
2. Click **OK**.
3. Display the Console tab and click **Enter**.
4. Type **root** to log in.
5. Enter the administrator password you created for all VAs during Workspace installation.
6. Type **/opt/vmware-hdva-installer/bin/zca-expand-lv** to run the script. The newly added disk is detected and added to the store logical volume by default.
7. Exit the server.

Upgrading a Workspace Environment

One nice thing about VMware Workspace is the simplicity to do in-place upgrades, with minimal disruption to the users. For the last couple of versions, VMware has included a command line to run in the configurator VA. You can do this from a Workspace environment running anything from an older version to the latest release.

You want to make sure that your environment can successfully resolve the following address: vapp-updates.vmware.com on port 80.

Before moving forward with the upgrade, you should validate the process. To do so, simply log in to the configurator VA via the command line, using `root` as the user, and then run the following command:

```
/usr/local/horizon/lib/menu/updatemgr.hzn check
```

The validation process will take a few minutes; wait for it to finish. When the process finishes, and if you don't get any errors, you're ready to do the upgrade. Simply retype the same command, but this time put `update` at the end:

```
/usr/local/horizon/lib/menu/updatemgr.hzn update
```

Enabling Workspace with NFS

When you add an NFS mount, this becomes the working data volume, the VMDK disk that is configured during install becomes a secondary data volume, and no new data files are added to the VMDK disk.

Before enabling Workspace with NFS, you need to create a directory on the NFS server that can be accessed from the data VA. You must identify the hostname or IP address and the directory when you mount the NFS volume.

Procedure:

1. Log in to the vSphere Client and select the Data server.
2. Click **OK**.
3. Display the Console tab and press **Enter**.
4. Type **root** to log in.

5. Enter the administrator password you created for all VAs during Workspace installation.

6. Change the directory:

   ```
   cd /opt/vmware-hdva-installer/bin
   ```

7. Mount the NFS volume by using the following command:

   ```
   ./mount-nfs-store.pl --nfs <nfs_serverhostname>:/<directory_to_use>
   ```

NOTE A new mount point is created, and the new volume is now the current primary volume for the data VA.

8. Verify the newly mounted NFS volume ID.

   a. Change to the Zimbra user by using the following command:

      ```
      su - zimbra
      ```

   b. Type `zmvolume -l` to see the volume ID.

Installing the Workspace Agent on Client Endpoints

This section outlines the detailed implementation procedures of the Workspace Client deployment.

Workspace Windows/OS X/iPad/Android Client Deployment

The easiest way to deploy the Workspace Client on a Windows machine is to point your browser to your Workspace download page. The URL is https://<Gateway-VA URL>/download. When you land on that page, you will see the possible choice for client installation. Workspace will recognize the OS of the client connecting to its download page and will suggest the proper client to install on the machine.

Figure 5.35 shows an example of a user that connected from a Windows machine and the view in the user's browser.

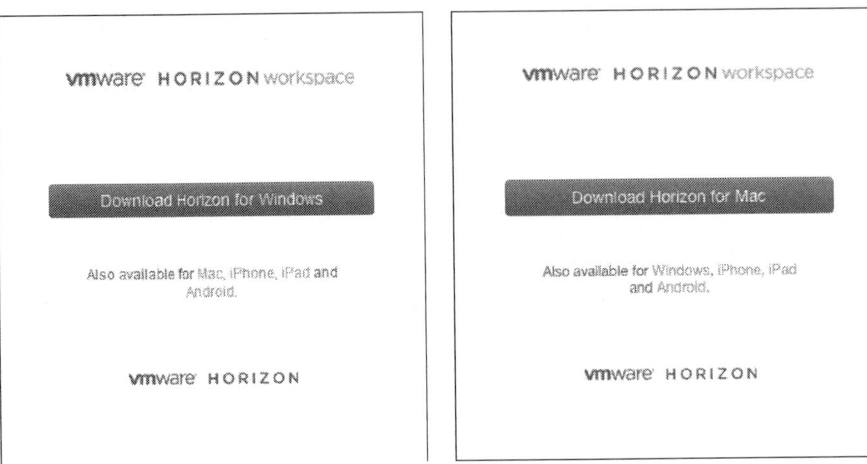

Figure 5.35 Client download page

NOTE It's the same process for an Android, iPhone, or iPad endpoint.

As an alternative, you can go on the Apple iTunes store (see Figure 5.36) or Google Play and look for VMware Workspace; it's a free download.

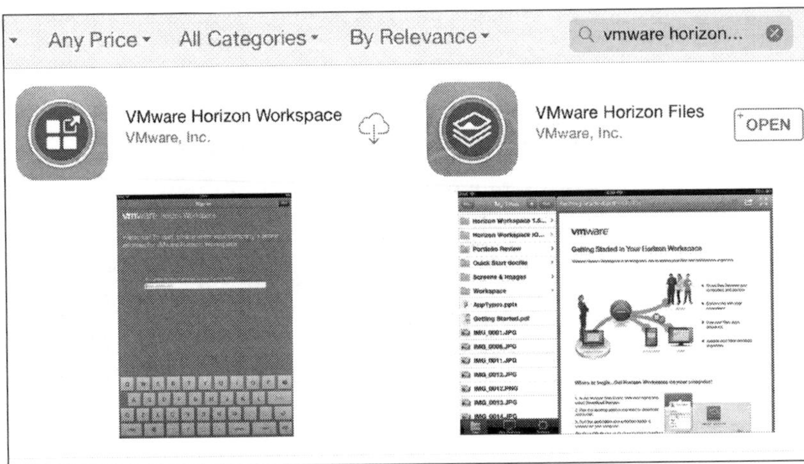

Figure 5.36 iPad client download

The important and easy part is that after you've downloaded the client (for additional details on integrating Windows Workspace clients, see Chapter 8), from whatever platform you've selected to do this, you need to enter only the following information:

- Gateway VA URL FQDN
- Username
- Password

On the Windows agent installation, the screen will look like that shown in Figure 5.37.

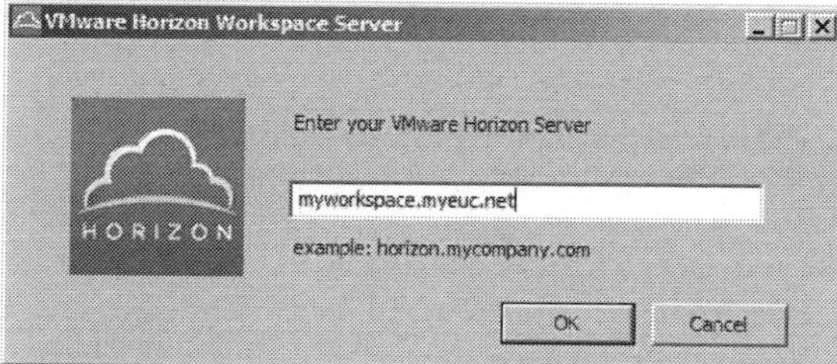

Figure 5.37 Workspace Client Wizard

Notice that you'll get a warning that there's a problem with the certificate if you haven't already deployed a valid, fully recognized certificate, as shown in Figure 5.38.

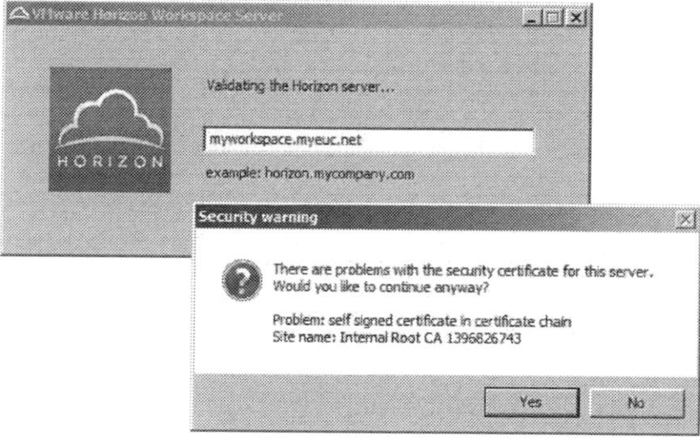

Figure 5.38 Workspace Client certificate notification

You will see from the onscreen information that you have a successful deployment, no reboot necessary.

Once successfully logged in, a user can do three things:

- Change the file location of the data synchronization
- Collect diagnostic information for the computer currently connecting to the environment
- Unlink the computer from the current Workspace connected environment

That's one of the strengths of Workspace: It is device aware and platform aware, so it gives you a consistent user experience across all your devices.

If you enter the information correctly, you are then logged in to your Workspace and you will see the files, the applications, and the desktops that are entitled to you.

The last two modules to configure are the mobile device and the Citrix XenApp integration. We cover these modules in the "Application Virtualization" chapter that you can download from the Pearson website: www.informit.com/title/9780133479089.

Using SSL Certificates in Workspace

SSL protects communications to Workspace and within it. During the Workspace web interface initialization, the configurator randomly generates a self-signed root CA certificate.

The Workspace Setup Wizard generates individual certificates for each VM in the vApp and chains those certificates to the newly generated root CA. Workspace uses the hostname as the CN within the certificate for all machines except the gateway. The Workspace Setup Wizard uses the Workspace FQDN to generate the SSL certificate for the gateway.

Because the initial SSL certificates in the vApp do not chain to a publicly available root CA, the generated root CA must be distributed to establish trust between Workspace and its clients. The initial Workspace Setup Wizard automatically distributes the root CA certificate to all VMs in the vApp to establish trust for intra-workspace communication.

If you deploy Workspace with our generated SSL certificates, the generated root CA certificate must be available as a trusted CA for any client who accesses Workspace. The clients can include end-user machines, load balancers, proxies, and so on. You can download the gateway's root CA from http://<gatewayhostname>/horizon_workspace_rootca.pem.

Applying an SSL Certificate from a Trusted Third-Party CA

All communication in the vApp is processed by the Workspace FQDN server. Workspace preloads the machines in the vApp to trust the major certificate vendors. As a result, if custom SSL certificates chain to one of the major certificate vendors, you can apply the new certificate by copying it to the load balancers, gateway, or connector.

If the Workspace FQDN points to a load balancer, the SSL certificate can be applied only to the load balancer. The gateway's root CA must be copied to the load balancer.

When you use multiple load balancers, you must copy the certificate to all of them. If you do not use a load balancer, the Workspace FQDN points to the gateway VA virtual machine. In this case, you must apply the SSL certificate to the gateway VA virtual machine.

Procedure:

1. Apply the certificate to the gateway VA virtual machine.
   a. Go to https://<configurator va>.
   b. Log in and click **SSL Certificate**.
   c. Copy the complete certificate chain and private key. Ensure that the certificate supports the FQDN hostname in the CN.
   d. Save the SSL certificate. The configurator copies the certificate to the gateway VA.

2. Apply the certificate to the connector VA virtual machine.
   a. Go to https://<connector va>/hc/admin.
   b. Log in and click **SSL Certificate**.
   c. Copy the complete certificate chain and private key. Ensure that the certificate supports the FQDN hostname in the CN.
   d. Save the SSL certificate. The configurator copies the certificate to the gateway VA.

Applying an SSL Certificate from an Internal or Nontrusted External Certificate Authority

Some enterprises use certificates generated by their own company or other CAs. These certificates have not been included in the trusted CA list. In this case, even if you apply the certificate correctly, some processes might not trust the certificate and will fail. You must apply the certificate using these steps.

Procedure:

1. Log in to the configurator VA as the root user.
2. Delete all *.pem files in the /usr/local/horizon/conf folder.
3. Copy your root CA and private key to this folder.
4. Run wizardssl.hzn from the /usr/local/horizon/lib/menu/secure folder.

You can now be sure that the VAs trust the new root certificate. You must apply the certificate on the gateway, load balancers, and any external connectors.

Summary

It is important to ensure that each component of the VMware Workspace environment is functioning properly. Each module is independent of each other, but to provide a full user experience to your end user, we strongly suggest leveraging all the modules of Workspace. Remember that a successful deployment will have user segmentation; therefore, knowing your users and what they do is the key to making your deployment succeed.

This chapter covered the initial configuration of Workspace. It showed how to work with publicly recognized and trusted certificates to make sure they are recognized in your environment, because we mentioned that you should always avoid the test certificate provided with the Workspace vApp.

This chapter also covered how to set up ThinApp packages. Using ThinApp is easy and straightforward. And now, because of the new HTTP download capabilities of Workspace, your user can also retrieve ThinApp packages without being on the corporate network. You also learned in this chapter how to configure Workspace files by using the default CoS and by creating a new one. The chapter also covered how to enable web applications (the easier module to set up). Even though this is an easy process, you can make your user fall in love very easily with this little gem. Being able to connect to multiple SaaS apps, not having to remember a dozen password or more, controlling your user access through your environment—who wouldn't want that? In today's organizations, many SaaS apps are in use, sometimes without IT even knowing about it. Some SaaS applications are illegal for corporate use and should not be used at all (for example, many file-sharing apps), but there are also legitimate applications that would benefit from Workspace. One example is ADP, which a lot of companies use to pay their employees; they fully support SAML authentication, and therefore it is easy to integrate with Workspace. Other application examples include Amex Travel and ServiceNow and SalesForce (as used in the example in the SaaS section). All of these are supported in the solution and are a lot easier for IT admin to manage if they have only one place to go to configure and manage all of these.

The chapter concluded by showing you how to configure the clients on the various platforms, and how to configure certificates in Workspace.

At this point, you have all the major infrastructure pieces of the VMware Workspace environment up and running. You should look at one other important piece of the VMware View platform: application virtualization. When you understand the benefit of application virtualization, you can integrate it into your View desktops and your secure Workspace.

Chapter 6

Integrating VMware View and Workspace

This chapter describes the integration between VMware View and VMware Workspace. Both solutions are autonomous and work well on their own. The strength of the VMware portfolio is the phenomenal integration it has done between each product. Once configured, you would believe from a user standpoint that it's one seamless solution and was purpose built for this, when in reality, they are two totally different solutions. This chapter covers the proper planning and the required steps to follow to deploy and integrate both solutions. We cover the workflow shown in Figure 6.1.

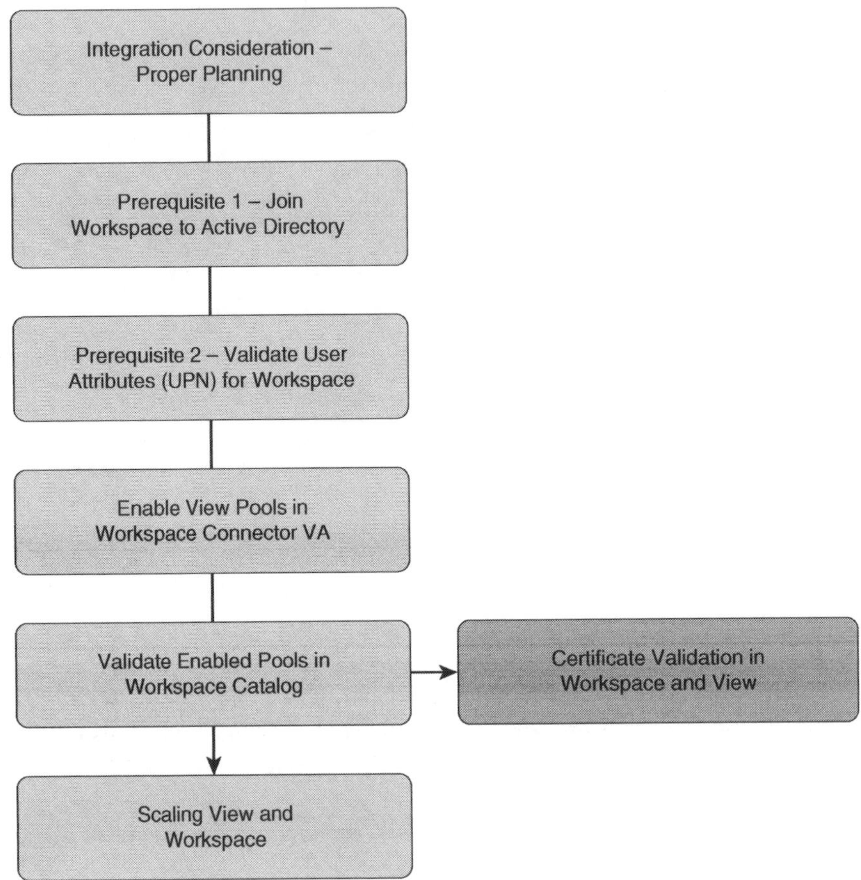

Figure 6.1 Workflow: Workspace and View integration

The end goal for your environment is to provide three key components to your user:

- Data
- Applications
- Desktops

The first two components were covered in Chapter 5. What we will focus on in this chapter is to add the third component, access to a corporate desktop from Workspace. Figure 6.2 demonstrates the possibly isolated and separated components coming together through Workspace and providing a unique experience to the end user.

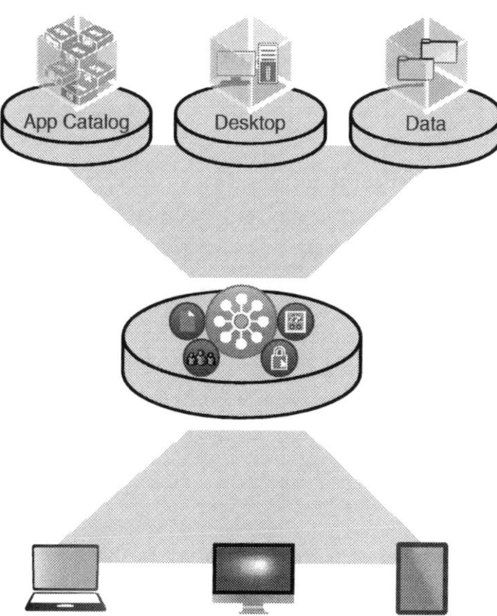

Figure 6.2 Secure workspace

We would like to think that data and applications are everything a user needs, no matter what type of device you're using, no matter where you're connecting from. However, the reality is that if you want to be successful in bringing desktop virtualization in your organization, you must consider a lot of legacy applications. Some of these old-school applications might not lend themselves well to a fully web-based interface. 3270 emulation, COBOL, and DOS are still required in today's corporate environment. (No, it's not a typo; we still see this today.) To that end, it's critical that you have a strategy to live with that gap for the foreseeable future. If you're lucky and you are in a corporate environment that's agile and fully embracing the desktop of the future, you might be able to reach 75% to 80% of your environment with only data and apps. If you're in a different type of organization, you might need to live with that "legacy PC gap" for the next couple of years. Might as well work with a solution that can integrate both sides, right?

VMware View and Workspace Integration Considerations

Looking at each solution individually will give you specific features that in many organizations are addressing what people are looking for. Looking at View, you will get what we've been delivering to users for the past 5+ years, a Windows desktop, virtualized and accessible from any device. Then, if you look at Workspace, you'll get the Dropbox/Box.ne/Skydrive functionality of file sharing that everybody loves, with one major difference (hosted on-premises). You'll get the App Store functionality that Apple made famous to consumers, but Workspace gives it a corporate twist by adding software-as-a-service (SaaS) integration with major web app vendors, also adding workflow approval, making sure that if there's a cost associated with the app that the organization is aware of it and a lot more.

Where you get the full strength of each product is when you integrate both of them together, striving for what the industry is asking for: access to your data, your applications, or your desktop from anywhere on any device. The desktop of the future is not here yet; we believe that what we are deploying today will not be the user environment that people will have as their corporate secure workspace in 10 years, but VMware took a strong stance by integrating these solutions. The gap between today's desktop and the Workspace environment of the future is slowly disappearing but that gap still exists and it might be there for the next 3 to 5 years, the driving factor, from our perspective, to bridge that gap will be when companies are able to completely get rid of the legacy desktop, which in most cases will also mean getting rid of all legacy applications.

The integration of both products requires for you to make sure that both versions are compatible. You should always refer to VMware site for the latest product support matrix. Keep the following site handy if you're working with VMware technologies: http://partnerweb.vmware.com/comp_guide2/sim/interop_matrix.php.

From the site, make sure you choose **Solution Interoperability**, and then you'll be able to combine the VMware Workspace solution with the VMware View solution and see which versions are compatible with each other. In Figure 6.3, we did a search on VMware Workspace 1.8 and VMware View 5.x.

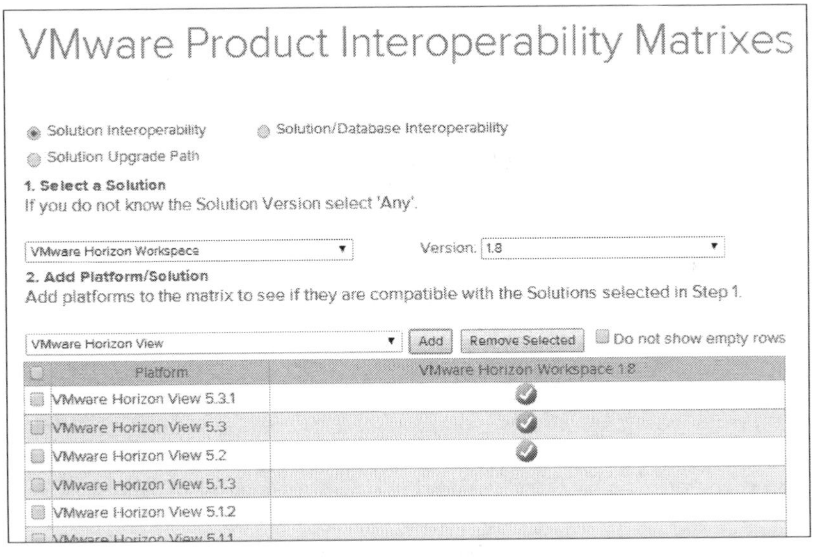

Figure 6.3 Interoperability matrix

VMware Workspace and View Integration

The process of integrating both products is fairly simple; you need a couple of prerequisites, and you'll be able to make them work together seamlessly. On the View side, only a Security Assertion Markup Language (SAML) authenticator needs to be added. The Workspace server will be querying the View Connection Server to retrieve pool information and displaying this information to properly entitled users. All the configuration steps are taking place on the Workspace side. Take a look at the following communication flow between both solutions, Figure 6.4 will give you a good understanding of the required connection points between each solution.

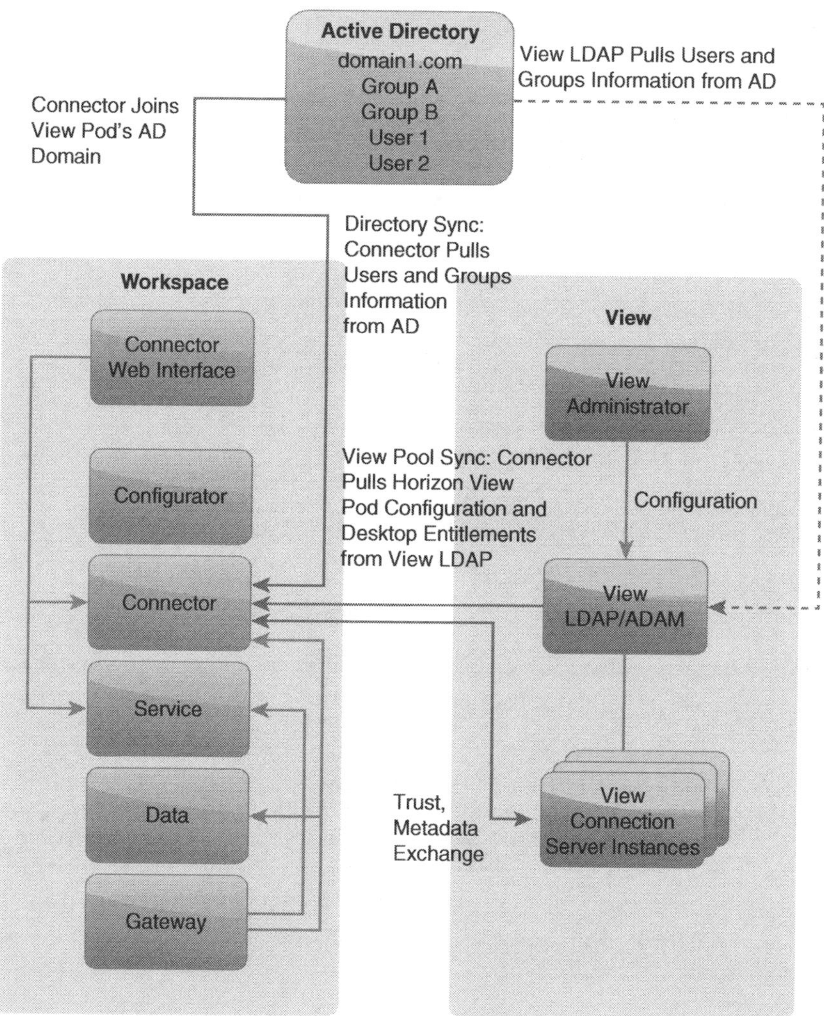

Figure 6.4 Workspace and View connection points

To start, log in to your Workspace Admin interface as an administrator. Make sure you log in to the gateway virtual appliance, which is usually the general name of the environment, something along the lines of MyWorkspace.domain.local. You could also have gone directly to the configurator module, but it is best to always follow the same path for administration, which makes it easier to follow the flow and remember where each component is configured.

Once logged in, you need to enable the View module; clicking the **Enable This Module** button will redirect you to the right place (see Figure 6.5).

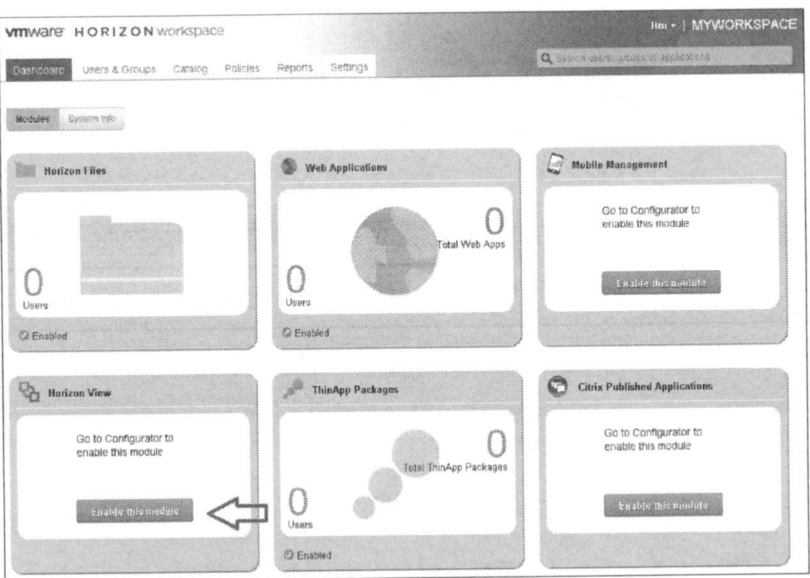

Figure 6.5 Enable View in Workspace connector

You will have to log in to the Configurator web-based Administrator interface with the password you set initially when the Workspace environment was set up.

After successful login, you will see a screen that is similar to the previous screen, but this time, you're in the actual configuration page in the connector virtual appliance web page.

Clicking again on the **Enable This Module** button of the View section will bring up the configuration of the View integration. This action will not automatically redirect you to the connector virtual appliance, but you can click the blue text and be redirected to the right page where you will have to verify some configuration items and also enable the View pools lookup (see Figure 6.6).

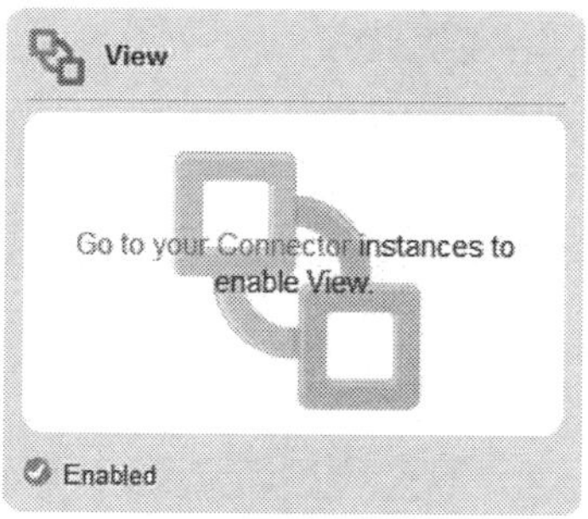

Figure 6.6 Module enabled

Alternatively, you could have reached the same web UI by going directly to the connector virtual appliance (https://<connectorVA-IP-Address>:8443/hc).

After you've reached the connector UI, the first step is to join Active Directory. For Workspace to be able to integrate with View, you need the Workspace environment to be domain joined. In the connector Web UI, display the Join Domain tab, and then check the **Join Domain** check box. The main reason for this integration is to seamlessly integrate Workspace Client into the desktop and use Kerberos authentication to single sign on to the Workspace services.

Provide the proper fully qualified domain name (FQDN) for the domain you want to integrate with, and then provide a username that has permission to join the domain.

You will notice that you have successfully completed this step if the button changes from Join Domain to Leave Domain and that the values were saved (notification on top of UI), as shown in Figure 6.7.

In a production environment, you wouldn't usually use a Domain Admin account. Best practice is to create a user specifically for this integration and grant domain join permission to that user. Note that this information is not stored on the connector. The user account is only used to complete the domain join, similar to the process used to join a Windows machine to the domain.

You can configure this security setting by opening the appropriate policy and expanding the console tree as such: Computer Configuration\Windows Settings\Security Settings\Local Policies\User Rights Assignment\, as shown in Figure 6.8.

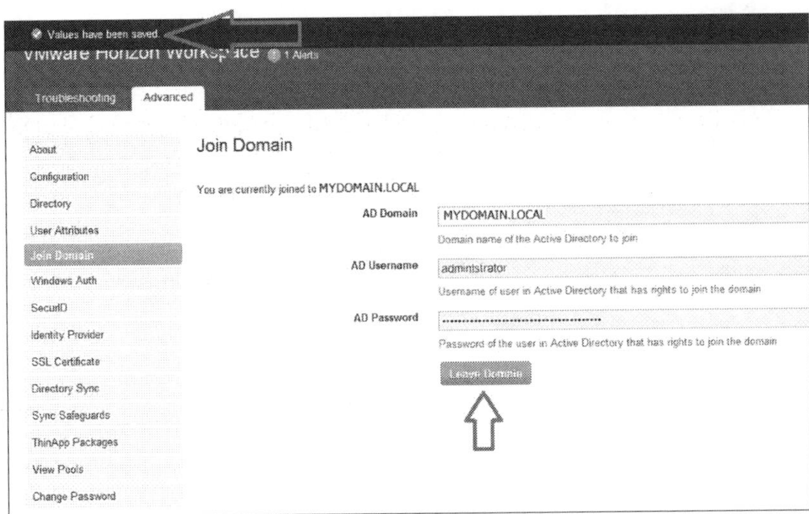

Figure 6.7 Domain join successful

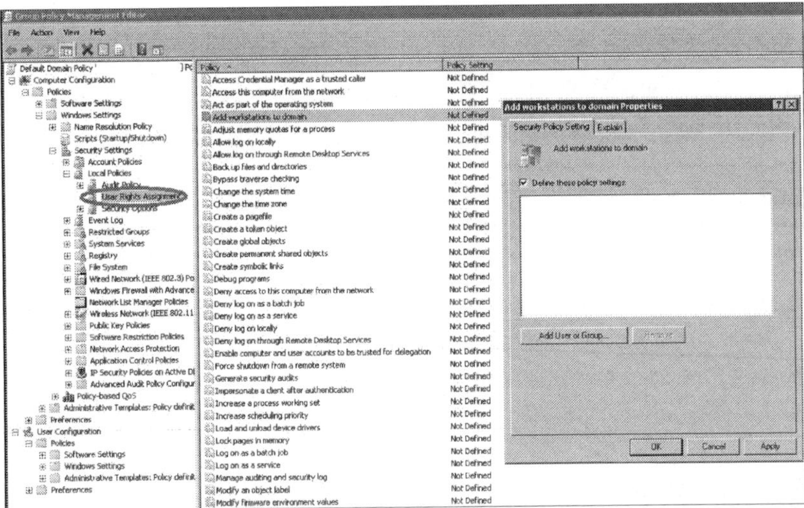

Figure 6.8 AD user rights validation

Users who have the Create Computer Objects permission on the Active Directory computers container can also create computer accounts in the domain. The distinction is that users with permissions on the container are not restricted to the creation of only 10 computer accounts. In addition, computer accounts that are created by means of Add

Workstations to Domain have Domain Administrators as the owner of the computer account, whereas computer accounts that are created by means of permissions on the computer's container have the creator as the owner of the computer account. If a user has permissions on the container and also has the Add Workstations to Domain user right, the computer is added based on the computer container permissions rather than on the user right.

The next step is to make sure that the UPN (user principal name) is checked in the User Attributes section, as shown in Figure 6.9; this is a requirement for View integration.

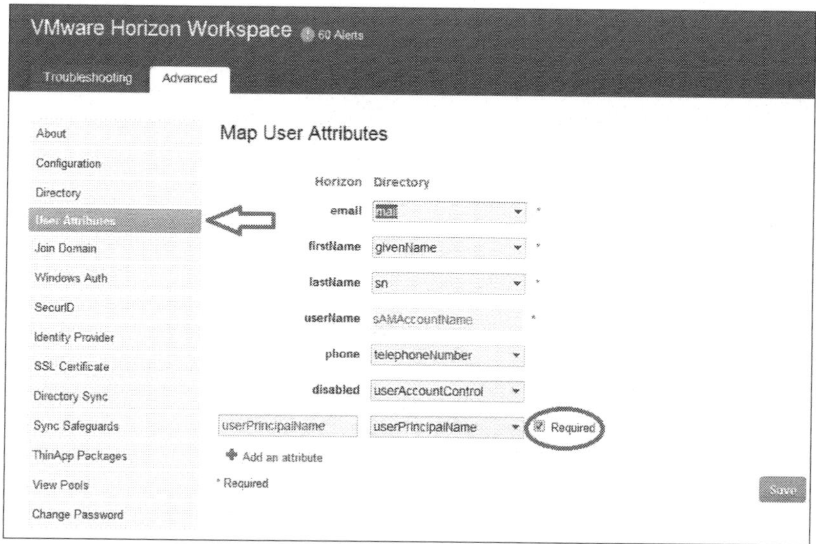

Figure 6.9 UPN validation

The last step in the configuration process for View integration is to connect to the View Server and synchronize the pool information.

Complete the following domain information for View (see Figure 6.10):

- **Check the Enable View Pools check box:** The Connection Server type is the FQDN of the View Connection Server instance with which you want to sync.
- **FQDN for Client Access:** Type the FQDN of the server or intermediate device, such as Security Server or load balancer that connects users to View desktops.
- **Username:** Choose an account that has the Administrators or Administrators (read-only) role in View Administrator.
- **Password:** Type the password associated with the Active Directory username.

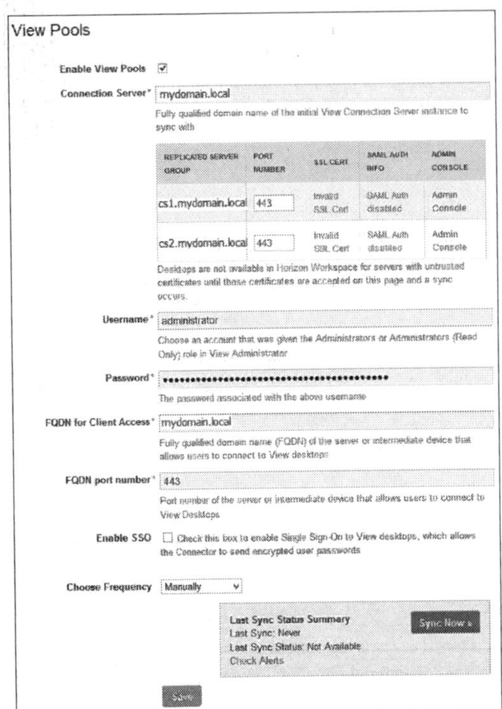

Figure 6.10 Enabling View pools

Click **Save** and **Sync Now** to propagate your View information to Workspace.

You can also decide to choose a sync interval, which we recommend for production deployments. Balancing the frequency of the synchronization and the resource it will consume from your domain controller is very important. In AD environments that have thousands and tens of thousands AD users, that synchronization will impact the connector performance; you definitely don't want to do this every hour.

Good practice, if you have an Active Directory that changes often, is to synchronize once a day, outside regular business hours, when the impact will be minimal on your environment. If you have an AD environment where changes don't happen often, you could also choose a longer period for your synchronization interval.

NOTE

If you want View integration to work in a multidomain environment, you must follow these steps:

- Verify that Workspace and the View Servers are joined to the same domain.
- Verify that the directory server host and the View Servers are joined to the same domain. The directory server host (defined on the Workspace Directory configuration page) must be an Active Directory host. Do not specify parent or sibling domain controller information.
- On the Workspace Directory configuration page, you must provide Global Catalog information to allow users in subdomains and sibling domains to access Workspace and View desktops.

Synchronizing View pools can be done automatically at scheduled intervals or can be done manually by going in the connector virtual appliance and clicking **Sync Now** on the View Pools tab.

Note that each time you change information in View, such as add an entitlement, add a user, and so on, you must force a sync to propagate the changes to Workspace or wait until the desired preconfigured synchronization interval.

After you enable View in the Configurator web interface, you can also sync the View pools. If used, this option must be enabled on all connectors, but you will only need to sync one of them:

1. Go to https://<ConnectorHostname>/hc/admin/ to open the Connector web interface.
2. Enter the admin password.
3. Click **View Pools** and click **Sync Now**.

Verify that you can sync View Pools and their entitlements from View Connection Server to Workspace:

- Log in to the Workspace Administrator web interface, https://<WorkspaceFQDN>/SAAS/login.
- Display the Catalog tab. If you have enabled any additional modules, such as Web Applications, you will see it there. For this part, we're interested in the View Pools section, as shown in Figure 6.11.

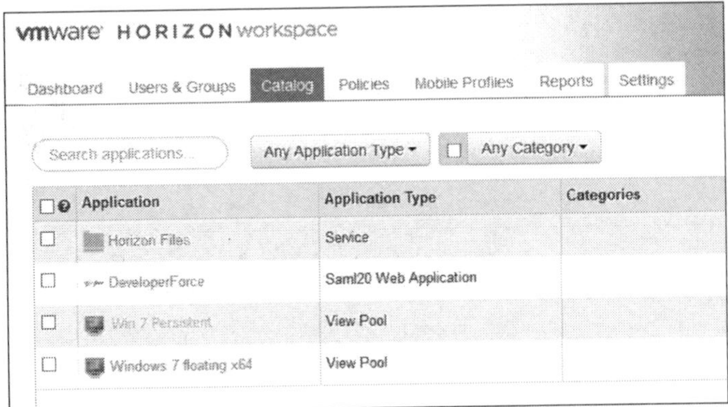

Figure 6.11 Workspace catalog showing View Pools

- Select a View pool and check the Details and Entitlements tabs, located below the name of the pool on the left side, as shown in Figure 6.12.

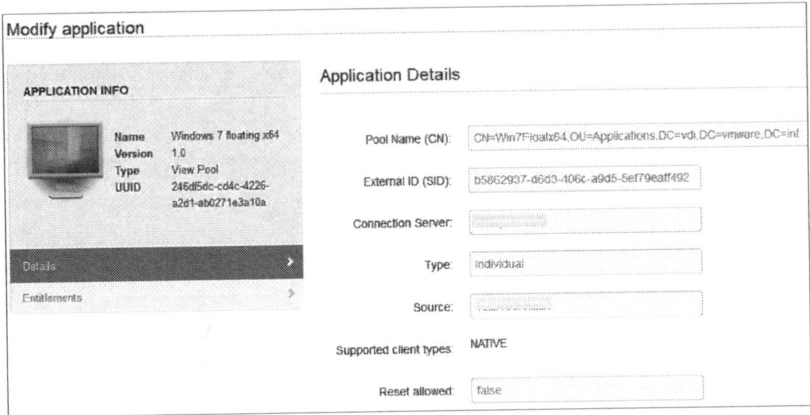

Figure 6.12 View pool details

Keep in mind that View pools are enabled in a Workspace environment. You do not entitle user access through Workspace; this process remains unchanged. You still complete the entitlements in View.

You have completed integration of the View and Workspace environment. You can now log in to the Workspace web interface and you will notice that your entitled desktops are now showing up with your applications. Remember that the integration between both solutions still require you to manage View pools through the View web administration console. In the Inventory section, under Pools, you can click any existing pool and validate the “entitlements.” See Chapter 4, “VMWare View Implementation,” for more information on pool entitlements.

If the user has any pools entitled to him, it will show up in the Workspace interface, as shown in Figure 6.13. Keep in mind that it will take another synchronization cycle for this new information to show up in the user Workspace. If the Workspace administrator does not want to wait for the interval to pass, he can always log in to the Workspace connector VA and synchronize manually. You can right-click on the pools the user has access to and log in to the desktop. You can also see from the picture that login through the web browser is not possible; this is because the Remote Experience agent has not been installed and configured in the View environment.

Figure 6.13 View desktops

The nice part about the integration is that from this view, in the Workspace web UI, right-clicking the pool and choosing **Open with View** launches the locally installed client and passes along the View desktop pool information, and if single sign on (SSO) is enabled, a feature that is configured in Workspace, it will automatically log you in to the desktop.

If no local clients are installed, it will offer to redirect you to the download page, so you can grab the proper client for your platform. For any reason, if you have a View Client installed locally and it doesn’t detect it, you will still be able to launch the client by choosing the Open View button, as shown in Figure 6.14.

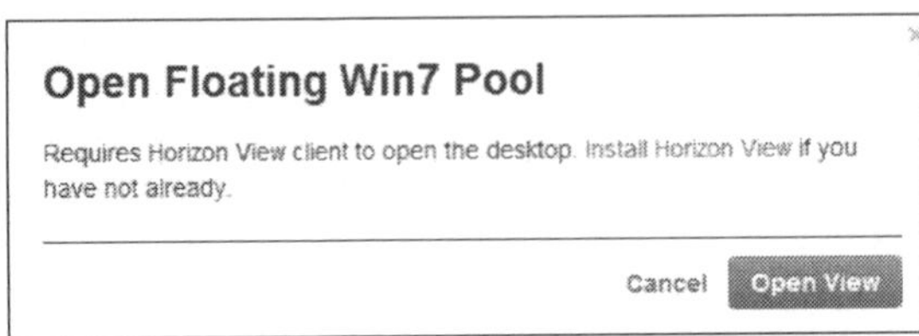

Figure 6.14 Client download

Troubleshooting Certificate Errors

You have completed the setup of your View Workspace to integrate the View desktop, but on the page where you save all the Connection Server configurations, you get one or two errors.

It might happen that you will have an error message mentioning that you have an invalid certificate for your View Connection Server or that your SAML authentication is disabled (see Figure 6.15). If you get this error message, it means that you have not properly configured the certificate for your View Server.

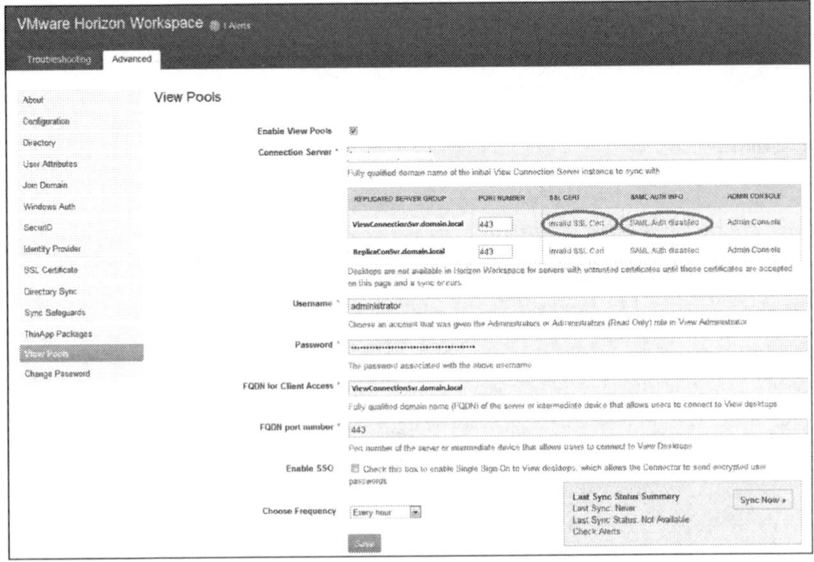

Figure 6.15 Certificate and SAML authentication

If you want to launch a View desktop from Workspace and use SSO, you must configure SAML authentication in the View Server:

1. Log in to the View Administrator web interface with an administrative user account.
2. Select **View Configuration, Servers** from the navigation panel to access the SAML 2.0 settings described in the following sections.
3. On the Connection Servers tab, select a Connection Server from the list, and then select **Edit, Authentication** (see Figure 6.16).

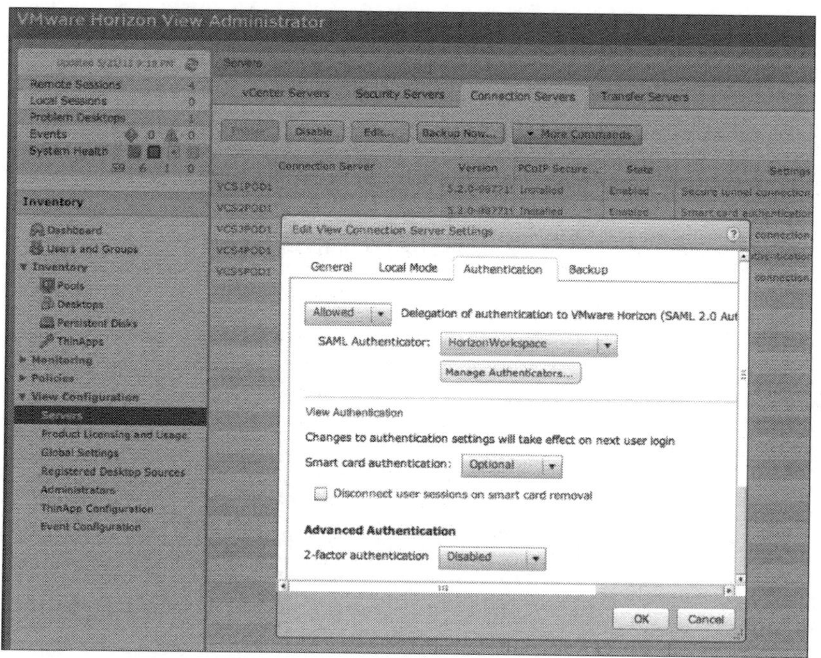

Figure 6.16 Enabling a SAML 2.0 Authenticator

4. Configure each Connection Server for which you want to use SAML 2.0 for authentication to.
5. Use the Delegation of Authentication to VMware (SAML 2.0 Authenticator) drop-down menu (see Figure 6.17) to enable and disable the SAML 2.0 Authenticator.

Figure 6.17 Required delegation

Be careful; setting this option to Required will force users to log in only from the Workspace environment. Choosing this option will also disable smartcard and two-factor authentication.

This is a good practice to put in place after you have deployed your environment and have been running it for a while and you're confident that all users are able to successfully log in to your Workspace environment.

A more lenient method is to start with the Allowed choice. This permits users to log in through the Workspace secure portal, but also permits users to log in via the regular client, if needed.

Add a SAML 2.0 Authenticator

There are two ways to add a new SAML 2.0 Authenticator:

1. On the SAML Authenticator drop-down menu, select **Create New Authenticator**.
2. Use the Manage Authenticators option, and click Add.

Both options display the Add SAML 2.0 Authenticator window shown in Figure 6.18.

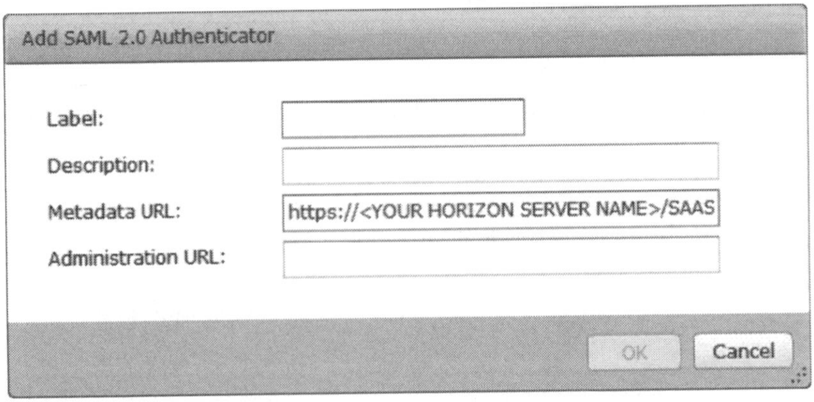

Figure 6.18 SAML Authenticator

The full length of the metadata URL looks something like this: https://<YOUR SERVER NAME>/SAAS/API/1.0/GET/metadata/idp.xml.

The Administration URL field is optional, but it is good practice to enter the login URL of your View web portal.

After you enter valid details, you must either accept the self-signed certificate (self-signed certificates are not recommended in a production environment) or use a trusted certificate for View and Workspace. After this, the SAML 2.0 Authenticator drop-down menu displays the newly created authenticator, which is now set as the selected authenticator. Note that SAML configurations are shared on all Connection Servers but must be enabled on each Connection Server.

Manage Authenticators

Use the **Manage Authenticators** options to add, edit, or remove SAML 2.0 Authenticators. Removing the last authenticator used by a View Connection Server in the View pod sets the SAML 2.0 Authenticator to Disabled. You cannot remove an Authenticator if it is being used by any View Connection Server in the View pod.

Select an Existing SAML 2.0 Authenticator

Select a SAML 2.0 Authenticator from the SAML Authenticator drop-down menu on each View Connection Server, and click **OK**.

Dashboard

When you create a valid SAML 2.0 Authenticator, the dashboard on the View Administrator displays the authenticator's health. You can select **Dashboard** on the Inventory, or select **System Health**, **Other Components**, **SAML 2.0 Authenticators**, as shown in Figure 6.19.

Selecting the SAML 2.0 Authenticator from the Dashboard displays a health authenticator panel. If there are no problems, the authenticator's health is green, as shown in Figure 6.20.

If there are issues, the health is shown as red. In Figure 6.21, the Status field indicates an untrusted certificate. When you validate and accept the certificate, the health status becomes green.

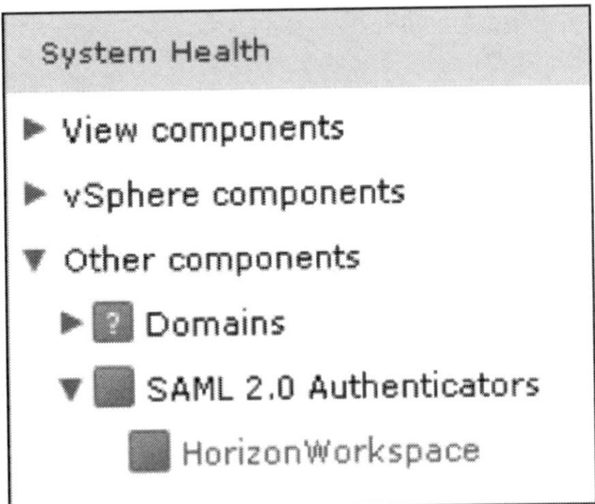

Figure 6.19 SAML validation

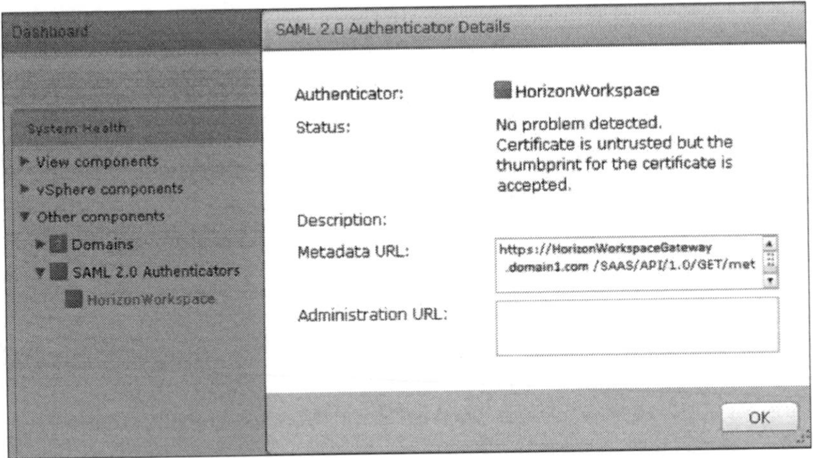

Figure 6.20 Health status

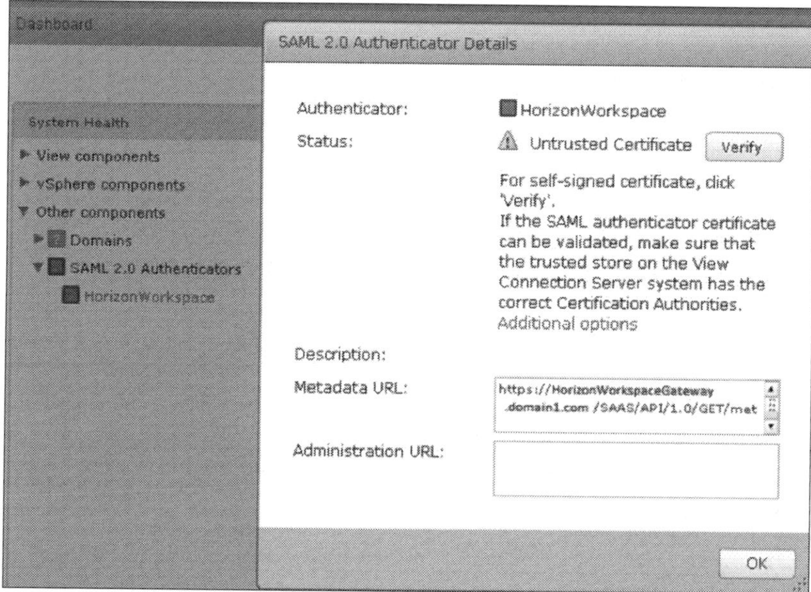

Figure 6.21 Certificate validation

An Authenticator's health can also display red if the gateway is not available or if there is an error in the metadata URL.

Workspace supports View desktops on desktops, laptops, and iPads; however, it does not support SSO on iPads.

NOTE

You have now configured both sides of the solution, fully integrating Workspace with View.

Scaling View and Workspace Deployment

Building View environments has been documented at length. It was covered in our first book, and we do not plan to dwell on that aspect. Instead, we recommend that you follow the VMware best practices and know your use cases; mileage will vary considerably depending on the use case you need to support.

If you're looking for more information on scaling VMware View environments, you can look to the *Architecture Planning Guide*, found on the VMware View Documentation Center (www.vmware.com/support/pubs/view_pubs.html).

In accordance with VMware's recommendation, a View pod can scale up to 10,000 seats per pod. Here again, you might be able to squeeze more users out of your pod if the majority of your users are task workers doing Office work and no videos. The flip side is that you might get a lot less users per pod if you have to support users who are "power hungry," typically requiring and consuming more bandwidth for things such as video and high-end graphics applications.

A rule of thumb is to have 2000 users per block and 5 blocks per pod, giving you a 10,000-user pod, as shown in Figure 6.22. If you need more users than that, you can repeat the process in 10,000-user increments.

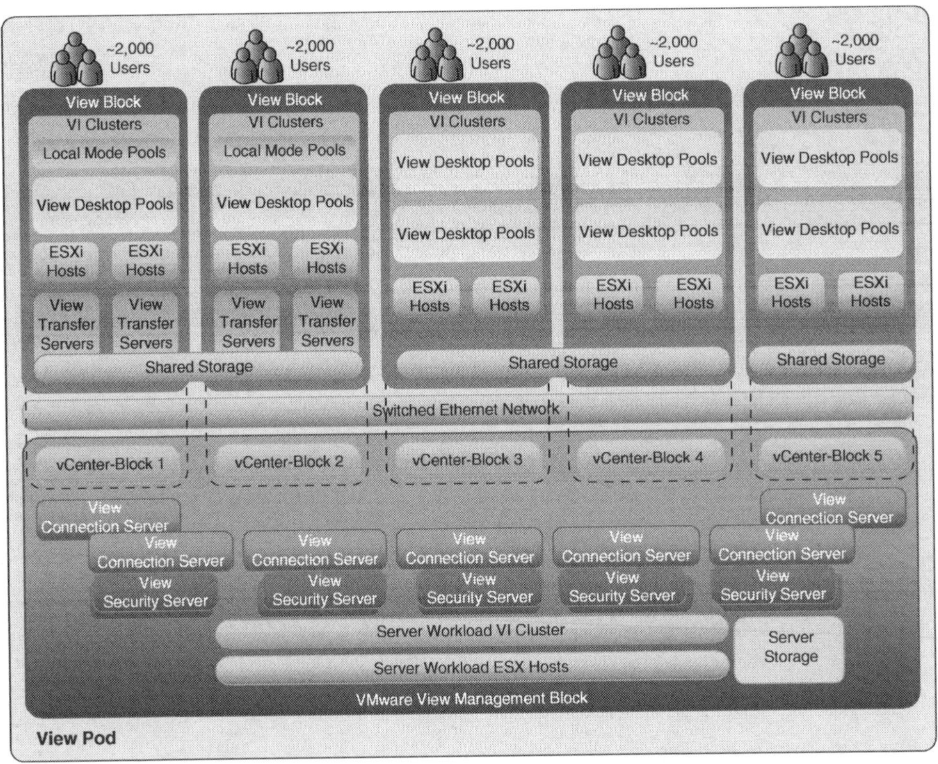

Figure 6.22 View pod

Workspace can scale in the thousands, as well. Planning the number of appliances required of each role is the key to having a successful deployment.

Figure 6.23 shows a view of the Workspace vApp. Let's take a closer look at each individual virtual appliance and how you can scale them to 10,000 users for a single pod.

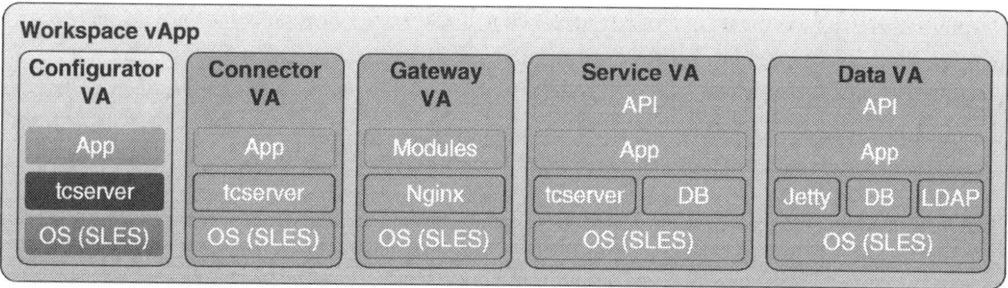

Figure 6.23 Workspace vApp

You will always have only one configurator virtual appliance per Workspace pod. Make sure that high availability (HA) is enabled on the VA and you will not need to do anything it else to it. This is the virtual appliance that keeps the heartbeat for all the VAs. It is also the module you use to add more VA to the vApp. Because it's not user facing, there will not be a lot of read or write input/output operations per second (IOPS) to that appliance.

The service virtual appliance will be more solicited. It is the virtual appliance that handles all the entitlements. It's the VA you will solicit when you access the Global Catalog and when you run reports, and it's the VA that will take care of device registration. Even though one single service VA can handle 100,000 users, we recommend any enterprise production deployment use at least two service VAs.

The connector virtual appliance is used for user authentication and integration with other services solution (like View). You might need to set up multiple connector VAs depending on the authentication type you want to support. You will require one connector VA per authentication type. For example, if you plan on using username and password but also plan on doing RSA authentication, you will need a minimum of 2 connector VAs. The connector virtual appliance can easily scale to 30,000 users. We recommend, similar to the service VA, to have at least two connector VAs per authentication type. Going back to our example, if you plan on doing username/password and RSA, this would mean that you should deploy four connectors for your pod.

The gateway virtual appliance provides a single namespace for all Workspace interaction. Because the gateway VA is involved in every interaction between the user and the various modules, it will receive a higher workload. The higher the number of users who hit the environment at the same time, the higher the load will be on the virtual appliance. We recommend one gateway VA for every 2000 users, and the number of gateway VAs might vary based on the load of your environment. We also recommend one gateway VA for every two data VAs you have.

The data virtual appliance needs to be sized a little differently. The file-sharing portion of Workspace is a model where the first data VA is the master data node, keeping a record of all the subsequent data VAs, and then any additional data VAs are user data nodes. In a production deployment, we recommend at least three data VAs to start with (one master and two user nodes). Each user data node requires its own dedicated volume. In a production deployment, VMware would support you only if you were using NFS for your data volumes. We recommend one data VA for every 1000 users in your Workspace pod.

It's important to understand that the data VA is the one that might vary the most, all depending on your type of users, the quantity of data, and the type of file sharing people do. Refer to the previous chapter for examples on how this will impact your storage associated with the data VAs.

The last piece of the puzzle to scale your environment to 10,000 users or more is to properly plan your database. We recommend using vPostgres, which is a very robust and reliable database that works really well with Workspace. Version 9.1 and later of that database will work with Workspace. The vPostgres database supports all the vSphere functionality, so we recommend using this DB virtual server and enabling HA on it. One single database can easily handle 10,000 users. From our testing, a typical 10,000-user deployment will create a database that will be between 80 and 100 GB in size.

Table 6.1 shows our recommendations when deploying for a 10,000-user Workspace pod.

Table 6.1 Recommendations for a 10,000-User Workspace Pod Deployment

Number	Description	vCPU*	RAM*	HDD*
1	Configurator VA	1	1	5 GB
1+1	Service VA	4	8	36 GB
1+1	Connector VA (authentication, Active Directory sync, View, and ThinApp integration)	2	4	12 GB
1+1	Connector VA (Kerberos)	2	4	12 GB
5+1	Gateway VA	6	8	9 GB
10	Data VA (1x master node, 2x data nodes) + files preview	6	16	300 GB

* Per virtual appliance, +1 for HA and business continuity/disaster recovery (BCDR)

Summary

View and Workspace work hand in hand to give your organization a solid and secure user workspace. You saw in this chapter how to configure the integration of both products.

At this point, you have all the major infrastructure pieces of the VMware View and Workspace environment up and running. You should now familiarize yourself with the SaaS aspect of Workspace and do a session discovery within your organization if you haven't done so already; we're almost certain that you will discover SaaS applications being used today by various groups within your environment. Adding these will be key to making sure that people use the Workspace environment daily. The more they use it, the easier it'll get. We have often seen Workspace administrators deploy the solution in their organization, start small, get to know the environment, and then it was a snowball effect: Everybody wanted it, and an avalanche of people asked to be able to use it. Make sure to be ready for that!

This chapter concluded by discussing how to scale a View and Workspace environment. Proper planning is key: Understand your use case, be ready to adjust your plan depending on workload, and above all else, plan for growth. Don't start your project with just the bare minimum and then be surprised that you are reaching bottlenecks or experiencing performance issues. Whenever possible, go for our recommended values and not the minimum specified by VMware.

Chapter 7

View Operations and Management

VMware View Operations

This chapter covers the operation of VMware View versus installation or architecture considerations. Perhaps the primary activity that you tend to repeat often is the creation and management of desktop pools, which are covered in this chapter. A few other functions also fall into the general category of management and operations, such as backing up the environment, patching, and replacing the certificates (all of which this chapter also covers).

Using View Access Groups

Before you start creating pools, take advantage of the ability to create access groups to organize your environment and to enable delegation of roles and responsibilities.

Let's consider the example of task-based workers and assume that they will use Windows Remote Desktop Services (RDS) pools. We are generalizing here, but you would use categories based on your analysis of your environment. Desktop pools are usually categorized by the function of the user, because the function tends to relate to a specific application workload, or by location if you are deploying a multisite architecture. In our example, you can create an access group called Task-Based Users and use it to further segregate the RDS Server pools within the VMware View Administrator console. You can then use the access group structure to delegate roles and responsibilities. Because it is likely that the team that manages your RDS Servers is not the same team that manages your desktops, this is a good use case for creating access groups. If you work in a fairly small organization, I still recommend using access groups, but just restricting their number. This way, you can delegate easily in the future. In this example, we use the category of Task-Based Users. To create the access group structure, follow these steps:

1. Log in to the VMware View Administrator console.
2. Browse to Inventory and Pools.
3. On the right pane, select **Access Group**, **New Access Group** from the drop-down, as shown in Figure 7.1.

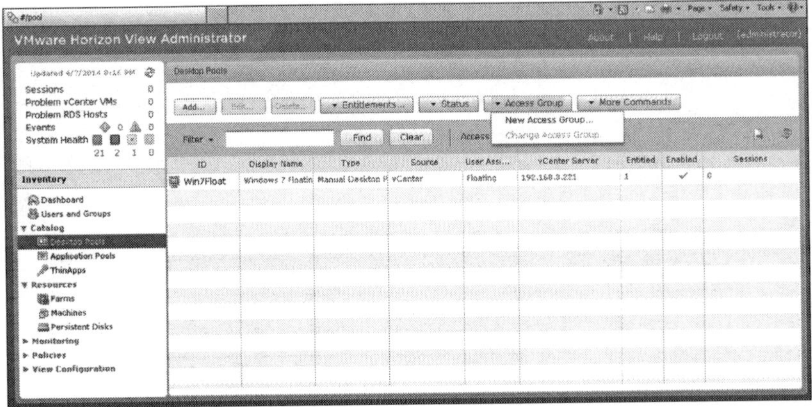

Figure 7.1 Creating access groups

4. Create the access groups that you need to organize your VMware View environment. It is ideal if you take the category details that you have created and paste them into the Description field, as shown in Figure 7.2.

Add Access Group

Name: * Marketing_Pool_01

Description:

OS: Windows 7 x86
Type: Stateless
vCPU: 1 vCPU

OK Cancel

Figure 7.2 Providing full descriptions

5. After you create your pool, under Pool Identification, you now see the access group you created to help categorize your environment properly, as shown in Figure 7.3. This feature also enables you to delegate roles and responsibilities for the access group.

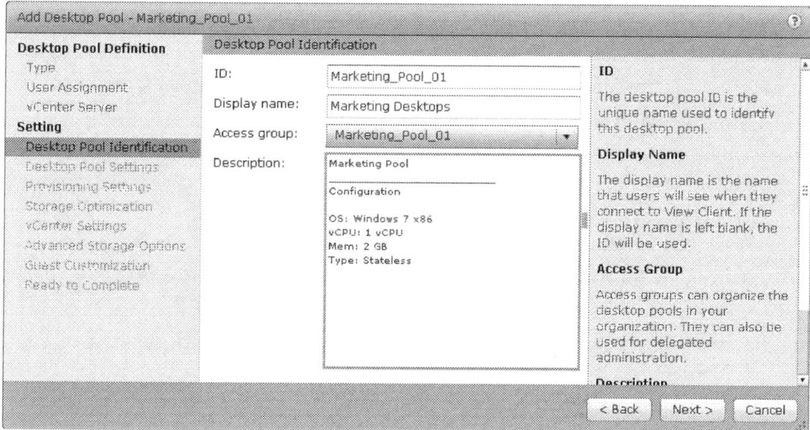

Figure 7.3 Access groups logically segregate your environment.

Types of Desktop Pools

Within VMware View, there are several types of desktop pools. Pools are used to describe clusters of desktop types that are assigned to users or groups of users. They are also used as objects in the View Management Console for the same purpose—to define desktop types, associate users, and entitle virtual applications. One type of desktop we have not covered is physical. It is possible to proxy physical desktops by installing the VMware Agent on the desktop and adding it to a pool for assignment. In addition, with View 5.1 and above, you can use View Persona on physical desktops. The process is the same in terms of installing the agent, but the creation of the pool varies slightly. We examine this topic further within this chapter.

Although the integration of physical desktops is no longer common due to the improvements in multimedia support in virtual desktops, it can still be used to transition from a PC blade environment to VMware View. For example, you can proxy PC blade users through the VMware View environment while you migrate from physical desktops to virtual ones and use View Persona to migrate the user settings.

Automated Desktop Pools

Automatic desktop pools are desktops that are provisioned and customized by VMware View automatically. They can be deployed either persistently or floating. When we talk about *persistence* or *floating* in this case, we are talking about the relationship between the user and the assigned desktop. If you choose persistent, the desktop is assigned to a specific user. You can select to do this automatically so that whatever desktop the user logs in to first becomes the assigned desktop. In addition, you can explicitly assign a desktop by defining a relationship between a desktop and user login as part of the deployment options, or you can manually assign desktops after they have been created through the View Administration console. Persistent pools can be used when the application load is tailored to an individual user or if there is a requirement to store some local data.

Nonpersistent, or floating, pools are assigned for the duration of the session. After a user logs off, the View desktop is available for other users. A floating desktop can be used when you have a large number of users but they do not sign on at the same time (for example, nursing stations in a hospital, management terminals on a manufacturing floor, or kiosk displays).

You can also set properties of the pools to allow for a dynamic and reactive creation of virtual desktops as they are assigned. For example, you can specify a minimum number of virtual desktops to be created when the pool first comes online. Desktops are created until the minimum number is reached. This capability ensures that an adequate number of desktops exist to service users.

You also can adjust the maximum setting for the number of virtual desktops that can exist in a pool. You can use this setting to make sure you do not overtask the supporting physical resources of the virtual desktop environment, such as the volume or logical unit number (LUN) on which the desktops are deployed.

Another setting that you can configure in a pool is the available number. The available number ensures that a constant number of virtual desktops exists to deal with demand. As the available number goes down, new virtual desktops are deployed to ensure the available number is maintained.

Within automated desktop pools, you can deploy full desktops or View Composer desktops. View Composer desktops are made up of linked clones. We discuss Composer later in this chapter.

Manual Desktop Pools

Manual desktop pools are created from existing machines or physical desktops. Machines may be managed by vCenter or unmanaged, as in the case of a physical device. If the users are allowed and the desktops are VMs managed by vCenter, manual desktop pools can also be used for offline virtual desktops. As with automated desktop pools, these manual pools can be persistent or floating. The source of either persistent or floating manual pools can be vCenter virtual machines (VMs) or physical machines.

Microsoft RDS Desktop Pool

RDS sessions can be managed by VMware View using the Microsoft RDS desktop type of pool. As explained in the preceding chapter, with recent releases of Windows, you can add many desktop attributes, such as themes, to give users the feeling they are using a dedicated and customizable desktop. With the release of View 6, native PCoIP support is available for RDS hosts.

Creating Desktop Pools

You can create a desktop pool within the VMware View Administrator console under Inventory and Pools. From the right pane, click **Add**.

You have three types of pools to choose from: automated, manual, or RDS. In the example in Figure 7.4, we selected **Automated Desktop Pool**. In the bottom-right corner, you see a list of supported features. This list varies, especially in the case of a Terminal Services pool.

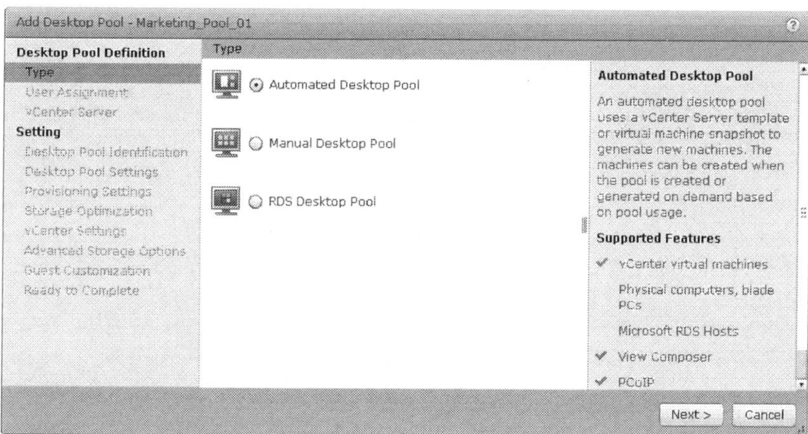

Figure 7.4 Types of pools

Within the type, desktops can be dedicated or floating. The setting really describes whether the relationship between the user and virtual desktop persists when the user logs off. Again, in the bottom right of this screen, you see how the features change depending on what options are selected as you build out the pool. In the example shown in Figure 7.5, we selected **Floating**. After the type is selected, click **Next**.

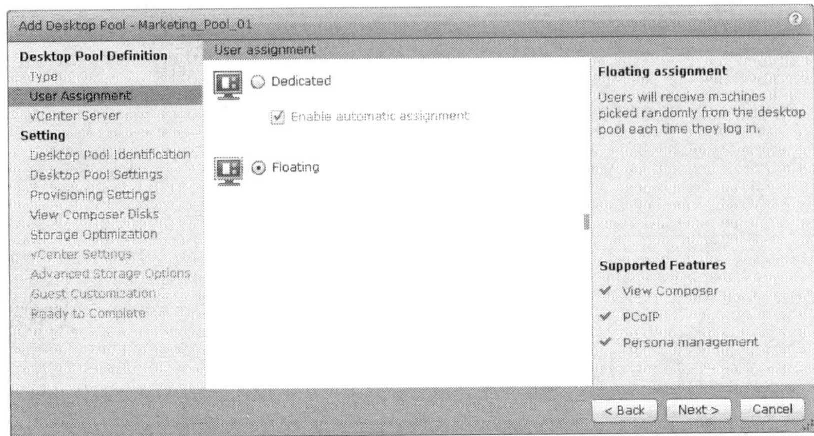

Figure 7.5 Dedicated or floating pool?

You can create full virtual machines or linked clones using View Composer. If you select View Composer, one of the features is storage savings, as shown in Figure 7.6. Choose either Full Virtual Machines or View Composer Linked Clones and click **Next**.

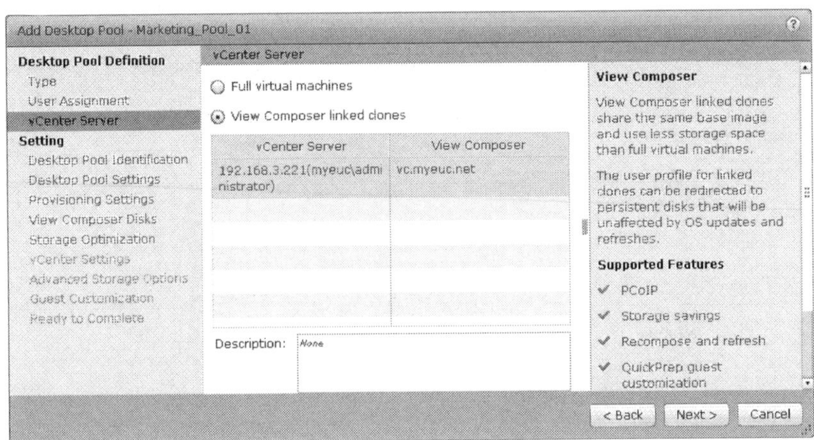

Figure 7.6 View Composer linked clones

Provide an ID (no spaces allowed), display name, view access group, and description; be complete, as shown in Figure 7.7. Configure the pool identification and click **Next**.

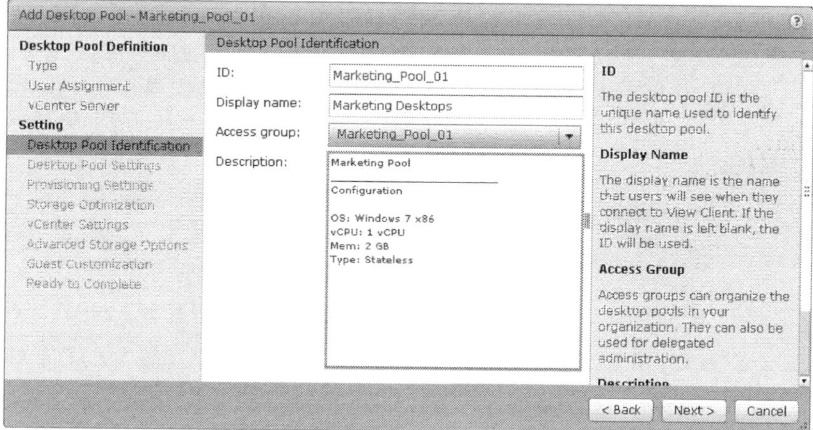

Figure 7.7 Pool identification

You can select numerous settings to control the pool, from power to display to Adobe Flash acceleration, as you can see in Figure 7.8. We review these settings after this example. Select **Desktop Pool Settings** and click **Next**.

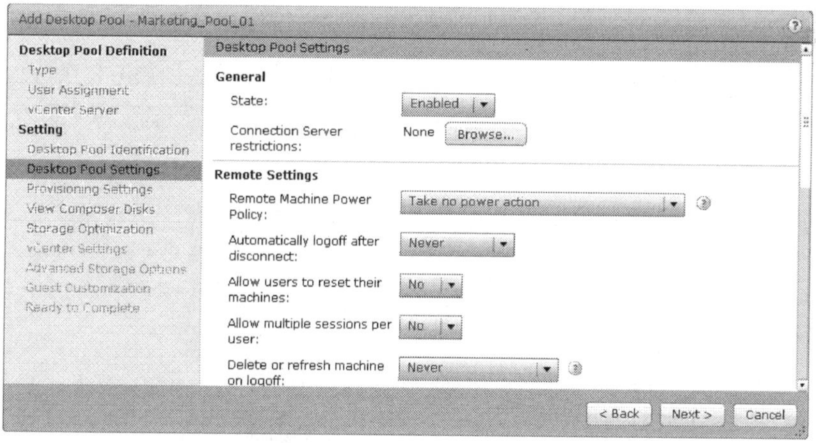

Figure 7.8 Pool settings

You can adjust the provisioning of the View desktops under the Provisioning Settings. For example, you can stop the provisioning when an error occurs or allow it to continue by deselecting the option because the default is to stop, as shown in Figure 7.9. You can define a standard naming pattern to keep the names of the View desktops standard and consistent. You also can set a maximum number of desktops allowed in the pool or a number of spare desktops. Setting a value for spare desktops forces desktops to be deployed in the event that all View desktops in the pool are in use. Plus, you can provision desktops as requested or demanded, which allows you to set a minimum number of available desktops to ensure users are not waiting on View Composer to finish provisioning. Alternatively, you can provision them all upfront. Select **Provisioning Settings** and click **Next**.

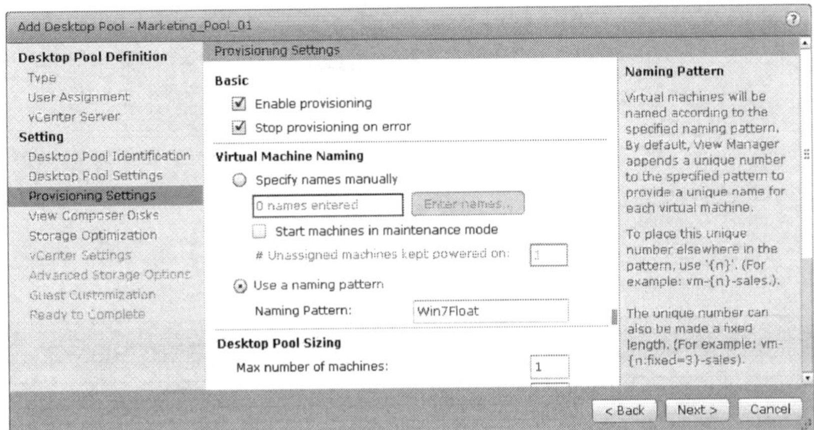

Figure 7.9 Provisioning settings

If you select View Composer Disks, you have an opportunity to tailor both the disposable file and the user data disk or persistent disk, as shown in Figure 7.10. The "Pool Settings" section later in this chapter covers these settings.

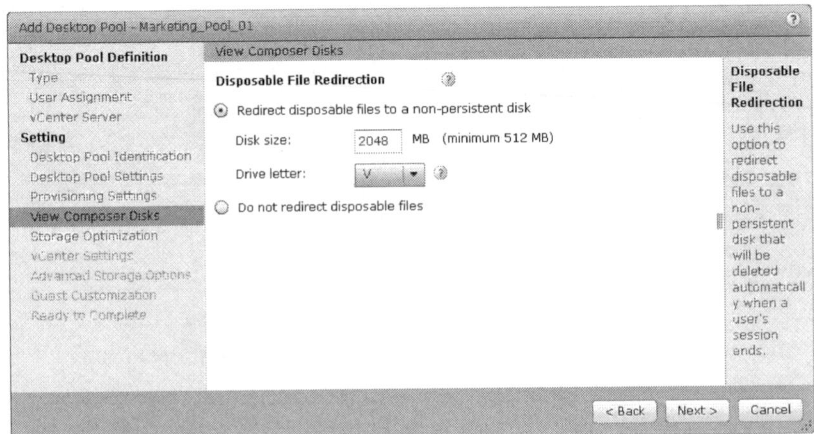

Figure 7.10 View Composer settings

Under the Storage Optimization section, we don't have Virtual SAN or Fast FS Clones (VAAI) configured. Leave the options unchecked, and click **Next**.

Under vCenter Settings (see Figure 7.11), you select the default image and the VM folder in vCenter under which you would like the VMs created, the host or cluster, resource pool, and datastore. View has added some additional options under the Datastore settings, which we discuss in the next section. Select a datastore here and click **Next**.

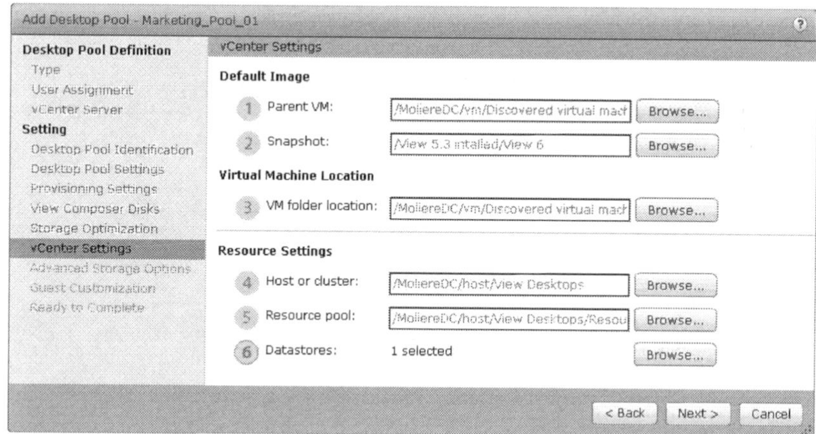

Figure 7.11 vCenter settings

In VMware View 5.3 and above, you can also take advantage of storage features supported in vSphere 5. One of these enhancements is a Content-Based Read Cache (CBRC) or Host-Based Cache, which is referred to as View Storage Accelerator (VSA) in the View Administrator console. This cache is local to the vSphere ESXi host and stores frequently used blocks of VM disk data. CBRC improves performance by offloading some of the I/O read requests to the local ESXi host versus sending them to the storage system or storage-area network (SAN). Using VSA, you can significantly reduce your peak read requests or input/output operations per second (IOPS) in your VMware View environment.

When VSA is enabled a disk digest file is created for each virtual machine disk (VMDK). You can enable VSA for both OS and user disks; however, VMware recommends that you enable it for the OS only.

The disk digest file creates hash values for all the blocks in the VMDK when the pool is created. When a user desktop reads a block, the hash value is checked to determine the block address. If it is in memory, it is returned to the user; otherwise, it is read from disk and placed into memory. The acceleration is done on reads only, so writes are always read from disk and used to update stale data in memory.

You must enable support of VSA through the View Administrator console by enabling it under the properties of your vCenter Server and enabling it under the properties of the desktop pool, as shown in Figure 7.12. To enable this support under the properties of the vCenter Server, follow these steps:

1. Open the View Administrator console and expand Server Configuration.
2. Select your vCenter Server and display the Storage tab.
3. Under Storage, select **Enable View Storage Accelerator**.

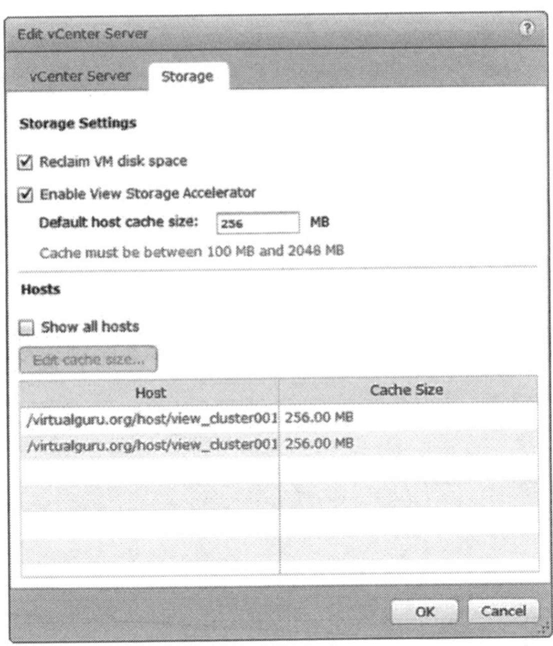

Figure 7.12 Enabling the VSA

When you enable it, you can specify how much memory is used across all hosts or on a per-host basis. The default is 1024 MB, but this can be changed from as little as 100 MB to 2048 MB. If you have different memory configurations on your hosts, configuring per host makes the most sense.

After enabling the VSA under the vCenter properties, you can selectively enable it under the pool settings, as shown in Figure 7.13. It provides the biggest benefit for shared disks that are read frequently, such as View Composer OS disks.

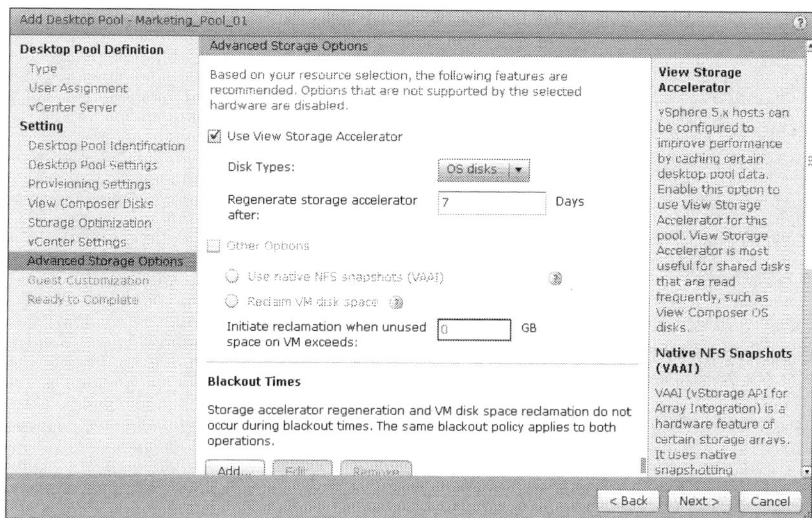

Figure 7.13 Advanced storage settings options

In addition, you can edit the advanced storage settings options after the deployment of a desktop pool by following these steps:

1. Open the View Administrator console and expand **Inventory**.
2. Select the pool from the right pane and click the **Edit** button.
3. Display the Pool Settings tab and Advanced Storage Options, which will display the window that enables you to select VSA, as shown in the figure.

Because it is cache, it must be regenerated on a regular basis. This activity can take up resources on the vSphere host, so you can enforce a "blackout" time period during which regeneration cannot occur, as shown in Figure 7.14.

In addition to the VSA, you can also turn on the reclaim disk space option under the advanced storage options, as shown in Figure 7.15. The reclaim option impacts only the OS disk in linked clones, but it enables ESXi to reclaim disk space without having to initiate a VMware View Refresh operation. You simply enable it and specify a threshold for how big the OS disk is allowed to grow before a reclaim event occurs; the default value is 1 GB. The blackout times you configure for the VSA also apply to reclaim operations. Reclaim is supported on vSphere 5.1 and later, although a patch is required. In addition, the VMs in the pool must be running on virtual hardware version 9 or later.

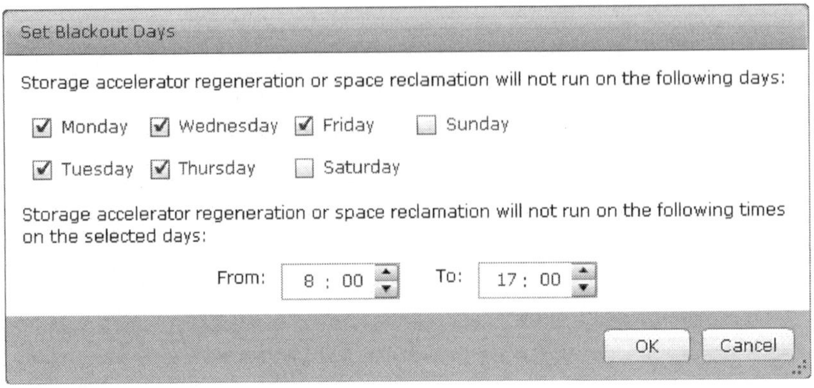

Figure 7.14 Blackout time period

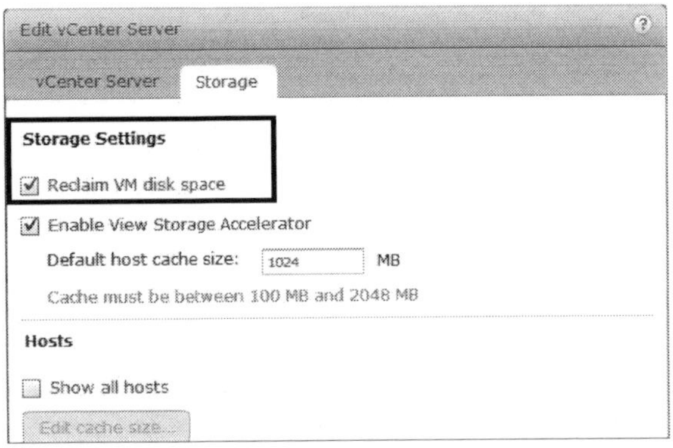

Figure 7.15 Reclaiming disk space

Each View desktop needs some form of customization to ensure that it deploys properly and is unique on the network. To customize the View desktop, you can use QuickPrep or Sysprep. See the section on pool settings so that you understand the differences between each. After the guest customizations, you can review your settings and click **Finish** to start the deployment of View desktops, as shown in Figure 7.16.

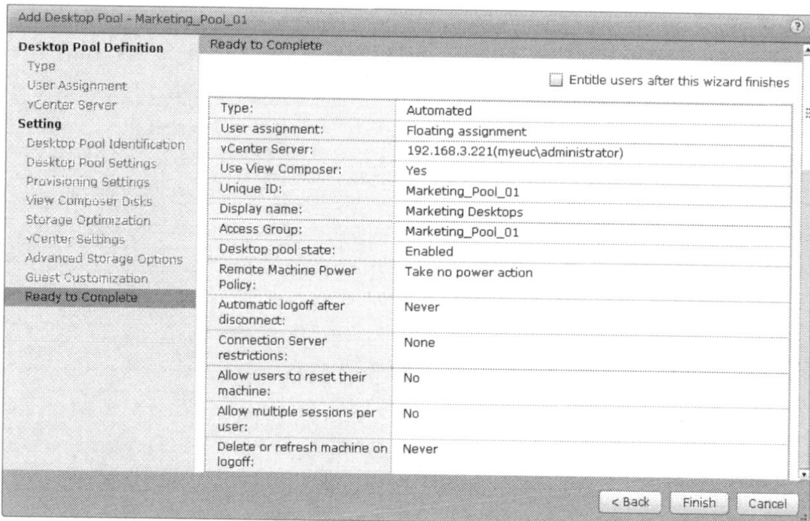

Figure 7.16 Click Finish to begin deploying desktops.

Power Settings

You can make a number of customizations to each pool that allow tighter control over the behavior of a VM, such as what happens when the user logs off. For example, it is possible to power off VMs when not in use to free up resources so that they are available for use by other virtual desktops in the environment. Some settings should be used with other settings. For example, powering off the VM makes sense provided that when you provisioned the pool, you set a value under Pool Sizing for the Number of Spare (Powered On) desktops, as shown in Figure 7.17, to ensure that users are not waiting for virtual desktops to boot. The other options within the pool are as follows:

- **Take No Power Action:** VMware View does not adjust the power option if the user powers down the VM.
- **Always Powered On:** VMware View does not power down the machine, and if it is powered down, the VM is automatically restarted.
- **Suspend When Not in Use:** When a user logs off, the virtual desktop is suspended. This option is also applied to floating desktops when the number of virtual desktops exceeds the setting in the available desktops counter.

- **Power Off When Not in Use:** If a virtual desktop is not in use, it is powered off. For example, if you deploy 10 desktops and 9 are not in use or logged off, View will power them off. I recommend that you combine this option with an available desktop number so that you avoid a situation in which you have users waiting for a VM to boot when connecting. Having a large number of VMs start at the same time can cause significant I/O to the storage system and is generally referred to as a boot storm. By using proper care in setting and tuning the power state options, you can avoid this situation in normal operations.

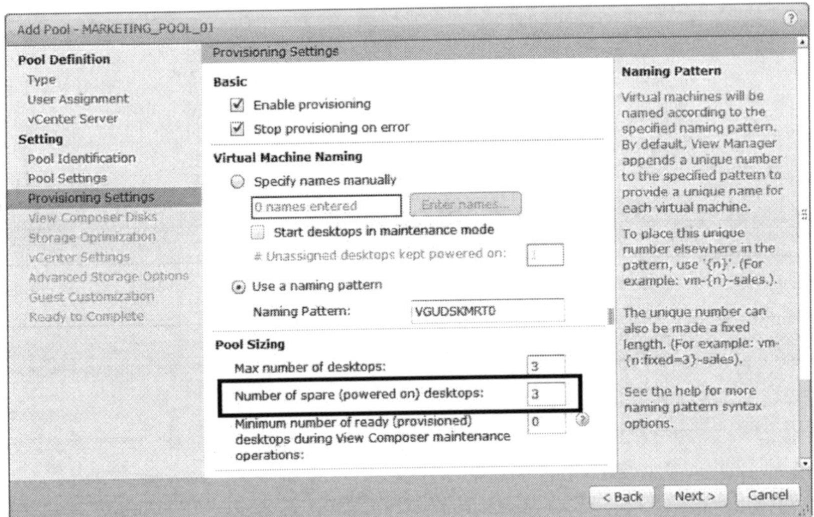

Figure 7.17 Number of spare (powered on) desktops

It is also recommended that because you are specifically defining what happens when a user logs off that you disable the user's ability to change the power state of the VM. You can do this through the Group Policy Object associated with the organizational units (OUs) in which the virtual desktops are deployed. Simply run the Group Policy Management tool and browse to the OU in which your View desktops are deployed. You should already have a Group Policy Object defined, but if you do not, create one by using the following procedure:

1. Select the OU (Horizon in Figure 7.18), right-click, select **Create a GPO in This Domain, and Link It Here**.

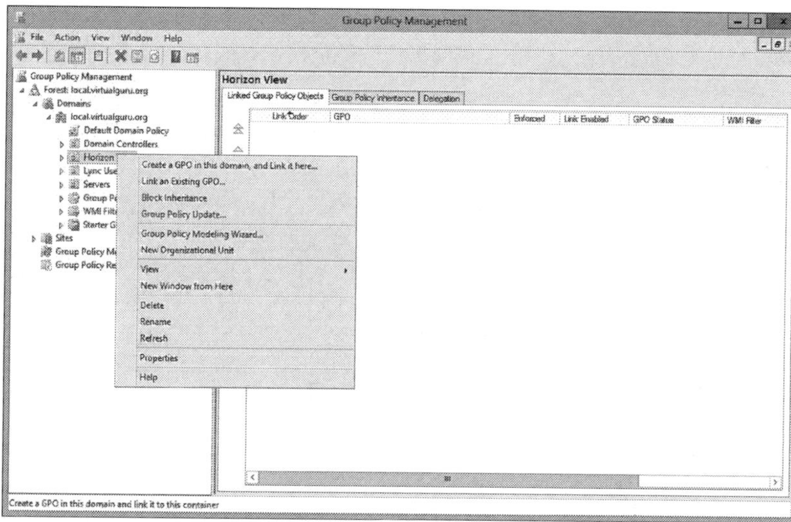

Figure 7.18 Creating a GPO

2. Provide a name for the Group Policy Object and click **OK**.
3. Select the Group Policy Object (in this example, it is named VMware Group Policy Object), right-click, and select **Edit**.
4. Browse to User Configuration, Administrative Templates: Policy Definitions and select the folder **Start Menu and Taskbar**.
5. Select the **Change Start Menu Start Button Policy** and enable it, and then change the action to remove the shutdown option. You can select Shutdown, Sleep, Logoff, Lock, Restart, Switch User, or Hibernate.
6. Click **Enabled**, as shown in Figure 7.19, and then click **OK**.

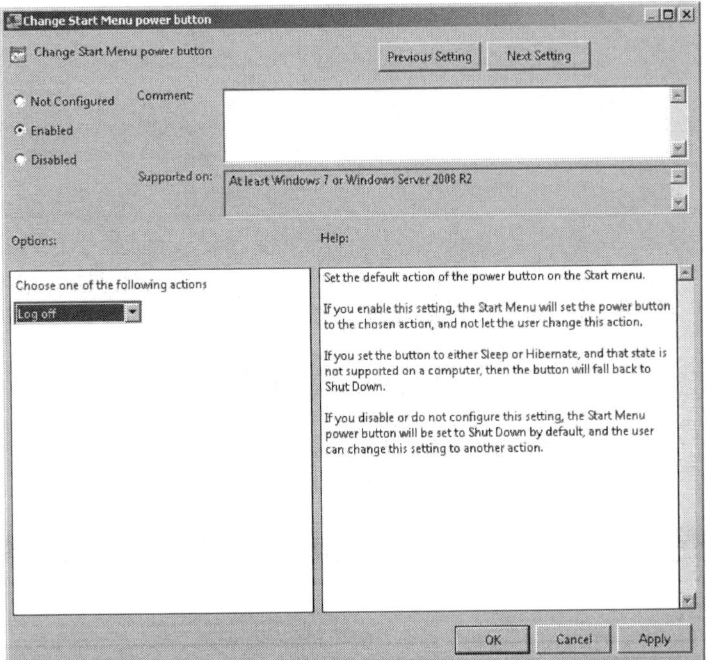

Figure 7.19 Enabling the policy

Pool Settings

It is important to understand all the settings when configuring a pool and where they would likely apply. Not all settings are available for each type of desktop. For example, for Windows RDS pools, many of the settings are not available because they are not supported. We step through each setting possible and provide a short description, and then give you some idea when they might apply. Because we have covered the types of pools, let's review the settings under the Pool Settings configuration page.

Pool settings are broken down into General, Remote Settings, Remote Display Protocol, and Adobe Flash Settings for Remote Sessions, as shown in Figure 7.20.

The first setting, which is the state of the pool, determines whether the pool is active or inactive. To activate a pool, set the state to **Enabled**. You can disable the pool if you need to perform maintenance, such as the refreshing of images.

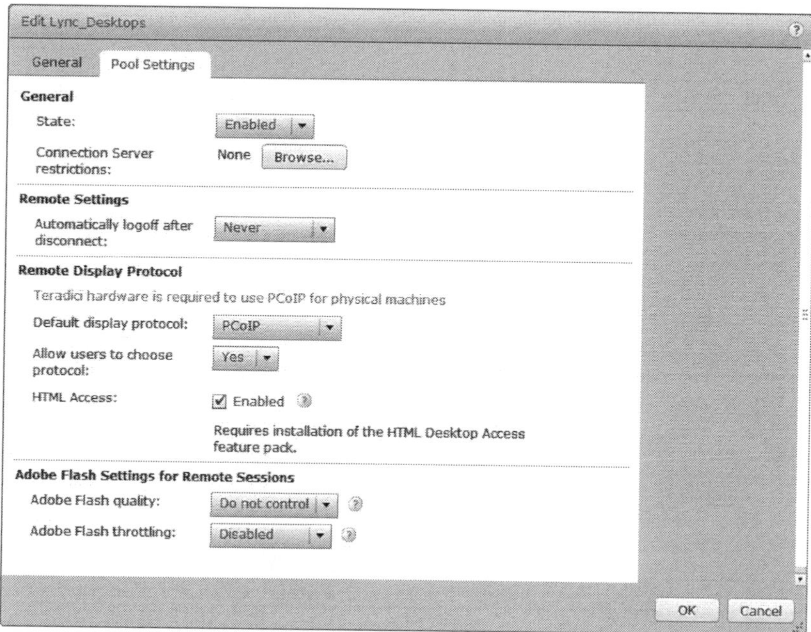

Figure 7.20 Pool settings

The next general setting is the capability to restrict the pool to only certain Connection Servers. The general use case is to separate Connection Servers that provide desktops to remote users from Connection Servers providing desktops to users internally. This setting also proves handy if you are a hosting provider and need to separate desktops by company, for example. To see the tags, you must first set them using this procedure:

1. In View Administrator, select **View Configuration**, **Servers**.
2. In View Connection Servers, select the **View Connection Server** instance and click **Edit**.
3. In the Tag text box shown in Figure 7.21, enter a tag. Separate multiple tags.
4. Click **OK** to save your changes.

The next group of options is in the Remote Settings pane, and the first is the power policy. You have the option of not adjusting what happens when the user logs off, always ensuring desktops are on, suspending them, or powering them off. These options are available from the drop-down menu, as shown in Figure 7.22.

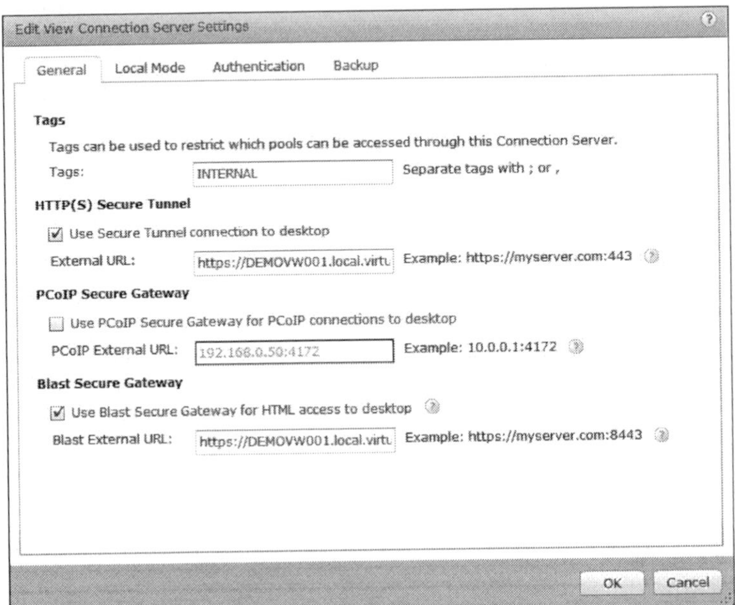

Figure 7.21 Connection Server restrictions

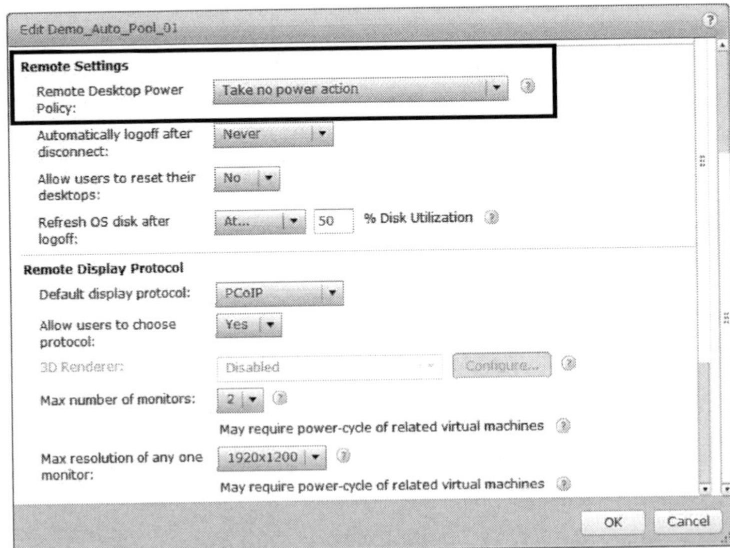

Figure 7.22 Remote desktop power policy

The next setting controls how long the desktop waits before logging off a disconnected user, as shown in Figure 7.23. The options are Immediately, Never, or After a Set Number of Minutes. Immediate is appropriate in a floating desktop pool in which it does not matter which desktop users log in to. If a pool provides remote access to users, you should allow for a certain number of minutes to compensate for some intermittent connectivity. If the users run batch processes that need to run for an extended period of time, Never might be the more appropriate selection.

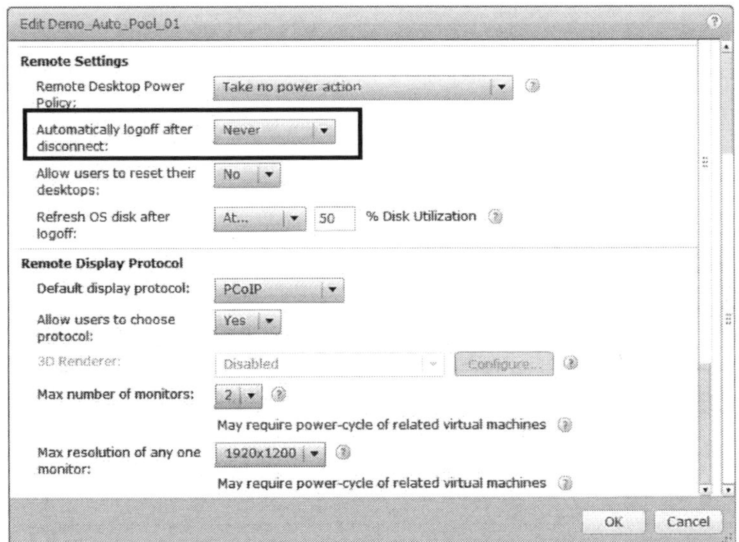

Figure 7.23 The Automatically Log Off After Disconnect option

The next available option (see Figure 7.24) determines whether an option to do a hard reset of the VM is available from the user interface (UI) to the user. This does not affect the user's ability to do an in-guest reboot within Windows.

The last item in the Remote Settings section is the Refresh OS Disk After Logoff, which allows you to complete a refresh operation selectively on a per-desktop basis versus initiating a refresh on the entire pool. This setting applies only to persistent linked clones. If the user association of the pool is set to floating, this option is not available. To configure it, you simply specify a percentage of the total size of the OS disk you would like to trigger the refresh. This only applies to Composer-based VMs and by default is set to Never. In this example, we set it to trigger when the OS disk is 50% utilized, as shown in Figure 7.25.

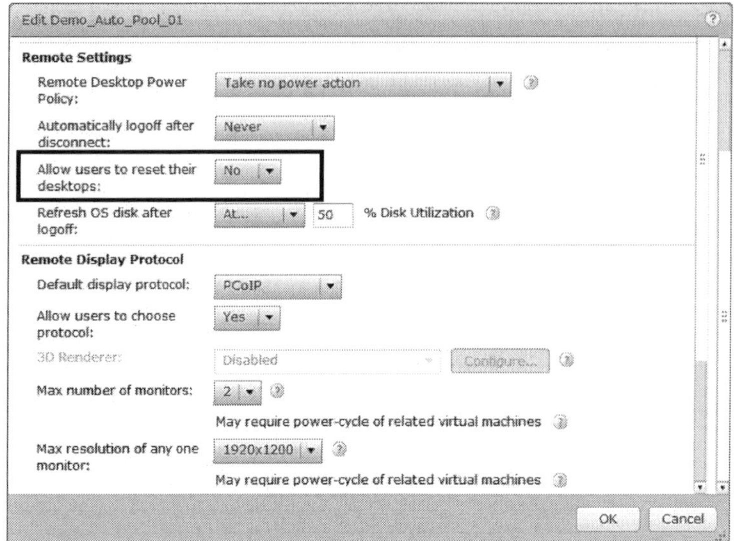

Figure 7.24 The Allow Users to Reset Their Desktops option

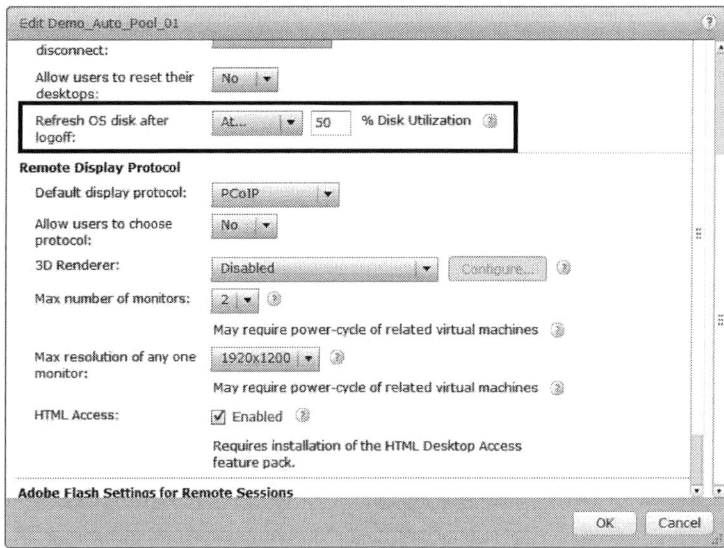

Figure 7.25 Refreshing the desktop after logoff

The next category of pool settings adjusts the display. In View 5, you can force either PCoIP, RDP, or allow users to select which one they would like. For most users, you should generally control the display protocol. If you do not segregate desktops specifically for remote access, you may allow users to choose, but it requires some education so that the users understand when to use which protocol.

In addition, you can turn on Windows 7 3D Rendering provided you have forced the PCoIP as the display protocol and you are using Windows 7 desktops, of course. Enabling this option restricts the number of monitors to two and the resolution maximum to 1920 × 1200 pixels. Enabling it also provides support for Windows Aero within the desktop. Enabling 3D Rendering and allowing a higher maximum resolution increases the number of pixels required to deliver the View desktop. This, in turn, has an impact on the overall network utilization of the PCoIP session. Take care that you thoroughly test these settings to ensure that a balance exists between the quality of the user experience and the overall network utilization.

Enabling this option allows you to adjust the vRAM setting within View, as shown in Figure 7.26, which adjusts the vRAM setting in the properties of the VM.

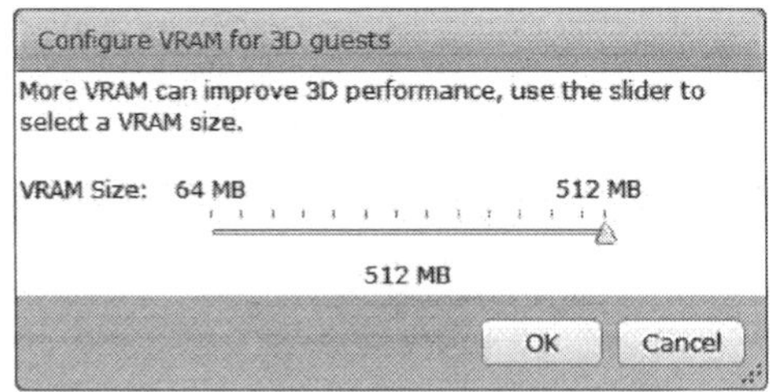

Figure 7.26 Adjusting vRAM settings

PCoIP supports a maximum of four monitors. You can select a maximum number between one and four for the desktop pool, as shown in Figure 7.26. If you force RDP, you do not have the option of adjusting the number of monitors or the resolution settings. The Max Monitors and Max Resolutions are designed to allow tuning of PCoIP. You can limit the resolution of display to one of the following:

1680 × 1050

1920 × 1200

2560 × 1600

Lowering the resolution reduces the number of pixel changes required, reducing the bandwidth compared to higher-resolution settings as well as lowering the amount of video RAM consumed by the VM. You might want to restrict the max resolution and the number of monitors to control general bandwidth utilization.

The last setting in the Remote Display Protocol section allows you to enable access to the View desktop over HTML using HTML 5. What is great about HTML access is that it is clientless access through your HTML 5–compliant web browser. Why wouldn't you enable this for every pool and avoid client-side software installations? VMware still recommends a native PCoIP client for a feature-rich end-user experience versus HTML access. It was initially released as an option pack for VMware View 5.2.

In the next section, Adobe Flash Settings for Remote Sessions, you are controlling Adobe Flash frame rates and bandwidth to manage traffic while still providing reasonable Flash video quality, as shown in Figure 7.27. Across the LAN the defaults may be acceptable, but for remote-access and WAN situations, you should adjust and test these settings.

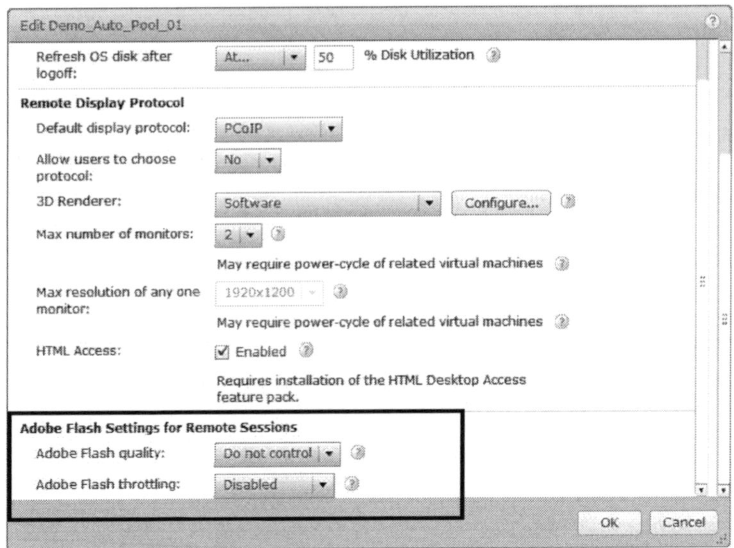

Figure 7.27 Adobe Flash settings

View Composer

In this section, we look at what types of VMDKs make up a View Composer–created VM. With Composer, you can separate user settings onto a second drive to allow them to persist. This capability is important because VMs created by Composer need the OS disk to be refreshed, rebalanced, and recomposed as part of normal operations. By not separating user data from the OS VMDK, you run the risk of user data loss when these activities are initiated.

Redirecting user data changes the default location of the user profile to a persistent disk. In addition, you can create a disposable disk or VMDK that becomes the default location of Windows temporary files. Persistent and disposable drives are thinly provisioned, so they consume space only as they are written to.

The VM sees these View Composer drives as additional local drives within the operating system. If you look at the persistent disk, you see the Users folder containing the profiles and a personality folder if you have integrated Persona. In addition, My Documents is redirected to the persistent disk so that the redirection is transparent to the users. If you look at the disposable disk, you see the Windows Temp folder. Both the persistent disk and Persona Management can be used together or independently. Using a persistent disk to provide localization of the profile speeds up login, but it may add an additional degree of complexity. Using a persistent disk to complement Persona Management creates a local persistent cache for the profile while also ensuring it is stored centrally on a file share. When a user requires a Persona profile, the majority of the data is locally available on the persistent disk. Only the differences between the unsynchronized data need to be downloaded from the central file share. If you are going to use them together, you need to ensure that the Remove Local Persona at Log Off policy is not enabled so that the Persona profile is not removed from the persistent disk. The other option is to forgo a persistent disk and just use View Persona to back up user data to a central repository.

Logically, the separation of VMDKs makes sense. The combination of the OS and internal VMDKs and snapshots enables you to refresh the operating system, the persistent disk allows you to keep user configuration activities so that they are not lost, and the nonpersistent disk flushes temporary files on reboot. What, then, is the internal disk for? The internal disk separates the unique machine information in a separate VMDK so that it can be managed properly. This disk is created when the machine is Sysprepped or Quick-Prepped. In addition, the disk stores the machine trust account that is used to authenticate a client machine to a domain controller. It is more generally referred to as the *computer account*. A computer account password is changed every 30 days by default (it is the same for all Windows versions from 2000 on up) and is set by default in the local policy of the operating system.

If you actually browse the directory store of the VM's folder, you see the VMDKs shown in Figure 7.28.

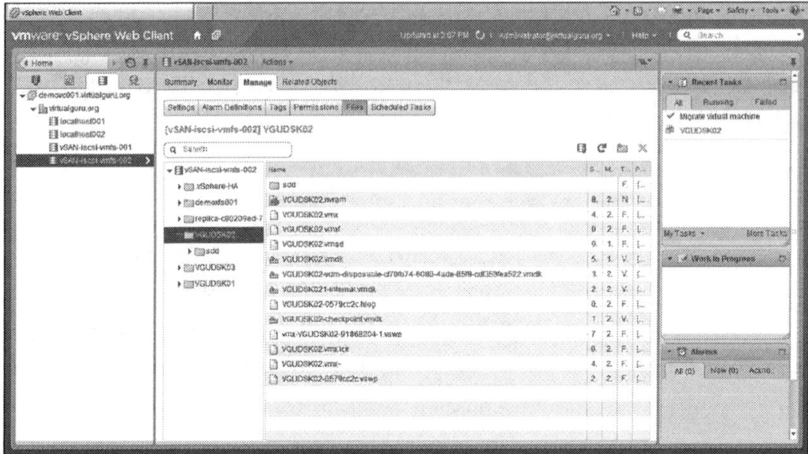

Figure 7.28 View Composer VMDKs

In this case, we have VGUDSK02.vmdk, which is the VM's virtual hard drive. We also have VGUDSK02-checkpoint.vmdk, which is the delta file. In addition we have a VMDK file that starts with VGUDSK02-vdm-disposable, which is where the nonpersistent data such as Windows temp files are stored. These files are deleted if the View Connection Server powers off the VM, but not if the user shuts down the desktop within Windows. We also have a VGUDSK02-internal.vmdk that stores the unique properties of the computer such as the computer account password to ensure connectivity to the domain is maintained when the OS disk is refreshed. Because the VGUDSK02-internal.vmdk persists, the relationship between the computer and domain is maintained.

Within a View Composer-created VM, an additional service called the VMware View Composer Guest Agent Server runs, as shown in Figure 7.29.

Services (Local)

Name	Description	Status	Startup Type	Log On As
Task Scheduler	Enables a us...	Running	Automatic	Local Syste...
TCP/IP NetBIOS Helper	Provides su...	Running	Automatic (T...	Local Service
Telephony	Provides Tel...		Manual	Network S...
Themes	Provides us...	Running	Automatic	Local Syste...
Thread Ordering Server	Provides or...		Manual	Local Service
Time Broker	Coordinates...	Running	Manual (Trig...	Local Service
Touch Keyboard and Handwriting Panel Service	Enables Tou...		Manual (Trig...	Local Syste...
UPnP Device Host	Allows UPn...	Running	Manual	Local Service
User Profile Service	This service ...	Running	Automatic	Local Syste...
vCenter Operations for View Agent	This service ...	Running	Automatic	Local Syste...
Virtual Disk	Provides m...		Manual	Local Syste...
VMware Horizon View Agent	Provides Vie...	Running	Automatic	Local Syste...
VMware Horizon View Script Host	Provides V...		Disabled	Local Syste...
VMware Snapshot Provider	VMware Sn...		Manual	Local Syste...
VMware Tools	Provides su...	Running	Automatic	Local Syste...
VMware View Composer Guest Agent Server	Provides V...	Running	Automatic	Local Syste...
VMware View Persona Management	This service ...	Running	Automatic	Local Syste...
Volume Shadow Copy	Manages an...		Manual	Local Syste...
WebClient	Enables Win...		Manual (Trig...	Local Service
Windows All-User Install Agent	Install AppX...		Manual (Trig...	Local Syste...
Windows Audio	Manages au...		Disabled	Local Service
Windows Audio Endpoint Builder	Manages au...		Disabled	Local Syste...
Windows Backup	Provides Wi...		Manual	Local Syste...
Windows Biometric Service	The Windo...		Manual	Local Syste...

Extended Standard

Figure 7.29 VMware View Composer Guest Agent Server

One of the things this service does is monitor changes to the computer account and ensure that any changes are updated to the internal VMDK. This ensures that if you run a recompose, for example, the computer account and its unique identity persist and are not corrupted in the Active Directory.

vCenter Settings

You have the option of specifying where on your storage system you want to store your replicas and OS disks. When creating a Composer pool under Storage Optimizations, you can specifically direct the OS disk and replicas to certain datastores; you can separate the location of the Replica and the Composer datastore as shown in Figure 7.30. The default location is to store the Replica and OS disk together on the same datastore.

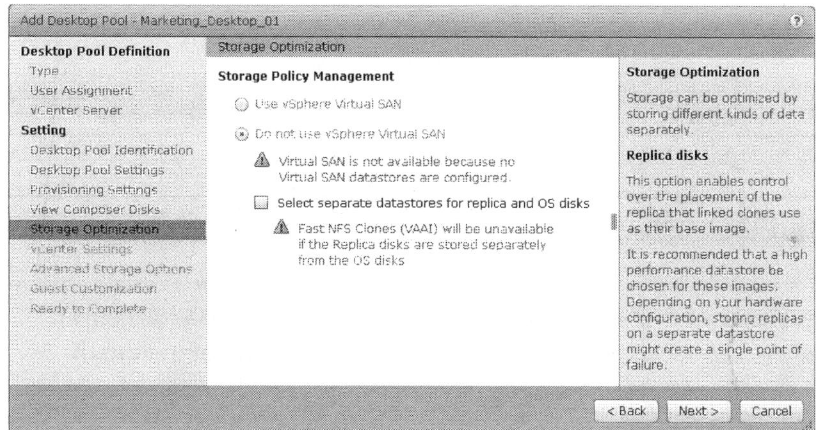

Figure 7.30 Storage optimizations

If you click **Select Separate Datastores for Replica and OS Disks**, on the following vCenter Settings page, under datastores using the Browse button, you can specify on which datastores you would like the Replica and OS disks. Because you have fine control on where certain components of View Composer are located, you can take advantage of all the innovations in solid-state drive (SSD) storage. New companies and technologies are allowing you to even more effectively manage I/O. Examples of these companies are Nexenta, PureStorage, and Fusion-I/O. You also can combine both local and shared datastores for this purpose. If you have included localized SSDs in your ESXi hosts, you can also deploy a Replica and Composer linked clones here.

VMware View also attempts to calculate the size required for the VMDKs created on the datastore selected; you can override the sizing calculation by changing the storage overcommit.

Storage overcommit adjusts how much capacity VMware View reserves for the dynamic growth of the files. It can be set to Conservative, Moderate, or Aggressive. Setting it to Aggressive, for example, increases the amount of overcapacity View factors into the deployment of VMs. Some storage systems do inline deduplication with very little impact to performance. If you have this underlying capability, you can get aggressive, but you should also be aware that depending on how your storage subsystem is designed, you could also be consolidating a larger number of I/Os.

- **None:** Storage is not overcommitted.
- **Conservative:** Four times the size of the datastore. This is the default level.
- **Moderate:** Seven times the size of the datastore.
- **Aggressive:** Fifteen times the size of the datastore.

At the bottom of this screen, you see the sizing estimated provided by VMware View. It is important to understand just how View sets the sizing so that you can understand how much is allocated by default. You can find additional information from VMware at www.vmware.com/files/pdf/view_storage_considerations.pdf.

- **Selected Free Space (GB):** This column shows how much free space is available in the selected datastores. This is just a sum of the real free space with no calculation applied.
- **Min Recommended (GB):** Based on the max number of desktops, View Administrator calculates the minimum you should have available on your storage and allows
  - Space for two replicas
  - Two times the memory of VM times the number of desktops
  - 20% of the size for persistent desktops times the number of desktops
- **50% Utilization (GB):** The calculation incorporates 50% OS disk growth compared to the parent VM disk for each desktop and allows
  - Space for two replicas
  - 50% of replica disk times the number of desktops
  - Memory of VM times the number of desktops
  - 50% of the size for the persistent desktops times the number of desktops

- **Max Recommended (GB):** This calculation determines that each desktop consumes the maximum disk space and allows
  - Space for two replicas
  - 100% of replica disk times the number of desktops
  - Memory of VM times the number of desktops
  - 100% of the size for persistent desktops times the number of desktops

Provisioning Settings

You can adjust how the VMs are provisioned using the provisioning settings. You are able to adjust the naming convention and provision all at once or provision on demand, for example. Why would you provision on demand? If you have a group of users who require access to computers periodically throughout the day but are not sitting in front of a computer, as a primary function, provisioning on demand ensures virtual desktops are available on request but conserves resources until needed. Let's look at these settings a little more closely.

The first part of the provisioning settings allow you to enable and stop provisioning on error (see Figure 7.31). Enabling the Stop on Provisioning option is a good idea while you are testing all the functionality of an environment.

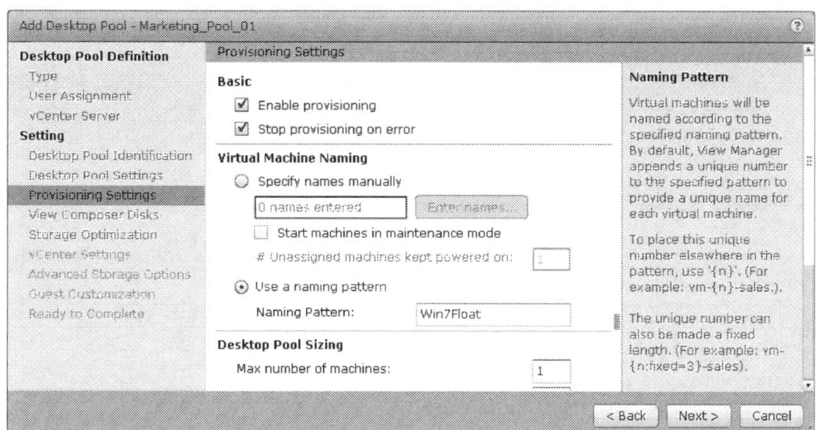

Figure 7.31 Provisioning settings

The second part of the provisioning settings allows you to specify a general naming pattern or get very specific and specify VM names manually, as shown in Figure 7.32. If you select a manual naming convention, you can start a desktop in maintenance mode, which denies a login until the desktop is taken out of maintenance mode. You can also associate specific users and start desktops in maintenance mode to allow additional applications to be loaded before users log in.

Enter Desktop Names

Enter names that will be used to create new virtual machines.

Each line must contain a unique desktop name. Optionally, for dedicated pools, a user name can be specified also. User names will be ignored for floating pools.

vdesktop1,virtualguru\jsmith
vdesktop2,virtualguru\jdoe
vdesktop3,virtualguru\msmall

Examples:

Desktop-001

Desktop-002-jdoe,abccorp.com\jdoe

Next > Cancel

Figure 7.32 VM naming

If this is a dedicated desktop pool, you can enter a list of names and associated users so that you can selectively control which user is assigned to which desktop, as shown in Figure 7.33. If this is a floating pool, user IDs are ignored. When you click **Next**, a lookup is performed in the Active Directory to ensure the users have associated accounts.

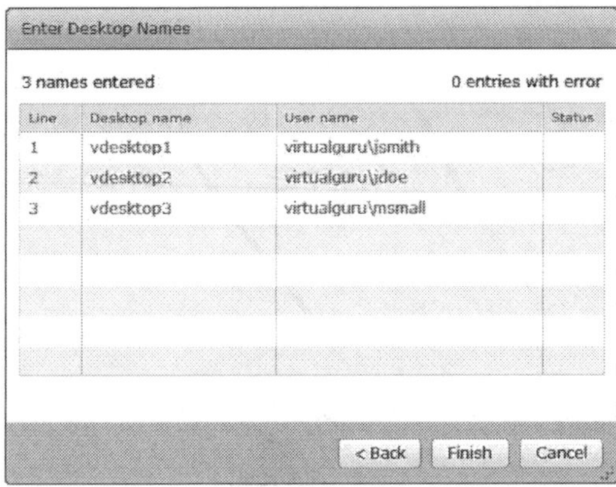

Figure 7.33 Associating users to desktops

Sysprep or QuickPrep?

With Composer, you can use QuickPrep or select a customization file within virtual center, which provides a full Sysprep to the VM. Sysprep, supplied by Microsoft, is designed to change the attributes of the computer to ensure the computer is unique within the environment. This includes the security ID (SID) of the computer. Each computer should have its own local unique SID number that gets updated when the computer joins a domain. The SID is a unique number that is used to identify the system to Windows. Sysprep goes through all files and registry keys on the computer and replaces the current local SID number of the computer with a new local SID. When you use VMware clones, it is possible for two computers to have the same SID. This is why it is necessary to apply a Sysprep to a VM to ensure that it has a unique SID.

Sysprep runs through all the files on the computer and replaces any SID references on the computer with new SIDs and therefore can take longer than QuickPrep. QuickPrep, provided by VMware, is used with View Composer-created VMs (in other words, linked clones). It changes the computer account and adds it to the Active Directory, taking much less time than Sysprep.

Due to the large provisioning time difference between using Sysprep and QuickPrep, you should use QuickPrep unless the applications that you are installing require a unique local SID. For example, some antivirus software requires a locally unique SID on each desktop to run properly.

Entitlement

After creating your desktop pools, you need to assign them to users. Within VMware View, this process is called *entitlement*. Entitlements associate a desktop pool with a selected group of users using Active Directory groups. The procedure for entitling users is as follows:

1. Log in to the VMware View Administrator console.
2. Browse to Inventory and Pools.
3. Select a pool of desktops from the right pane.
4. Select **Entitlements**.
5. You have the option of searching by user or group. Simply deselect the **User or Group** check box and click **Add**. Generally, you should associate pools of desktops to Active Directory groups and not individual users.
6. Enter a name or description and select **Find** to search for the AD group or user.
7. Select the group and click **OK** and **OK** again to entitle the desktops.

Replicas

A *replica* is a read-only copy of the parent VM and contains a snapshot file of the original configuration. View Composer uses the replica to create the linked clone View desktops. The replica is used to right-size the VM by moving from the parent VM format to a thin-provisioned VM. From VMware View 4.5 and on, you can store replicas in separate datastores.

This enables you to store the replica on high performance disk on the SAN or local SSDs. It is from the replica that the linked clone tree is built. Keep in mind, though, that if you use a local disk, the linked clone tree also resides on the local disk.

The use of local SSDs should be reserved for stateless View desktops in a nonpersistent environment. The point of using a local SSD is to take advantage of the extremely high I/O capabilities of the technology.

When you use View Composer, desktops are created from a replica, a linked clone is created for each VM, and a snapshot is taken to create a checkpoint to enable a refresh or rollback operation.

Now that you have a basic understanding of the makeup of the Composer VMs, you can look a little more in depth at the operational management. In View Composer, you can do several activities to manage the desktops.

Refresh

As the VM grows, the size and storage requirements of the linked clones increase. To reclaim this space and reduce the size of the virtual desktops, you can initiate a *refresh*. A refresh essentially reverts the machine to the snapshot that was created when the VM was deployed.

The OS disk is reduced in size as the machine is reverted to its initial creation size, reclaiming the space. Because the VM's machine-specific information is stored in the internal VMDK, this change can happen without having to re-create the computer account in the Active Directory because the trust relationship between the View desktop and the Active Directory is maintained.

You can control how the refresh is initiated. For example you can determine how long it is delayed and adjust the notification provided to users. Let's go through the steps to apply a refresh to the desktop pool:

1. Within the VMware View Administrator console, browse to Inventory and then Pools.
2. Double-click the pool you want to refresh on the right.
3. Display the Inventory tab to refresh individual desktops or the Settings tab to do the entire pool.

You can select individual desktops from the Inventory tab if you like. From the Inventory tab, under the View Composer drop-down menu, you can select operational tasks such as Refresh, Recompose, Rebalance, or Publish.

You can reschedule the day and time in which the activity takes place (the default is current day and current time) and force or wait for users to log off. You cannot change the grace period for logoff here, but you can see it and update it in the global settings if it needs to be adjusted.

Recompose

A *recompose* is designed to replace the OS disk of the VM, but it has limitations. You cannot recompose to a different operating system. For example, if your linked clones are using a Windows 7 OS, you cannot recompose to a Windows XP OS. Before you can recompose, you must either change the existing parent VM or create a new one to introduce the linked clones. After the parent has been updated or created, View goes through a similar process to the creation of a new pool. A replica is created first, and then the linked clones are built from the replica. A recompose operation generally follows your image refresh or rebuild cycles, which typically happen every 6 months to a year.

Because a new OS disk is used, a new vdm-initial-checkpoint snapshot is created for use in future refresh operations. The persistent disk with all the user configurations is not replaced as a part of the recompose, allowing the OS to change but preserving the users' settings. Because it is a new OS, the sysprep Or QuickPrep process is rerun, and a new internal disk is created. A recompose can use a lot of resources in the virtual desktop environment, so it is generally recommended that you initiate a recompose after work hours. The process is similar to a refresh, except that you select Recompose from the View Composer drop-down. The exact process to initiate a recompose is as follows:

1. In View Administrator, browse to Inventory and then Pools.
2. Select the pool to recompose by double-clicking the pool ID in the left column.
3. Choose whether to recompose the whole pool or selected desktops.
4. On the selected pool's page, display the Settings tab and select **View Composer and Recompose**. To recompose specific desktops, select individual desktops from the pool by displaying the Inventory tab. Select the desktops to recompose and select **View Composer and Recompose**.
5. Click **Finish**.

Rebalance

A *rebalance* of View desktops redistributes linked clones among available datastores based on the amount of free space available (see http://kb.vmware.com/selfservice/microsites/search.do?language=en_US&cmd=displayKC&externalId=1021506). This is the only way to move linked clone trees between datastores. The redistribution takes place only if there is an unequal amount of space across datastores. When you rebalance a pool of desktops, the first thing View does is put the VM in maintenance mode so that no one can log in. View then determines what to move based on the amount of space in the datacenters. View separates the OS and persistent disks from the Composer desktop. It then removes the OS and persistent disks and creates a new replica and tree in the datastore. If a replica does not exist in the datastore, it is created first, unless a specific datastore has been identified for replica storage. View deletes the OS disk and creates a new OS linked to the replica. Because this is a new OS disk, Sysprep or QuickPrep is run and a new machine is created. When this process is complete, a new initial-vdm-checkpoint snapshot is created, and the VM's status is updated from provisioned to available. Be aware that the activity you are starting may involve copying a number of full VMs to many datastores plus snapshots and delta files to create the replicas and View desktops. The impact of this process can be very heavy in a large environment, so it should be performed within a maintenance window. The persistent disks are moved from the original target virtual desktop to the new one, so the user configuration information is maintained through the process:

1. In View Administrator, browse to Inventory and then Pools.
2. Select the pool to rebalance by double-clicking the pool ID in the left column.
3. Choose whether to rebalance the whole pool or selected desktops.
4. On the selected pool's page, display the Settings tab and select **View Composer and Rebalance**. To rebalance selected desktops. display the Inventory tab. To rebalance specific desktops, select the desktops to rebalance and select **View Composer and Rebalance**.
5. To rebalance specific desktops, select the desktops to rebalance and select **View Composer and Rebalance**.
6. Click **Finish**.

Managing Persistent Disks

It is possible to manage persistent disks on an individual basis. From an operations perspective, you might need to do this if you want to preserve settings from a virtual desktop that has had a problem to be able to copy them to a new one you have re-created. You need to detach and reattach the persistent disk to preserve the settings.

If you have integrated Persona Management, the user configurations and profile are available centrally from the file repository, so there is less need to reattach persistent disks. This capability can come in handy, however, from time to time. For example, if a user is having issues with a persistent desktop, the help desk can ask that user to log off and reassign the user to another desktop to which you have reattached the user's persistent disk. Because View Persona ensures the user's settings transfer to the new View desktop, there is minimal impact to the user. While the user is working, troubleshooting can be performed on the problematic virtual desktop.

All persistent disks are organized into a single view under the Inventory and Persistent Disks section in the VMware View Administrator console. If you look in the right pane, you see all your persistent disks and what state they are in (attached or detached). You also see the desktop, pool, datastore, and the current capacity of the persistent disk.

You can select any disk from the Attached tab and detach its persistent disk. When you do, the associated VM is deleted and removed from inventory. When you detach, you are prompted to keep the disk on the current datastore or move it to another. If you move it to another datastore, you are asked to select a VM folder that the persistent disk should be moved to. From the Detached tab, you can view the detached persistent disks, refresh the inventory, and create new VMs to be reattached to the persistent disks. This capability is a substantial improvement over older releases of View, which required scripts to be run to reassociate user data disks.

The operational procedures to detach and attach persistent disks are as follows:

1. In View Administrator, click **Inventory** and **Persistent Disks**.
2. Select the persistent disk to detach.
3. Click **Detach**.
4. Choose where to store the persistent disk.
5. Use the current datastore. Store the persistent disk on the datastore where it is currently located.
6. Move to the following datastore. Select a new datastore on which to store the persistent disk. Click **Browse**.
7. Click the down arrow and select a new datastore from the Choose a Datastore menu.
8. The View Composer persistent disk is saved on the datastore. The associated linked clone desktop is deleted and removed from inventory.

Provided the desktop you want to reattach it to is the same OS, you can reattach it as follows:

1. In View Administrator, click **Inventory** and **Persistent Disks**.
2. Display the Detached tab.
3. Select the persistent disk.
4. Click **Attach**.
5. Select a linked clone desktop on which to attach the persistent disk.
6. Select **Attach as a Secondary Disk**.
7. Click **Finish**.

IMPORTANT

Double-check the permissions on the persistent disk to ensure that System and Administrators have full access. You should also ensure that the local user group has Read & Execute, List Folder Contents and Read, and the special permission Create Folder and Write Data.

After the desktop is joined to the domain, the domain users group is added to the local users group, ensuring the user has the appropriate access to download or create a profile. From the same Detached tab, you can select a detached disk and re-create a desktop OS by selecting the persistent disk and clicking the Recreate Desktop button.

Backing Up View

The practice of redirecting user data to file servers versus backing up user content on their desktops is the same on virtual as it is on physical desktops. Rather than backing up each virtual desktop, you will employ user, group, and profile management to centralize the content on a file server and back up from that point. This exception to backing up View desktops is when you have stateful desktops or desktops in which user configurations or data is stored within the virtual desktop. Although it is still simpler to employ folder redirection and Persona Management to centralize user data for backup even with stateful, it is possible that the View desktops configuration and toolset is unique to the requirements of a single user (for example, developer desktops in which the developer installs and customizes the configuration for their specific need). In this case, the stateful desktop should be backed up.

Whether to back up a desktop is largely determined by the nature of its use and whether it is a full clone or linked clone. There is little value in backing up a linked clone, but it may make sense on a full clone. For example, if the full clone desktop is highly customized when it is initially deployed by the developer, but changes very little after that, once a week might be overkill.

The opposite of a stateful desktop is, of course, a stateless desktop. A stateless desktop does not contain any unique user configuration or data and therefore does not require backup.

There are, however, a few components of the View architecture that you should take steps to protect by having backup policies. This section examines which components of the View architecture are critical and therefore warrant backup. The components that you should consider backing up include the following:

- View Connection Server
    - Including AD-LDS datastore
- View Composer
    - Including database
- View Transfer Server and offline desktop file repository
- The central repository of ThinApp packages
- User Persona file repository
- vCenter database

VMware recommends that with respect to the AD-LDS and vCenter and Composer databases that you back them up in the following order:

1. View Connection Server AD-LDS
2. View Composer database
3. Back up vCenter database

You can use traditional backup tools for backing up the OS, file repositories, and databases, but there is a specific process for backing up the AD-LDS datastore and a sequence recommended by VMware. In addition, by default, each Connection and Composer Server automatically backs up the AD-LDS database locally every day at midnight to a text file that is kept for 7 days. To back up the AD-LDS database manually, you need to ensure that there are no operational desktop pool processes in progress such as a refresh, recompose, creation, or deletion of View desktop instances. For desktop pools that are autoprovisioning VMs based on min and max settings, for example, it is important to turn off the provisioning during the backup. To back up the AD-LDS database, complete the following steps:

1. Log in to the VMware View Administrator console by browsing to the URL https:\\[FQDN of View Server]\admin.
2. Expand the Inventory menu and select **Pools**.
3. Select each automated pool and right-click and select **Disable Provisioning**.
4. After you have verified that all operational activity has been temporarily disabled, you can run the AD-LDS database export utility. You can find this utility on the VMware View Server within C:\Program Files\VMware\VMware View\Server\tools\bin; it is called vdmexport.exe.

The tool exports the content in LDAP Data Interchange Format (LDIF), which is a text-based format for exchanging LDAP information. To run the tool, just execute the utility and redirect the content to a file with an .ldf extension. For example:

```
vdmexport.exe>Viewconfig.ldf
```

Although you learned how to here, doing this process manually is not very practical (and it is fully automated by View). You can, however, automate many of the processes within View. VMware provides VMware View PowerCLI cmdlets. When you install the View Connection Server, a View PowerCLI console is also installed. When you first run the View PowerCLI, though, you will receive errors because PowerShell's default settings restrict unsigned or untrusted scripts. To enable the scripts, open Windows PowerShell and follow this process:

1. To verify the current policy, type **Get-ExecutionPolicy**. You should see that the default setting is restricted.
2. To update the current policy, type **Set-ExecutionPolicy Unrestricted**.
3. When prompted, type **Y** to confirm that you want to update the policy.
4. To verify that the policy is now unrestricted, type **Get-ExecutionPolicy** one more time and you should see that it is now unrestricted.

You can now close the Windows PowerShell console and open the View PowerCLI console.

It is possible to disable provisioning using PowerCLI commands. To explain how, we provide an example, but this is not intended to be an extensive review of VMware View PowerCLI. For detailed information on the VMware View PowerCLI, refer to VMware's online documentation. In this example, we update an automated pool that has been created using View Composer. To update an automated Composer desktop pool, you will use the Update-AutomaticLinkedClonePool cmdlet. Because it is likely that you will have a variety of pool types, you want to ensure that you disable provisioning on the appropriate type and specific pool. You can specify a specific pool by providing the pool's unique ID, which is the name of the pool within View (and not the display named presented to the users). In this example, we are disabling provisioning on an automated linked clone pool called CALL_CENTER:

```
Update-AutomaticLinkedClonePool -pool_id CALL_CENTER -isProvisioningEnabled
$false
```

You can reenable provisioning by changing the value to `$true`, as shown in the following example:

```
Update-AutomaticLinkedClonePool -pool_id CALL_CENTER -isProvisioningEnabled
$true
```

Replacing Certificates

When you first install View, it uses self-signed certificates. VMware does not recommend that you use these in production. In a highly secure environment, updating certificates may be required on a regular basis as the certificates expire. This section covers how to replace certificates on the VMware View Server as well as the Composer and Security Server. A Transfer Server does not really use certificates, so replacing them would be of no net benefit.

At a high level, the process that you will follow is to create a Certificate Signing Request (CSR) config file that is used to generate the CSR to request a certificate. Once you receive the signed certificate you will import it and then configure View to use it. This process is outlined in Figure 7.34.

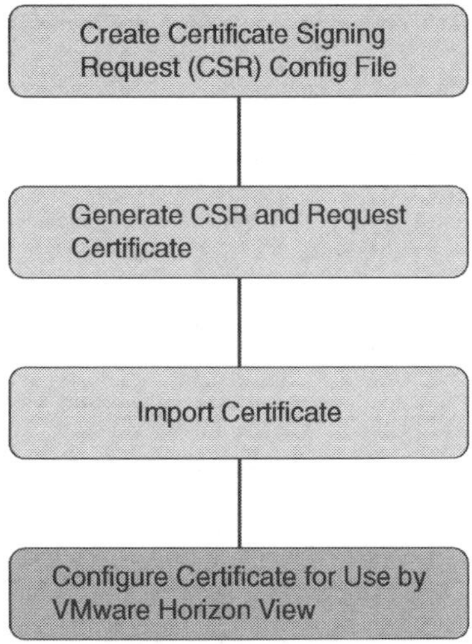

Figure 7.34 Updating certificates

The first part of the process starts with creating a configuration file from which to generate the CSR, as shown in the example request.inf file. The Subject line contains the distinguished name and location of the View Server.

In addition, you can adjust the key length to increase the security of the certificate:

```
;----------------- request.inf -----------------
[Version]
Signature="$Windows NT$
[NewRequest]
Subject = "CN=demovw001.virtualguru.org, OU=IT, O=virtualguru,L=Newmarket,
S=Ontario, C=CA"
; Replace View_Server_FQDN with the FQDN of the View server.
; Replace the remaining Subject attributes.
KeySpec = 1
KeyLength = 2048
; KeyLength is usually chosen from 2048, 3072, or 4096. A KeyLength
; of 1024 is also supported, but it is not recommended.
Exportable = TRUE
MachineKeySet = TRUE
SMIME = False
PrivateKeyArchive = FALSE
UserProtected = FALSE
UseExistingKeySet = FALSE
ProviderName = "Microsoft RSA SChannel Cryptographic Provider"
ProviderType = 12
RequestType = PKCS10
KeyUsage = 0xa0
[EnhancedKeyUsageExtension]
OID=1.3.6.1.5.5.7.3.1 ; this is for Server Authentication
;-----------------------------------------------
```

Create this file, adjust the appropriate values, and save it within a directory on the View Server (for example, c:\cert\request.inf).

After you have the input file, you can use the Microsoft Certificate Request Utility certreq.exe to generate the CSR using the following command syntax from within the directory (in our example, c:\cert):

```
certreq -new request.inf [output file]
```

The utility will generate a CSR within the output file you specified. It is this file that you will submit to the third-party certificate authority (CA) to receive the certificate file. If you maintain your own Windows CA, you can create your own certificate internally. To continue our example, we will use a Microsoft CA.

From the Microsoft CA's website, select **Request a Certificate**, as shown in Figure 7.35.

Figure 7.35 Requesting a certificate

On the Advanced Certificate Request web page, submit a certificate request by using a base-64-encoded CMC or PKCS #10 file, or submit a renewal request by using a base-64-encloded PKCS #7 file, as shown in Figure 7.36.

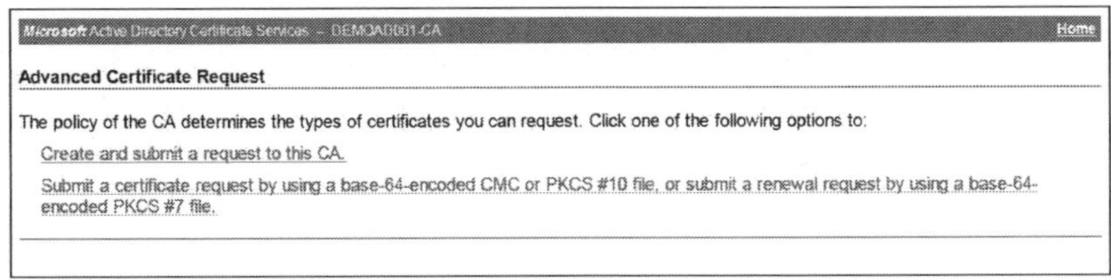

Figure 7.36 Advanced certificate request

On the Request a Certificate web page, click the **Or, Submit an Advanced Certificate Request** link.

On the Submit a Certificate Request or Renewal Request web page, paste the contents of your CSR into the Saved Request window and select the drop-down under the Certificate Template heading and ensure that the Certificate Template being used is Web Server, as shown in Figure 7.37, and click **Submit**.

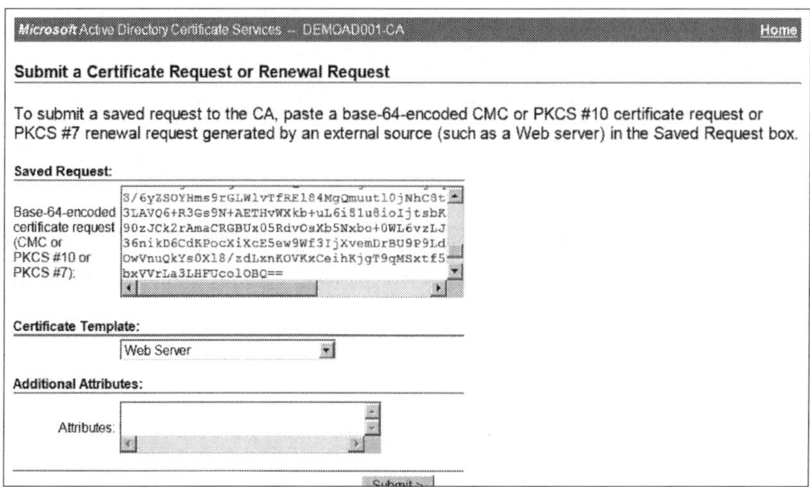

Figure 7.37 Submitting a certificate request

On the Certificate Issued page, leave the default **Der Encoded**, and click the **Download Certificate** link. Ensure that you save the certificate on the View Server (in our example, back in the c:\cert directory).

To import the certificate to the View Server, you can use the certreq.exe utility by using the following command:

```
certreq.exe -accept [certificate name]
```

The utility imports the certificate, but View does not start using until you rename it. To rename it, follow these steps on the View Server. If you have multiple View Servers, you will need to run the process on each server:

1. Run an Management Console (MMC) by typing **MMC** in the Search Program and Files box from the Start menu of the View Server.

2. From the MMC console, select **File**, **Add/Remove Snap-In**.

3. Select **Certificates** from the Available Snap-Ins options and click **Add**.

4. When prompted for which account will be managed by the snap-in, select **Computer Account**, and then click **Finish**.

5. When prompted to select the computer, accept the default **Local Computer**, and then click **Finish** and **OK**.

6. From the MMC, expand **Certificates** and **Personal** and **Certificates**.
7. Right-click the original certificate and select **Properties** and rename to the friendly name **vdmold**.
8. Right-click the new certificate and select **Properties** and add a friendly name called **vdm** and restart the Connection Server.
9. After the reboot, log in to the Connection Server and ensure that under the Dashboard the System Health for the Connection or Security Server shows green, as shown in Figure 7.38.

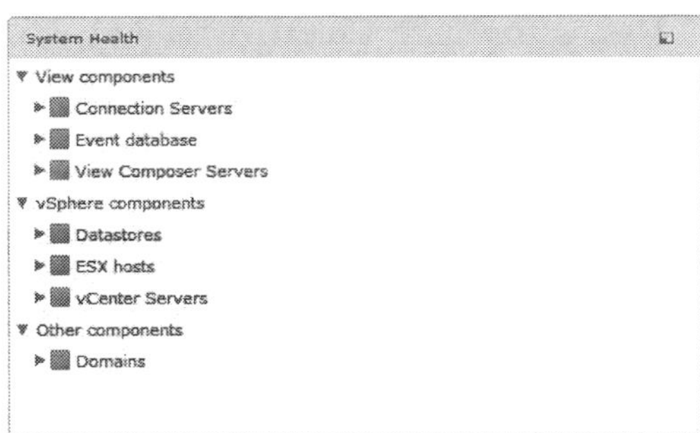

Figure 7.38 Verifying the certificate is accepted

Composer and Certificates

The processes of replacing the certificate on the Composer Server is similar except that you do not need to change the common name but you do have to run the SviConfig utility to bind the updated certificate to the port that Composer uses. The syntax for the utility is as follows:

```
sviconfig -operation=ReplaceCertificate -delete=[false/true]
```

The false or true statement determines whether as part of the process the existing certificate is deleted. False prevents the deletion, and true deletes the certificate when the binding is updated.

Summary

This chapter examined the operational steps in creating, configuring, and managing VMware pools. You looked at what it takes to perform backups of key View components and also replace and update the certificates. Although the steps here are important, they are no substitute for having a good operational process. This involves ensuring that you have predetermined operational windows, for example, so that you can do pool refreshes or rebalances and not impact end-user activity in the environment.

VMware View provides a set of tools that add a lot of capabilities, but it is up to you to integrate them in a way that minimizes disruptions. As with any hosted environment, disruptions to service are amplified in a large VMware View environment. A well-managed change management process for effecting change in your View environment goes a long way to ensuring that users have confidence in the solution and that it remains stable and provides good performance.

Chapter 8

VMware Workspace Operations

Operation of VMware Workspace

Several components of VMware Workspace require operational management, including entitling users, catalog and client management, and integrating additional services. This chapter reviews some of the more common operational procedures you are likely to complete when managing VMware Workspace, as shown in Figure 8.1. This chapter covers many of the processes in which you are likely to engage when running a Workspace environment, but you should refer to VMware documentation for additional details.

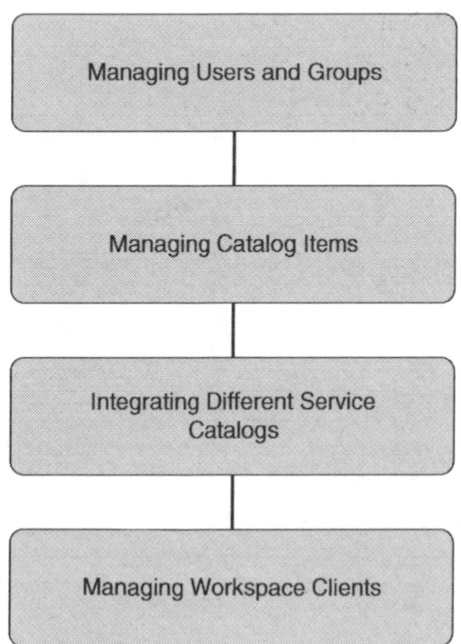

Figure 8.1 Common administrative tasks

This is not a complete list of operational procedures, but merely a starting point from which to build your operational proficiency. Workspace consists of several virtual appliances (VAs) that each performs a separate function; most administrative tasks can be performed from the Administrator web page. You can access this web page by using the Active Directory (AD) administrative account through the URL https://HorizonWorkspaceFQDN/admin. When you log in, you are presented with the initial dashboard of enabled modules and several tabs for managing operational activities in VMware Workspace, as shown in Figure 8.2. By default, the account you used to connect and sync to your Active Directory is the initial administrative account.

If for some reason you cannot access the Administrator web page using the AD account, you can use the default admin account along with the password you specified during the web-based user interface configuration as part of the installation. If using this account, you must log in to a different URL: https://HorizonWorkspaceFQDN/SAAS/login/0. You learn how to set up different administrators in the section "Users & Groups," later in this chapter.

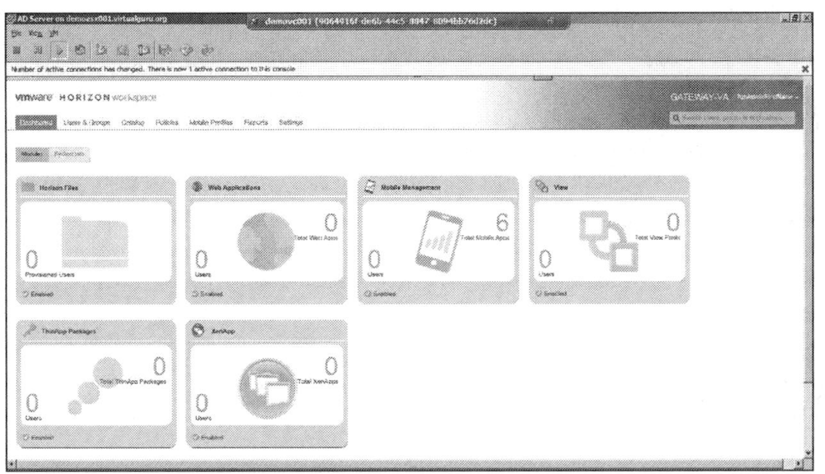

Figure 8.2 Administrator web page

The first tab on the Administrator web interface page is the Dashboard tab, which provides information on what modules you enabled for use in Workspace. New to Workspace 1.8 is the capability to integrate Citrix XenApp Farm. With the integration of Remote Desktop Session Host (RDSH) into the next release of Workspace (the VMware name for this feature is either RDS Pools or App Remoting), however, you will have several options to deliver applications from servers. See the e-chapter available for download for additional information about the integration of App Remoting and VMware Workspace. One other module that is likely to undergo significant change is Mobile Management. This is because VMware has recently acquired AirWatch, which is a leader in mobile device management (MDM) according to Gartner. Because overlap exists between AirWatch and the integrated Mobile Management of Workspace, it is not yet clear what the overall strategy will be. Because it is yet to be determined, this chapter focuses on the other administrative tasks that are common to VMware Workspace.

The second tab available from the Administrator web page is the Users & Groups tab. This is where you can manage users and groups, including those imported from Active Directory (AD) or those added as guest users. For additional information, see the "Users & Groups" section.

The catalog is a collection of all the resources to which you can entitle users. The nature of the catalog determines whether Workspace controls entitlement. For example, entitlement for VMware View desktops is done from within the View Administrator console instead of from within Workspace.

The Policies tab controls both access and mobile policy sets. Access policies control which applications can be accessed from which network segments. Mobile policies control what is allowed and not allowed from the mobile workspace.

Mobile Profiles enables you to preset certain default settings for Exchange, virtual private network (VPN), and WiFi connections. Reports enables you to run reports to both audit and troubleshoot the Workspace environment. The final tab, Settings, links back to the configurator VA and controls general settings across the Workspace environment. The following sections take a look at each tab in depth and review how to perform some common administrative items.

Dashboard

In addition to displaying which modules are enabled, the Dashboard tab provides a snapshot of how many applications, users, and groups are under management and the status of object synchronization. To display the system info, click the **System Info** link to bring up the current status, as shown in Figure 8.3.

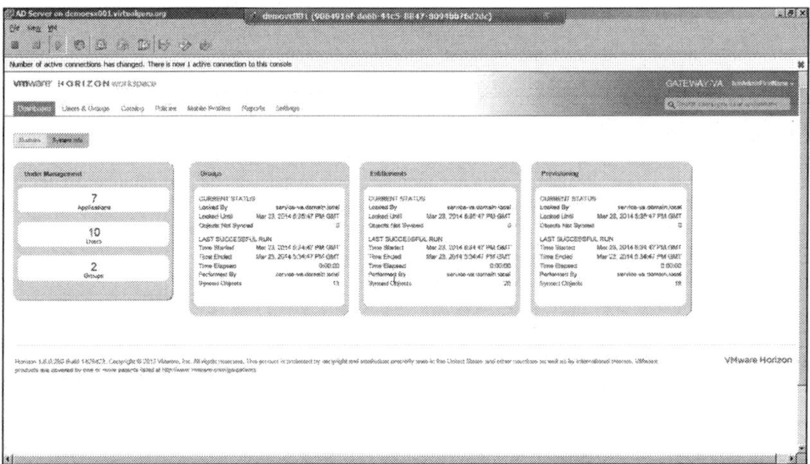

Figure 8.3 System Info link

Users & Groups

On the Users & Groups tab, you can control both Workspace-defined users and groups as well as AD-defined users and groups. Some limitations apply, though. For example, although it is possible to create Workspace groups, you cannot create AD groups from Workspace. In addition, you can control access to resources for AD users and guest users, but you cannot create these types of users.

Guest users are users located outside the company who may be defined only by their email address or a user who is within an AD server that is not synced to Workspace and so is not known. Guest users are most commonly created by users to share files outside the organization. The Guest Users page lists the email address, last login time, and access status of every guest user associated with Workspace. You can delete, lock out access, or unblock locked access for guest users. To manage guest users, follow these steps:

1. Log in to the Administrator website of VMware Workspace.
2. Click the **Users & Groups** link at the top of the page.
3. Select **Guest Users**, as shown in Figure 8.4.

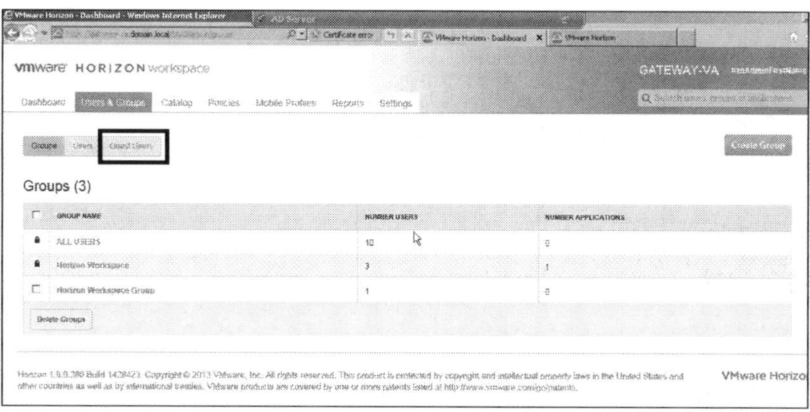

Figure 8.4 Selecting guest users

4. To delete a guest user, check the check box for the guest user and click **Delete Users**.
5. In addition to deleting, you can lock or unlock guest access by clicking **Lock** or **Unlock** for each guest user you want to affect.

In addition to guest users, you can control groups and users. Workspace groups are defined within Workspace and can be created and deleted from the Administrator web console. You can also add users to Workspace groups from within the Administrator web console. To create a Workspace group and add a user from the AD, complete the following steps:

1. Log in to the Administrator website of VMware Workspace.
2. Click the **Users & Groups** link at the top of the page.
3. In the upper-right corner of the page, click **Create Group**.
4. Provide a name and description and click **Add**.

5. Select the newly created group.
6. Click the **Users in this Group** link.
7. Click the **Modify Users in This Group** link on the right of the page.
8. On the Modify Users in This Group page, you can add users or groups looking for or excluding specific attributes, such as email or first name, for example. Or you can add or exclude specific users. For example, to add a specific user, select **Additional Specific Users** and type their names in the input box, as shown in Figure 8.5, and then click **Next** and **Finish**.

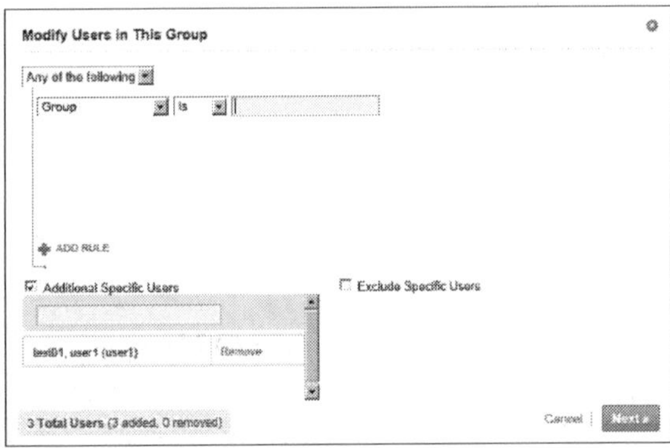

Figure 8.5 Adding specific users

Entitlement

You build a user's or group's Workspace by entitling them to catalog items. For example, after you have integrated Workspace and VMware View, you can entitle a group to the View Desktop Pools catalog. This will present the Computers tab in the user's Workspace, giving the user access from within Workspace to View. Upcoming plans for VMware Workspace will blend the applications and computers onto a single tab. Care must be taken with the word *entitlement* in this particular case because the Workspace entitlement does not supersede the entitlement done within View. The user must first be entitled to the desktop pool in View before the entitlement done in Workspace. You can entitle users to different catalog resources from within their group or from the catalog item. To entitle a group, complete the following steps:

1. Log in to the administrator website of VMware Workspace.
2. Click the **Users & Groups** link at the top of the page.
3. Select the group to which you would like to add the entitlement.

4. Select **Entitlements** and **Add Entitlement**.
5. From the drop-down list, select the application type (Web Applications, ThinApp Packages, and so on), and then click **Save**.

The second area in which you can entitle access is as a property of the catalog item itself. To entitle the resource directly, complete the following steps:

1. Log in to the Administrator website of VMware Workspace.
2. Click the **Catalog** link at the top of the page.
3. Select the Catalog item to which you would like to add the entitlement.
4. Select **Entitlements** and either **Add User Entitlement** or **Add Group Entitlement**.
5. Type the name of the user or group, or browse to it and click **Save**.

Remove Users

You can remove users from Workspace by unentitling them to resources. Of course, disabling their account within the Active Directory or the identity provider would also prevent them from logging in. In addition to disabling accounts or unentitlement, you can also remotely wipe user data by reviewing which Workspaces are assigned to the user and selectively removing data. You can do so using these steps:

1. Log in to the Administrator website of VMware Workspace.
2. Click the **Users & Groups** link at the top of the page.
3. Select the group, and then select **Users in This Group** to display the list of users.
4. Select **Entitlements**, and then click the **Unentitlement** link on any catalog items to which you want to restrict access.
5. To do a remote wipe of the user's data, click the **Workspaces** link and then the **Delete** link to remove any stored data from the device.

Catalog & Modules

Within Workspace, you can create catalogs of mobile and Cloud-based applications in addition to integrating Windows-based application delivery technologies such as View, ThinApp, and Citrix. Because Chapter 6, "Integrating VMware View and Workspace," covers the integration of Workspace and View, we focus here on ThinApp integration as it is directly related to View.

An important step in the development of catalogs is understanding what services your users need access to and how you organize these requirements into Workspaces. In developing your service catalog, you can preselect applications that appear to the user or allow users to add only applications they select or a combination of the two. Within Workspace, this behavior is controlled by selecting which deployment type should be used. The options are Automatic and User-Activated. With some catalog resource types, there is no capability to have the user select the application, so the deployment type is preset to Automatic and cannot be changed. Although the configuration of a catalog varies by resource, let's take a look at how we create and integrate ThinApp packages with Workspace so that we can create ThinApp catalogs. Keep in mind that Workspace users will need the VMware Workspace Client for Windows to launch the ThinApp applications.

ThinApp Integration

The process to integrate ThinApp starts with ensuring that you have a file repository configured, which is essentially a file share with the correct permissions, as shown in Figure 8.6. A ThinApp file repository requires the following permissions:

- Read access for the domain computers group for file and sharing permissions
- Read and Execute NTFS permissions for the users who will launch the packages

When packaging applications for Workspace, you must be aware of a few things that differ from typical ThinApp packaging steps. The first is to select the **Manage with VMware Horizon Workspace** option, as shown in Figure 8.7, when using the ThinApp Setup Capture utility. The URL is optional, but it enables you to specify where the user can download the Workspace Client to allow them to run the ThinApp application. When you copy over the ThinApp'd package, you must copy everything in the Bin directory from the ThinApp packaging desktop to a subfolder on the share. For example, if I ThinApp'd notepad++.exe within my Bin directory on the ThinApp packaging desktop, I would have a notepad++.dat and notepad++.exe. I would then copy this information to a share in its own folder (for example, \\demofs01.virtualguru.org\ThinApp\Notepad++\).

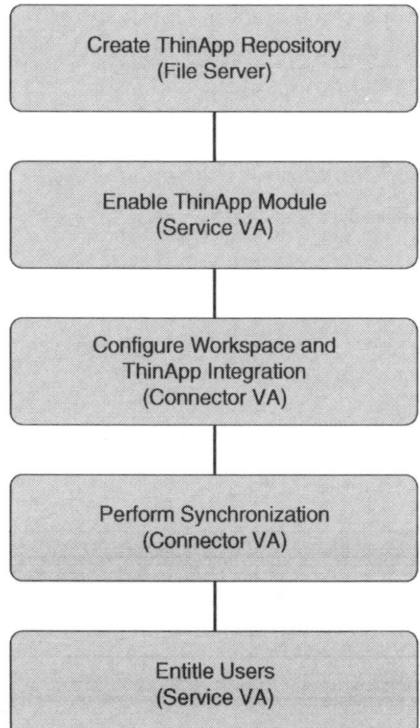

Figure 8.6 Integrating ThinApp

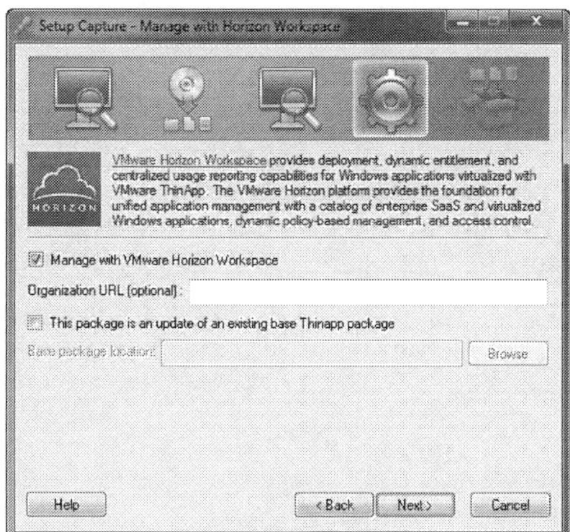

Figure 8.7 Selecting Manage with VMware Horizon Workspace

When the file repository is created and we have some applications packaged, we will enable the ThinApp module through the Administrator website on the service VA. When the ThinApp module is enabled, we must update the configuration on the connector VA. To update the configuration, browse to the connector VA and complete these steps:

1. Display the Advanced tab, and then select the **Join Domain** option from the list.
2. Check the **Join Domain** check box and provide the name of the domain and a username and password, and click **Join Domain**. If it's successful, you should see a message that tells you that you are currently joined to the domain.
3. Select the **Packaged Apps - ThinApp** option and check the **Enable packaged Applications** check box.
4. Provide the file repository path (for example, \\demofs01.virtualguru.org\ThinApp).
5. Choose the synchronization frequency you want from the drop-down list; possible options are every hour or once a week, day, or manually. (Note that *manually* means that you must perform the synchronization yourself.) If you are using Microsoft Distributed File System (DFS)—a Microsoft service that uses distributed folders, replication, and a single namespace to provide location transparency and data redundancy—it requires a username and password, so you should enable account-based access and provide the account information. In addition, if you are planning to deploy applications over the web, account-based access is required.
6. Click **Save** and the **Sync Now** button and verify (by reviewing the status) that the sync is successful and that you now have ThinApp package information.

When you enable ThinApp packaging on the connector VA, you can find any alerts related to the synchronization under the Troubleshooting tab under Packaged Apps (ThinApp) Alerts. Ensure that all your ThinApp packages are imported and processed without errors. In addition, if you go back to the Administrator web console on the service VA, you should see that the ThinApp module shows all ThinApp packages, which can now be entitled to your Workspace users. You will also find the new ThinApp packages under the Catalog page, listed under the application type of ThinApp Package. At this point, you are ready to entitle your users and test. Entitling ThinApp does not significantly differ from entitling other catalog items. However, you can deploy the package automatically or use user-activated deployment. In addition, and as mentioned, the users will need the Workspace Client software to test.

Policies

In VMware Workspace, there are two types of policies: mobile and access. We will steer clear of mobile ones and focus this section on the access policy sets. To understand the access policy sets that can be applied to web applications in your catalog, you need some background on the Security Assertion Markup Language (SAML). SAML is a secure XML-based communication protocol for enabling identity approval between third-party organizations. The primary use case is for single sign on across the Web. SAML eliminates the need to have separate accounts and passwords for each software-as-a-service (SaaS), web, or SAML-capable software application you use. SAML delivers higher security because it reduces multiple accounts for each service, reduces the number of phishing exploits by reducing the number of user logins, and is seamless to the end users. It enables enterprise organizations to integrate Cloud-based SaaS, web, and SAML application solutions without introducing additional user accounts and management points.

SAML Overview

SAML involves interaction between the user, the account database, and the authentication mechanism (that is, Active Directory), which is more commonly referred to as the identity provider (IDP) and the hosted application or service provider (SP), as shown in Figure 8.8.

Figure 8.8 SAML components: user, IDP, and SP

SAML is called into action when a user attempts to access SaaS, web, or SAML-capable applications by clicking a link in a portal, for example, or by browsing to a website. When that happens, Federated Identity software running at the IDP validates the user's identity, and that user is authorized to use that SaaS application. A SAML token that includes only enough information to enable the user is communicated between the IDP and the SP. The SP Federated Identity software determines that the IDP is trusted and that the user is valid, and then creates a session enabling access. This whole process is seamless to the end user. From the user perspective, they click the link and are granted access. SAML is an open standard, so it enables interoperability and is widely adopted by SaaS providers.

VMware Workspace provides three default authentication methods: Kerberos, password, and SecurId. The Password authentication method is commonly used to support Active Directory authentication. You can view the three default IDPs under the Workspace Administrator web console as follows:

1. Log in to the services VA (https://service-va.virtualguru.org/admin).
2. Display the Settings tab and select **Authentication Methods**.

You will notice the three defaults as well as the ability to add additional authentication methods. (Even though you can extend authentication methods, VMware officially supports only the three defaults at the time of this writing.) You will also notice that each has an associated authentication score. The default setup is this: The more hardened the authentication method, the higher the score. For example, password is 1, Kerberos is 2, and SecurId is 3.

You can use any one of these default authentication methods to create an IDP. The first IDP is created during installation and is called hznConnector; it uses the password authentication method to integrate your Active Directory. It is listed on the Save page as an authentication method under the identity providers.

The last piece of background information you need is to understand network ranges. Network ranges enable you to define a network segment and associate a specific identity provider. For example, you may create a network range that specifies your internal networks and associate it with the default hznConnector IDP and create a network range for external IPs to associate a SecurId IDP. After you define your network ranges, you can associate them as follows:

1. Log in to the services VA (https://service-va.virtualguru.org/admin).
2. Display the Settings tab and select **Identity Providers**.
3. Select **Edit** on the row of the provider you would like to associate with a certain network range.
4. From the Network Ranges section, select the range you want to associate, and click **Save**.

Access policies allow you to take an IDP, authentication score, and network range and define restrictions that control access. For example, in Figure 8.9, we have created an access policy set called Low Risk that contains a policy called Low Risk for the internal network with a minimum authentication score of 1 and a TTL (Time To Live) of 8 hours.

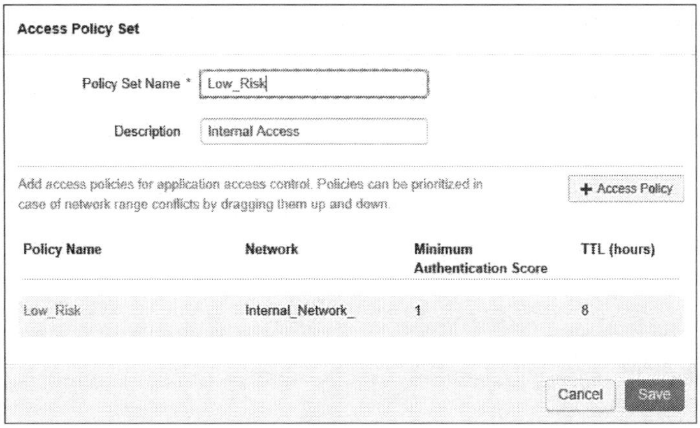

Figure 8.9 Policy set example

When you have a policy set, it can be assigned to any web application within your catalog to control access. Note that they do only apply to web applications. Applying an access policy is a straightforward process. Just select the web application and, under the access policies, select which policy you want applied, and save the changes. When a user logs in to Workspace, you might have different access policies for different web applications. Suppose, for example, that you have one highly secure application that you enable for authentication level 3 (SecurId) versus the default authentication level 1 (password/AD) for the default login. When users click the sensitive application, they are redirected to the SecurId server so that they can authenticate to the higher-level identity provider. The TTL is started, and they are allowed to use the sensitive application for the TTL limit specified. When the TTL expires, the user is asked to reauthenticate.

Auditing and Tracking

VMware Workspace enables you to audit user, administrative, and entitlement events. Because Workspace is designed to be a universal broker between your users and all applications irrespective of where they are hosted, auditing enables you to get a good view of overall user activity. In addition to tracking, you can assign a cost to a catalog item and use the Workspace software development kit (SDK) to integrate into an existing licensing system. Auditing must first be enabled before you can generate auditing reports:

1. Log in to the service VA (https://service-va.virtualguru.org/admin).
2. Display the Settings tab and select **Auditing**.
3. Check the **Enable Auditing** check box.
4. To view audited events, display the Reports tab and the select **Audit Events**.

You can specify any number of criteria to enable you to narrow the search of audited events, such as by user, type of event, action, and object, or by using a range of time. In addition to auditing events, you can associate costs and meter licenses to certain catalog items. To configure licensing parameters for a catalog resource, complete these steps:

1. Log in to the service VA (https://service-va.virtualguru.org/admin).
2. Display the Catalog tab and select the application type **ThinApp** (for example).
3. Select the ThinApp package you want to configure, and click **Licensing**.
4. Select **Edit** and specify the licensing pricing, type, cost per license, and number of licenses, as shown in Figure 8.10.

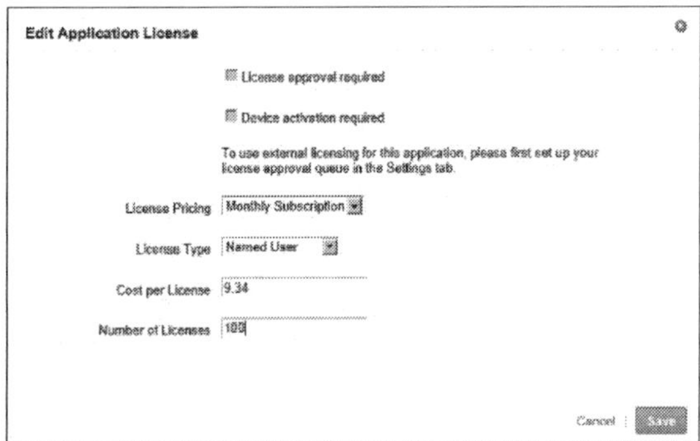

Figure 8.10 Edit application licensing

Workspace Clients

Mobile clients for Android are available from Google Play and for the Apple iOS from iTunes. For users to access the Workspace desktop clients, however, you must place the installer files in the download directory and the auto-update directory on the data VA virtual machines (VMs). Once the files are put in the directories, Apple and Windows users can download these client files from their Workspace user portal.

The clients will poll the Workspace server to determine whether a new version has been added to the auto-update directory. If a new client is found, the client is automatically updated. Users must have administrative privileges on their desktop to install the client; otherwise, you must use a software distribution tool to push the software to the client devices. Adding Workspace clients is a four-step process, as shown in Figure 8.11.

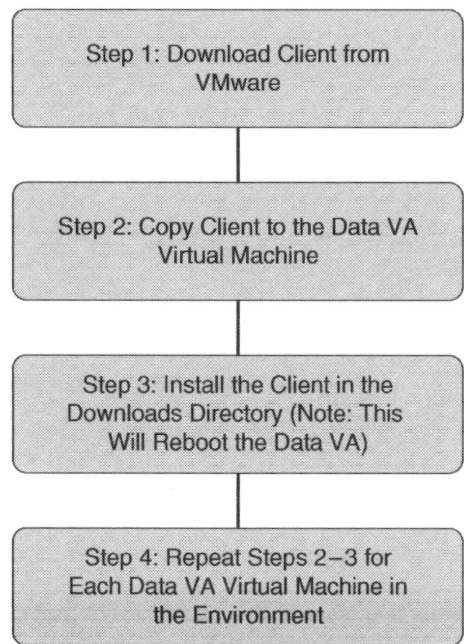

Figure 8.11 Adding Workspace clients

In Step 3, you run the following command, assuming that you have downloaded the file to the /tmp directory of the data VA in Step 2:

```
/opt/vmware-hdva-installer/bin/check-client-updates.pl --install
--clientfile /tmp/[client file name].zip
```

Take care when you run this command because it will reboot the data VA after it has installed the client software into the proper directories.

On the desktop clients, it is possible to configure single sign on (SSO). This is done by updating a parameter on the service VA virtual machine. If SSO is not enabled, users will have to log in to their Workspace first. The configurator parameter can be found in the runtime-config.properties file located in the /usr/local/horizon/conf/ directory. You will need to add the following line to the file:

```
apply.login.ota=true
```

After you have added the line to the runtime-config.properties file, you must restart the service VA virtual machine using the following command:

```
/etc/init.d/horizon-frontend restart
```

Horizon Files

With Horizon Files, you can enable a Cloud storage and collaboration service for your Workspace users. When Horizon Files is enabled for a user, a Horizon Files folder is created on their system. Any files or folders placed in the Horizon Files folder are synced to Workspace, enabling the user to view and preview, share, and sync files across systems. The storage of these files can be on a data VA virtual machine or a Network File System (NFS). A data VA virtual machine is recommended for every 1000 users in your environment. For scaled-out environments, VMware recommends using a network-attached storage (NAS) with NFS storage. If you transition from a local virtual machine disk (VMDK) to NFS, when you add the mount point, the volume on the VMDK gets marked as a secondary storage location, and no new files are added to it.

From an operations perspective, the management of Horizon Files requires that your users are entitled and have enough space and that any net new data VA virtual machine is added and properly configured. In addition, you need to ensure that when the additional space is added through a new data VA, it is visible to Workspace. In addition to managing storage, you can remove access by de-provisioning users through unentitlement and can force a remote wipe to remove user data from their device.

During the installation of VMware Workspace, you will notice that a VM called datava-template is created with the vApp that remains powered off. This VM is the template for creating additional data VA virtual machines to add additional capacity to your environment.

Enable Horizon Files

To break down the operational activity, let's first review the setup of Horizon Files, and then the addition of additional space or data VAs, and finally removing a user's access securely. To set up Horizon Files, you need to complete the steps shown in Figure 8.12.

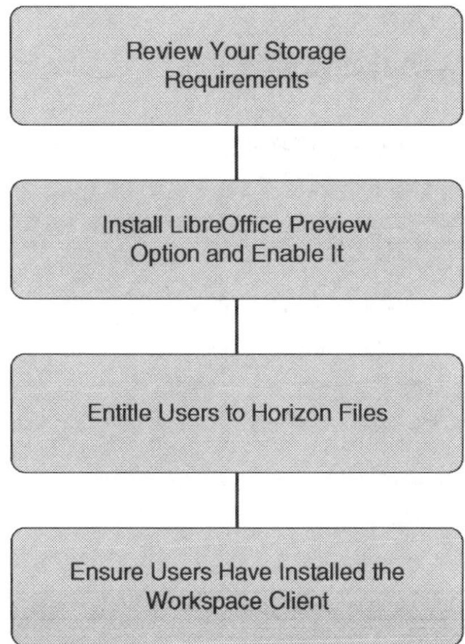

Figure 8.12 Enabling Horizon Files

By default, the data VA is provisioned with approximately 175 GB of storage, but only 1 GB is designated for Horizon Files blob storage. VMware recommends that you allocate 2.5 times the storage set in the users quota. Quotas can be set by applying a Class of Service (COS) to Horizon Files. The default one does not enforce a quota. To review or add a new COS, complete the following steps:

1. Log in to the services VA (https://service-va.virtualguru.org/admin).
2. Display the Catalog tab, and select **Services** from the Application Type drop-down.
3. Click **Horizon Files**, and then click **Class of Service**.

You have the option of adding a new CoS or copying or editing the default one. If we look at the default one by selecting **Edit** from the default CoS row, we will see the default setting of no quota, as shown in Figure 8.13.

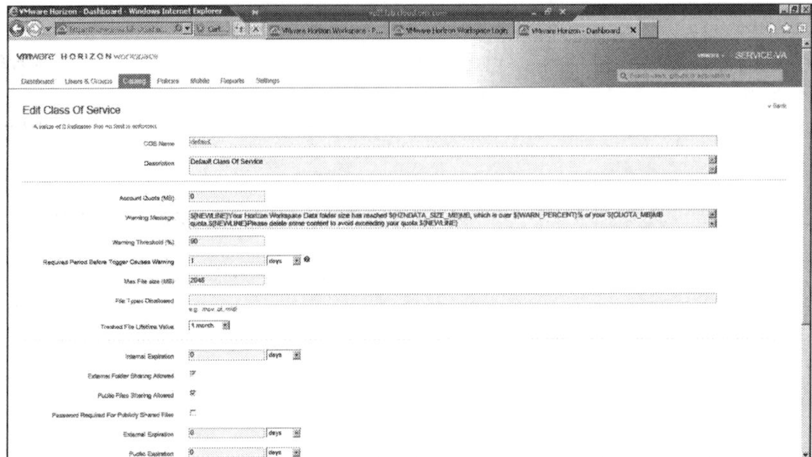

Figure 8.13 Default quota

To add space, you simply add additional hard disks to the data VA virtual machine. When you add the additional hard disks, they are not immediately made available to Horizon Files. To bring them online, you must log in to the console of the data VA and run the following command:

```
/opt/vmware-hdva-installer/bin/zca-expand-lv
```

To work with various types of files in the environment, VMware uses LibreOffice Preview or Microsoft Windows Preview if your company is licensed for Microsoft Office. The MSI (Microsoft Installer) for Microsoft Windows Preview is called VMware-Horizon-Data-Preview-Server, and you can download it from the data VA from the following directory location:

```
/opt/zimbra/jetty/webapps/zimbra/downloads/
```

This file should be installed on a Microsoft Windows 2008 R2 server on which you have disabled User Access Control (UAC) and installed the Microsoft Office 64-bit version of 2010 Professional or later. During the setup, you must provide a password and specify the number of worker threads. The last part of the process is to point Workspace at the Preview server, which must be done from the data VA console and requires the following steps:

1. Change to the Zimbra user by running `su - zimbra`.
2. Run the configuration utility to point to the Microsoft Preview server:

   ```
   /opt/zimbra/bin/zmlocalconfig -e ms_converter_url=http://[Preview Server IP]
   ```

3. Restart the mailboxd daemon:

```
/opt/zimbra/bin/zmmailboxdctl restart
```

4. You then need to run the zmprov utility to modify each CoS, including the default one:

```
/opt/zimbra/zmprov mc [COS] hrzndataConverterHints UseMsPDFConverter
```

Even if you decide to use the Microsoft Preview option, you still need to install Libre-Office Preview, so most customers tend to use LibreOffice. The installation of LibreOffice is much more straightforward and can again be done from the data VA console as follows::

1. Run the LibreOffice installer:

```
/opt/zimbra/libexec/libreoffice-installer.sh
```

2. Change to the Zimbra user by running `su - zimbra`.

3. Restart the mailboxd daemon to enable LibreOffice:

```
/opt/zimbra/bin/zmmailboxdctl restart
```

The last part of the process is to entitle users and ensure they are running the VMware Workspace desktop client. The entitlement process can be done from within the Horizon Files catalog page on the Administrator website and is similar to other entitlement processes already described.

Add Additional Data VAs

For capacity and load balancing, you will need to add an additional data VA. When adding additional data VAs, you must consider several things, such as controlling where users are provisioned and ensuring that the new data VA is brought online properly. You can control where users are provisioned by adding additional classes of service, as described in the section "Enable Horizon Files." One of the CoS options is the host pool, which enables you to associate the fully qualified domain name (FQDN) of a data VA to the service class. By specifying different host pools in different classes of services, you can control where users are provisioned. Keep in mind, however, that the first data VA is always the master and stores all the metadata for the user accounts; all data VAs created after the first are used for file storage only.

The process of adding a data VA involves running a command from the configurator VA:

```
/usr/local/horizon/bin/hznAdminTool addvm --type=DATA -ip=[new data-va IP]
```

After the data VA is deployed, you must add the LibreOffice Preview software as described in the section "Enable Horizon Files." After you have installed LibreOffice, complete the following steps:

1. On each gateway VA, run the `memcached restart` command:

   ```
   /etc/rc.d/memcached restart
   ```

2. Log in to the configurator web page URL at https://configurator-va and open the Systems Information page.
3. Find the newly deployed data VA and click **Exit Maintenance Mode** under the Actions box.

Ensure that there is a green check box under the status of the new data VA, and after this, the extra storage space is ready for use. You can perform other operational procedures, such as removing a data VA, but these are really the most operational processes. For additional information, refer to VMware's online documentation at http://pubs.vmware.com.

System Diagnostics

VMware Workspace provides enhanced system diagnostics of not just the Workspace environment but also the underlying vCenter. You can access these system diagnostics by logging in to the configurator VA and selecting the **System Diagnostics** option. The system diagnostics enable you to examine a higher level of detail to help identify the source of the problem, as shown in Figure 8.14.

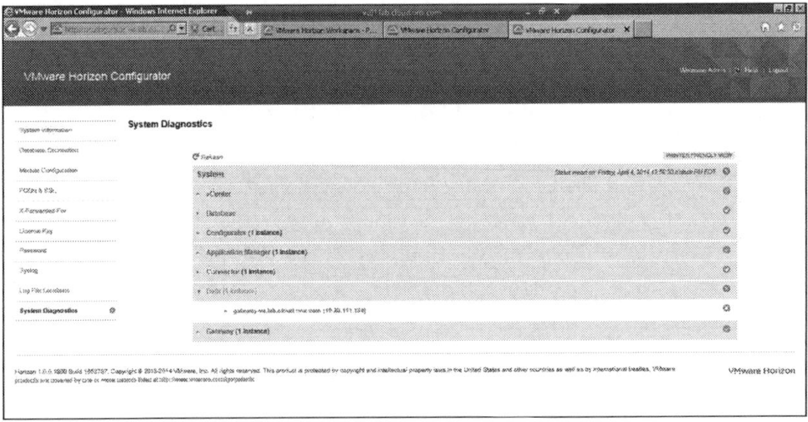

Figure 8.14 System Diagnostics page

Summary

Although this chapter has not covered every possible operational process you might encounter in administering your VMware Workspace environment, you have learned the common ones as well as the ThinApp catalog items. The discussion here purposely stayed away from the MDM features because these are likely to change significantly after the integration of AirWatch is completed. Each web application tends to be unique, but there are several good examples available on VMware's blog site that you can use as examples. The most important element of integrating web applications that require authentication is the understanding of SAML, which you read about in this chapter. Take time in your lab or proof-of-concept environment to get used to the standard operating procedures described in this chapter; doing so will give you the confidence to look at more complex integration between Workspace and third-party Cloud providers. Many of the large Cloud service providers have well-documented federation procedures to enable you to integrate their services.

Chapter 9

VMware Horizon Mirage

This chapter describes the recommended approach to prepare for a deployment of all the components of Horizon Mirage. This product came from an acquisition VMware made in mid 2012 from a company called Wanova. The idea behind the acquisition, as we've been told, was to address a broader market than just the virtual desktop space. VMware was looking into reaching the physical PCs as well as the virtual desktops and provide one solution to manage both types of endpoints. In the physical PC game, there is a multitude of solutions currently on the market to manage the end-to-end lifecycle of a PC. Horizon Mirage is not a PC lifecycle management solution (PCLM), but it does a good job at providing single-image management, automated OS migration, desktop recovery, and hardware refresh. This chapter covers each of these use cases and explains how you can get the most out of Horizon Mirage.

VMware Horizon Mirage Deployment and Design Considerations

Building a solid Horizon Mirage environment, like the other solutions previously discussed, requires strong planning and focus. After the initial product is deployed and configured, you can go in multiple directions. This chapter guides you based on the following use cases:

- Build and deploy a OS layer
- Build and deploy an application layer
- Migrate a Windows desktop (physical and virtual)
- Setup desktop recovery (BC/DR)
- Plan for a hardware refresh

You will learn about each of these in detail in the following pages. The chapter concludes by covering at a high-level the branch office use case, but without delving too deeply into the subject; you'll learn why at the end. Figure 9-1 shows a workflow that is a good approach to a Mirage deployment.

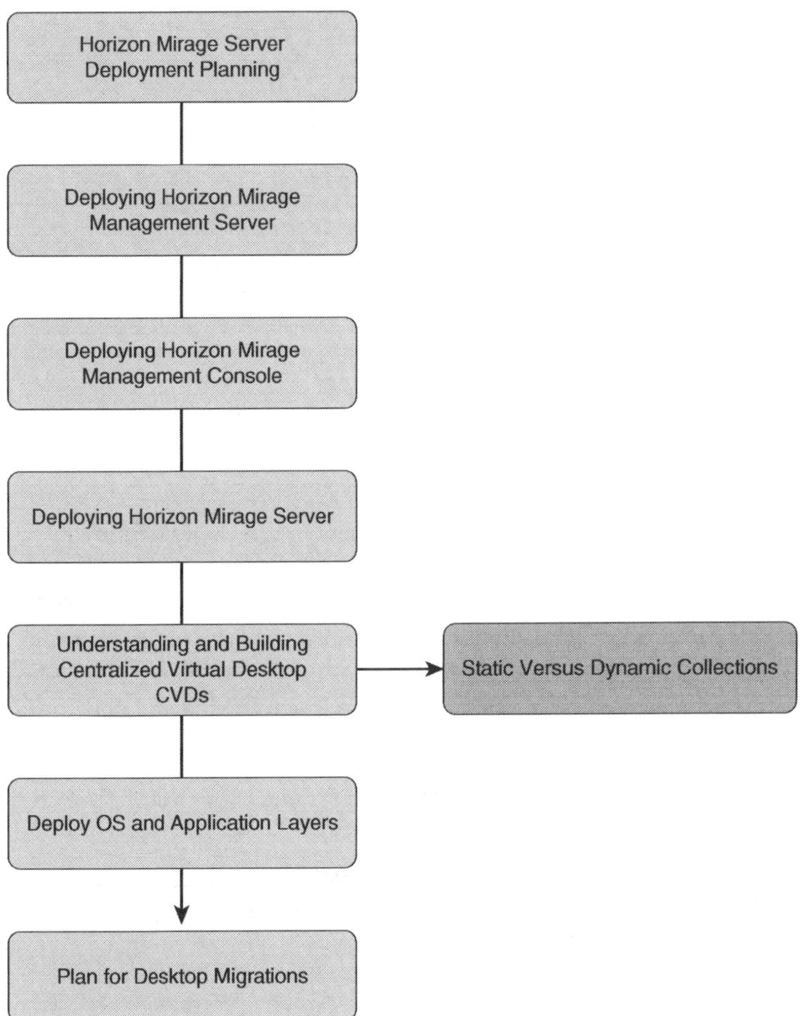

Figure 9.1 Horizon Mirage deployment workflow

Horizon Mirage Planning

When planning for a deployment that will involve reaching out to a potentially large number of PCs (perhaps even doing a backup of them and deploying a new image to those PCs), multiple things will be impacted, mostly the network and disk.

Being able to estimate the network requirements for a Mirage deployment is key; the use case that will solicit the most amount of bandwidth will be desktop centralization or desktop backup (different name, same functionality). So, your first task is to identify the network from the endpoints you want to centralize and the Horizon Mirage Server.

Your second task is to identify the storage you will require for the centralization of the endpoints and the different layers you will create.

Horizon Mirage Components

In a Mirage deployment, you will usually find the following components. The number of each will vary depending on the size of your deployment. Keep in mind that in this chapter we are sizing our deployment for 500 desktops and following the use case listed at the beginning of the chapter.

Horizon Mirage is a solution used to centralize the entire desktop contents in the datacenter for management and protection purposes, distribute the running of desktop workloads to the endpoints, and optimize the transfer of data between them. The Horizon Mirage components integrate into a typical distributed infrastructure. The following list describes the relationships between the system components:

- **Horizon Mirage Server:** The Horizon Mirage Servers manage the storage and delivery of base layers, app layers, and centralized virtual desktops (CVD) to clients and consolidates monitoring and management communications. You can deploy multiple servers as a server cluster to manage endpoint devices for larger enterprise organizations.
- **Horizon Mirage Management Server:** The Management Server is the main component that controls and manages the Horizon Mirage Server cluster.
- **Horizon Mirage Management Console:** The graphical user interface used to perform scalable maintenance, management, and monitoring of deployed endpoints.
- **Horizon Mirage Web Management:** The Horizon Mirage Web Management enables help-desk personnel to respond to service queries, and the Dashboard feature assists the protection manager role to ensure that user devices are protected. The web Management mirrors Horizon Mirage Management Console functionality.

- **Single-instance store (SiS):** External storage accessible to the Mirage Server cluster. Consumed capacity varies, depending on the file duplication level across CVDs, base layers, and the number of snapshots stored.
- **Centralized virtual desktop (CVD):** Represents the complete logical contents of each PC. This data is migrated to the Horizon Mirage Server and becomes the authoritative copy of the contents of each PC. You can use the CVD to centrally manage, update, patch, back up, troubleshoot, restore, and audit the desktop in the datacenter. A CVD consists of the following components:
  - A base layer defined by the administrator, which includes the OS image plus core applications. A base layer is used as a template for a large group of endpoints.
  - App layers defined by the administrator, including sets of one or more departmental or line-of-business applications and any updates or patches for already installed applications suitable for deployments to a large number of endpoints.
  - A drive profile defined by the administrator, which specifies a group of drivers for use with the specific hardware platforms. These drivers are applied to devices when the hardware platforms match the criteria that the administrator defines in the driver profile.
  - User-installed applications and machine state, including unique identifier, hostname, and configuration changes to the machine registry, dynamic link libraries (DLLs), and configuration files.
  - Changes to data, applications, or the machine state made by end user are propagated to the datacenter. Conversely, all changes the administrator makes to the base layer or app layers in the datacenter are propagated to the endpoints.
- **Horizon Mirage reference machine:** A Horizon Mirage reference machine is used to create a standard desktop base layer for a set of CVDs. This layer usually includes OS updates, service packs and patches, corporate applications for all target end users to use, and corporate configurations and policies. A reference machine is also used to capture app layers, which contain departmental or line-of-business applications and any updates or patches for already installed applications. You can maintain and update reference machines over time over the LAN or WAN, using a Horizon Mirage reference CVD in the datacenter. You can use the reference CVD at any time as a source for base and app layer capture.
- **Horizon Mirage branch reflector (optional):** A Horizon Mirage branch reflector is a peering service role that you can enable on any endpoint device. A branch reflector can then serve adjacent clients in the process of downloading and updating base or app layers on the site, instead of the clients downloading directly from the Horizon

Mirage Server cluster. Using a branch reflector can significantly reduce bandwidth use during mass base or app layer updates or other base or app layer download scenarios. The branch reflector also assists in downloading hardware drivers.

- **Horizon Mirage file portal:** End users can use appropriate login credentials and the Horizon Mirage file portal to access their data from any web browser. The file portal front-end component runs on any server machines that have IIS 7.0 or later installed, and the back-end component runs on the Management Server.

Prerequisites

Many components are involved in a Horizon Mirage deployment. Review Tables 9-1, 9-2, and 9-3 before moving forward with an actual deployment. Throughout this chapter, you will read about the deployment of 500 desktops. You might need to adjust with additional components if you plan to scale your deployment at a higher level than this.

Table 9-1 Environment Hardware

Number	Item	Specifications
500	Horizon Mirage Client	Enterprise class laptops and desktops. Minimum requirements: RAM: 512 MB (for Windows XP with SP2 or SP3 32-bit) 1 GB (for Windows 7 Professional or Enterprise, 32-bit and 64-bit) Free space: At least 5 GB for normal client operations
1+1*	Horizon Mirage Server node (virtual or physical server) (primary + failover)	Windows Server 2008 R2 Standard Edition, 64-bit. Domain membership required. Minimum requirements: RAM: 16 GB. CPU: 2x quad-core processor, 2.26-GHz Intel core speed or equivalent. System drive capacity: 146 GB. This includes a 100-GB allocation for the Horizon Mirage network cache. Note that this does not include Horizon Mirage SiS. See Horizon Mirage storage prerequisites discussed later. 2x Gigabit Ethernet port. Note that it is recommended to access the client network and storage network on separate dedicated ports.

Number	Item	Specifications
1	Horizon Mirage Management Server	Windows Server 2008 R2 Standard Edition, 64-bit Domain membership required
1 or more	Horizon Mirage Management Console	The Horizon Mirage Management Console can be installed on any Windows 7 machine in your environment. We recommend installing it at least on one of the Mirage Servers, and then on any administrative machine you will use for your deployment. Network connectivity to Horizon Mirage Management Server.
1	Horizon Mirage Web Management (optional)	It is recommended that you set up an additional Windows server (2008 R2 or 2012) with IIS Server installed to host the Horizon Mirage Web Management and the file portal. This is an optional component but highly recommended.

* +1 indicated for the Mirage Server and Management Server is to ensure that you have failover for your infrastructure. If you deploy Horizon Mirage as a virtual server, you can definitely leverage vSphere high availability (HA), but we also recommend having at least two servers for your production deployment; it makes the solution more robust.

You might need more servers, as discussed a little later in this chapter.

Table 9-2 Environment Software

Item	Specifications
Horizon Mirage Client	.NET Framework 3.5 SP1. Windows XP Professional with SP2 or SP3, 32-bit. Windows 7 Professional or Enterprise, 32-bit and 64-bit.
Horizon Mirage Server	Microsoft .NET Framework 3.5 SP1 64-bit. The file portal requires IIS 7.0 (or later) as well as the IIS 6 Management Compatibility role and ASP.NET feature (both options that are not selected by default when IIS is installed).
Horizon Mirage Management Server	Microsoft .NET Framework 3.5 SP1 64-bit
Management Console	Microsoft .NET Framework version 3.5 SP1. Microsoft Management Console (MMC) 3.0 (see http://support.microsoft.com/?kbid=907265).

Reference machine	Horizon Mirage Client. (Check Horizon Mirage documentation for the latest version.) Windows XP Professional with SP2 or SP3, 32-bit. Windows 7 Professional or Enterprise, 32-bit and 64-bit. Operating system and applications installed on the reference machine must use volume licenses and be designed for multiuser, multimachine deployment. Note: The reference machine should not include the following: Applications that install and use hardware-specific licenses. Applications that install and use local user accounts and/or local groups. Software that uses a proprietary update service. Such software must be installed directly on endpoints.

Table 9-3 Database and Ports

Item	Specifications
Database software	Microsoft SQL Server 2008 64-bit R2. All editions are supported (Express, Standard, and Enterprise) (http://msdn.microsoft.com/en-us/evalcenter/ff978728.aspx).
Database permissions	Microsoft SQL Server must be set up with Windows Authentication. The Windows account used for installing Horizon Mirage must have dbcreator privileges. The user account running the Horizon Mirage Server services must be configured with access privileges to the Horizon Mirage database.
Ports	8000: TCP/IP or SSL/TLS (External): Communications between Horizon Mirage Clients and Horizon Mirage Servers 8001: TCP/IP (External): Communication between the Branch reflector and the local peers at the remote site. 8443: TCP/IP (External: With SOAP message-level security): Communication between Horizon Mirage Management Console and Horizon Mirage Management service 135, 445: TCP/IP (Internal): To control communication between Horizon Mirage Management Service and Horizon Mirage Server. 8444: TCP/IP (Internal): Communication between the IIS server and the Horizon Mirage Management Server.

Storage Considerations

The Horizon Mirage Server cluster requires storage, which we recommend be either network-attached storage (NAS) connected using a Common Internet File System (CIFS) network share or NAS access via CIFS, and they must support alternative data streams. The discussion about architecture in this chapter explains what should be used for a deployment of 500 desktops based on the use case introduced at the beginning of this chapter (backup/centralization, and OS/app layering).

External Dependencies

In a Horizon Mirage deployment, the infrastructure needs to rely on a few other components. These components were listed in the previous tables. To ensure that none are missed, we are including them here:

- **Active Directory:** All the Mirage Servers need to be part of the domain. In theory, it might be possible to work without it, but in most cases Mirage will be managing enterprise desktops connected to an Active Directory domain. All the desktops you will want to manage are part of a domain; Horizon Mirage Servers need to be part of that same domain.
- **SQL Server:** In a small proof-of-concept or lab deployment, you might get away with SQL Server Express. This would save you a license cost. For a production deployment, however, you should use SQL Server 2008 R2 as your official Mirage database.

Mirage Architecture

Mirage Server (or a cluster of Mirage Servers) manages desktop images in the datacenter and orchestrates uploads and downloads between datacenter desktop images and Mirage-managed endpoints. Storage disks in the datacenter contain the desktop images and base and application layers. The Mirage database contains pointers to the base and application layers and desktop images in storage, and also an inventory of what is on the endpoints. The database catalogs the information; the storage contains the actual information. Each Mirage-managed physical or virtual computer has the Mirage Client installed, which communicates closely with the Mirage Server to synchronize the datacenter desktop image with changes to the endpoint. Figure 9-2 shows the architecture for the Horizon Mirage.

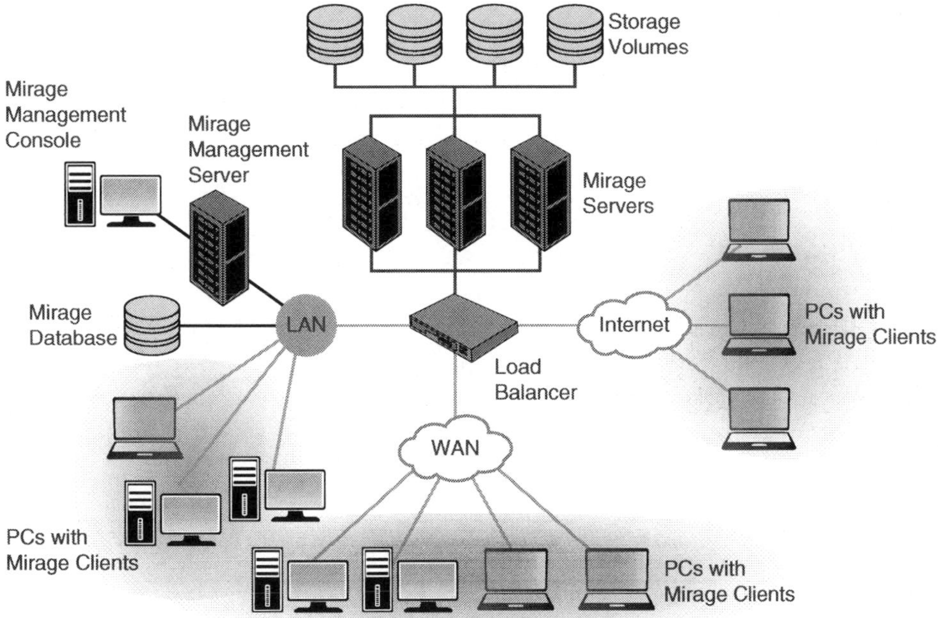

Figure 9-2 Horizon Mirage Architecture

Deploying Horizon Mirage Management Server

The first server you want to deploy is the Mirage Management Server. As discussed before, it's the server that manages desktop images in the datacenter and orchestrates uploads and downloads between datacenter desktop images and Mirage-managed endpoints.

The Horizon Mirage installation file comes in the form of an archive, from the VMware download site. Download the file and extract all the files contained within the archive. Once downloaded, click the MSI package called VMware_Horizon_Mirage_xxx.xxxxx.zip. (The X's are the version number.) After you have extracted the files, you will have five folders:

- BootUSB, tools to create a USB boot disk for Mirage Clients
- Client, the clients installation file, x86 and x64
- EdgeServer, folder with the executables installation files for Mirage Edge Server
- Server, the installation files for all the server components
- WebManagement, Web Management software (to install with IIS server)

At this stage, we're interested in the Server folder. As a prerequisite to the installation of the Horizon Mirage Management Server, you need to make sure that you have a SQL server available where you have permission to create a database and have permission for the Mirage Service account to interact with that server. Make sure that you know the SQL server name and the instance name (by default, MSSQLSERVER or MSSQL or SQLEXPRESS). The installation file is called mirage.management.server.x64.xxxxx. It is an MSI package, so just double-click it to launch installation. You will see that the installation process is straightforward (as long as you have met all the prerequisites and have all the information handy). As mentioned before, one of the few requirements for the Windows Server 2008 R2 where you will install Horizon Mirage is to make sure that .NET Framework 3.5 is installed (see Figure 9-3). In contrast with a regular Windows desktop, installing .NET Framework 3.5 on a server will require that you complete this through the Features Wizard. If you have started with a plain install of that server, you will also be prompted to add the required dependent role.

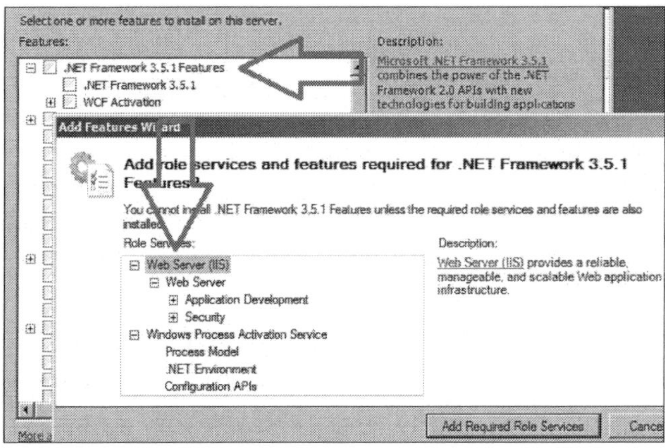

Figure 9-3 .NET Framework server feature

Again here, if this is a plain installation of Windows Server 2008 R2, you will also get prompted to add the related IIS feature. Because we will be configuring the Mirage file portal later in this chapter, we might as well configure the required IIS feature you will need for the file portal to work. In a production deployment of scale, design best practice is to separate this role on a different, dedicated server. For a smaller deployment like the one in this book, we can make an exception and keep this role on the same server. Figure 9-4 shows you the role services for the IIS Web Server component.

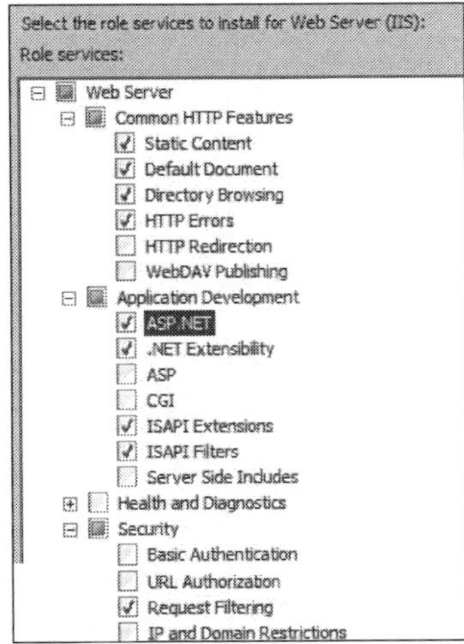

Figure 9-4 IIS required services for the Mirage file portal

Notice that the default Role services are not all checked; be sure to check all the Service roles displayed in this figure.

Going back to the Horizon Mirage Management Server installation, after you have clicked the installation file, you will need to accept the end-user license agreement (EULA). Then, you are asked to provide the SQL server name and the instance name (which you noted in the prerequisites step).

Make sure that you check the **Create new storage areas** check box, and as you will see in the wizard (see Figure 9-5), if you're using a network share (which we recommended earlier that you should), be sure to utilize a Universal Naming Convention (UNC) path with proper access permission.

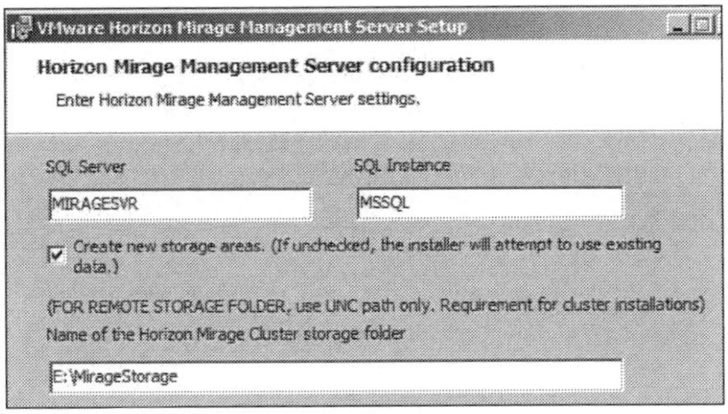

Figure 9-5 Mirage storage area

In this example, we're pointing to local storage. In a production environment, however, you should go with a network share, CIFS or otherwise.

The next screen asks you for proper credentials to connect to Active Directory; our recommendation is to use a service account that has domain admin privilege. Recommended security best practice is to create a dedicated account for your deployment. Give it Domain Admin rights and use that account for your deployment. Do the same for the group when asked to specify a group for the deployment; it would be best practice to create a dedicated group for the deployment, something along the lines of MirageAdmins, for example (something that can easily be identified if you need to do any kind of log inspection in the future).

Click **Next**, and then click **Install**. There are no other options to configure at this point (as mentioned, very straightforward).

The next step is to install the Mirage Management console. This installation requires no special configuration and no parameters to enter. Just launch the file mirage.management.console.x64.xxxxx and follow the onscreen wizard.

We highly recommend deploying the console on the Management Server and also on at least one of your administrator Windows 7 management desktops. Installing it on the Management Server is just for initial testing and configuration. In a production deployment, you will most likely do all your management from your administrator's PC.

Before we move on to installing the Mirage Server, let's go in the Management Console and configure the Horizon Mirage Management Server.

Once the console is open, right-click **VMware Horizon Mirage** and choose **Add System** (see Figure 9-6). If you are doing this from the server itself, you can then enter **Localhost** in the message box that will appear. If you are doing this from a Windows 7 administrative machine where you deployed the Management Console, make sure to use the hostname of the Mirage Management Server.

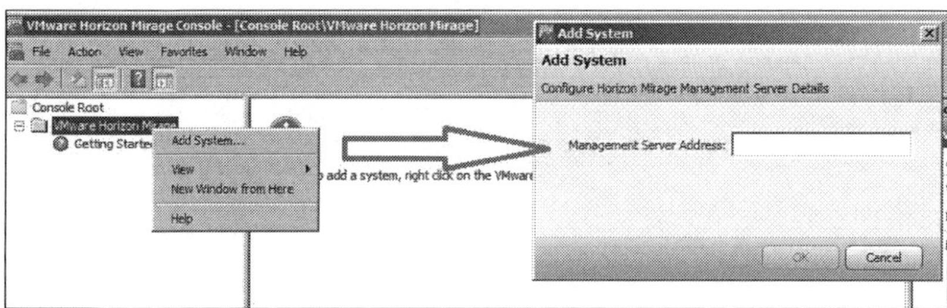

Figure 9-6 Adding the Mirage Management Server

Now, we should configure the system. Go in the System Configuration section, select it, and then right-click it and choose **Settings**. The first tab (General) is the main one and is the one that requires the most amount of configuration.

First, let's configure snapshots. Horizon Mirage snapshots are a centrally retained point-in-time image of CVD content, including OS, applications, and user data, which enables complete restoration of a specific endpoint or a specific file. The Horizon Mirage Server generates snapshots and keeps generations of snapshots available according to a retention policy. It is important to note that the number of snapshots you keep will impact the storage you will need on the server.

For example, in the hour intervals, if you put a number there, this will mean that Mirage will keep that number of consecutively generated snapshots that the system keeps. The default number is zero, as shown in Figure 9-7.

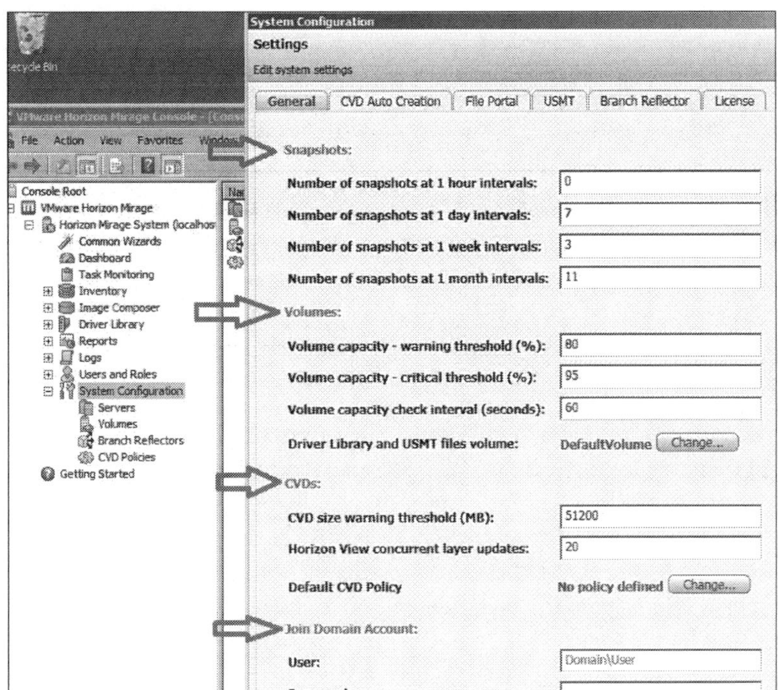

Figure 9-7 Mirage Management Server settings

If you were to put a different value (for example, 8), this would mean that the system always keeps the latest eight successful CVD snapshots in this category. Historical snapshots older than the latest eight are discarded. However, if daily snapshot retention is defined (as shown in Figure 9-7), whenever a first snapshot of a new day is created, the oldest snapshot in the hourly category becomes a candidate as the newest daily snapshot. The default number of hourly snapshots is zero, meaning new snapshots are not kept as they are created.

So, if all four categories were used, you would have the following:

- Last successful hourly becomes candidate for first daily.
- Last successful daily becomes candidate for first weekly.
- Last successful weekly becomes candidate for first monthly.

The next category is to configure the CVDs. The size warning threshold is important again here, to properly keep tract of storage used and when some CVDs might fall out of policy. The number there indicates the maximum size to expect from a CVD. If this number is exceeded, the Mirage administrator is alerted. Reminder: To be successful, know and understand your use case. So, because you know your organization environment, you will be able to figure out the disk space size utilized by the biggest desktop within that environment and put a number in the size warning treshold that makes sense for you.

The volumes section is straightforward; all fields relate to the storage area you created earlier. You want to make sure that you are warned when that storage space is getting full. Put numbers in there that you feel confident will give you sufficient reaction time when it reaches the defined threshold. The Driver Library and USMT file volume button enable you to choose where these files will be located. Look at the default setting and decide whether that location works for you. By default, it uses the same storage area you created during the initial installation.

The next setting is new starting with Horizon Mirage 4.3. In a physical PC management world, you do not need to worry as much about the concurrent number of layer operations being done; all endpoints use local resources available to them on physical PCs. In a virtual world, where all the desktops run on vSphere servers in the datacenter, it is important to know how many layers should be done concurrently; we've seen cases where setting a number too high could potentially bring a server to its knees. The default number is 20, which we think is too high to start with. If you're going to manage virtual desktops, a good rule of thumb to start with is to put two concurrent layer updates at a time per physical vSphere host you have. Typically in a Horizon View cluster, you will have more than one host. If you have three hosts, for example, you could put 6 in that field and feel safe that your environment will not be crippled by these layer updates. Naturally, the more you use the solution, the more comfortable you'll become with a higher number; the key is to monitor server performance. The upside of a higher number is that the number of machines that receive their layer update will be higher, in turn making the whole deployment of that layer quicker. The lower the number, the more time it will take to finish deploying that layer.

The next section covers the default CVD policy. For now, if it is your initial installation of the product, you will find that you have two policies already created: the default Mirage CVD policy, and another one optimized for Horizon View desktops. We discuss both policies later in this chapter. For now, though, you can choose the first policy.

The last section in this tab is to configure the account you will use to join the domain. This is important; you need that account when doing any operations that use domain join operations, and Mirage needs to be able to automatically insert the machine account into the domain. We recommend using the same account you used earlier, a Domain Admin account dedicated to Horizon Mirage (keeping in mind that this account would not be used for anything other than Mirage administrative operations and should be closely monitored by normal audit operations).

The CVD Auto Creation tab and the File Portal tab stay unchanged for now; we will configure each of these later.

The USMT tab is very important. USMT stands for User State Migration Tool, which is a Microsoft tool that Horizon Mirage leverages during migration operation to migrate the user profile from the old machine to the new one. For example, you have a user running on Windows XP, he has a domain account, and he has configured and personalized his desktop to his liking (changed background image, saved files in his documents and settings, and so on). You migrate that user to Windows 7 (you learn how later), and you want that user to keep his personal things (a customization that makes him good). That's the main goal of USMT: to migrate information from a Windows XP profile to a Windows 7 profile.

You need to go on the Microsoft.com website to retrieve the USMT tool. Starting with Horizon Mirage 4.4, you can use USMT 4.0 and 5.0 with the solution. In most cases, version 4 of USMT will be used. However, if you need to manage Windows 8.1 OS, you need version 5.0 of USMT.

We will not change the Branch Reflector tab information for now, and the last tab is the License tab, which you previously filled in when setting up the server.

You have completed the basic configuration of Horizon Mirage Management Server. Let's move on to the Mirage Server installation and configuration.

Horizon Mirage Server

As previously mentioned, the Horizon Mirage Server manages the storage and delivery of base layers, app layers, and CVDs to clients and consolidates monitoring and management communications.

From the folder where you extracted your RAR archive before, go back in the Server folder and locate the file named mirage.server.x64.xxxxx. The next step is to log in to your virtual or physical Windows 2008 R2 server. Keep in mind that in a production deployment, the Horizon Mirage Management Server and the Horizon Server are not on the same server. (See the hardware specifications earlier in this chapter.)

After you've accepted the EULA, you will see a screen in the wizard that looks like the one from the Mirage Server installation screen. You are asked to enter the SQL server information and the SQL instance name. This is the same information you entered in the previous installation. Then, be sure to check the **Create new local cache area** box.

The Horizon Mirage cache is storage of popular blocks of information that Mirage keeps to perform data deduplication over the WAN. When large files are transferred, their blocks are kept in the cache, and the next time similar files need to be transferred, the server obtains the blocks from the cache instead of over the network. It is good practice to keep the cache on fast storage (for example, on a local drive or even on a solid-state drive [SSD]).

You do not need to back up that folder; the default size suggested by VMware is 100 GB. This might appear to be a big number for cache, but it is used often in a mixed deployment, and you will be glad to have put a number there that will bring the bandwidth chatter down.

The next screen asks you to enter transport configuration information. In a production deployment, it is definitely recommended to have a certificate for the Mirage Server; this ensures additional security of the connection, which is sent in clear text otherwise.

The last configuration step is to enter the Mirage Service account and password. You should use the same account used earlier, dedicated to Mirage. You click **Install** and **Finish** when done.

Note that when you have completed the installation of the Mirage Server, you must reboot that server for all the changes to take effect.

You have now completed the basic installation of a Horizon Mirage deployment. The next section covers the process of building the CVDs, which includes centralization of the endpoint, creation of reference machines, and deployment of OS layers.

Mirage Day-to-Day Administration

One feature of Horizon Mirage is that it enables you to centralize an endpoint. Centralizing an endpoint means that you basically do a snapshot at a specific point in time of the whole machine and send that blob of data to your SiS. There are two distinct reasons to do this. The first one is when you plan a migration of a critical PC from a particular OS to a newer one (in our case, going from Windows XP to Windows 7). Organizations that manage data outside of the endpoint might not need to do centralization before OS migration, but any endpoint deemed critical should be centralized before migration. Centralizing an endpoint before doing any operations on it will permit a rollback in case of failure or other reasons. The second, less frequent use case is to make backups of the endpoint at regular intervals. This will happen to a few of your users. Keep in mind that activating this for all your users, even with data deduplication, would consume a lot of disk space. So, not to sound like a broken record, but it's all about knowing your use case. Constant endpoint backup, at regularly timed intervals, is required for a very few number of people within an organization, especially if your environment has a good data and application processes.

So, find out which of your users need this feature active all the time and also which of your users might require this for a one-time migration.

After you have properly identified each group, you can start centralizing the desktop.

The first step is to install the Mirage Client on the endpoint. Just log in with an account that has local administrative permissions (a requirement to install any software, courtesy of Microsoft), and then install the client from the Client folder (going back to the zip archive previously expanded). There's no other option to specify for a client but the hostname or IP address of the Mirage Server, as shown in Figure 9-8.

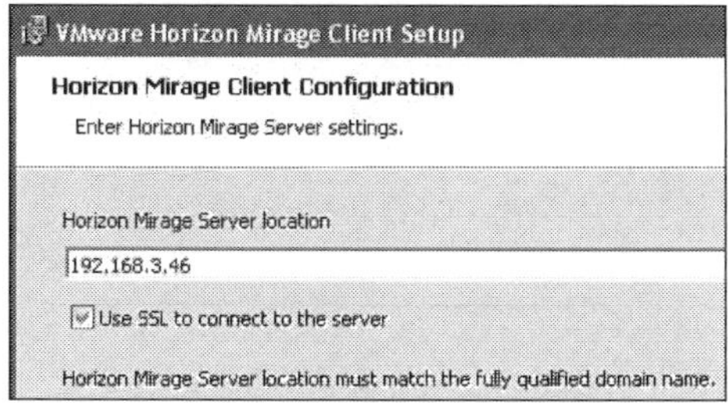

Figure 9-8 Mirage Client installation

Once the installation is complete, you can leave the endpoint as is, or you can reboot it to shorten the upload cycles. If you do not reboot the endpoint, it will follow the upload policy you created previously and send its information at the next synchronization cycle, as shown in Figure 9-9. If you reboot the client right away, it will send the information upon reboot.

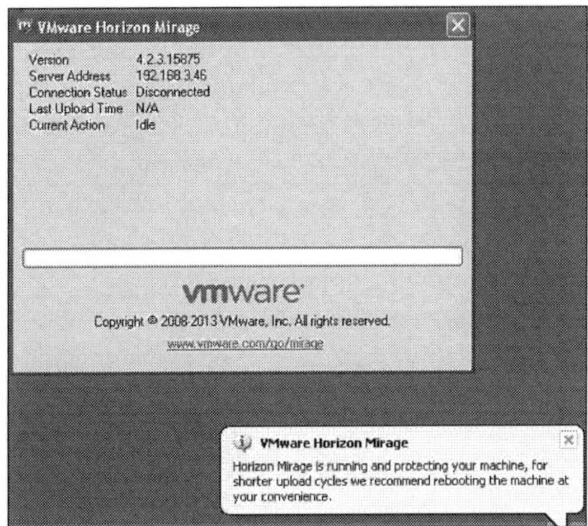

Figure 9-9 Pending client reboot

One very cool feature of the Horizon Mirage Client is to always keep the latest version installed. It will detect, as soon as can reach the Horizon Mirage Server, whether it's running the latest version of the client. You do not need to worry about upgrading your Mirage Client; as long as the endpoint can reach the Mirage Server, it will update itself automatically. In Figure 9-10, we installed on an endpoint an older version of a client, and after installation completed, it exchanged information with the Mirage Server, saw that it did not have the latest version, pulled down the latest version, and installed itself automatically.

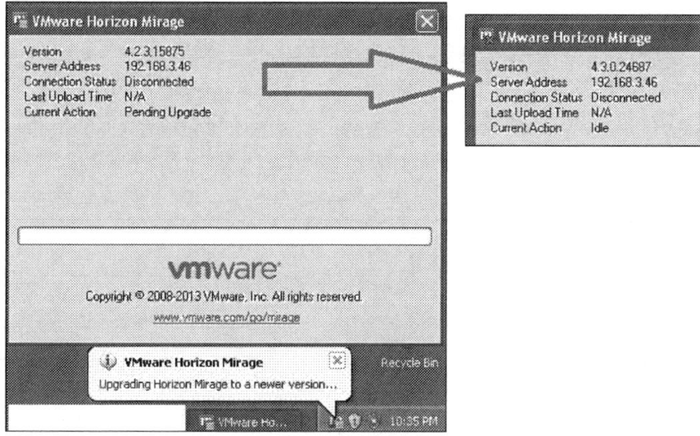

Figure 9-10 Automatic Mirage Client upgrade

After you've completed the installation of the Mirage Client, after the next upload cycle, you will see the endpoint appear in the Pending Devices section of the console (see Figure 9-11). Let's centralize the endpoint by clicking it and choosing **Centralize Endpoint**. Next, you will have to choose the Horizon Mirage CVD upload policy that is appropriate for that endpoint, and then click **Next**. In Figure 9-11, you will see that you could apply directly a base OS layer to the endpoint. For the current centralization, we will not automatically deploy a base layer, but we will come back to that process later.

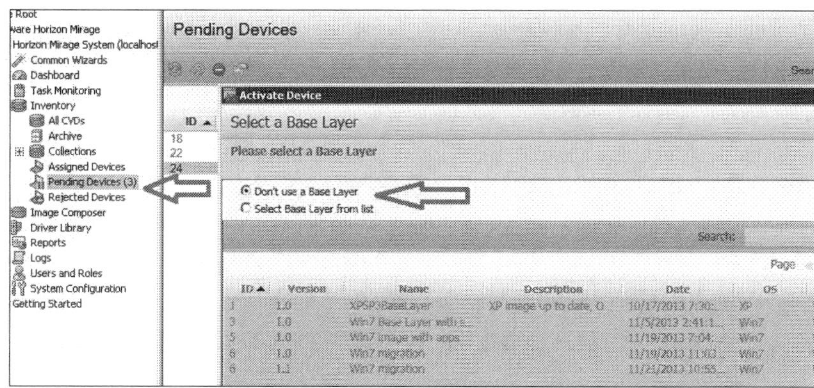

Figure 9-11 Pending devices: base layer

The next screen asks you to choose the volume. By default, it offers to automatically choose the volume. If you have configured more than one volume, you might need to change the choice from automatic to manually choose a volume. At the compatibility check screen, click **Next**. You will then be at the Summary screen, where you click **Finish**. Once that is done, the Mirage Server automatically starts to centralize the endpoint, sending the command to the endpoint. Centralization time varies based on a lot of factors; it depends on how many centralizations you start concurrently at any given time, and it also depends on bandwidth and on the endpoint itself (resources of that machine).

Not a lot indicates that the centralization process is occurring; that specific task does not appear in the Task Monitoring section. It shows up only in the All CVDs container. To view the current centralization process, click **All CVDs**, and then you will see the progress of the endpoint currently being centralized, as shown in Figure 9-12.

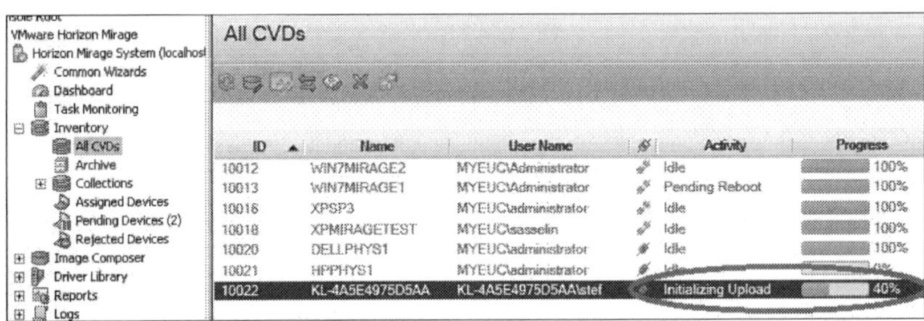

Figure 9-12 Endpoint centralization

Horizon Mirage Endpoint Restoration

The centralization process should complete eventually. The time it takes to centralize an endpoint depends on the number of endpoint being centralized, bandwidth, and available resources. Another important factor that influences centralization time is whether the data is already present. For example, if you are centralizing a lot of Windows XP endpoints, the base operating system will be similar in a lot of cases. Horizon Mirage can deduplicate the information and send only unique data back to the SiS, greatly reducing the total amount of data being sent.

You can now go in the Mirage Management Console and restore the endpoint. You can do this for any endpoints that were successfully centralized. Choose an endpoint, right-click it, and choose **Revert to Snapshot**.

This is a scenario where you centralized someone's endpoint and something happened to it (a hardware or software failure). You need that person to be able to go back to a point in time where the PC was working properly. This process of Mirage is very good because it will restore the snapshot, copying the files over without a lot of impact to the end user. There's a good chance that the end user is unable to work at this point anyway; if the user can still continue to do work, this is a very useful feature.

As shown in Figure 9-13, the Revert to Snapshot Wizard contains only one available snapshot. If your environment has been running for a while, you might have more than one here. Be sure to choose the one that works for your user.

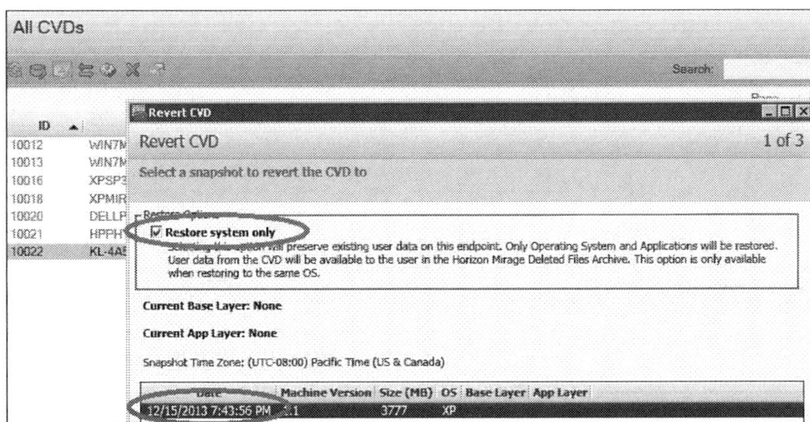

Figure 9-13 Revert to snapshot

The other important decision point is whether you will restore everything or just the system. This is very important; if you decide to restore everything, you uncheck the **Restore system only** check box. The end result will be that the user will go back to the point in time mentioned in the snapshot window. The side effect is that if the user has saved any files locally since or if he installed any applications, those changes will be lost.

That discussion needs to happen before the action is triggered with the user. That person will understand that he will go back in time to a working state, but very often he won't understand the consequences of a full restore compared to a system-only restore.

Horizon Mirage Base Layer

One of the main goals of Horizon Mirage is to build a base OS layer that you will distribute to all the managed endpoints in your organization. In that layer, you should find the basic operating system, patched with all the Microsoft updates and up-to-date. You should put there any common applications you find in all the desktops within your organization (for example, basic applications such as Adobe Reader, Flash Player, a compression utility of some sort, and in most cases, Microsoft Office). Ensure that you build a clean image, one that has no unwanted clutter. You also want to build an image that has the basic drivers in them but nothing too specific. We will build a driver library later in this chapter. One common mistake is to forget to put at least a network driver for the endpoints to keep communication with the Horizon Mirage Server. In the end, if there's no network connectivity, there will be no interaction between the endpoints and the server, so the end result is that the process will not complete successfully.

Horizon Mirage base layer provisioning is not the same as doing a migration. Base layer provisioning reimages the endpoint, so you can only provision the same OS to the same OS. If you want to push a CVD to an endpoint from a different OS (for example, XP to Windows 7), you must follow the Migration Wizard in Mirage, which is covered later in this chapter.

We like to use a virtual image. It provides more flexibility in the image creation, and it also allows you to have multiple stages of the image-building process because of the built-in snapshot functionality of VMware Workstation or Fusion or even vSphere. If you build a solid reference image combined with a good driver library (*good* meaning to accurately reflect your organization hardware), a virtual image will work great. If you are unsure about the hardware, you should build reference images based on groups of hardware. This will give you more images to manage but better results when pushing base layers to your endpoints.

Let's dig in by going in the Mirage Management Console to build the reference machine. We will assume that you have built the reference machine the way you want it to look like and that you have installed the Mirage Client on it. Now the reference machine should be in the Pending Devices section of your Inventory section.

Right-click the machine and choose to create a CVD reference machine, as indicated in Figure 9-14.

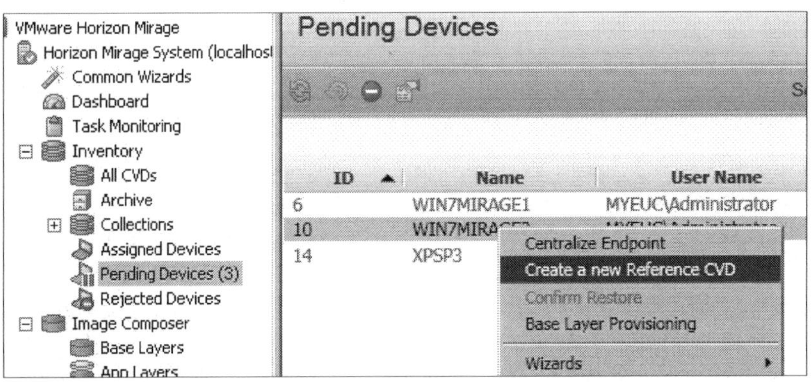

Figure 9-14 Create a new reference CVD

Two choices will appear: base layer and app layer. The app layer, if you've been following the steps since the beginning of the chapter, should still be grayed out (as explained a little later in this chapter).

On the next screen, you choose the CVD upload policy. Make sure to use the one that will link to this Reference CVD and all endpoints that will later be using this base layer. Then, the next screen gives you the choice to use a base layer. In this case, we will not use a base layer, and here is why.

You could have a use case where you are building a reference machine but it is not quite at the level you want it to be. For example, you have a physical HP desktop running Windows 7 Pro. It's been managed by Mirage for a while now; that specific model is used in a lot of different groups within your organization. What you want to do is push an up-to-date version of Windows 7 Pro to that HP desktop to make sure that it receives all the latest Microsoft updates, all the base common software, and the proper drivers. Then, you want to use that machine as a new reference machine for all future HP desktops of the same model. Hence, building one cleanly and efficiently, everything being done remotely, you can now push that reference CVD to all other HP desktops of the same model and rest assured that they will have the same look and feel, while keeping the user data.

Now, back to our reference machine build process. The next screen is the choice of the Mirage volume. Here again, you can let Mirage choose the volume automatically for you or you can manually choose it. The last screen is the compatibility check. If there's anything wrong with the choices you've made and if the image has a missing component, it will list it here; otherwise, it will be a green check mark next to it, and there will be nothing to configure on the page.

You have now created your first reference machine. The process will take a while to complete; you can monitor the creation process by going in the Task Monitoring section of the Mirage Management Console.

Now that you have the reference CVD, you need to capture the base layer. The base layer is a snapshot in time of the reference CVD. It contains everything from that machine and makes it ready to deploy to other endpoints.

We recommend going through the Common Wizards section and clicking the **Capture Base Layer** button. Once the wizard starts, choose to use an existing CVD. We will use the one we just finished creating in the previous steps. Choose **Use an Existing Reference CVD** and click **Next**. The next screen offers you a choice of the existing CVDs; pick the one we just created and click **Next**. Give the layer a name, something meaningful to distinguish it when you will see it listed among all the other base layers, and then click **Next**. The next screen is the Check Compatibility screen. This is where it will validate information like the type of Windows license. After ensuring that you have passed all the compatibility checks, click **Next**. A summary page will then appear. Click **Finish**. Figure 9-15 shows two base layers completed in a Mirage environment.

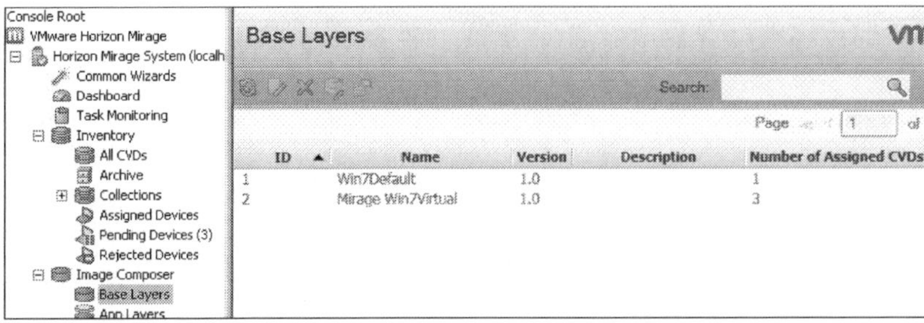

Figure 9-15 Base layers example

When the process is complete, you are now ready to deploy that new base layer to your endpoints.

Deploying Mirage Base Layer

At this point, you have created one or more base OS layers and are ready to deploy those layers to your organization endpoints. We first discuss how to deploy a single layer, and then we cover the more elaborated scenarios of creating static and dynamic CVD collections. You can deploy a base layer either by going in your Pending Devices section and choosing an endpoint listed there or by going to the All CVDs section and choosing an endpoint there. If you decide to start with an endpoint that's pending, right-click it and choose base layer provisioning; this will open up the wizard so that you can provision that endpoint. Remember that base layer provisioning does not mean the same thing as XP to Windows 7 migration. Remember that deploying a base layer will reimage the endpoint.

The process to deploy a single base OS layer begins by going in the All CVDs section or the Collections section (you will learn how to build a collection later in this chapter) and choosing the endpoint. Once the wizard is started, you need to choose the layer you want to apply to that endpoint. Clicking the layer will display all its properties at the bottom of the page, information like the installed programs, the services, drivers, and license keys information. You can even compare the base layer by clicking the **Compare Programs with Layers** button shown in Figure 9-16.

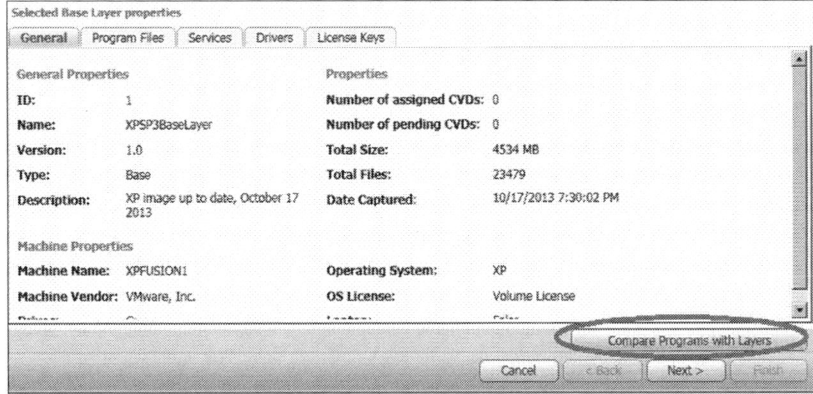

Figure 9-16 Base layer comparison

This will launch a web browser and show you the differences between the reference CVD and the endpoint you are provisioning. This is a useful feature and should be used to validate your deployment. Make sure that you don't make any big *faux pas* or miss something obvious.

The next page shows your image validation (if the endpoint types are similar and OS is the same). The last page gives you a brief summary, and you are now ready to apply the base OS layer to that endpoint. Keep in mind that depending on the differences between the endpoint you're provisioning to and the reference CVD, a reboot might be required; it depends on the content of the layer you're pushing.

Horizon Mirage Layer Updates

Microsoft and other software vendors share important information with us occasionally (every second Tuesday of the month in Microsoft's case), telling us how many patches we need to apply to the operating system. Those patches can range from very few, noncritical if we're lucky, all the way to high-critical viruses, preventing pandemic proportion if we're unlucky. So, you will most likely need to update the base layer or layers once a month, if not more often. Horizon Mirage provides a simple way to update the layer and, even more fun, an easy way to bring all the endpoints linked to that layer up-to-date as well.

To update a base layer, go in the Reference CVDs section and choose the endpoint that has been updated. Right-click it and choose **Capture Base Layers**. You then have two choices: create a new base layer or update an existing one. In our case, let's say that the CVD was just updated with a dozen Microsoft security fixes and is now up-to-date, so we want to update the layer with a minor version revision, as shown in Figure 9-17.

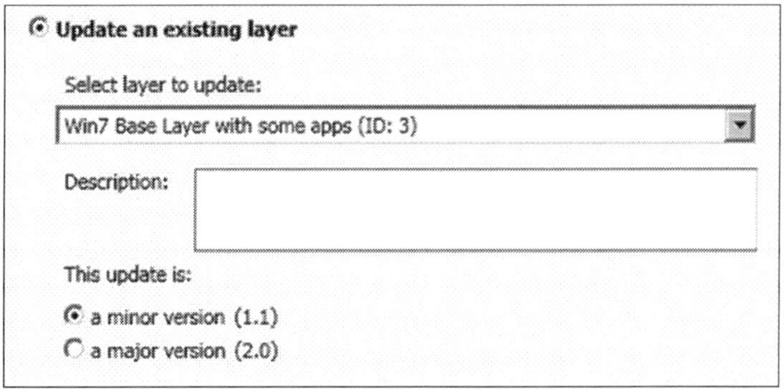

Figure 9-17 Base layer update

Go through the rest of the wizard and click **Finish**. After doing so, you will have a new base layer (in our case, version 1.1), and you are ready to deploy it to your endpoints.

Horizon Mirage Endpoint Migration

Now that we have covered the base layer provisioning, let's take a look the migration of an endpoint. A successful migration requires the following:

- Horizon Mirage Windows 7 reference CVD or a base layer containing a Windows 7 image
- User State Migration Tool (USMT) deployed
- Endpoint to migrate (XP or Vista)

We will assume that you have all these ready, and we will talk about the migration itself. In the Horizon Mirage Management Console, in the Common Wizards section, click the **Windows 7 Migration** button to start the wizard. On the first screen that appears, select the CVDs that you want to migrate or select the collection. You can multiselect CVDs, migrating them all at once, or you can choose to migrate only one CVD.

The next step is to choose the base layer you want to apply to the endpoint. You have two important choices. You can choose to download and apply the base layer or only download the base layer. The key thing to remember is that you want to control when the user will have downtime. If you can plan and schedule user downtime, let them know what's coming and when, you will most likely have happier users. If you choose to only download the base layer, it will copy everything over but not start the migration process. If you choose to download and apply, the migration process will start when the download has completed.

The next screen presents you with the existing app layers (if you have any). Here, you can choose the applications you want added to the targeted endpoint when the migration is being done, fully automating the endpoint migration (OS, data, and applications). Then, you will get the Target Machine Name screen. This is where you specify where to place the CVD in your Active Directory; in most cases, it will stay in the same OU, but at least you get the opportunity to change this if you need to. The field at the bottom is the Join Domain Account. Make sure that the account listed here (which we configured during initial setup) still has proper rights to add computer accounts to the domain.

The last page gives you a summary, as shown in Figure 9-18. If you think you missed something or some information is incorrect, you can always go back. When you click **Finish**, the process starts, and the endpoint begins its migration.

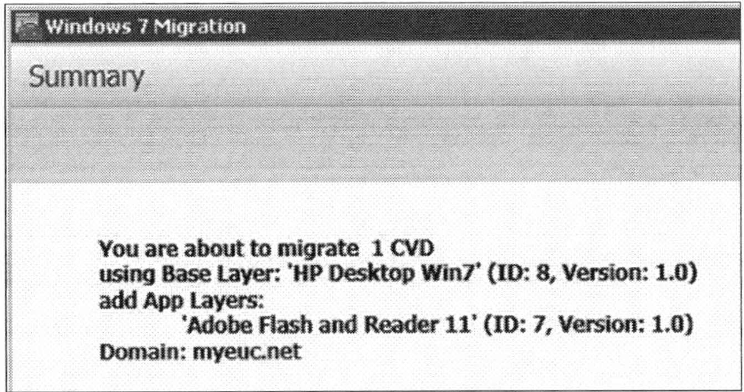

Figure 9-18 CVD migration

You can also go on the endpoint and look at the Mirage Client status. Because this is a full desktop OS migration, including applications and data, the end user will lose access to its machine at some point while this is happening. The good news is that user downtime is minimal and the user will see the steps; Horizon Mirage displays onscreen the steps it's going through. There are no details on the steps, but here is a list of those steps from our understanding:

1. Centralization: The Mirage Client takes a VSS snapshot, scans all files that match the upload policy, and calculates MD5 signature of the file. This results in an upload manifest. This manifest is then sent to the server, which calculates what actually needs to be uploaded, taking into account all the files that the server all ready has (deduplication), and sends the deduplication manifest to the client.

2. The client then uploads the files.

3. The client will from now on start an upload cycle as described previously once the time passed from the last upload is greater than the time specified in the assigned policy.
4. Each time the client connects to the server, it checks what it has to do. Most times, the chosen action is to upload, but if you assign a layer (or start Windows 7 migration), it will do that instead.
5. Once you assign a layer (or Windows 7 migration, in this case), the client will again take a VSS and scan all the files that match the upload policy.
6. The server sends a manifest of the layer that should be downloaded, and this time it's the client that calculates which files actually need to be downloaded. It's important to note that if there hasn't been a successful upload within the assigned upload interval (from the policy) or 6 hours, the client will first start an upload before the layer assignment.
7. The client then starts the download of the layer. It first scans for branch reflectors.
8. The client downloads the entire image.
9. While the layer is being downloaded, the client starts processing the downloaded files and prepares the layer for deployment.

   Mirage does not run generalization tools on the layer at the capture, but rather on the deployment. This will include removing the machine name from the layer, for example. Some drivers will be removed from the layer, as non-PnP drivers and legacy drivers from the layer won't necessarily match the CVD. Remove some registry keys for known software according to their guidelines for creating images. One example is McAfee ePO agent.
10. The resulting registry hives that will be applied after the layer assignment are saved and the pivot files are generated.
11. The Mirage Client asks for a reboot. Because the resulting registry hives and pivot file were already created, and changes from now on won't be reflected on these files, it is critical that the client boots ASAP.
12. The machine will boot, and the pivot will come into play. The pivot (in case of Windows 7 migration) will move the old XP or Vista into <Volume>:\Windows.old and move the downloaded layer into <Volume>.
13. The pivot will also fix the MBR if needed; this happens in a Windows 7 migration.
14. The CVD boots in Windows 7.
15. Post-installation processing starts running.

16. Another boot occurs, because the Plug-and-Play detection process and joining a domain require such a reboot.
17. The machine was migrated to Windows 7.
18. The CVD starts an upload. The server uses this upload as a way to know that the layer assignment was successful.
19. From an end-user standpoint, the user will continue to work until the pivot happens. Figure 9-19 shows what the user sees when the process has started.

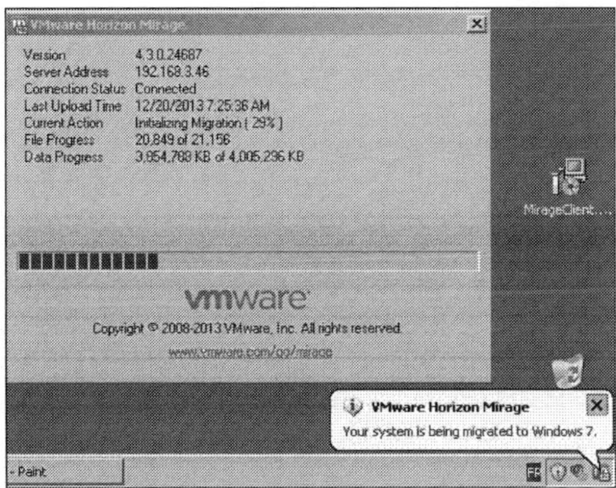

Figure 9-19 Horizon Mirage endpoint migration notification

After all of these steps have been completed, the user will be at the login screen of his migrated endpoint, domain joined, application installed, and data migrated.

Horizon Mirage File Portal

We decided to put this section here because this is a feature that is used by the end user, and when the centralization that we made completes, you will be able to have your end user try the file portal.

Installing the Horizon Mirage file portal is straightforward. Go back to your Horizon Mirage installation folder. Look for a file called mirage.WebAccess.x64.xxxxx. Install the component on the Horizon Mirage server; follow the onscreen wizard and click **Install**.

Once complete, you can validate that the installation was successful by going in the IIS Server Management Console, under the Sites web folder and look for the Explorer virtual folder.

The other step you need to complete is to go to the Horizon Mirage Management Console, under System Configuration Properties, and display the File Portal tab. You need to enable the file portal, and then specify the Horizon Mirage URL. You can either enter the fully qualified domain name (FQDN) or the IP address for the Horizon Mirage server and add **/Explorer** at the end. It should look similar to Figure 9-20.

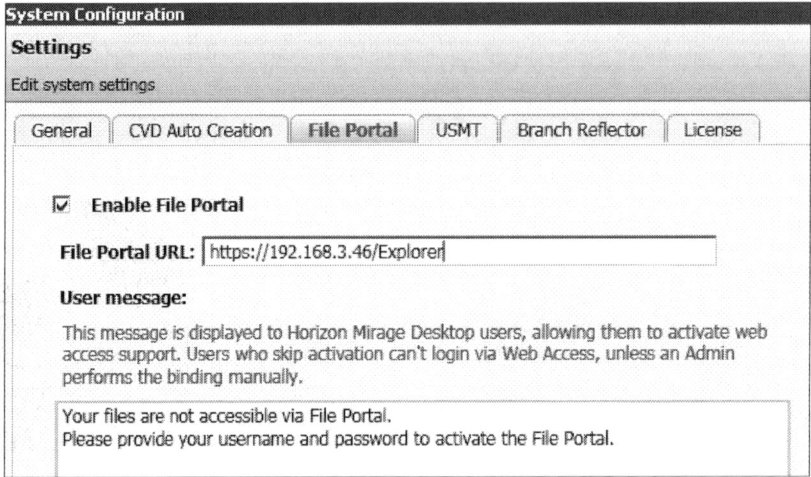

Figure 9-20 Horizon Mirage file portal

Enabling this file portal will permit users to go in that file portal and look at their files and do a file restore if they want to. Keep in mind that they will be able to restore files that follow the upload policy we set up earlier in this chapter, and remember that any files outside of the profile will not be included.

If you have used/logged in more than one CVD, you will have more than one profile stored (if using local profiles on those CVDs and not centralized profile through a third party or Microsoft roaming profiles).

If this is the case, you will have a list of multiple PCs. You choose the PC you want to inspect and click on it. From there, the users will go and navigate to the folder structure, look at the files they want to retrieve, and obtain them.

Also keep in mind that you might have more than one version of that file; make sure that you remind your user to look at the file time stamp. Figure 9-21 shows what a Horizon Mirage user sees from a browser when logging in to the file portal.

Figure 9-21 Horizon Mirage file portal

Enabling the Horizon Mirage file portal brings down the recovery time for users to get to their files. It is a great self-service tool; it helps users become independent with regard to file restore, and it will make the IT administrator look like a rock star. It's an easy feature to implement; it's very visible to end users.

This feature is also available through the Windows Explorer of the CVD, the end-user PC. Ask your user to test the feature or test it yourself. In Windows Explorer, right-click a file and you should see a screen similar to that shown in Figure 9-22.

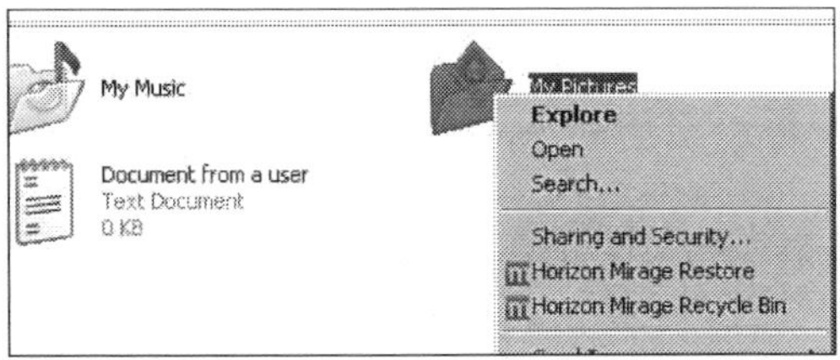

Figure 9-22 Horizon Mirage user file restore

The difference between the two options is easy. If the file is still there, you can do a Horizon Mirage restore. If the file is no longer accessible, you need to inspect the Horizon Mirage Recycle Bin for that file.

Horizon Mirage Web Management

You first need to set up Horizon Mirage Web Management on the server side. At the beginning of this chapter, we extracted a set of folders. From the Mirage Server, go into the WebManagement folder and look for the file mirage.webmanagement.x64.xxxxx. (The X's are the build number.) Here again, as in the previous installation, it is pretty straightforward. Launch the MSI package and follow the wizard. You don't really have anything to configure. Just specify the name of the Mirage Server, nothing more.

Once installed, you can go in the IIS console and validate that the Web Management components were installed by looking for the Horizon Mirage Virtual Folder under the Sites Web folder.

You should then go into a web browser and access the Web Management interface. To do so, point to Horizon Mirage Server folder https://HorizonMirageServer/Horizon Mirage. You will see something that will look like Figure 9-23. Keep in mind that at the time of this writing, the Mirage Console had more features than the Web Management console. VMware is working on getting feature parity for the Web Management console, but they are not there yet.

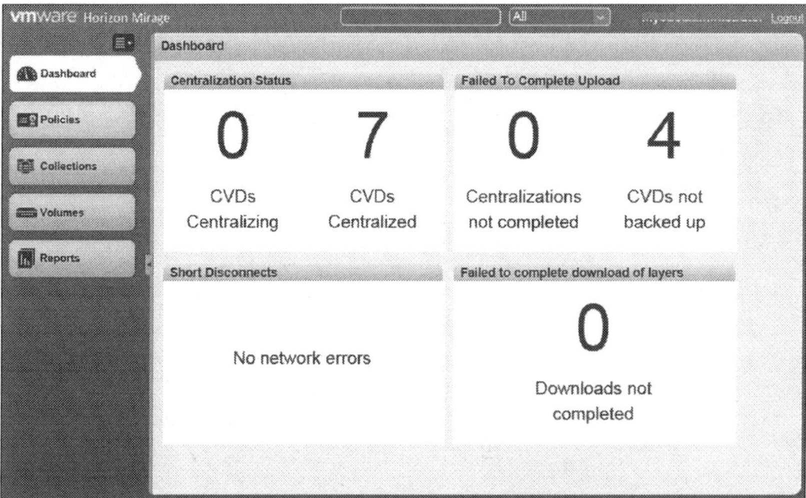

Figure 9-23 Horizon Mirage Web Management console

Horizon Mirage Driver Library

Building a solid driver library will make your Horizon Mirage deployment even better. The less the user or the IT department has to worry about a PC, the better the user's life will be. Mirage comes with a driver library feature; it's the place where you will build profiles based on your organization, a common set of hardware configurations, and then assign those profiles to CVDs to make sure that they have the latest and greatest drivers with their physical PCs. You can approach building the library in a couple of different ways. Our recommendation is that whenever a manufacturer is able to supply you with a complete driver list for a specific brand and model, in the form of a CAB file, you should use that CAB file. Remember that you will need to extract the CAB file (keeping the folder structure) before using it with Mirage.

Let's take a look at building one of those profiles and then assigning it to a CVD.

We also recommend keeping a folder hierarchy that enables you to easily recognize manufacturer, make, model, and OS version. Figure 9-24 shows the folder structure we used in our deployment.

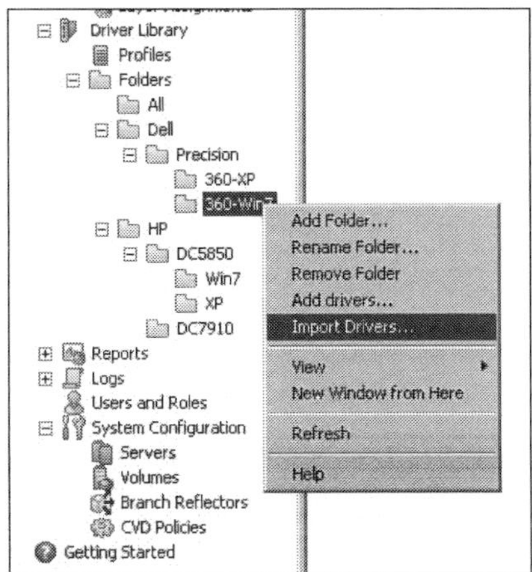

Figure 9-24 Driver library folder structure

As previously mentioned, there's a few way to add drivers; let's do a CAB file import. First, make sure that you download the proper CAB file from your hardware manufacturer. In our example, we grabbed the CAB for a Dell Precision Optiplex 360, XP, and Windows 7 drivers. We also grabbed the drivers for HP workstations, models DC5850 and DC7910. We prepared a staging folder on our network where we extracted the CAB files to follow the structure shown. Then, from the Horizon Mirage Console, we chose one of the sets of files we wanted to import into Mirage, right-clicked the folder, and chose **Import Drivers**. If you do this, Horizon Mirage will then prompt you for a UNC path where the files are located. To follow our example, it should look something like \\Fileserver\Servershare\Dell\Precision\360-Win7. If you're confident about your folder structure, you could even do one massive import. Because there is no stopping the process once it starts, however, we advise that you do this one model at a time. If you're doing this from a local drive on the Mirage Server, simply make sure to use the UNC form to point to your server and be sure to have access to the right path. For example, a local drive could be \\MirageHostname\D$.

Importing a driver library might take a while, especially if you have chosen a model that has a lot of different components for the same model. You can always go into the Task Monitor section of Mirage and look at the progress. When the import completes, go back in the folder you chose to import and look at the end result.

The next step is to assign a profile to a CVD or set of CVDs. Under the Driver Library, in the Profile section, right-click and choose **Add**. A wizard will appear and display two tabs: the General tab, where you will enter the name of the profile you're creating and a description; and a Rules tab. The Rules tab is very powerful with Mirage; you can build rules to have very specific scope or keep it very general, if you want to catch multiple types of hardware. In Figure 9-25, we're using it to catch the HP PCs and want to make sure that the driver profile we've built will only apply to these CVDs. The rules can contain specific text or it can be wildcard by using the Condition Contains statement.

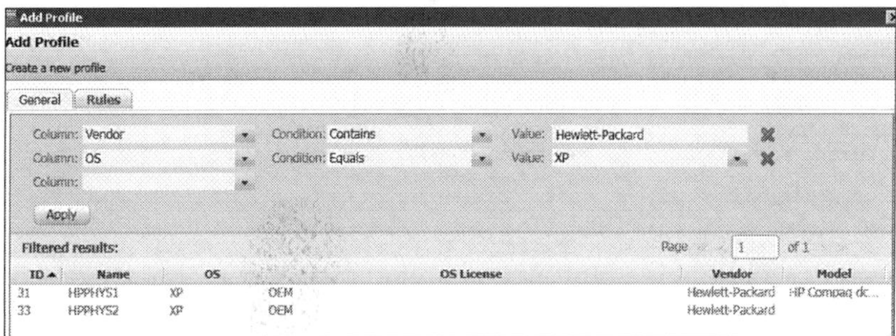

Figure 9-25 Profile creation rules

After you have built a driver profile, you can see it in action when you launch any of the following Mirage tasks:

- Centralization
- Migration
- Hardware migration/restore
- Machine cleanup
- Base layer update
- Manually applying a driver update

If you want to see the profile applied right away, you can easily go to All CVDs and choose one of the machines for which you have built a profile, right-click it and choose **Apply Driver Library**. You can then also go on the client side and see it being applied, as shown in Figure 9-26.

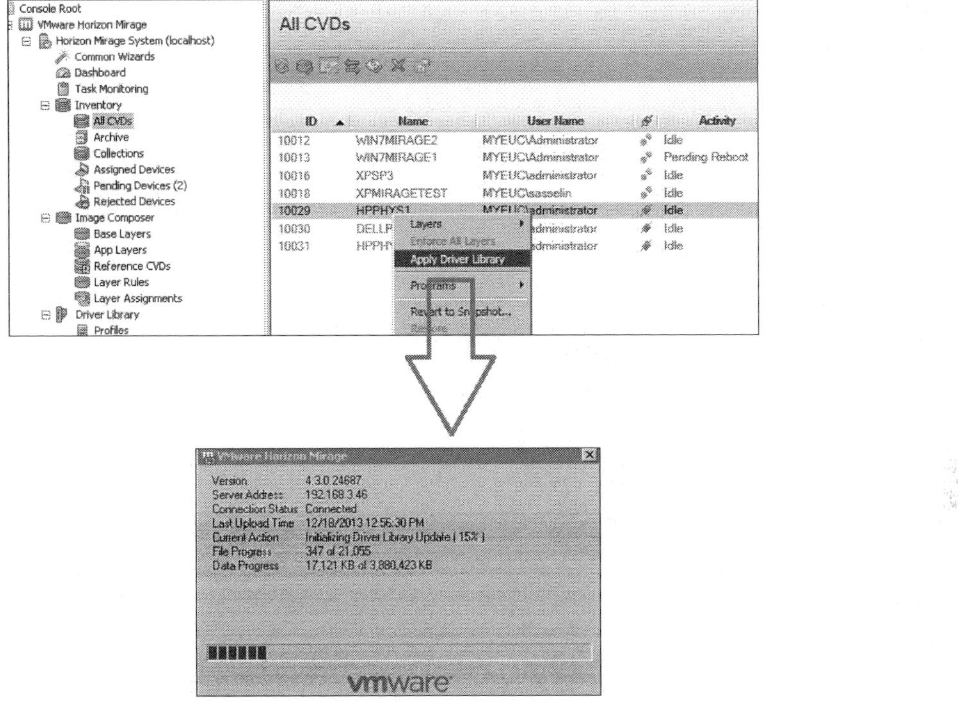

Figure 9-26 Driver profile applied

Remember that the more complex the driver library profile rules, the more detailed you can be to hit specific hardware vendors and models. It is a delicate balance between being too narrow and missing the target CVDs and being too broad and hitting CVDs that do not need those specific drivers. The more you do it, the better you'll get at building those rules. We found this information very useful to update drivers remotely even when no maintenance was being done on the CVDs.

Horizon Mirage Collections

Collections are a key part of Horizon Mirage. They enable you to group machines per type, per model, or per business unit (AD OUs, for example). This will help push base layers or app layers that are targeted to specific endpoints and make your deployment and management of the environment smoother.

There are two types of collections: static and dynamic. A static collection is pretty self-explanatory. It's when you have a group where you will manually add endpoints into that collection. Let's create a static collection by right-clicking **Collections** under Inventory, and choosing **Add Collection**. The only way to configure at this point is to give the collection a proper name and description, and then click **OK**.

Next, go in the All CVDs section, choose an endpoint that would fit into the newly created static collection, right-click the endpoint and choose **Manage Collections**, as shown in Figure 9-27. Doing so brings up a pop-up window where you specify to which collection you want the endpoint to be added.

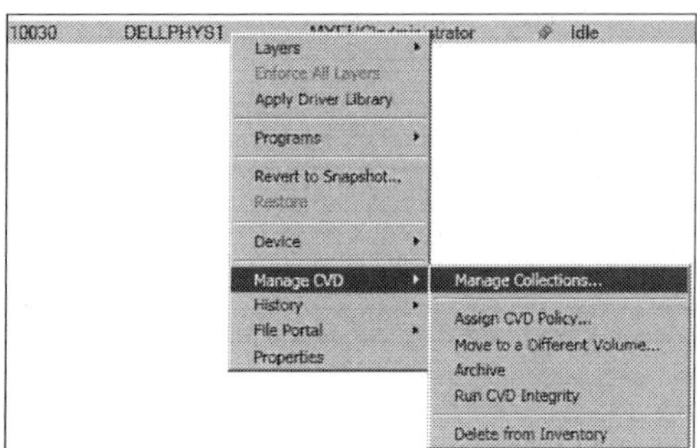

Figure 9-27 Endpoint static collection

Once the collection is created, right-click it; you will then see all the actions you can run against that collection. You can assign a layer, you can assign an upload policy; you can apply a driver library, you can suspend network operations, you can sync the devices within the collection, and you can even reboot all the endpoints within the collection. You should get to know how to build and properly manage collections; they will save you a lot of time on endpoint management.

The next type is the dynamic collection. This is very useful if you plan on managing endpoints that are added over time where you don't have all the information but you know stuff like the machine nomenclature or the machine types or model. So, for instance, you can build a dynamic collection for all your HP desktops of a specific model within the organization, assign layers (base and app) and drivers to it, and then, any new endpoints coming online in Horizon Mirage will automatically be added to that static collection and receive the assignment from it.

As shown in Figure 9-28, we built a dynamic collection to target HP desktop model DC7900. After that, we could assign a driver profile and push a base layer to it; all within a few clicks, after carefully preparing all the necessary components of course.

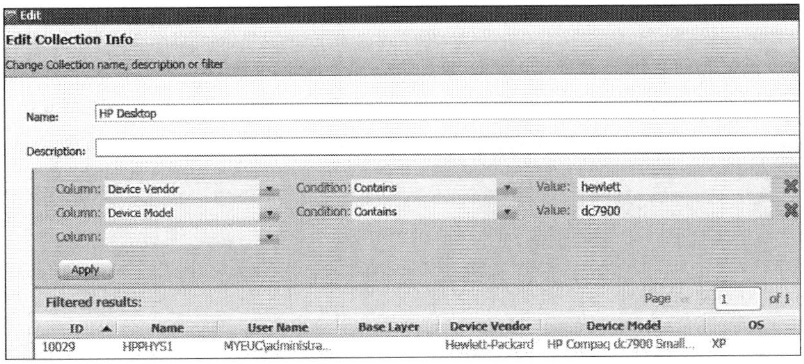

Figure 9-28 Dynamic collections

Horizon Mirage Application Layers

Another useful component of the solution is to be able to build application layers. We strongly recommend using a virtual image for this. It makes it a lot easier to do snapshots and to delete and revert back to a clean image. Of course, you need to keep capture state if you think you will need to update the application later (for a common application like Microsoft Office, for example).

To start application layer capture, the CVD has to be in the Pending Devices list. After validating this, you can go in the Common Wizards section and click the **Capture Application Layer** button. Doing so starts the wizard for application capture. The first screen asks you to select the pending device. You then choose the upload policy to use with it. The next screen will be the volume choice; we recommend that you keep the **Automatic selection** option. The next screen is the compatibility check, where it will inspect the endpoint to make sure that no conflict exists. The last page is the summary page, where you will see all the choices from the previous screen. When you click **Finish**, it starts the whole process. By now, you are familiar with these steps, which is why we have not added additional screenshots here. You can now go in the Task Monitoring screen to see the progress of this process, or you can also go on the endpoint and you will see the Horizon Mirage status of the capture, as shown in Figure 9-29.

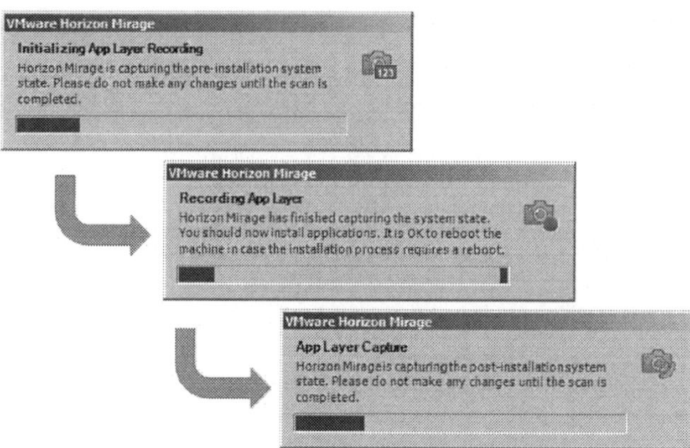

Figure 9-29 Endpoint application capture state

When the preparation is complete, you are now ready to install the application on the CVD. Installation is done like you would normally do; that part does not change from a normal installation on a physical or virtual desktop.

When you have completed the installation and customized/configured everything you want to inside the application, it is time to complete the capture process. You start this by going back to the Horizon Mirage Console. In the Reference CVDs section, look for the endpoint you've been using for the capture. Right-click it and choose **Finalize App Layer Capture**, as shown in Figure 9-30.

Reference CVDs

ID	Name	User Name		Activity	Progress
10017	WIN7MIRAGEVPC	MYEUC\Administrator		Idle	100%
10032	HPPHYS2	MYEUC\administrator		Idle	100%
10033	VMWAREDEMO-PC	MYEUC\Administrator		Recording App La...	0%

Capture Base Layer...
Finalize App Layer Capture...

Figure 9-30 Finalizing the app layer capture

Horizon Mirage will inspect the endpoint and look for any applications that were installed. It will display the applications it finds in the wizard. One interesting use case is that you could potentially build one application layer for multiple applications. For example, you have an HR department where all the employees of that department require the same basic set of applications. You could build one application layer that contains all these applications, and then the distribution would not change. That's the beauty of Horizon Mirage: An application layer can be one or multiple applications in the same layer; you get to decide the lifecycle of the application. Keep in mind that if you build an application layer that contains multiple apps and then you need to update one of these apps, you will need to update the whole layer. So, be sure to keep a snapshot of that in the virtual machine you used to do your capture.

When the application layer capture is complete, you will see your newly created app layer in the App Layers section under Image Composer. You can then assign that layer to any managed CVDs.

From a best practice standpoint, here is what we recommend you do:

1. Install the Mirage Client on your virtual desktop.
2. Take a snapshot of the VM before you do anything else.
3. Install any precapture software you need but do not want to capture (could be things like .NET Framework, Java, and so on). It could also be applications that are already part of the base layer that you might need to install the new applications.
4. Start the application layer capture by choosing your VM in the Pending Devices.
5. Install one or more applications in the VM.
6. Finalize the application capture, going back to Horizon Mirage, in the Reference CVDs section, and choosing your VM.
7. Reset your VM to a previous snapshot or keep to current state (depends on the purpose of the VM and the evolution of the applications within that VM).

The VM will automatically go back in the Pending Devices section once the app layer capture is complete.

Note that the app layer will need to be done by the operating system you have. You cannot build an app layer on Windows XP and use it on Windows 7. It's one app layer per different OS you have.

Horizon Mirage Reports

The Report section of Horizon Mirage is pretty self-explanatory:

- The storage report describes storage use on the selected volume or volumes. To run the report, select the report from the Reports node, click **Generate Report**, select **volumes**, and click **OK**. To view the report, select the report line and click the **View Report** icon on the report list toolbar.
- The base layer dry-run report compares the content of the base layer and the CVD.

- An application-level report describes projected applications that are added to, updated in, or deleted from an endpoint device when the selected layer changes are applied. It compares the applications installed on the layers and the CVD and provides a general view of the result for the change in layers.
- A Program Executable (PE)-level report analyzes the outcome of removing or updating a PE file. It projects affected software modules, such as DLL files, when a base layer is downloaded to an endpoint device client, and details whether each affected module is downgraded.
- The CVD Integrity report verifies that a CVD is consistent and free of corruption and can continue to reside in the system and be used for restore and other purposes.

Horizon Mirage Logs

Horizon Mirage comes with three types of logs. The first one, the Event Log, lists important system events as propagated from the server and clients. The second one, Transaction Log, records logical operations between the Horizon Mirage Server and Client. You can use the Transaction Log to monitor the progress of updates coming from and to the server. The third log, Manager Journal, collects and tracks audit event history. An audit event is created for any administrator action that results in a system setting or configuration change. This includes actions performed using the Management Console or through a CLI. Read-only actions do not create audit events. Audit events provide the operation time, name, and details, and the username.

We like the Transaction Log (shown in Figure 9-31) because it helps keep track of a lot of useful information about the CVDs. Going into that section will show you the type of event that happened to the CVD (for example, an incremental update or a Windows 7 Migration or a drivers and tools update). It will also show you the state of the transaction, successful or failed, and then the interesting part, the quantity of data in total and the data actually transferred. If you scroll to the right of the logs, you will also see the start and end time of that transaction (also very useful to track the time it took for a specific operation to complete).

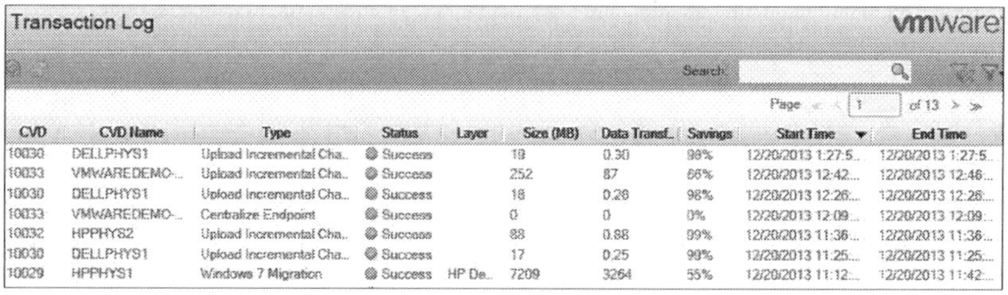

Transaction Log vmware

Search:

Page 1 of 13

CVD	CVD Name	Type	Status	Layer	Size (MB)	Data Transf...	Savings	Start Time	End Time
10030	DELLPHYS1	Upload Incremental Cha...	Success		18	0.30	98%	12/20/2013 1:27:5...	12/20/2013 1:27:5...
10033	VMWAREDEMO-...	Upload Incremental Cha...	Success		252	87	66%	12/20/2013 12:42...	12/20/2013 12:46:...
10030	DELLPHYS1	Upload Incremental Cha...	Success		18	0.29	98%	12/20/2013 12:26:...	12/20/2013 12:26:...
10033	VMWAREDEMO-...	Centralize Endpoint	Success		0	0	0%	12/20/2013 12:09:...	12/20/2013 12:09:...
10032	HPPHYS2	Upload Incremental Cha...	Success		88	0.88	99%	12/20/2013 11:36:...	12/20/2013 11:36:...
10030	DELLPHYS1	Upload Incremental Cha...	Success		17	0.25	98%	12/20/2013 11:25:...	12/20/2013 11:25:...
10029	HPPHYS1	Windows 7 Migration	Success	HP De...	7209	3264	55%	12/20/2013 11:12:...	12/20/2013 11:42:...

Figure 9-31 Transaction logs

Summary

Horizon Mirage provides a strong solution to manage end-user desktops. It is important to fully comprehend the use cases that work well with this solution. We have seen projects fail with this solution when the organization tried to get the product to do things it is not good at doing or is not designed to do. We have seen other organizations where proper planning was not done and they fell short in resources (network, disk, and so on). We discussed in this chapter the good and strong use case for Mirage. We talked about base layer provisioning, application layering, and how you can group multiple applications in one layer (when it makes sense to do so).

This chapter also covered OS migration, a very good use case for Mirage: how to prepare for it, what to include, and how to classify CVDs. You also learned how to build a driver library; this will make or break a lot of organization when deploying Mirage. Lack of a good driver library will slow deployments of the solution, and missing/outdated drivers will cause havoc and in some cases will strongly hinder the solution. In some cases, it might even cripple the endpoint to the point that it cannot successfully talk to Horizon Mirage (for example, a missing network driver during an OS migration).

The chapter concluded by covering the various reports and the logs accessible with Mirage.

Chapter 10

Multimedia

To deliver a successful VMware View environment, you must have a strong focus on the end-user experience. Although a virtual desktop environment is largely a datacenter-delivered service, you must be very conscious of how this service is consumed by the end user. The reason that this issue is so crucial is that you are making a change to something that most users consider a personal device: their desktop. Is it a big change? A View desktop presents itself as a physical desktop, so it should be more of a form-factor change from physical to virtual versus an end-user change. To carry out this change successfully, you must understand how the desktop performs from the users' perspective in addition to an IT or infrastructure perspective. If you have implemented changes similar to virtual desktop technology, such as server-based computing (VMware App Remoting, Citrix, or Terminal Services) technologies, you will understand the risks of not getting the end-user experience right. As with any new technology, you can avoid some general issues if you investigate them properly upfront. These intangible issues have less to do with technology and more to do with the users' perception of change. They include the following:

- When a change is made to end users' desktops, users blame any and all problems with performance on the virtual desktop platform.
- As the instrument of change, you are likely guilty until you can prove that the issue is unrelated to the desktop.
- When you make the change, any prior issues in the physical desktop environment quickly become your problem even if they have existed for some period of time.
- Due to the highly variable and intermittent nature of issues in a virtual desktop environment, it is important to look at end-user experience upfront and to have a set of tools to measure these issues on an ongoing basis. We discuss ongoing monitoring in Chapter 12, "Performance and Monitoring of VMware Horizon." In this chapter, we look at how to quantify the end-user experience.

How Do You Deliver a Rich End-User Experience?

Today, information is delivered in a variety of ways, including audio, video, and rich text and graphics. Rich video and graphical experiences have become the norm for users' viewing, understanding, and developing data. For your VMware View environment to be successful, you must appreciate and deliver a desktop that provides a rich end-user experience.

To provide this experience, you must first understand it. When you understand it, you can determine how it should be optimized to deliver good performance. The primary method for delivering visual information in a VMware View environment is PC over IP (PCoIP), so we spend much of the focus in this chapter addressing how it has been enhanced in VMware View 5 and what you can do to ensure it performs well under a variety of different scenarios. Display, however, is not the only aspect of providing a rich end-user experience. It can also entail bidirectional audio communication, such as Voice over IP (VoIP) and ensuring that general performance and functionality are all available within the virtual desktop.

VMware View 5.x contains many additional methods to control the PCoIP protocol and the bandwidth it uses. You can more finely tune the PCoIP protocol to ensure a great user experience under a wider range of environmental conditions. Throttling PCoIP is not a new capability, but the settings are more visible and more granular than any other release prior to View 5.1. To tune your environment, you need a controlled environment where you can adjust settings, simulate poor network conditions, and ensure that the changes you are making are properly set. This goes for any tuning you are going to do of the VMware View environment.

Different levels of enhanced graphics can be achieved in a virtual desktop; choosing the right solution that makes sense for you is key. VMware provides three different levels to achieve this. (At the time of this writing, however, the third level was not yet officially supported. We were still able to do testing on it, though, and provide data about that later in this chapter.)

The three levels of accelerated or enhanced graphics in View are as follows:

1. Software rendering
2. Virtual shared graphics acceleration
3. Virtual dedicated graphics acceleration

Software rendering will be used with task workers, people who require more horsepower than the normal desktop but who do not need capacity to run applications like AutoCAD. This is usually "out-of-the-box" functionality and built right in to the software rendering engine. These are users who need to display videos in normal quality, who might use Windows AERO (a distinctive visual style that combines the appearance of lightweight, translucent windows with powerful graphic advances) or other lightweight graphics applications that require DirectX or OpenGL.

Then you will have other users who require a little bit more graphic horsepower to run resource-intensive applications like AutoCAD or Google Earth. These users need shared graphics (vSGA). This is where you share a 3D graphics card among multiple users, as covered later in the chapter.

The third scenario is where you have users who require even more graphic horsepower. They need a dedicated 3D graphics cards for their resource-intensive applications, and vSGA is not enough. This will happen when applications such as AutoCAD or MapleSIM go to their limit, rendering rich and complex drawings, where users must be able to scroll and pan without losing a single frame. For this scenario, you need to dedicate a full 3D graphics card to that user, as also covered later in this chapter.

Figure 10.1 summarizes the 3D graphics and video possible with View, potential configurations, and the use cases where it makes sense to use those configurations.

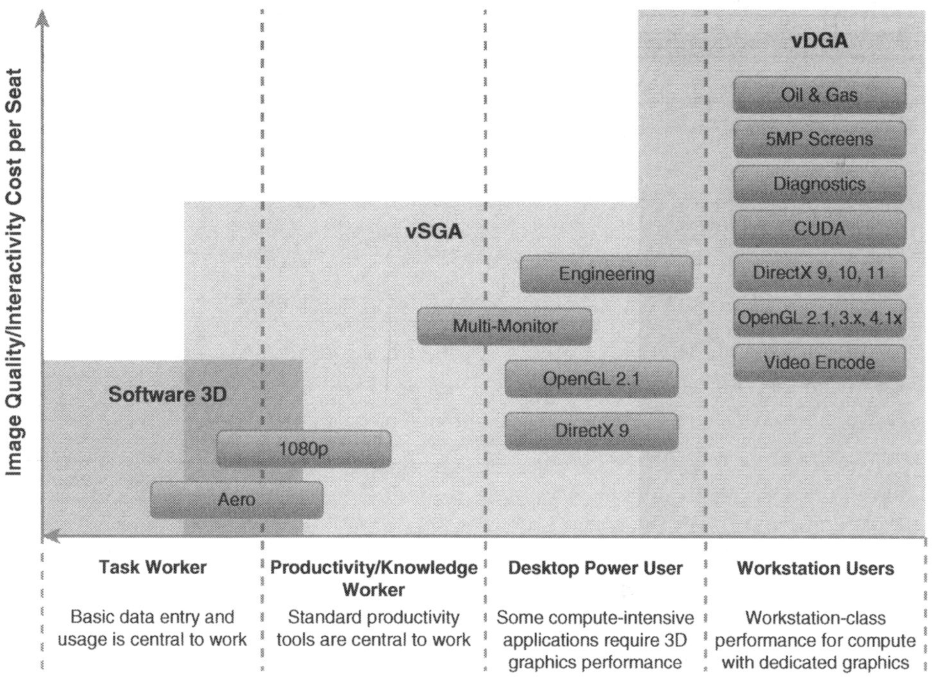

Figure 10.1 VMware View 3D graphics

The first scenario we want to cover to provide enhanced graphics is software rendering. VMware View takes advantage of vSphere 5's support for nonhardware-accelerated 3D graphics. Support is provided for DirectX 9 and OpenGL 2.1. This feature in ESXi enables View to run applications requiring OpenGL or DirectX without a video offload card or physical graphical processing unit (GPU).

In addition to software options, you have hardware options for improving the rendering and performance of PCoIP. Teradici released a set of adapter cards that can be installed in a vSphere ESXi host; these cards enable you to offload the PCoIP image encoding tasks, reducing the load on the servers' CPUs. Later in the chapter, we also cover how you can combine this card with the 3D graphics card, providing an even stronger graphic delivery solution to the users.

The Teradici APEX 2800 Server Offload Card enables you to ensure a greater consistency in graphics performance of your View desktop. The card dynamically offloads the most active 64 View desktop displays. In so doing, it enables an even greater consolidation ratio. The card ships as a PCI Express card that is inserted into the ESXi server. After it is physically installed, you install the drivers on the ESXi host and then enable the hardware acceleration in VMware View Administrator. You enable the hardware acceleration under the VMware View Administrator's Policies and Global Policies by selecting Edit. Ensure that the PCoIP Hardware Acceleration is set to **Allow** (the default). The final step is to install the drivers for the Teradici APEX 2800 card within the View desktops. You can find additional details on Teradici's website at www.teradici.com/pcoip/pcoip-products/teradici-apex-2800.php. The cards are fully supported on ESXi 4.1 and later and VMware View 4.6 and later.

To improve the end-user experience, View 5 provides continuity services. If the user is suddenly disconnected from the session, the PCoIP protocol tries for up to 30 seconds to reconnect or restore the connection without having the user relaunch the connection.

Your desktops and settings should be tuned to deal with the conditions you are going to see in your production environment before the final production version is delivered. This chapter covers a few ways you can do that. The goal is to build a contained environment in which you can inject latency and packet loss, for example, to change settings and quantify the benefit before you put the virtual desktop in front of users. A number of tools are readily available to do this, in addition to the ones mentioned here, such as Shunra or WANem. In a large-scale environment, using third-party tools designed for this purpose is recommended, but because each environment has its own approach, we wanted to combine some freely available tools to create a test environment.

This approach enables you to test and verify any number of settings from audio and video to graphics and multimedia performance. It also ensures that the results are reproducible in a way that is much more difficult when you are dealing with a live environment.

vSGA, Virtual Shared Graphics Acceleration

The next use case is to leverage a 3D graphics card, shared among multiple users. This is useful in a setup like a virtual classroom that requires more graphics-intensive applications to run (for example, AutoCAD or MapleSim). The SVGA 3D graphics driver provides support for DirectX 9.0c and OpenGL 2.1. This driver is supported on Windows 7 for 2D and 3D, and is used for both software 3D and vSGA. One of the benefits of VMware SVGA 3D for both software 2D and 3D and vSGA implementations is that a virtual machine (VM) can dynamically switch between software or hardware acceleration without you having to reconfigure it. It is also a major factor in why live VMware vSphere vMotion on the VM is supported even when providing hardware-accelerated graphics using vSGA. Having a standard driver in your image greatly simplifies management and deployment of your View desktops.

We were fortunate enough to be able to work with a team of very experienced IT resources at La Cité Collegiale (www.collegelacite.ca), a college located in Ottawa, Canada that has approximately 1,700 employees and 5,000 full-time students (thanks especially to Yves Bourgeois and Luc Lacasse). Their use case was pretty straightforward: They needed to be able to support virtual classrooms for engineering and multimedia students. When the project started, they were at a crossroads where their hardware was due for a major refresh, and the choice needed to be made to either replace the existing with more powerful hardware or go virtual and maintain one centralized environment only. They went virtual and decided to deploy VMware View. They installed 3D graphics NVIDIA K1 and K2 cards in their server, and added APEX 2800 cards on top for higher density.

This combined design enabled them to achieve very high virtual desktop performance for those resource-intensive graphics applications. To obtain the list of cards officially supported by NVIDIA, visit their website (www.nvidia.com) and search for VMware vSphere ESXi 5.5 drivers. (At the time of this writing, 5.5 was the general availability release; you can just update the version with the latest release of ESXi.)

The supported cards from NVIDIA are as follows:

- Quadro Series (4000, 5000, 6000)
- GRID Series (K1, K2)
- M-Class (M2070-Q)

Note that the cards are certified by NVIDIA because it is the owner of the driver for ESXi. VMware does not have a list of cards; it relies on NVIDIA to test and produce a driver that will work with vSphere for the vSGA capabilities.

It's important to understand that when using those capabilities, you must have a good grasp of the number of users who will actually be able to leverage the card at any given moment. This will drive the View pool you build. You don't want to create desktop pools of 50 users, assign them to a card, and end up being able to have only four to eight VMs in the whole pool being able to use the capabilities of the card. The ESXi host reserves GPU hardware resources on a first-come, first-served basis as VMs are powered on. If all GPU hardware resources are already reserved, additional VMs will be unable to power on if they are explicitly set to use hardware 3D rendering. If the VMs are set to automatic, the VMs will be powered on using software 3D rendering.

For example, the NVIDIA Quadro 6000 comes with 6 GB of RAM. The maximum amount of video memory that can be used by a VM (this might change in the future) is currently 512 MB. The good thing about using these cards is that vSphere takes half the load of the allocated memory. So, if you assign 512 MB to a VM, 256 MB will come from the card and 256 MB will come from the host. A rapid calculation 6 GB of RAM divided by 256 MB will give you a maximum of 24 VMs assigned to that single card. Remember that you will also need to reserve the same amount of memory on the ESXi host. Being able to leverage this card for 24 VMs really brings down the cost of using such hardware. On top of those resources being shared, you potentially could have 40+ users linked to a single card at any given time. In a classroom scenario, that might not necessarily work, because the students will be logged on at the same time and probably doing similar work (that is, have a similar workload requirement). In other scenarios, however, like in a hospital, this becomes an appealing solution for doctors and nurses who need those kind of resources for X-ray applications.

Configuring ESXi for sVGA

Adding a 3D graphics card to ESXi is straightforward. You need to make sure that you use one of the cards mentioned in the chapter earlier or visit the NVIDIA site for a list of updated officially supported cards. You must install the proper driver on the ESXi host, then configure vSphere to work with the card, and then properly configure the pool in View.

The first step is to physically install the card in your host. Once it's done and the host is booted, you can verify that the card is actually detected by EXi by running the following command:

```
esxcli hardware pci list -c 0x0300 -m 0xf
```

Look for the vendor name and the device name. Make sure that it's the right information. Then, you must install the proper vSphere installation bundle (VIB) driver. You can obtain this from the NVIDIA website (www.nvidia.com). After downloading the driver, you need to upload it to your host in the datastore. We then recommend that you put the host in maintenance; this is required for the driver installation to be successful.

After uploading the driver to the datastore, open a Secure Shell (SSH) session and run the following command:

```
esxcli software vib install --no-sig-check -d /<path to nVidia VIB bundle>/
vib-name.zip
```

The path should not contain the less than (<) and greater than (>) characters; this is just an example. The `--no-sig-check` is to prevent any errors that might happen from the driver not being properly signed. At the end of the installation, you should see a message stating that the operation finished successfully. Although a reboot is not absolutely necessary, VMware recommends you reboot to test the Xorg service to make sure that it starts properly. You can find more information about the installation and the validation in the *Virtual Machine Graphics Acceleration Deployment Guide*, which was written by a knowledgeable technical resource, Simon Long, very active in the desktop virtualization community (www.simonlong.co.uk).

Another quick command you can run from the SSH session, after the reboot, is to verify all the installed VIBs. The command for this is as follows:

```
esxcli software vib list
```

If the environment is up and running properly, you will see among all the VIBs your NVIDIA driver listed, as shown in Figure 10.2.

Figure 10.2 NVIDIA driver in ESXi

In the case of La Cité Collegiale, as discussed earlier, we also added an APEX card to the environment, as shown in Figure 10.3.

Figure 10.3 Teradici APEX driver in ESXi

VMware View with vSGA

Now that you have configured the vSphere side, you are ready to go in your View environment and configure your desktop pool to leverage the 3D graphics card. You want to keep a couple of prerequisites in mind:

- The desktops must be Windows 7 (32-bit or 64-bit) or later.
- The pool must use PCoIP as the default display protocol.
- Users must not be allowed to choose their own protocols.
- The desktop VMs must be Virtual Hardware Version 9 or later.

You want to make sure that you don't leave the desktop to automatic for video RAM sizing; you will end up with virtual desktops that might have very low numbers assigned to them. Go into the settings of the image and set a manual number to reflect your requirements. You will notice if your VM is powered on that you cannot change this setting. You must turn off the VM to make those changes, as shown in Figure 10.4. After you've configured the virtual desktops, you can verify the video memory on it.

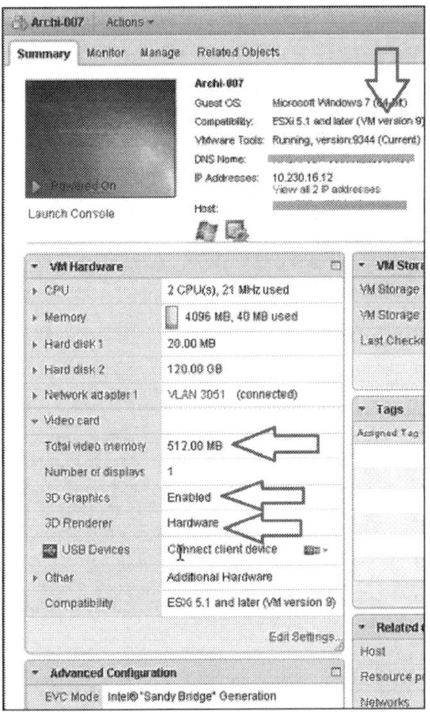

Figure 10.4 Virtual desktop configuration

NOTE VRAM settings that you configure in View Administrator take precedence over the VRAM settings that are configured for the VMs in vSphere Client or vSphere Web Client. Select the **Manage Using vSphere Client** option to prevent this.

The maximum resolution that can be used (in the current release of View) with 3D hardware acceleration turned on is 1920 × 1200, and you cannot use more than two monitors.

VMware recommends setting the 3D rendering option to **Automatic**. We suggest having a smaller pool, more focused on user segmentation; make sure that the user in that pool requires those resources and set the 3D Renderer option to **Hardware**, as shown in Figure 10.5. This will ensure that all users within the pool have access to the 3D graphics card when required. For a classroom setup, this makes more sense; you do not want your users to switch to software rendering when they could be using hardware acceleration. It goes back to the use case and balancing the cost versus the performance you will get with these cards.

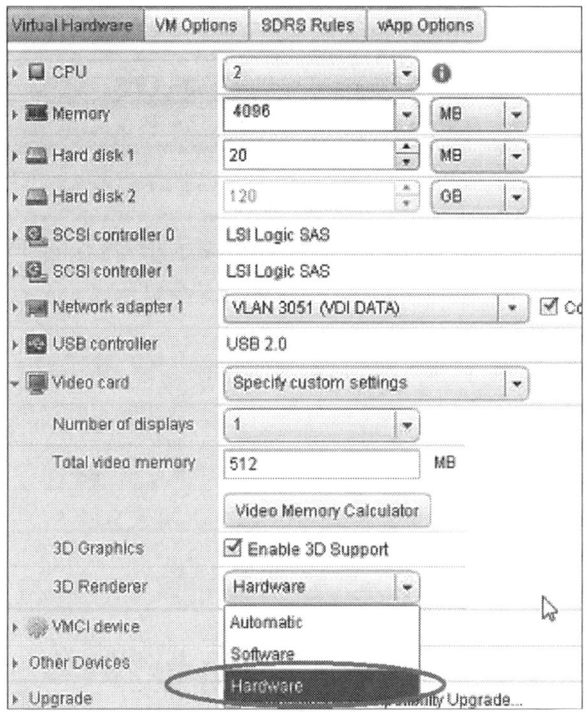

Figure 10.5 View pool configuration

To complete this section, we just wanted to make sure that you saw how powerful this can be, if configured properly. We encourage you to go on YouTube and look for videos of people who have made such a successful deployment. You can watch La Cité Collegiale's video of its real-world deployment of the solution at www.youtube.com/watch?v=zralQRBZHv0.

vDGA, Virtual Direct Graphics Acceleration

vDGA is a graphics-acceleration capability provided by VMware ESXi for delivering high-end workstation graphics for use cases where a discrete GPU (graphics processing unit, also referred to as a PCI device or video card) is needed. vDGA dedicates a single GPU to a single VM for high performance. vDGA configurations do not use the VMware SVGA 3D driver; instead, they use the native graphics card driver installed directly in the guest OS. You can refer to the *Virtual Machine Graphics Acceleration Deployment Guide*, available from VMware's website, for configuration information with this use case.

So far, from our experience, we have not seen scenarios where vSGA, properly configured, did not address the capacity requirements of the users.

We have seen a lot of testing on vDGA. If you do a quick search on YouTube for videos, just entering vDGA and VMware View, you will get a lot of hits. So far, almost all the testing has been to show the capabilities of doing vDGA with gaming and complex animation. It makes sense because these are two of the more demanding scenarios from a resource standpoint, but balancing the cost of the solution with the benefits, you might want to keep vDGA for unique, special cases where cost is not an issue. We do not think you want to invest thousands of dollars so that your user can play *Call of Duty* faster.

When doing vDGA, keep in mind that you enable the host for GPU passthrough; this means direct access to ESXi kernel. You will be at the mercy of the quality of the drivers and the applications that you install within the virtual desktops. Also keep in mind that you will not be able to vMotion those desktops. We have seen cases where, in rare situations, you could purple screen the host when pushing the envelope of the available resources.

Enhancements in PCoIP

In the initial release of the View Virtual Desktop Manager (VDM), the display protocol options were limited to Microsoft's Remote Desktop Protocol (RDP) and HP's Remote Graphics Software (RGS). Because both were developed by the original equipment manufacturer (OEM), VMware decided to develop a third option designed to deliver a graphics rich desktop experience over a User Datagram Protocol (UDP) network. The leader at the time in digital television graphics chips was Teradici. VMware signed an agreement to develop the physical graphics card technology as a software solution, and the PCoIP protocol for VMware was born. Unlike other remote graphics protocols, PCoIP transfers pixels versus caching bitmaps. This makes it more similar to high-definition TV (HDTV) technologies than to its predecessors, Citrix's ICA or Microsoft's RDP.

When you look at the quality of graphics in a display and speed of rendering the display, you are essentially compressing the image and then restoring it to the display. Although lossless compression is superior for many kinds of images, it is critical only in certain situations. For example, you would not want to use lossy compression for an X-ray program for radiology; because the details are critical, you would use lossless. Basically, lossless image compression means that all the data from the original file is preserved.

Lossy compression, in contrast, removes some data from the original file and saves the image with a reduced file size. To provide a high-quality screen, PCoIP monitors the type of data, such as text or image, and applies the correct compression algorithm. For example, you would not want to apply a lossy compression algorithm to text because you might deliver blurred or unfocused text to the screen.

The lossless compression has been significantly improved in the PCoIP protocol in View 5. This improved algorithm can deliver up to 75% reduction in bandwidth requirements from earlier releases. You can also more fully control the build to lossless algorithm to deliver a good user experience even when less bandwidth is available.

Your ability to control the build to lossless provides a significant improvement over prior versions of View.

In addition to compressing pixels, PCoIP uses special filtering to ensure that only the portions of the screen that change are sent rather than the entire screen. These portions are sent in 8 × 8 pixel blocks. In addition, PCoIP caches image blocks on the client device and uses temporal analysis to reuse this cached data to avoid resending the same information. For example, imagine a user is paging forward and backward through a PDF file within a VMware View session. Much of the screen refresh information could be more efficiently reused from cache rather than reset across the network. The inclusion of the client-side cache saves bandwidth over earlier versions of View and the PCoIP protocol.

VMware View provides a series of image quality controls that enable you to adjust the clarity of the image to tradeoff between less bandwidth and rendering of the screen. These controls are among a few that impact the lossless nature of PCoIP. Recall that lossless builds a screen by sending all the data so that there is no loss of image pixels, translating to higher quality. If you are deploying VMware View at a hospital, for example, this quality can be critical if the data involves medical images that are being used by doctors to form a prognosis.

If the user is using general office and business applications, this build to lossless is often overkill. The capability to tune lossless behavior is provided in VMware View 5. The options are whether to build to lossless or perceptually lossless. In many cases, perceptually lossless is not discernible to the end user. To see the effects of these settings, however, you need to be able to simulate poor network conditions so that the effect is measurable.

From a delivery perspective, it is a great to understand how these adjustments work in a controlled scenario so that you can have confidence that you are tuning the right settings for the right use cases. This is to say, what is optimal in one use case may not be optimal in another. For example, if you have high latency, you tune and optimize the desktop session much differently than if it is being delivered on a high-speed corporate network. You tune per use case, and different use cases have different optimization settings.

Building a Performance Test Environment

You must be able to do two things in a controlled test environment. You need to inject real-world delays and simulate "real" end-user activity. No single tool set gives you everything, but you can take utilities that have been accepted by the community and use them to build your controlled environment. These tools can be deployed in your virtualization environment at little or no cost. One question that comes to mind is why take the added effort to build out this controlled testing environment? Why not just deploy and tweak in the live VMware View environment?

Chapter 1, "The New End-User Model," talked about the double-edged sword for virtual desktop environments; it can be a huge benefit to the management of desktops, but if poorly implemented, it may not be accepted by the end users. Building a performance test environment is about doing your homework to ensure that you have done everything possible to ensure the success of the technology. You might be able to crunch the exam and pass the test, but if you fail, you may not get another opportunity to take it.

In the performance test environment in this chapter, we are going to use the VMware environment, WANem, View Planner, Wireshark, and for detailed analysis, PCoIP Log Viewer:

- WANem is software running on a Linux distribution called Knoppix. WANem can be used to emulate network link qualities (bandwidth size, packet loss, jitter, and latency) to test how a technology performs under simulated real-world scenarios. WANem is launched through a LiveCD or bootable ISO or media file. (You can download WANem from http://wanem.sourceforge.net/.)
- View Planner is a VMware benchmarking tool that allows you to automate and simulate user workload in a VMware View environment. This tool is useful for

assessing load versus session tuning. View planner is publicly available for download from www.vmware.com/ca/en/products/view-planner.

- Wireshark is a third-party packet sniffer that enables you to profile your network to ensure that you are getting accurate information on what the real conditions are on the network. (You can download Wireshark from www.wireshark.org/download.html.)
- PCoIP Log Viewer is a tool developed by a member of the developer community (Chuck Hirstius) for parsing and reading PCoIP log files. (You can download PCoIP Log Viewer from http://mindfluxinc.net/?p=195.)

You do not need to be a network expert to use WANem, but you do need to understand the basics of what you will be adjusting:

- Jitter is the one-way packet delay variation (PDV). It is a measure of the variation between one-way packet latency. For example, if within a transaction one packet takes 9 ms and the second takes 11 ms to reach its destination, the jitter is the variation between the first packet and second packet. The less jitter there is on a network, the more predictable the one-way network latency is.
- Latency is the time taken for a packet stream to travel between source and destination. When you are injecting latency, it is important to take into account the round-trip nature of network packets. If you are trying to emulate 30 ms of latency because your ping test on the network shows a delay of 30 ms of latency, you configure your emulation device for 15 ms to provide a round-trip time of 30 ms.
- Bandwidth is the amount of data that can be carried from one point to another within a time period (typically 1 second). It is usually expressed in bits or bytes (8 bits/byte).
- Packet loss occurs when one or more packets fail to reach their destination.

It is the combination of these four measurements that determines how the transmission is affected. To simulate how the virtual desktop will perform, you need to understand how to identify what your current network is experiencing so that you can configure your simulated network in the controlled environment to fine-tune your VMware View environment.

The environment you are going to build involves creating a path to the View environment that forces the connection to go through the WANem virtual appliance (VA). It, of course, does not have to be a completely isolated View environment because you are testing for session improvements to ensure you have a rich user experience versus capacity of load testing. A single VMware View desktop allows you to create the environment needed.

The environment requires a physical desktop where you run the View Client and the metrics and monitoring tools. To configure this environment, you should create a networking-facing vSwitch and an internal vSwitch and a virtual desktop running internally from the perspective of the WANem VA. Logically, the environment should look like that shown in Figure 10.6.

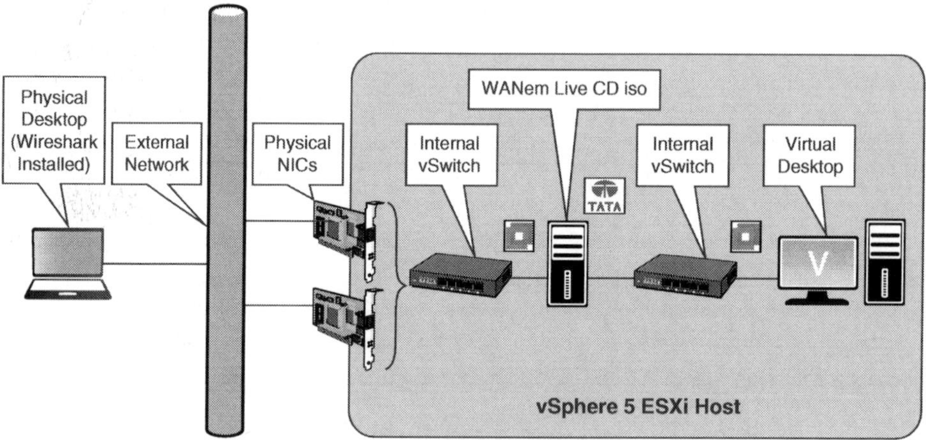

Figure 10.6 End-user performance testing environment

From the physical desktop to the internal virtual desktop should be a Layer 2 network, or it should be essentially flat. This ensures that nothing will introduce a delay over your network path other than what you introduce yourself through WANem. WANem can be downloaded as a VA or boot ISO running Knoppix. The VA is based on VMware Server or Workstation and essentially is the bare minimum required to boot from the Knoppix live Linux CD.

The WANem ISO downloads in tarball format (this format allows you to combine multiple files in a single "tarball"), so you might need to have a compression tool such as WinZip, 7-Zip, or WinRAR handy to extract the ISO. You can also download the VA, which also contains the ISO file, so either is okay. You create a WANem VA that boots from the ISO, and when done, you need to configure it in bridge mode. Bridge mode keeps everything at a Layer 2 level and essentially creates a tunnel to the View desktop on the internal vSwitch. This is the most straightforward approach because essentially you do not have to redirect any traffic; it just flows to and from the View desktop.

For example, add IP addresses to the environment and clarify the internal virtual desktop requirement, as shown in Figure 10.7.

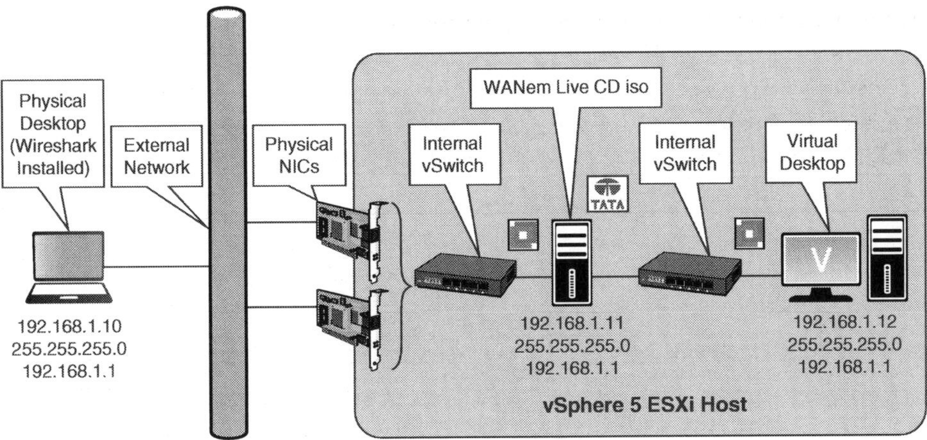

Figure 10.7 End-user performance testing environment with IPs

In the case of the WANem appliance, it has two interfaces that will be bridged. The bridge is configured with an IP, but the individual interfaces are not. Figure 10.8 shows this configuration from the perspective of the ESXi hosts.

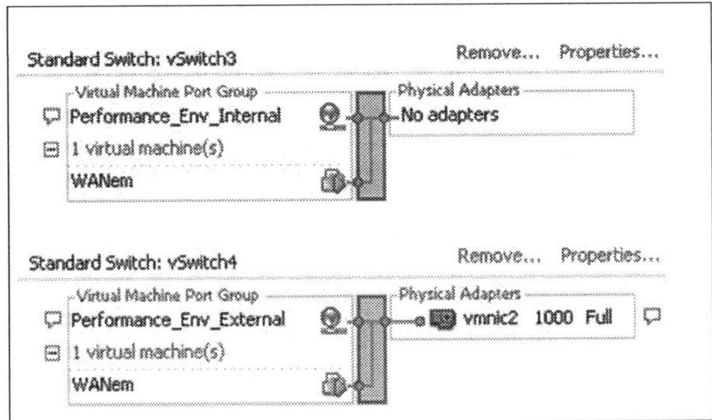

Figure 10.8 Internal and external switches

You can see that one of WANem's interfaces is connected to the internal switch, and the second interface is connected to the external switch, exactly as you intended.

Installing and Configuring WANem

The resources for the WANem appliance should be exclusively reserved to ensure that you can manage the VA even when you are introducing a high degree of overhead to the network. This means ensuring that the memory reservations are set on the WANem appliance to ensure the emulator has adequate resources. WANem requires a minimum of 512 MB of memory, which should be reserved to ensure the appliance has sufficient resources for your testing. To create the WANem VA, create a VM with the following properties:

- Linux operating system based on Ubuntu
- 1 vCPU
- 512 MB of memory
- Two virtual network adapters

Assuming that you are not using the VA, configure the VM to boot from the Knoppix ISO. You will likely want to copy the ISO file locally to the host.

After configuring the VM, follow these steps to configure WANem to operate in bridging mode:

1. Boot the VM from the Knoppix ISO file. Press **Enter** to start the boot process from DVD.

2. You want to hard-code the IP addresses. So, when prompted to configure the system using DHCP, type **n** for no (see Figure 10.9).

```
Autoconfiguring devices...                              Done.
Mouse is ImPS/2 Generic Wheel Mouse at /dev/input/mice
 Accelerated MKXORGCONFIG . (Backgrounding)
 Video is VMware Inc Abstract SVGA II Adapter, using Xorg(vmware) Server
 Monitor is Generic Monitor, H:28.0-96.0kHz, V:50.0-76.0Hz
 Using Modes   "1024x768" "800x600" "640x480" Modes
Scanning for Harddisk partitions and creating /etc/fstab... Done.
Network device eth0 detected, DHCP broadcasting for IP. (Backgrounding)
Network device eth1 detected, DHCP broadcasting for IP. (Backgrounding)
run commands are started : setup_dialog,setup_ja,Done.
INIT: Entering runlevel: 3
Do you want to configure all interfaces via DHCP(y/n): n_
```

Figure 10.9 Configuring interfaces by IP

3. Because you do not want to associate IP addresses to the individual interfaces but configure them as a bridge, you also need to escape the wizard configuration of the individual interfaces. Simply press **Esc** to go back to the command prompt.

4. Before you configure the interfaces, you must supply a password for the root account. Supply and confirm the password you want to use.

5. You must exit to the underlying Linux shell to configure the interfaces. This step is quite simple to do; you simply type **exit2shell** at the prompt.

6. It is important to bring up both interfaces so that you configure and add them to the bridge. You bring up each interface in turn by typing **ifconfig eth0 0.0.0.0 up** and the same for the second interface, **ifconfig eth1 0.0.0.0 up**, as shown in Figure 10.10.

WANemControl@PERC>exit2shell
Type 'wanem' to return to WANem console
root!tty1:/# ifconfig eth0 0.0.0.0 up
root!tty1:/# ifconfig eth1 0.0.0.0 up

Figure 10.10 Bringing up the interfaces

You are ready to configure the bridge so that traffic can flow through the interfaces.

7. You must first use the bridge control utility to add a new bridge br0 by typing **brctl addbr br0**.

8. Now that you have created the bridge, you can add the two interfaces to it to establish the working configuration. Again, you use the bridge configuration utility and add the devices by typing **brctl addif br0 eth0** and **brctl addif br0 eth1**.

9. You need a management interface to adjust the network emulation to simulate the latency. You apply the IP address using the ifconfig utility to the bridge by entering the command **ifconfig br0 10.0.1.4 netmask 255.255.255.0**.

   To go back to the WANem module, simply type **wanem**.

10. To verify whether everything is reachable and good, simply open an Internet browser and browse to the IP addresses configured on the bridge. If everything is working, you should get the message shown in Figure 10.11.

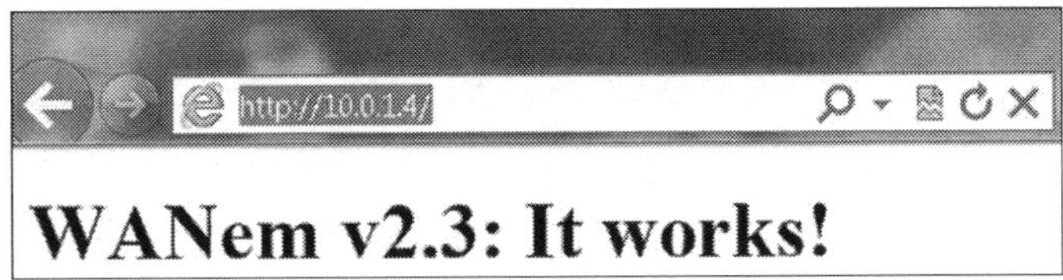

Figure 10.11 Verifying WANem

To adjust the settings, browse to the WANem IP: WANem (http://[IP Address] / WANem).

To adjust latency only, select **Basic Mode**. Ensure that you have the bridge selected and choose a bandwidth type to emulate on each interface. You can add delay or latency by specifying it in the Delay column for each interface and apply the settings (see Figure 10.12).

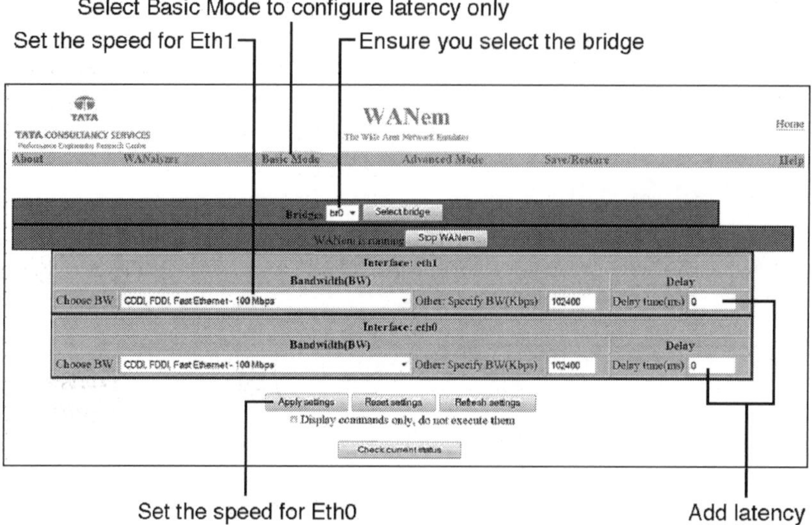

Figure 10.12 Configuring WANem

To add qualities such as jitter or packet loss, you need to go to the Advanced Mode screen and select a specific interface. You can add delay and loss settings under the Delay and Loss columns (see Figure 10.13). Don't forget to apply your settings to have them take effect. You can verify the latency by running a ping test from the physical desktop where you are launching the View Client to the virtual desktop. You should see a fairly consistent pattern of latency. It varies a little due to the interjection of WANem on the network stream and the time it takes the appliance to process the packets.

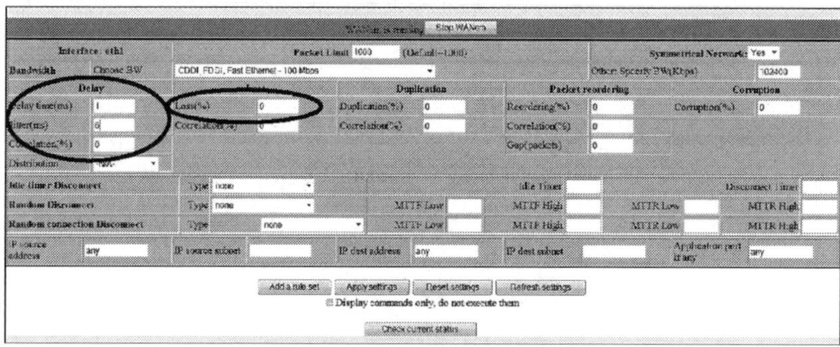

Figure 10.13 Configuring network delay and packet loss

Installing and Configuring Wireshark

Although you now have a method to simulate distance and see how a VM performs, you will want a better level of visibility on the traffic you are impacting. One of my favorite tools for viewing packet streams is Wireshark. Wireshark is a packet sniffer that enables you to zero in on certain traffic streams. In this case, you should look at PCoIP traffic between the virtual and physical desktops. When you install Wireshark, it installs WinPcap, which enables your network device to run in promiscuous mode. Promiscuous mode enables you to see the network traffic through the Wireshark interface. To install Wireshark, download it from wireshark.org and follow these steps:

1. Launch the installer, and on the Welcome screen, click **Next**.
2. On the next screen, you can choose what components you want. Because the defaults are good, just click **Next**.
3. On the Additional Task screen, you can create additional shortcuts to launch Wireshark and associate the trace extensions; this setting is checked by default. Click **Next**.
4. Select the destination and click **Next**.
5. On the next screen, you are prompted to install WinPcap, which is necessary, so click **Next**.
6. Click **Next** on the WinPcap Installer screen and Next on the Welcome screen.
7. Agree to the license terms and click **Install** on the next screen. You have the option of automatically starting WinPcap at boot time, but this is not necessary.
8. Click **Finish** on the WinPcap installation screen, which takes you back to the Wireshark Installer. Click **Next** to proceed with the installation.
9. On the Completing Installation screen, select the option Run Wireshark and click **Finish**.

When you launch Wireshark, you are prompted to start a capture on an interface. Simply select the appropriate interface, and you are taken to the capture window (see Figure 10.14).

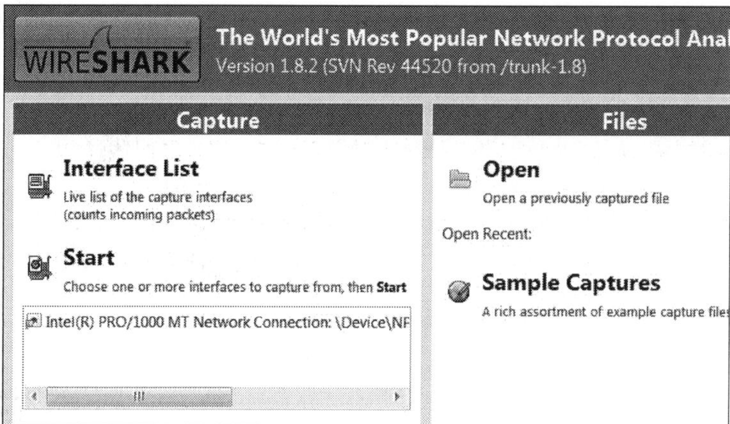

Figure 10.14 Selecting the interface

Because you want to look at PCoIP traffic in a graphical way, you should drill down and use filters to target just the traffic that you want to see. From the capture window, select **Statistics** and then **IO Graphs**.

Now you have a graphical representation of the network flow, but you should adjust the Unit setting from Packets/Tick to Bytes/Tick (see Figure 10.15).

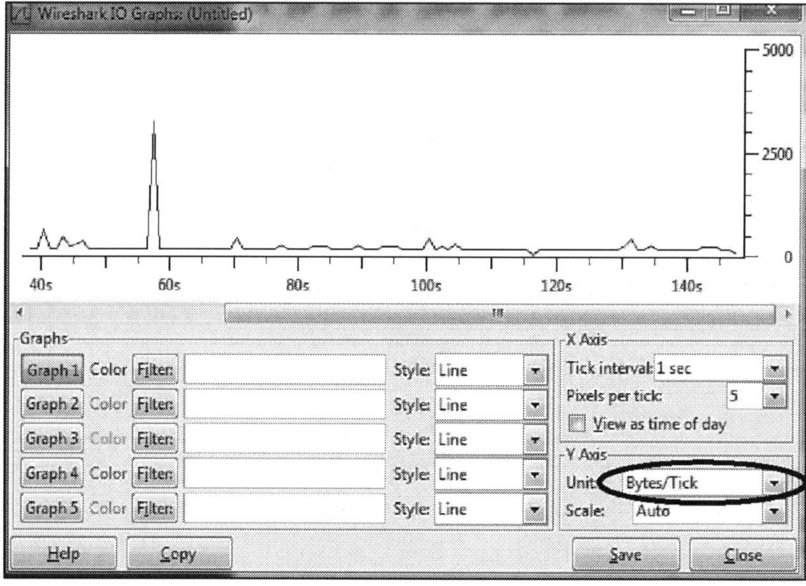

Figure 10.15 Adjusting to Bytes/Tick

The final task is to apply filters so that you are capturing only the PCoIP stream. Specifically, you want to capture traffic to and from the client and virtual desktop. To add an IP filter for a specific address, you simply enter **ip.addr ==** *IP ADDRESS*.

For example, if your IP address is 10.0.1.3, you enter **ip.addr == 10.0.1.3**. (Note that there is no space between the double equal signs.)

Of course, you want the traffic to and from both machines, so you must add a second IP address. To concatenate or add the second IP address, you specify **&&** and the second IP. If your VM address is 10.0.1.8, your final notation is as follows:

```
ip.addr == 10.0.1.3 && ip.addr == 10.0.1.8
```

This gets you the traffic only between these two points, but you should be specific to the PCoIP protocol. The PCoIP protocol is UDP based and uses only UDP port 50002 on the VM and UDP port 4172 on the client side. To filter only the UDP traffic on those two ports, you just append the UDP port filters to the following statement:

```
&& udp.port == 50002 && udp.port == 4172
```

In the example (see Figure 10.16), the complete statement is this:

```
ip.addr == 10.0.1.3 && ip.addr == 10.0.1.8 && udp.port == 50002 && udp.port
== 4172
```

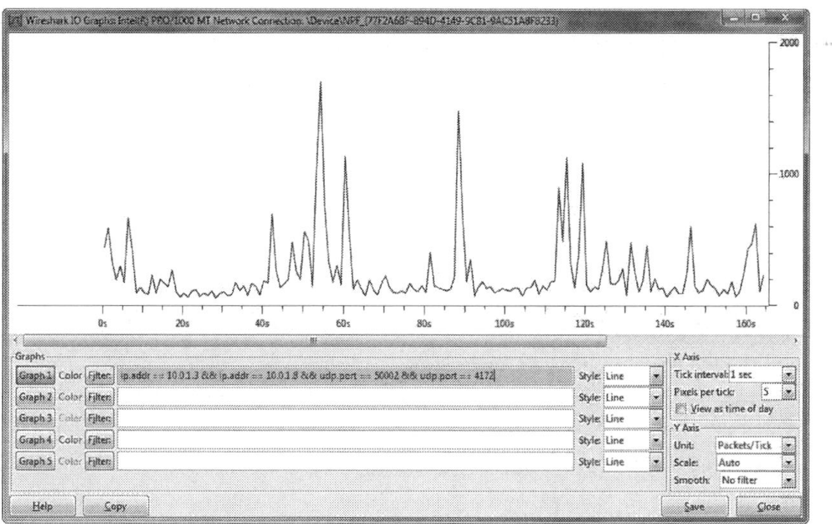

Figure 10.16 Real-time PCoIP information

You are now looking only at the PCoIP traffic between your client and VM. Now you can tune the environment and see the relative impact you are having on traffic and how it impacts your overall user experience. With Wireshark, you get a general sense of the live traffic flow while you make adjustments. It is also useful to go back and analyze your PCoIP stream if you are troubleshooting or want a detailed breakdown of the changes you are making. The testing described here will give you results on PCoIP. To validate you have full bandwidth evaluation, make sure that you cover other protocols, such as universal serial bus (USB) communication and multimedia redirection (MMR). To have a good understanding of the full bandwidth calculation, always consider this.

Tuning PCoIP

Before we go into how to tune, perhaps we should cover when to tune. PCoIP is a real-time protocol that adapts based on existing network conditions. Before you start adjusting the settings, make sure that you have already followed best practices, such as wrapping quality of service (QoS) around the PCoIP data stream and ensuring that your desktop image is properly tuned. Network QoS enables a network to handle application traffic in a way that meets the service requirements of the stream. Within QoS, you can set up a series of queues that enable you to prioritize real-time traffic over other network traffic.

Altering parameters can have unexpected results if you cannot measure the change. This is why we started creating a tuning environment. Keep in mind that as you tune, you are trading off on performance versus impact to the end-user experience. You might have certain virtual desktops that require tuning and others that do not. Keep this in mind when you are setting up your organization units (OUs) for the View desktops because most of the tuning parameters are applied through Active Directory (AD) policy.

As mentioned, you tune PCoIP through the AD using templates provided with VMware View. It is similar to the process of enabling Persona Management. You can find the PCoIP templates in the following location:

<install_directory>\VMware\VMwareView\Server\extras\GroupPolicyFiles\pcoip.adm

To import them into the AD, follow these steps:

1. Open your Group Policy Management Console.
2. Right-click your View Desktop OU and create or link a GPO policy.
3. Enter a name such as View PCoIP Tuning Policy.
4. Right-click the new policy and select **Edit**.
5. Browse to Administrative Templates and select **Add/Remove Templates**.

6. Click **Add** again, browse to the location on the View Server, and select the pcoip.adm template. (In Windows 2003, a template has an *.adm extension; for Windows 2008, the extension has been changed to *.admx.)
7. Expand the Administrative Templates and PCoIP Session Variables.

Tuning Parameters

As you adjust the tuning parameters, review how they affect the controlled performance tuning environment. For it to be clear, you should adjust each individually and then run a `gpupdate /force` command on the VM so that the policy is applied to the session. In some cases, you may have to restart the user session to see any differences.

Enabling the Build-to-Lossless feature actually disables the build to lossless and requires that you acknowledge this when you enable it (see Figure 10.17). You should enable this feature when the quality of the image is not critical. Keep in mind that you will likely have a percentage of desktops on which graphics quality is not critical and a portion on which it is. In general, enabling this feature is not noticeable to most users who are not modeling or reviewing medical information.

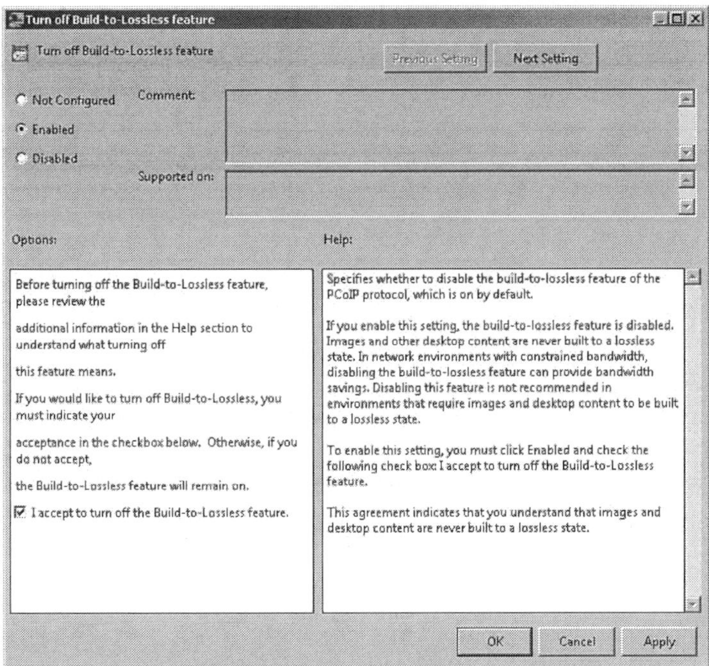

Figure 10.17 Enabling Build-to-Lossless

Setting the session bandwidth limit can prove helpful in low-bandwidth situations or on highly utilized LAN connections. VMware recommends that you set it to 10% lower than the maximum bandwidth rate. For example, on a Fast Ethernet connection of 100 Mbps, the kilobits per second is equal to 102,204. The default setting is 90,000 Kbps, which is roughly 10% below the maximum throughput for Fast Ethernet (see Figure 10.18).

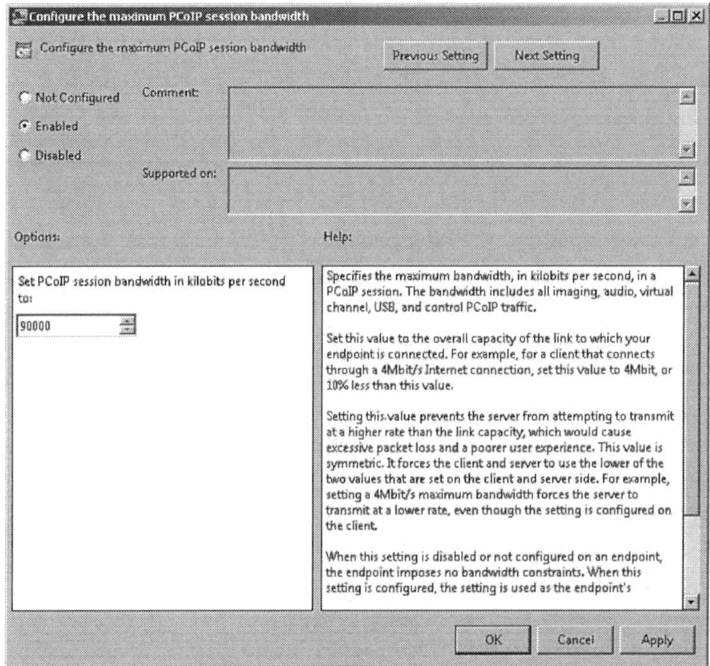

Figure 10.18 Session bandwidth limits

Setting the PCoIP session bandwidth floor is like setting a minimum reservation for the display traffic. It can be helpful if there is a large amount of packet loss on the network, such as wireless or 3G or 4G networks.

When you get into detailed configuration of the PCoIP protocol, that is where the PCoIP Log Viewer can be an invaluable asset because it breaks down the PCoIP traffic so that you know how to adjust the bandwidth floor setting in the policy, as shown in Figure 10.19.

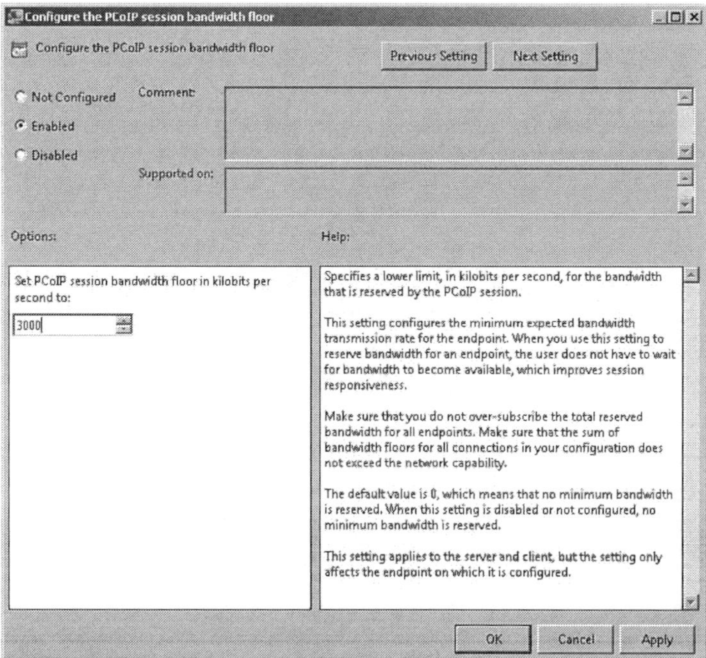

Figure 10.19 Configuring the bandwidth floor

Configuring image quality can be important to ensure a good user experience. The default maximum value for image quality is 90%. The maximum value limits the image quality of the changed regions of the display. Over a WAN, VMware recommends that you adjust this number down to 50% to 60% to reduce the bandwidth requirement of the session. On a LAN, a minor adjustment may improve the user experience without a noticeable difference to the user. The minimum value of the display sets the minimum quality of the images. This can be used in limited-bandwidth environments when you want to ensure a certain quality of image. For example, if you are using medical imaging or a healthcare application, you might want to ensure that the image is a certain quality before displaying. The minimum value cannot exceed the maximum value.

The other image quality setting is the frame rate, which determines the maximum frames per second (FPS). The default setting of 30 frames is ideal for good network conditions. You should adjust the frame rate from 30 to 10 to 15 frames in WAN network conditions (see Figure 10.20). You can also adjust this setting up as high as 120 FPS, but you must be careful to ensure your network conditions can support a higher frame rate.

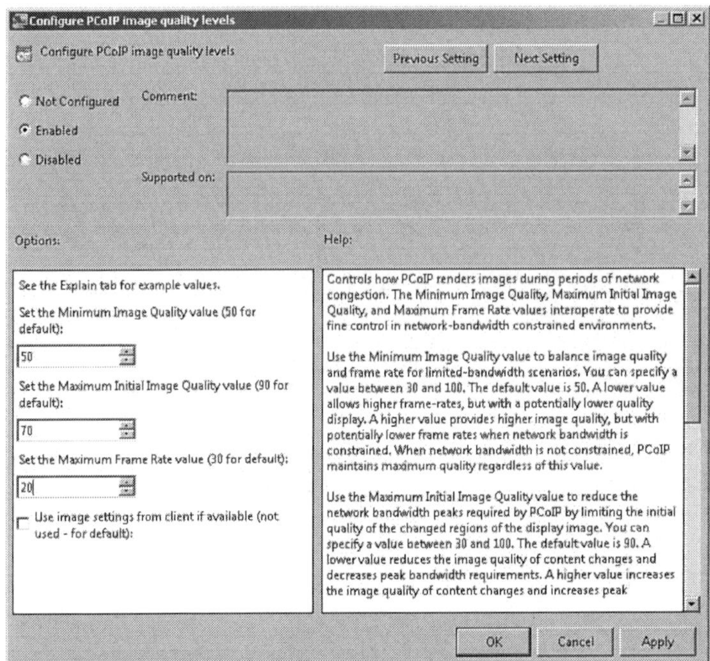

Figure 10.20 Image quality levels

Audio quality can be adjusted to set a predefined limit on the amount of bandwidth that the audio stream can use in kilobits per second (Kbps). You can adjust audio between 50 and 450 Kbps, but it requires fine-tuning and testing to determine what the tradeoff is between audio quality and bandwidth savings (see Figure 10.21). If audio is not required, you can turn it off.

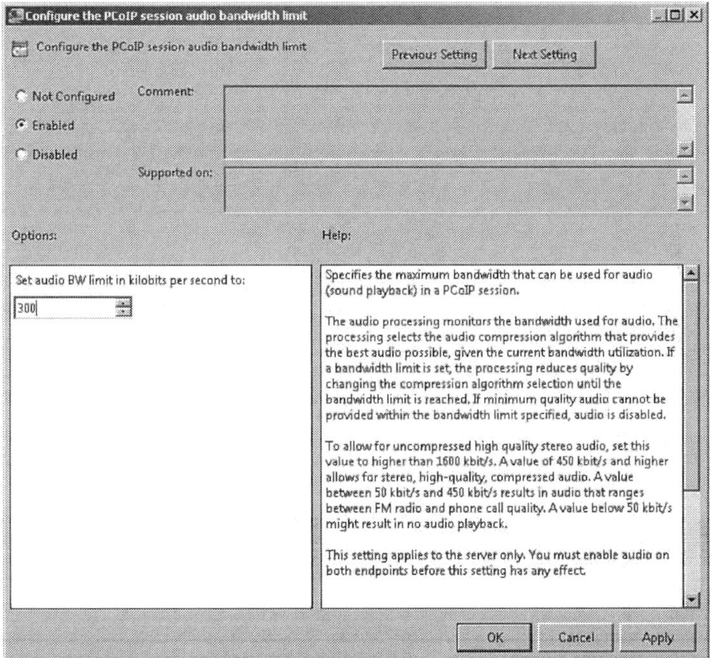

Figure 10.21 Audio bandwidth

One of the new features of PCoIP is a client-side image cache. You can adjust the size of this cache from the default of 250 MB. If you are using thin clients that have a restricted cache setting, you should adjust this value to match what is available in the thin clients. Attempting to use a larger cache than what is supported could lead to disconnects and timeouts (see Figure 10.22).

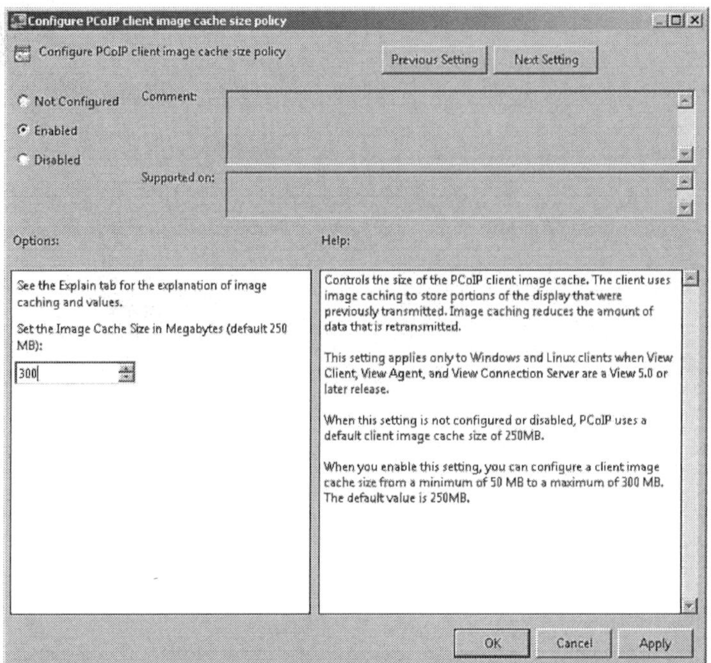

Figure 10.22 Adjusting the image cache

You also can adjust more settings, but these are some of the major ones that impact both user experience and performance. Use your performance-tuning environment to test and adjust so that you find the best combination of performance and utilization. In all cases, I have found that it is a good idea to adjust the settings from the defaults to either provide bandwidth savings or improve the overall user experience.

Further Analysis

If you need to break down the PCoIP protocol further, a number of good third-party tools are available. One of the best that is freely available is the PCoIP Log Viewer. PCoIP creates log files that are stored in C:\ProgramData\VMware\VDM\Logs by default. There are agent and server log files. The server logs are the ones that contain a wealth of information on how PCoIP is performing on the network. The PCoIP Log Viewer provides a parser and a viewer for looking at these log files. At the beginning of 2014, a new version was released that simplifies parsing and viewing these files. Now, everything is done within the Log Viewer tool. The viewer is based on Java and requires you to have Java installed on the machine from which you want to run it. The tool was developed by Chuck Hirstius and can be downloaded from http://mindfluxinc.net/.

Also note that Oracle decided, starting with Java 7 Update 51, to block any applications that are using a self-signed certificate to run. If you're like most people and have left the default configuration and if you're using that version of Java or a newer one, you will need to lower your security settings for the Java application to launch. Click **PCoIP-LogViewer.jnlp** to begin the installation. The first time you run the file, it downloads the remaining files from mindfluxinc.net. After you open it a second time, it checks to see whether any updates are available. If a connection to the Internet is not available, it takes much longer to launch but does launch after a period of time.

After the PCoIP Log Viewer is installed, two options present themselves to you; you can either connect to a live session or open a log file, as shown in Figure 10.23.

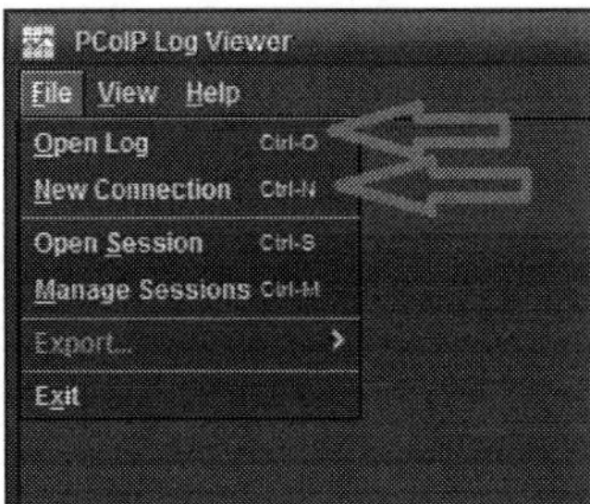

Figure 10.23 PCoIP Log Viewer

With the Log Viewer, you have access to specific information on bandwidth, PCoIP connection quality, packet count, latency, client-side performance, and so on. It is important, however, to understand how to interpret the information to make the necessary adjustments. Under the menu of the items, you see a series of tabs: Server, Network, Options, and Displays. The Server tab provides information on where the PCoIP Server service is running, such as the OS and CPU information.

The Network tab provides the IP address of the VM running the PCoIP Server services, the link speed, and maximum transmission unit (MTU) size, which is the size of the largest packet the network can transmit.

The Options tab shows you what options have been configured for the PCoIP session. These options are either the defaults if you have not adjusted them or the adjusted values.

The Displays tab shows you information on the display, such as how many are in use, the number that are allowed, and the image quality settings.

PCoIP Bandwidth Utilization

The details of the PCoIP Log Viewer are displayed in a graph that identifies key aspects of how the PCoIP protocol is functioning. These details allow you to troubleshoot certain issues and tune specific values. The first graph (see Figure 10.24) is the PCoIP Bandwidth Utilization graph. This graph displays any limit. In this example, we set a limit of 90,000 Kbps or 10% less than the total. You also see the plateau or ideal utilization of the session when all the virtual channels are considered. You can also break down traffic from the VM and to the VM as well as the overage.

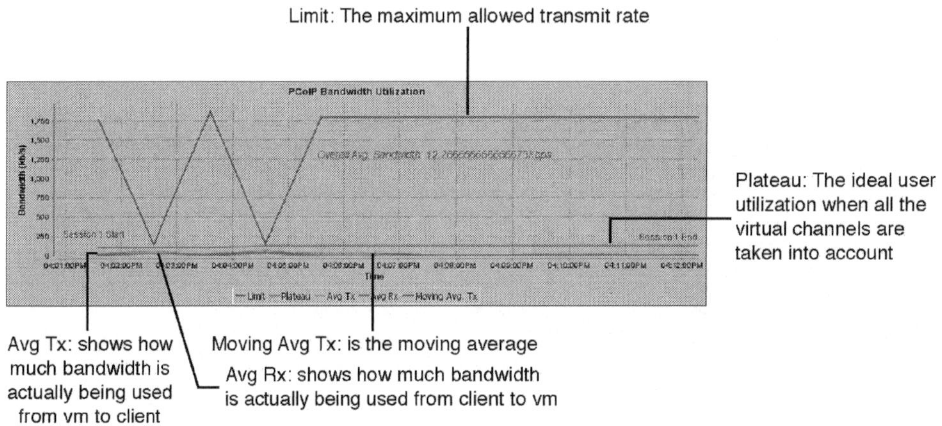

Figure 10.24 Bandwidth Utilization graph

PCoIP Connection Quality

The PCoIP Connection Quality graph tells you about packet loss from the PCoIP server running on the VM and also from the client to the PCoIP Server service. A large number of transmit losses occur when PCoIP is doing some rate limiting.

PCoIP Packet Counts

The PCoIP Packet Counts graph provides a better breakdown between image, audio, and other packets (see Figure 10.25). It enables you to see the changes when you are adjusting the PCoIP tuning options that affect image and audio in relation to the other channels.

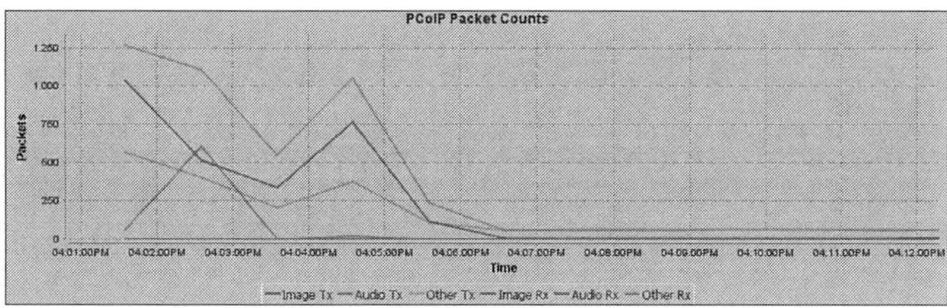

Figure 10.25 Packet Counts graph

PCoIP Connection Latency

Latency is the round-trip time from PCoIP Server service to the client and the variance between each measured round trip. It is shown in the Connection Latency graph (see Figure 10.26).

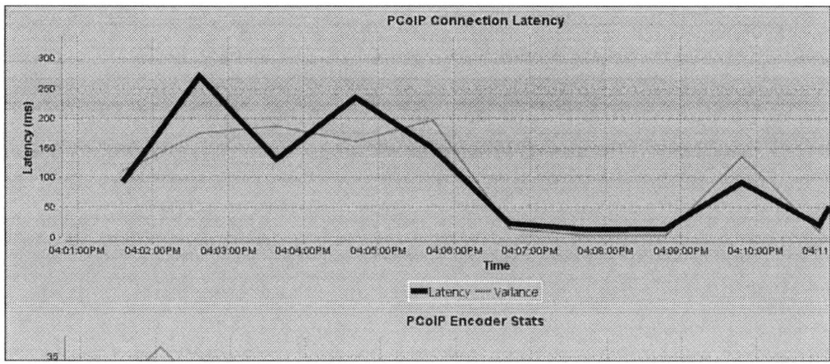

Figure 10.26 Connection Latency graph

Encoding Graphs

The architecture of PCoIP is based on a process that encodes the pixels using algorithms and a client that decodes the information to translate it to the screen. The encoder is the PCoIP Server service that is installed on the View virtual desktop when the agent is installed. The decoder is the View client that is installed on the access point. The next series of graphs deals with the performance of the Encoder and Decoder running in the VM and client, respectively.

The PCoIP Encoder stats measure the performance of the Encoder in encoding packets to send to the View client for decoding. The encoding is measured in UDP packets in frames per second (FPS) and video sample rate of flips (see Figure 10.27). The Quality Table measures the level of quality for the build to lossless. Generally a lower Quality Table number is considered better. A lower number translates to fewer dropped packets and lower rate-limiting activity. A high quality number usually corresponds to a poorer user experience. You can use this graph to lower the frames per second for better bandwidth while keeping an eye on the Quality Table.

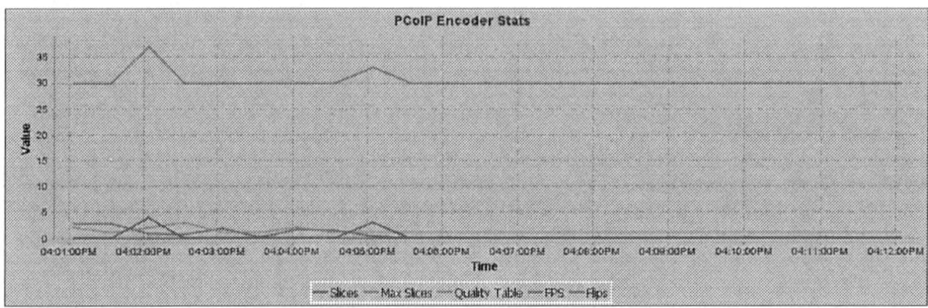

Figure 10.27 Encoder Stats graph

The PCoIP Encoder Stats graph tells you how many pixels have changed in the last 30 seconds. The PCoIP Encoder Stats—Delta Bits tells you how many lossless packets (Delta Build Bits) you have in relation to general data packets (Delta Bits). A high number of lossless data packets generally translates to a good overall user experience. The PCoIP Encoder Stats—Encoder Performance tells you how much compression is happening in the Bits Per Pixel line graph. The lower the bits per pixel value, the higher the compression ratio is. The final graph tells you about client performance. If the Client decode rate is less than the average transfer rate found in the PCoIP Bandwidth Utilization graph, that may indicate a client processing problem.

Although the PCoIP Log Viewer can be used for real-time data, I prefer to use Wireshark to get a sense of the traffic rate and then the viewer to better understand how PCoIP is reacting to the network. The Log Viewer requires a number of changes to support real-time data; these changes are fine in the controlled performance-tuning environment built previously, but more of a security risk to measure in production. The steps to enable real-time monitoring are included here but are not recommended for use in a production environment:

1. You must allow DCOM traffic through all Windows firewalls (View desktop to the PC running the PCoIP Log Viewer).

2. The Remote Registry Service must be started and set to automatic startup.
3. You must change permissions on the following registry so that administrators have full control:

```
HKEY_CLASSES_ROOT\CLSID\{76A64158-CB41-11d1-8B02-00600806D9B6}
```

Configuring these settings in production makes the desktop vulnerable to a security exploit.

You can use a combination of these tools to tune, measure, and apply your configurations to maximize the user experience while still getting the most out of your bandwidth. One issue you need to also review is overall performance. So far, this chapter has focused on session tuning, but you must also understand the overall performance of the environment to ensure the user experience is optimal.

The Impact of Load

To ensure a rich end-user experience, you must have accounted for load properly in your design and architecture. Load is generally measured in terms of input/output per second (IOPS) in a View environment, which refers to the number of reads and writes on the storage system. Load is a difficult thing to quantify until you have deployed virtual desktops into production. You should have a benchmark of relative performance of the environment ahead of that time to ensure the virtual desktops will perform well for users in production. This benchmark should be gathered by observing the resource utilized by the virtual desktop over a period of time.

VMware released the View Planner, which enables you to benchmark an environment under a simulated workload. Although the result is not identical to what you will experience in production, it gives us a representation of how it may perform under pre-scripted conditions. The value of benchmarking is that it further reduces your risk that users will not get a good user experience and ensures the environment has adequate resource capacity.

View Planner consists of a virtual desktop infrastructure (VDI) controller VA, client and desktop VMs, and your virtual infrastructure, as shown in Figure 10.28. You can leverage AD and View Server or choose not to, depending on the type of test you are running.

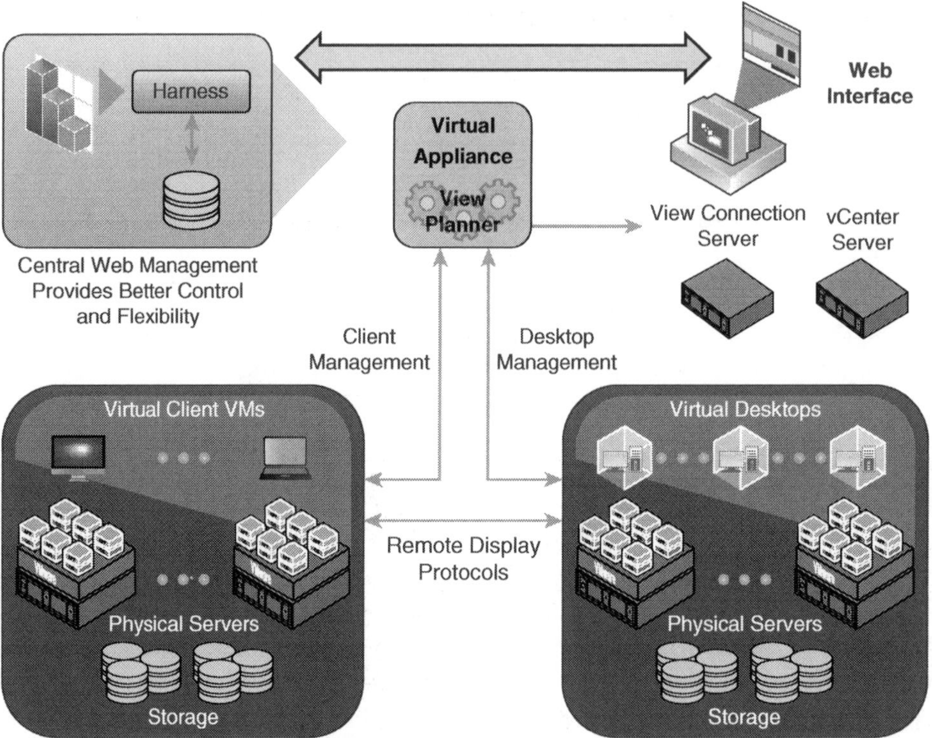

Figure 10.28 View Planner architecture

VMware View Planner enables you to conduct three types of tests, depending on the amount of infrastructure you are willing to commit and what you are most interested in stressing:

- Remote mode requires one client per VM and is closest to a real-world simulation. It requires the most amount of infrastructure for load testing.
- Passive client mode allows multiple VMs per client. This requires less infrastructure for your load testing but still incorporates a client component.
- Local mode requires no client VMs but still enables you to simulate a "real" workload for benchmark testing. It requires the least commitment to infrastructure.

For a complete list of hardware and software requirements, refer to VMware's documentation.

Setting Up VMware ViewPlanner

View Planner comes as an OVF file you simply download and import into your virtualization environment, as shown in Figure 10.29. After the installation, you need to run a series of commands from the console to prepare the appliance.

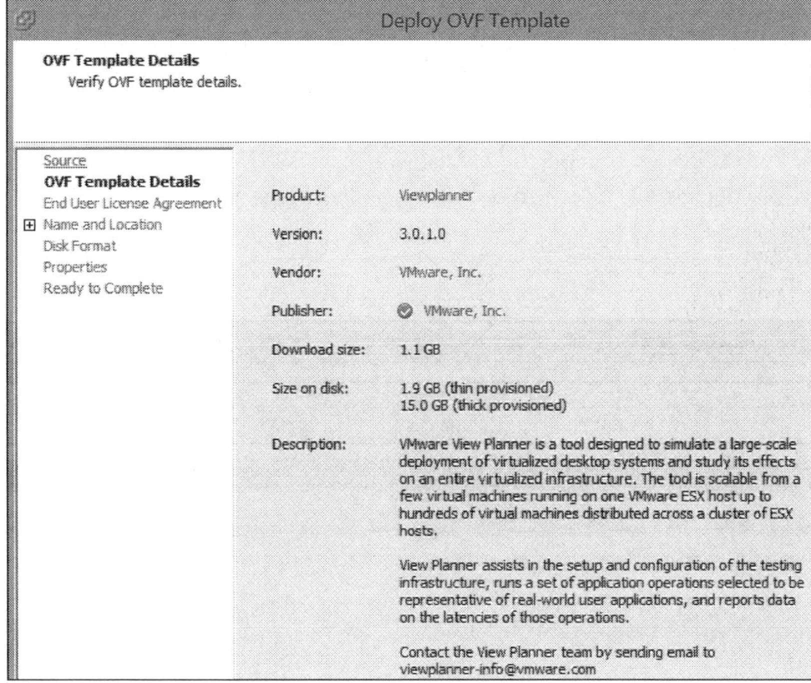

Figure 10.29 Importing the virtual appliance

After importing the appliance and entering the proper IP information, you must prepare it. You prepare the appliance by running the following commands:

1. Boot the appliance and, if prompted, type **yes** to accept the license agreement.
2. Log in to the appliance using **root** and password **vmware**.
3. Change to the /root/ViewPlanner directory by running **cd /root/ViewPlanner**.
4. Set the path for Python by running **source setup.sh**.
5. Hard-code an IP address using the Python script and the following syntax:

```
python ./harness_setup.pyc -i [IP ADDRESS] -m [NETMASK] -g [GATEWAY]
-d {DOMAIN NAME] -n [DNS SERVER]
```

After configuring the appliance, you can browse to the web page and log in using **root** and the default password **abc123**.

After you log in, you need to configure connections to the vCenter, View, and AD servers. What connections you need to configure are determined by whether you are running a remote, passive, or local mode test. For example, for a local mode test, you do not need an AD server, but you still need to put a dummy entry in the AD portion (for example, 127.0.0.1). After you put entries in the configuration section, click **Save** to have them saved and stored.

To have the View Planner automate the workload and deployment, you need to install several bundles on your AD, View, client, and virtual workstations. These bundles install Python and the various default scripts to run the components. These bundles are available as downloadable packages from the View Planner VA under the Packages section, as shown in Figure 10.30.

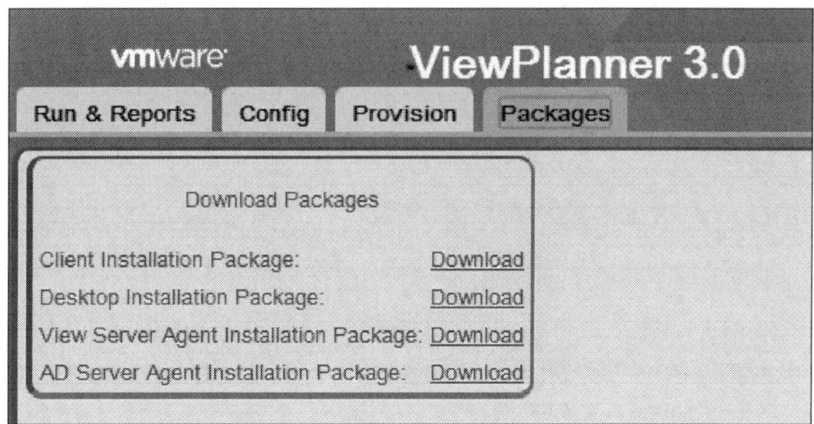

Figure 10.30 Downloading View Planner components

You also need to make some configuration adjustments to the VMs and View Servers. For an extensive list, refer to the documentation. At a high level, you need to configure the following:

- VMware View Server.
- Install the View Server Agent Installation Package.
- Set PowerShell execution to unrestricted using the following command from the PowerShell window:

  ```
  Set-ExecutionPolicy unrestricted
  ```

- Configure an external URL for the VMware View Server by logging in to the View Administrator console, View Configuration, Servers. Select **View Server** and click **Edit** and enter an external URL in the format https://*View Server IP*:443.
- Golden master image.
- Install Windows 7 or Windows XP image. (Note that you must ensure either Microsoft Key Management Services exists in the environment or that the image has a Multiple Activation Key [MAK].)
- Ensure that you have a second E: drive labeled datadisk for user data.
- You need to install the desktop bundle Python package.

Many more optimizations that you can tweak are suggested in the deployment guide.

Setting Up the Client Desktop

To test the client desktop, you need to create a separate client template. The reason is that both the client machines and VMs are virtualized in the load testing done by View Planner. In addition to a client desktop, you need to install the Client Installation Package on the client machine.

When everything is prepped, you are ready to configure the provisioning settings. You have the option of using vCenter or View Composer. Just enter the vCenter information or View or both.

After you have everything properly staged, you can create a profile that defines which applications to run, how many iterations, and the pauses (think time) between iterations. You simply specify a profile name, click which applications you want to instantiate, specify the iterations and think time, and save the profile.

When you have a profile, you can specify the number of VMs to run, which workload profile, and what percentage of the total number of VMs should run this specific profile. You can build a variety of different types of profiles to simulate light, medium, and heavy users to ensure that you have properly stressed the environment.

At this point, you have looked at session tuning and load testing to ensure that you have validated session and overall performance of the environment. Proper testing and tuning ensures your environment can deliver a rich end-user experience.

The public version of the View Planner does not have all the extensive configuration options of the Partner version. Refer to this site for all the details: www.vmware.com/ca/en/products/view-planner.

Summary

This chapter discussed the importance of measuring the end-user experience to fine-tune each use case. You looked at the different scenarios possible with VMware View, going from software rendering, then including a 3D graphics card to share among multiple users, all the way up to dedicating a full GPU to a virtual desktop.

You looked at tools to help quantify this by simulating distance through the use of WANem to apply latency, packet loss, and jitter to your PCoIP stream. You should now understand how to use standard networking tools such as Wireshark to look at real-time PCoIP traffic flows. In addition, you looked at the PCoIP Log Viewer utility to break down and analyze each of the components that work to deliver the PCoIP protocol from the View desktop to the client. You also reviewed a tool to simulate IOPS in the View environment so that you can load test your virtual desktop environment. I cannot stress enough the importance of ensuring that you have taken the time to use these tools or tools like these to examine how things like PCoIP perform in different use cases and how your virtual desktop environment will perform under various load stresses.

Chapter 11

Integrating Lync and VMware View

Microsoft Lync and VMware View

This chapter covers the integrations Microsoft has made to ensure Lync performs better in a virtual desktop environment. Microsoft Lync 2010 supported Voice over IP (VoIP) but not video when integrated with VMware View. With Microsoft Lync 2013, Microsoft has changed the architecture to enable support of voice and video. To provide an example in this chapter, we review the specifics around configuring Lync to work with VMware View and how you can troubleshoot if you run into problems. The configuration of Lync 2013 used in this chapter is suitable for proof-of-concept (PoC) environments, but it is not meant to be an extensive examination of deploying an enterprise Lync 2013 infrastructure. For this, you need to refer to Microsoft's online documentation. It will, however, let you set up and review how this works in a VMware View environment so that you can review the details of the configuration.

One of the challenges for integrating VoIP and video can be described using the following example. In this example, let's look at two users who are sitting side by side in a branch using View desktops with Lync installed. Using a default installation within the virtual desktops, all the components of Lync would be installed in the View instance. A call to User B initiated by User A would travel from the client device to the datacenter to the second View instance and back out to user A, as shown in Figure 11.1. This type of traffic flow is called *hairpinning*.

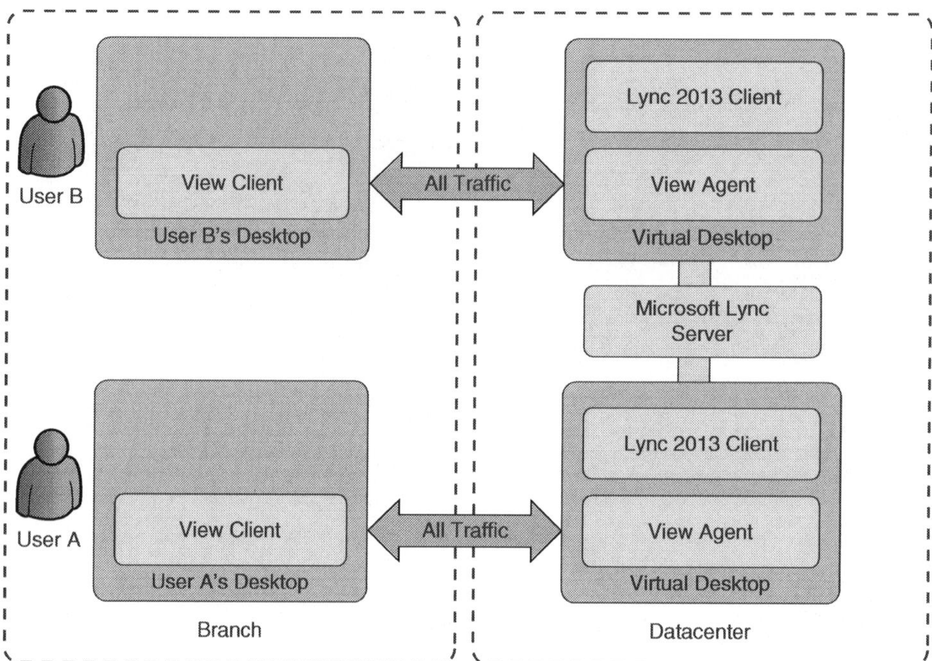

Figure 11.1 Hairpinning

In VoIP, hairpinning is a process in which a phone set connects to a private branch exchange (PBX) and then back out to another phone set to carry out a call. The entire communication takes place over a path that is longer than the shortest possible circuit between the two endpoints.

All telephone systems make use of hairpinning connections. In VoIP, hairpinning can often be avoided if two endpoints can be connected directly. This direct link is called shuffling. Hairpin connections are considered inefficient and can be especially problematic when using virtual desktops because the default route is usually the longest point between two clients.

To support VoIP in virtual desktop infrastructure (VDI), integrated thin client and VoIP systems were used to support shuffling. When you look at it shuffling is very similar to multimedia redirection (MMR), in which the video is redirected to the local client for rendering and made to appear as if it's running in a unified session. In the case of shuffling, the VoIP traffic is redirected to the client-side device so that a direct connection can be made along the shortest possible route. If we look at our example again, a shuffled connection would initiate a VoIP call directly from User B's client to User A's client, as shown in Figure 11.2.

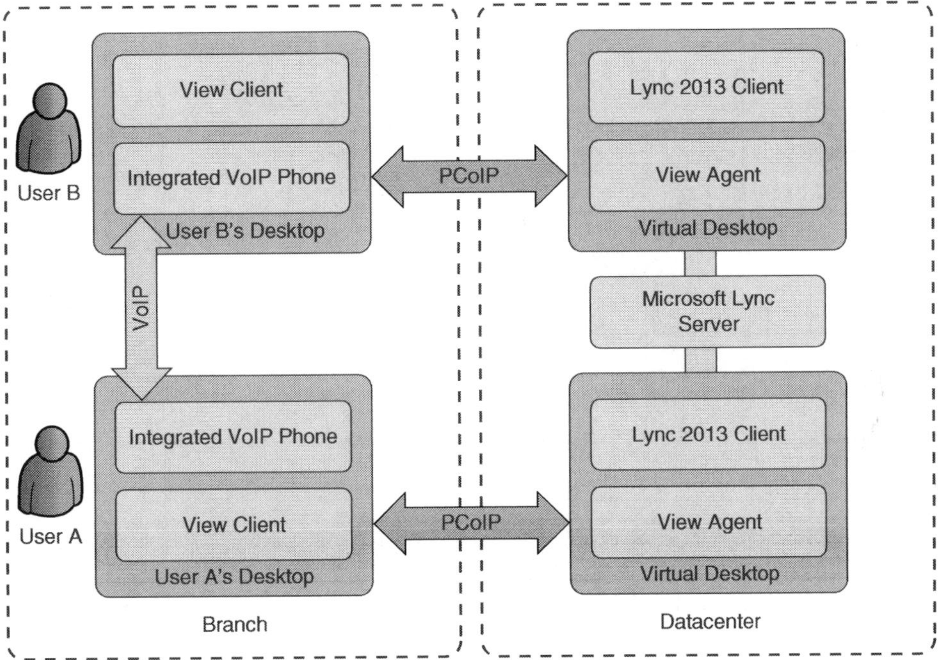

Figure 11.2 Shuffling in virtual desktop environments

Microsoft Lync 2013

You can enable support for video and audio with Microsoft Lync 2013. Microsoft has created a Lync VDI plug-in that enables you to redirect or shuffle audio and video between client connections versus hairpinning them through the datacenter. In Figure 11.3, we see these components working together. User B is using a Lync 2013 Client installed natively on his desktop, and User A is using a View Desktop with the Lync 2013 Client installed. In addition, User A has the Lync VDI plug-in installed locally on his desktop in addition to running the View Client. When User B establishes a video conferencing session with User A, the audio/video is sent directly to User A's desktop.

The advantage of this architecture is that the audio and video is not sent over the PC over IP (PCoIP) connection, reducing the load and latency. Because it is a direct connection, the performance should match that of the native Lync 2013 Client. Note that on User A's desktop the Lync VDI plug-in is used in place of the full Microsoft 2013 Lync Client. This is because the VDI plug-in and Lync Client cannot be installed on the same device together.

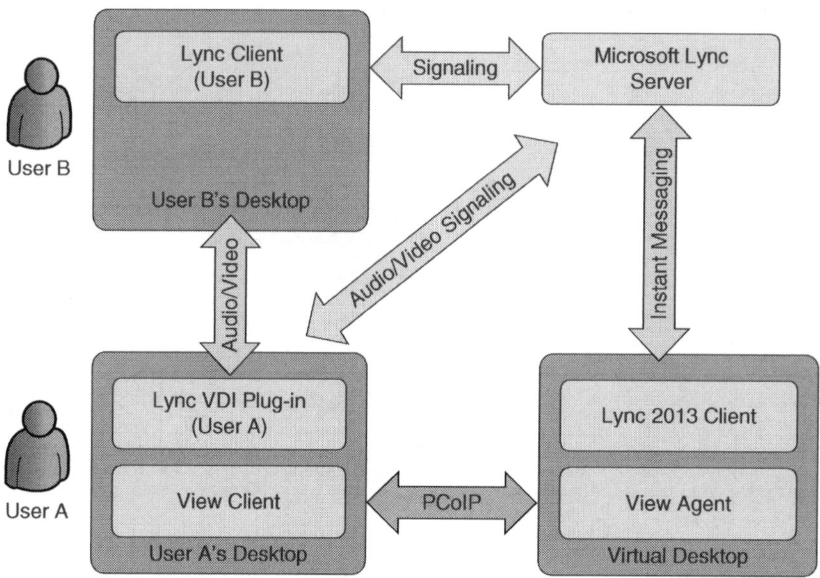

Figure 11.3 Shuffling in virtual desktop environments

Creating a Lync Environment

Installing Lync is a multistep process with many interdependencies and prerequisites to get you up and running. To enable you to test the environment, the steps required to deploy an integrated Lync 2013 and VMware View environment are provided. Only the basic features of Lync are enabled to verify that the redirection occurs. For additional features and details about Lync, refer to Microsoft's online documentation.

Preparing for Lync 2013

To avoid problems, you should set up a number of prerequisites before beginning the installation. Lync requires certificates and Domain Name System (DNS) entries to install properly. In addition, you need an Active Directory server as well as a Standard front-end Lync 2013 server. To provide a certificate, you can use Microsoft Certificate Authority if you install this role. In this example, we are using a Microsoft Windows 2012 for the AD server and for the Lync 2013 server. The AD server runs the following roles:

- Active Directory Certificate Services
- Active Directory Domain Services
- DNS Server

To add a role on a Microsoft Windows 2012 server, just follow these steps:

1. Log in to the Microsoft Windows 2012 desktop.
2. From the taskbar, click the **Server Manager** icon (Note that the default behavior is for Server Manager to launch by default on login, so it might open automatically.)
3. From the Server Manager dashboard, select **Manage** from the menu and select **Add Roles and Features**.

Lync requires several entries in DNS in addition to a host record for the server. To make it easier for users to join meetings or access Lync Administrator tools, simple URLs are used. Because this configuration example uses a single front-end Lync server, all the URLs point back to the same server. The simple URLs that need to be defined are meet, dialing, and admin. Verify that you have an A record and reverse DNS entry for your Lync server, and then add the additional A record, as shown in Figure 11.4.

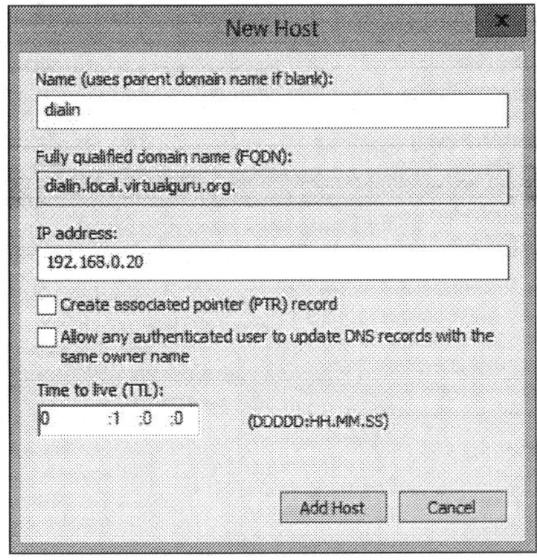

Figure 11.4 Adding DNS records for Lync simple URLS

You can add these records by completing the following steps:

1. Open DNS Manager.
2. Expand the Forward Lookup Zone folder and select your DNS domain.
3. Right-click and select **New Host (A or AAAA)**.

NOTE You do not need to create the associated PTR (pointer) record because you have one already for the Lync server itself.

In addition to the simple URL DNS records, you also need to create a service record for the Session Initiation Protocol (SIP) service running on the Lync server. SIP is a communications protocol used for managing voice and video calls over an IP network. In actual fact, in a production Lync environment, it is likely that you will have multiple SIP service records for internal, external, or federated service partners. In this example, though, we are only testing the integration between View and Lync internally, so we will create an internal SIP service record. Within DNS Manager, you do not automatically see service records unless you select to view the advanced configuration items as well. You can do this by selecting **View** from the menu bar in DNS Manager and then selecting the **Advanced** option from the drop-down menu. When you select the advanced options, you will notice that you have additional folders displayed under your domain space, such as _sites, _tcp, _udp. Because SIP runs over IP, you can add the service record using the following steps:

1. Open DNS Manager.
2. Expand the Forward Lookup Zone folder and expand your DNS domain.
3. Select the _tcp folder and right-click and select **Other New Records**.
4. Under Select a Resource Record Type, scroll down until you see the **Service Location (SRV)**, as shown in Figure 11.5.

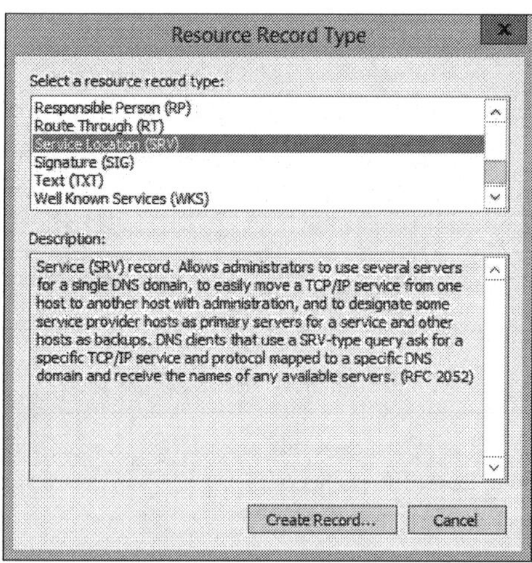

Figure 11.5 Adding a Service Location record

5. Input the following information: the service name is **_sipinternaltls**; the protocol is **_tcp**; the port is **5061**; and the host offering this service is the fully qualified domain of your Lync server, as shown in Figure 11.6.

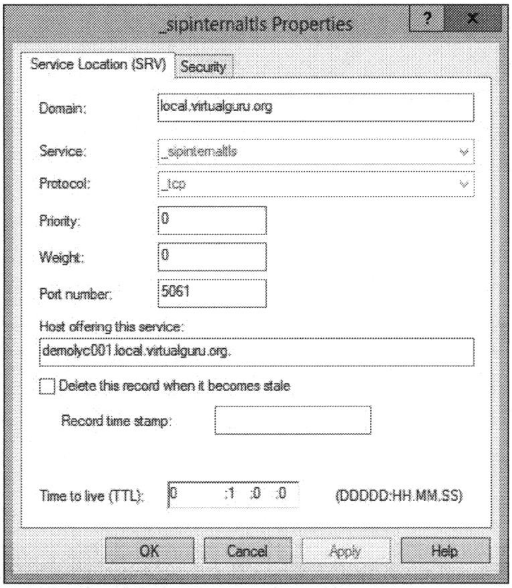

Figure 11.6 Creating the _sipinternaltls service record

Lync 2013

Perhaps the most difficult part of installing a Lync 2013 server is ensuring that you have all the prerequisites installed. For the most part, this is a matter of using the Add Roles and Features option described in the first part of this section, with the exception of the steps to add .NET 3.5 and perhaps adding the certificates. Let's cover both those items so that you can complete them and verify that you have all the prerequisites.

Earlier in the chapter, we added the Active Directory Certificate Services to our AD server. The installer will use this service to apply a certificate to the Lync server.

Windows 2012 and .NET Framework 3.5

The process to install .NET Framework 3.5 differs a little bit under Windows 2012 from earlier Windows releases. This is because by default the source files are stored in a different location on the media and must be prepared before adding it as a feature using the Add Roles and Features Wizard. To avoid any problems, ensure that your Lync server has a valid connection to the network, and then run the Deployment Image and Servicing and Management (`dism`) command specifying the source files on the installation media. For example, if your install media is on the D: drive, you run the following command:

```
dism /online /enable-feature /featurename:NetFX3 /all /source:d:\sources\
sxs /LimitAccess
```

You should see `dism` enable the feature, as shown in Figure 11.7.

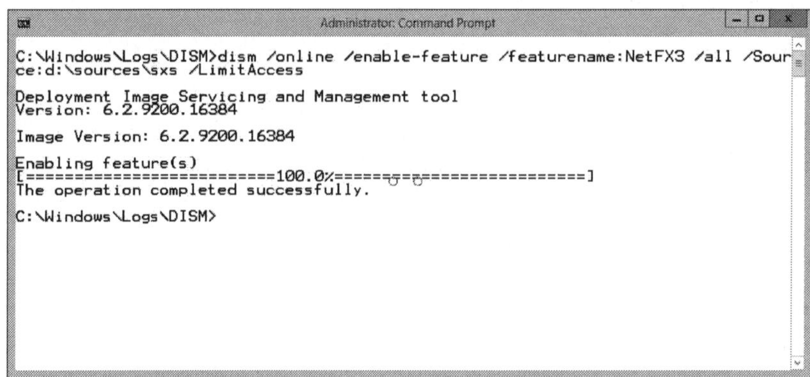

Figure 11.7 Running `dism` to enable .NET Framework 3.5

After preparing the .NET Framework, it is a matter of installing the extensive prerequisites using the Roles and Features Wizard. Lync 2013 requires the following roles and features:

Roles

- File and storage services
    - File and iSCSI services
        - File server
- Web server (IIS) role, including the following features:
    - Common HTTP features installed
        - Static
        - Default doc
        - HTTPS errors
    - Health and diagnostics
        - HTTP logging
        - Logging tools
        - Tracing
    - Performance
        - Static content compression
        - Dynamics content compression

- Security
    - Request filtering
    - Client cert mapping authentication
    - Windows Authentication
- Management tools
    - IIS management console
    - IIS management scripts and tools
- Application development
    - ASP.NET 3.5
    - .NET extensibility 3.5
    - ASP.NET 4.5
    - .NET extensibility 4.5
    - ISAPI extensions
    - ISAPI Filters

Features

- Message queuing and message queuing services
- Remote server administration tools and role administration tools and Active Directory Domain Services (AD DS) and Active Directory Lightweight Directory Services (AD LDS) tools
- User interfaces and infrastructure and desktop experience
- Windows Identity Foundation 3.5
- .NET Framework 3.5
    - .NET Framework 3.5
    - HTTP activation
    - Non-HTTP activation

When installing the .NET Framework 3.5, you must click the **Specify an Alternate Source Path** link on the Confirm Installation Selections page of the Add Roles and Features Wizard, as shown in Figure 11.8.

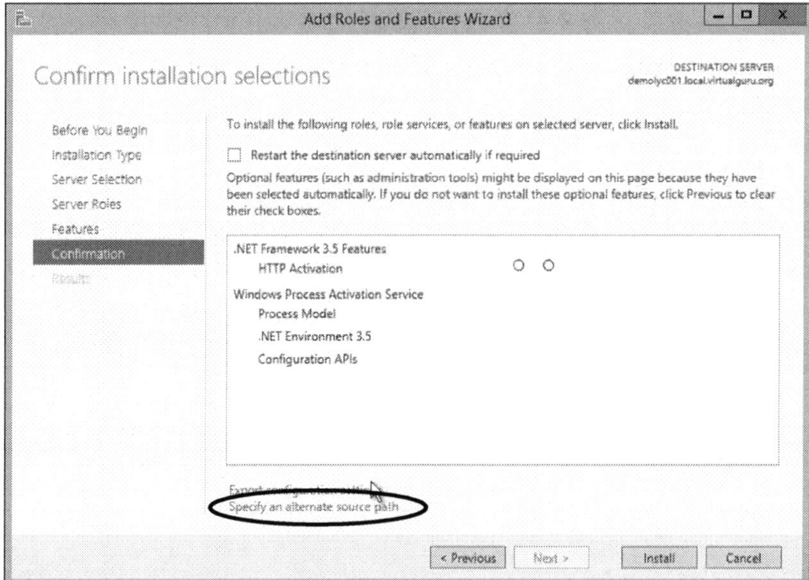

Figure 11.8 Specifying an alternative source path

When prompted, you specify **D:\Sources\SxS** (assuming D: is the installation media drive), as shown in Figure 11.9.

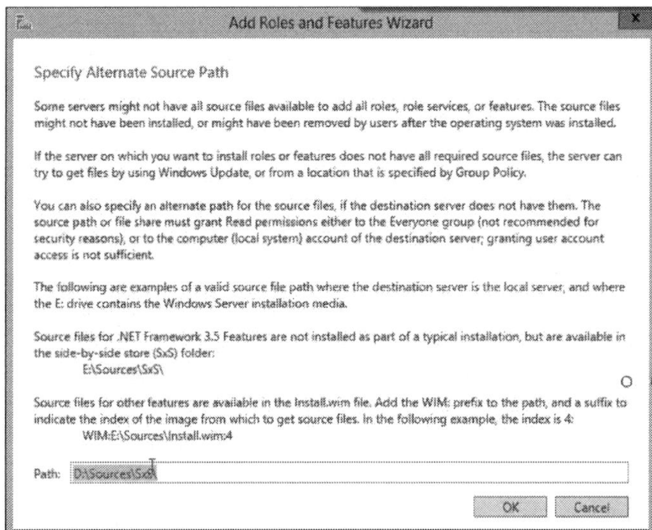

Figure 11.9 Specifying the path D:\Sources\SxS

The last feature you need is the .NET Framework 4.5, along with all options.

In addition, Lync's management console leverages Microsoft Silverlight, so you should install it on the server.

Installing Lync Server

The actual installation involves installing the core components, preparing the Active Directory, installing a local configuration store, and defining whether it is an enterprise or standard pool. (An enterprise pool can contain as many as 20 computers and is designed for high-availability and load-balanced environments.) A standard pool is suitable for testing and smaller environments and defines a single server for all services.

As mentioned previously, an enterprise configuration is beyond the scope and focus of this book, so the example configures a standard pool to ensure that you can test Lync integration with VMware View.

To install and configure Lync, complete the following steps:

1. Launch setup.exe from the Lync 2013 installation media.
2. When prompted to install Visual C++, select Yes (because it is a requirement for Lync).
3. You can accept the default installation location C:\Program Files\Microsoft Lync Server 2013 or select Browse to specify an alternate location. Once a location is specified, click Install.
4. Click **I Accept the Terms in the Licensing Agreement**, and then click **OK** to start the installation.

The installation should start the Lync 2013 Deployment Wizard. However, if it does not, you can press the **Windows** button on your keyboard to bring up Windows Tiles and select the Lync 2013 Deployment Wizard, as shown in Figure 11.10.

When the Lync Server 2013 Deployment Wizard runs, it will take a few moments to determine at what stage the deployment is. From under the Deploy pane, select **Prepare Active Directory** and complete the following steps on the Prepare Active Directory for Lync Server page, as shown in Figure 11.11.

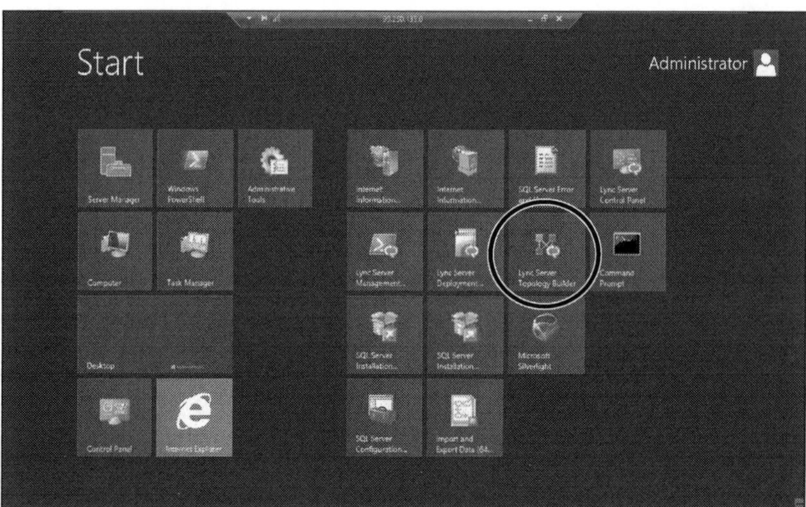

Figure 11.10 Launching the Lync Deployment Wizard

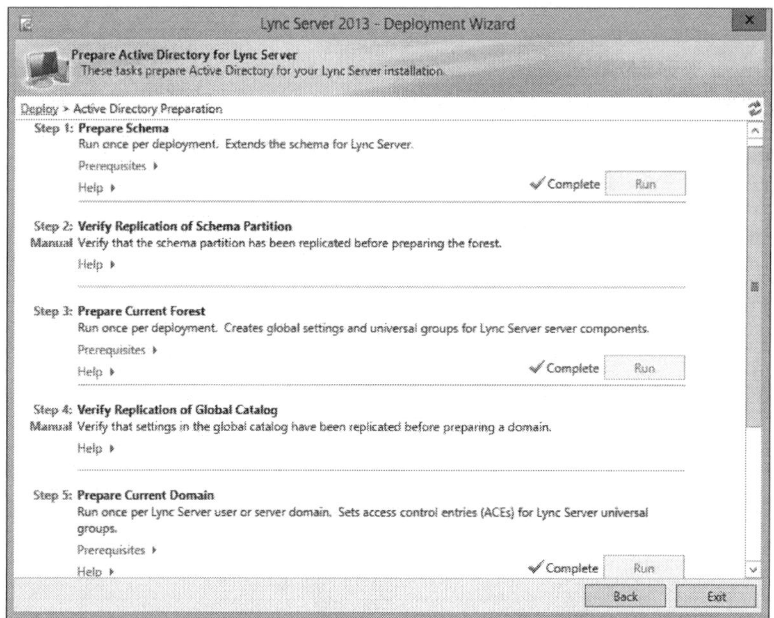

Figure 11.11 Preparing Active Directory for Lync server

1. Under Prepare Schema, select **Run**.
2. If you have more than one AD server, you must run Step 2: Verify Replication of Schema Partition by selecting **Run**. If you have only a single AD server, you do not need to run this step.
3. Select **Run** under Step 3: Prepare Current Forest.
4. Select **Next**, **Local Domain**, **Next** to prepare the AD forest.
5. Step 4: Verify Replication of the Global Catalog is a reminder that if you have more than one AD server you should check to see whether the newly created Lync objects are available on other AD servers. The easiest way is to check that any of the newly created Communication Server (CS) groups have replicated across your environment. To verify, perform the following steps:
    a. On a remote domain controller, run Active Directory Users and Computers.
    b. Click **Users** and look at any of the CS groups in the right pane, as shown in Figure 11.12. If you do not see any of the new Lync objects, you may have to force replication.

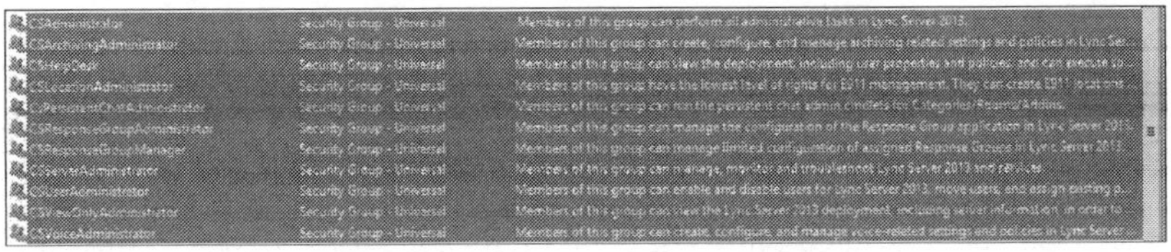

Figure 11.12 Lync CS objects

6. Under Step 5: Prepare Current Domain, click **Next**.
7. Step 6: Verify Replication in the Domain actually verifies that the schema changes in Step 1 have been properly replicated if you have more than one AD server. The verification process involves running a commandlet in the Lync Server Management Shell. To verify whether Step 1 was successful, complete the following:
    a. Press the **Windows** button to bring up the installed application tiles and select the **Lync Server Management Shell**.
    b. Run the following command, substituting the correct values for your environment:

```
Get-CsAdDomain -Domain [DOMAIN NAME] -GlobalSettingDomainController
[FQDN of AD Server]
i.e.
Get-CsAdDomain -Domain virtualguru.org -GlobalSettingDomainController
ad01.virtualguru.org
```

The command returns `LC_DOMAIN_SETTINGS_STATE_READY is successful.`

8. Step 7: Add Users to Provide Administrative Access to the Lync Server Control Panel involves adding administrator accounts to the newly created CSAdministrators group. To add users, complete the following steps:
    a. On a domain controller, run Active Directory Users and Computers.
    b. Right-click **CSAdministrators** and select **Properties**.
    c. Display the Members tab and click the **Add** button.
    d. In the Enter Object Names to Select box, type the names of the users you want to add, and then click **OK** and **OK** again.
9. After Step 7, click the **Back** button to go back to the Lync Server 2013 Deployment Wizard.

Now that we have installed the files and prepared the AD for Lync, we are ready to prepare our server. To prepare the server, click the **Prepare First Standard Edition Server** link from the Lync Server 2013 Deployment Wizard, as shown in Figure 11.13. In this example, we are installing all components on a single server so that we have the installer use SQL Server Express Edition and create the RTC databases used to store persistent user data and other Lync server installation files.

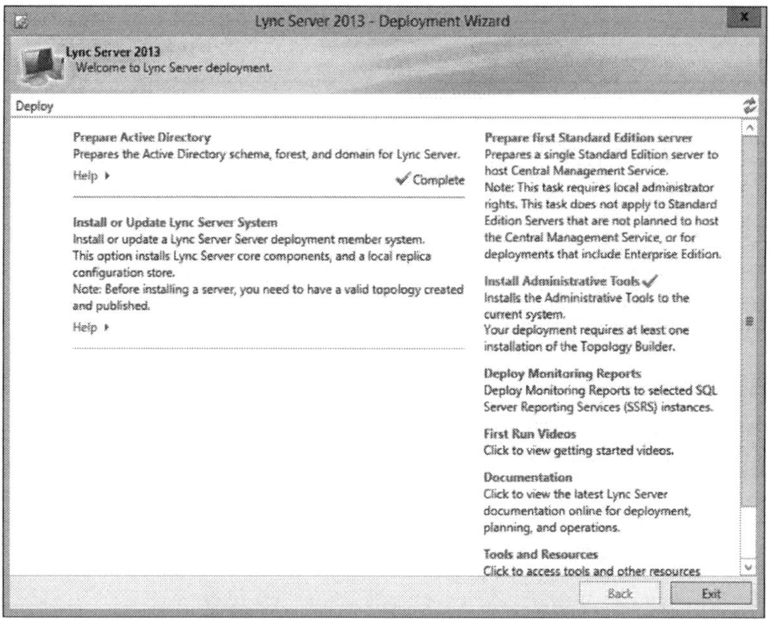

Figure 11.13 Preparing the first Standard Edition server

When this process completes, click the **Install Administrative Tools** link on the Lync Server 2013 Deployment Wizard.

Build and Publish a Lync Topology

The next part of the deployment process is to build and publish a Lync topology. For this, we will use one of the newly installed Lync administrative tools: the Lync Server Topology Builder. To launch the builder, create a topology, and publish it, complete the following steps:

1. Press the **Windows** button to bring up the installed application tiles and select **Lync Server Topology Application**.
2. Select **New Topology**, as shown in Figure 11.14, and click **OK**.

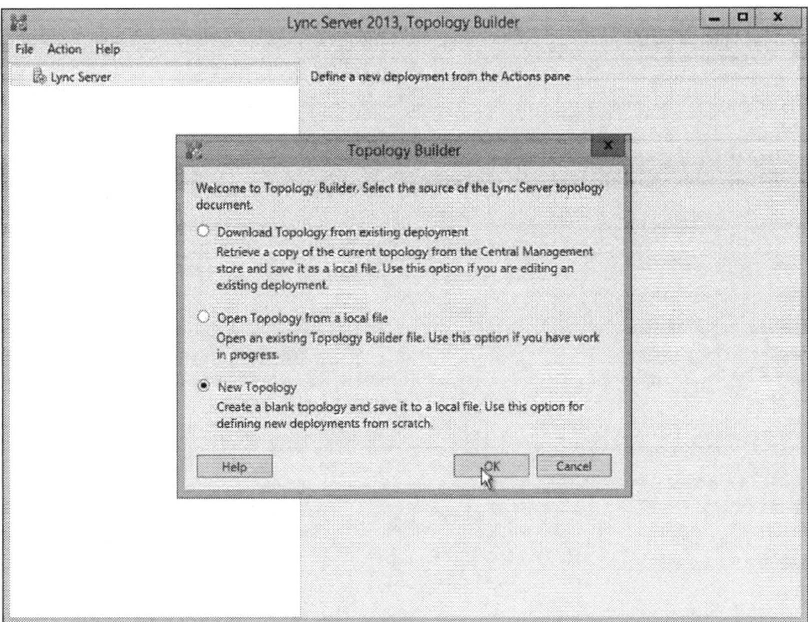

Figure 11.14 Selecting New Topology

3. Specify a filename under the Save New Topology As window and click **Save**.
4. Under Create New Topology, specify the primary SIP domain, as shown in Figure 11.15, and click **Next**.

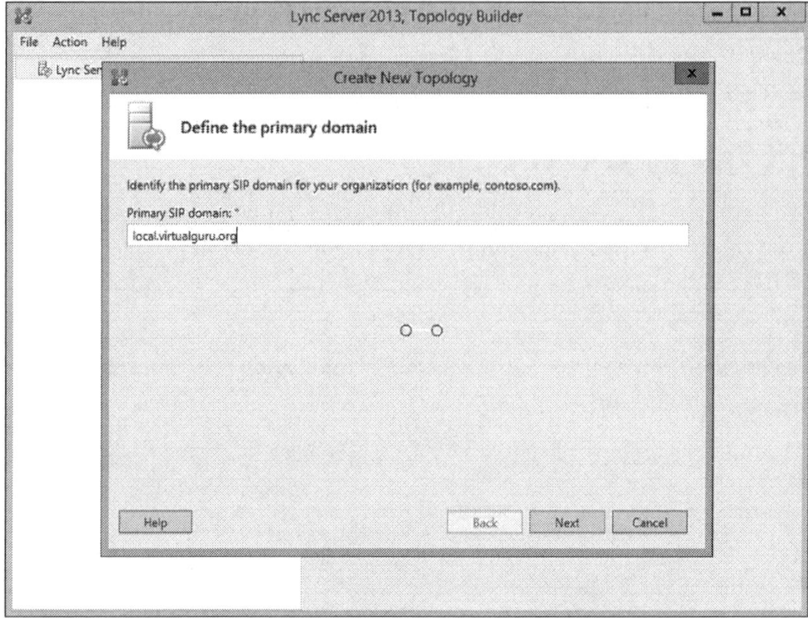

Figure 11.15 Defining the primary domain

5. The next screen lets you enable other domains for SIP; if this is the only domain, click **Next**; otherwise, add the domains under the Additional SIP Domains text box and click **Add** and then **Next**.

6. On the Define the First Site screen, provide a name and description of the site you want to create, and click **Next**.

7. On the Specify Site Details screen, provide the city, state/province, and the country/region code, and click **Next**.

8. On the final screen, ensure that the default, **Open the New Front End Wizard When This Wizard Is Finished**, is selected, and then click **Finish**.

9. On the Define the New Front End Pool Welcome screen, click **Next**.

10. On the Define the Front End Pool FQDN screen, specify the pool FQDN (for a Standard Edition this will be the FQDN of the server) and ensure that **Standard Edition Server** is selected and click **Next**.

11. On the Select Features screen, select **Conferencing**, **Enterprise Voice**, and **Call Admission Control** for testing purposes, and then click **Next**, as shown in Figure 11.16.

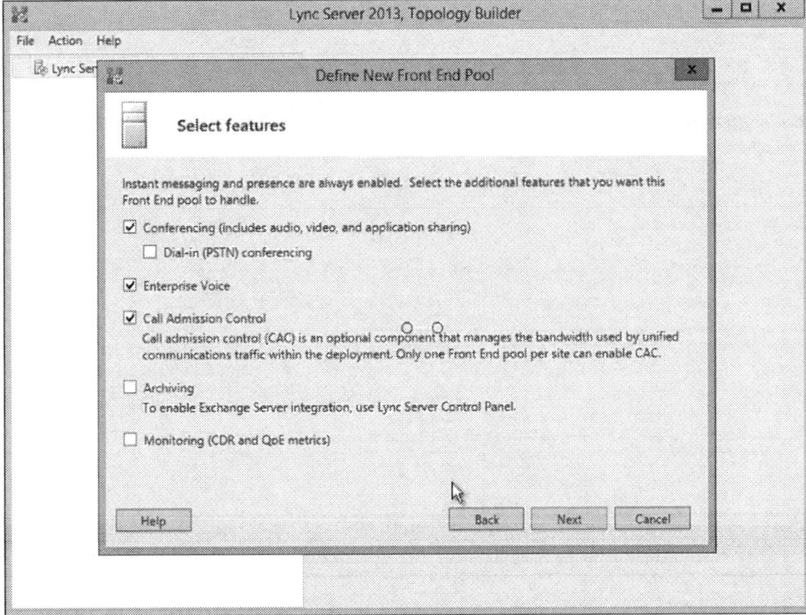

Figure 11.16 Selecting features

12. On the Select Collocated Server Roles screen, select **Collocate Mediation Server** because we have only one server, and then click **Next**.
13. On the Associate Server Roles with this Front End Pool screen, we will not enable the media component on the edge pool, so you can click **Next**.
14. Because we are using SQL Express, the default server store location [localhost]\rtc is fine, so we can click **Next**.
15. Because we have not yet defined a file store, ensure that the default **Define a New File Store** is selected and that the default name is **share**, and then click **Next**.
16. Because we have a single server, the default external base URL of the local host is correct, so you can click **Next**.
17. On the Select Office Web Apps Server screen, we will leave the default **Associate Pool with an Office Web Apps Server** selected and click **New**.
18. For the Office web app server, add **owa** to the beginning of the domain name, as shown in Figure 11.17, and click **OK**, and then click **Finish** to complete the process.

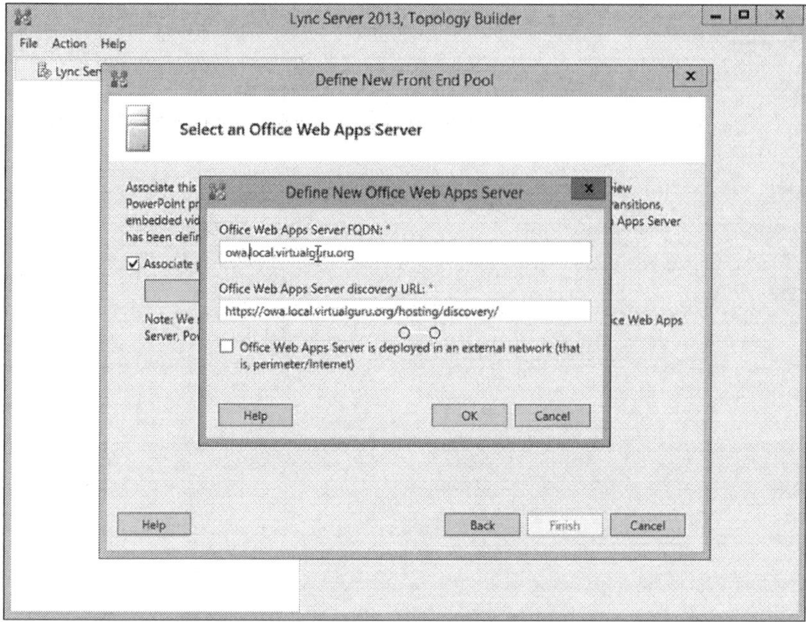

Figure 11.17 Defining a new Office web apps server

This process creates a new file store on the local server with a default name of share, but it does not grant permission to the appropriate RTC objects for the share. If you did not add the File and Storage Services role, you can do so now and manually create the share. Once created, you should grant permission to the following RTC objects with read and write access:

- RTCComponentUniversalServices
- RTCHSUniversalServices
- RTCUniversalServerAdmins
- RTCUniversalConfigReplicator

To add these RTC objects, complete the following steps:

1. Run Server Manager and from the pane on the right, expand File and Storage Services and Shares.
2. Select the share and from the Volume pane, select **Tasks** and **Advanced Security Settings for Share**.
3. Display the Permissions tab and click **Add**.

4. On the Permission Entry for Share screen, choose **Select a Principal**.
5. Under Enter the Object Name, type the name of the RTC object and click **OK**.
6. Under Basic Permissions, ensure that only **Read** and **Write** are selected, and then click **OK**.
7. On the Advanced Security Settings for Share screen, click **Apply** and **OK**.

Within our Lync Server 2013 Topology Builder, if we expand the Lync server, we should see our newly created topology, as shown in Figure 11.18.

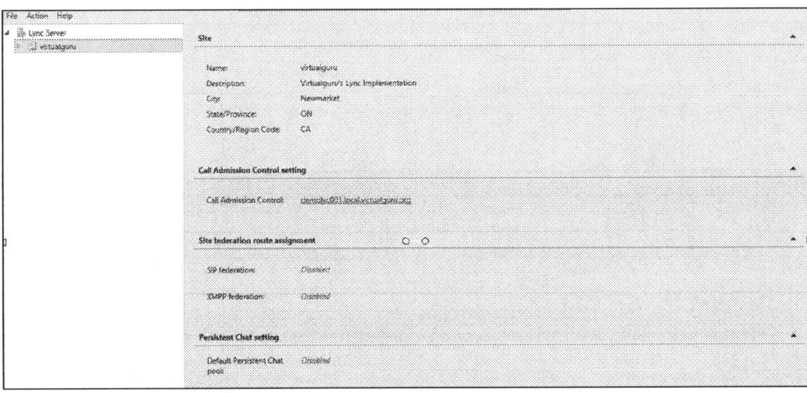

Figure 11.18 New Lync server topology

Before we publish this topology, however, we will want to update the admin URL. We can do this by selecting the top-level topology Lync server and selecting **Edit Properties**. From the left, select **Simple URLs** and scroll down. Under Administrative Access URL enter the URL representing the DNS record for the Admin console, which in this case is https://admin.local.virtualguru.org, as shown in Figure 11.19.

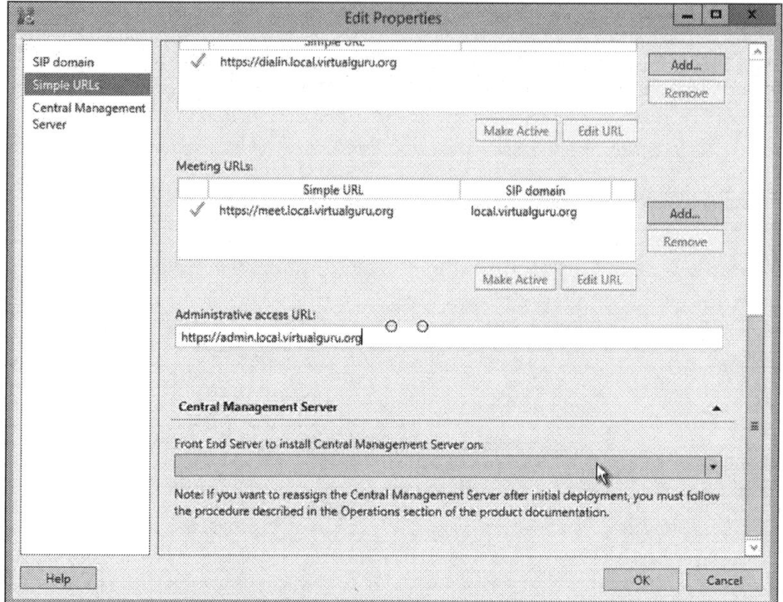

Figure 11.19 Administrative access URL

Further down on this page, you will see the option to select the Central Management Server, which is, of course, itself; select the drop-down and select the local server, which in our example is **demolyc001.local.virtualguru.org virtualguru**.

After selecting both these settings, click **OK**. We are now ready to publish our topology, which we can do right from the Lync Server 2013 Topology Builder by selecting **Action** from the **File** menu and then **Publish Topology**, which launches the Publish Topology Wizard. To complete the wizard, follow these steps:

1. Click **Next** on the initial page to have the wizard verify the installation.
2. Ensure that the Central Management Server is the local front-end server (that is, demolyc001.local.virtualguru.org virtualguru), and click **Next**.
3. Verify that all the steps complete successfully, and then click **Finish**.

With a topology published, we can now complete the final four steps to finish installing Lync 2013. To run the final four installation and configuration routines, select the **Install or Update Lync Server System** from the Lync Server 2013 Deployment Wizard. This displays the remaining four steps to finalize the installation of Lync 2013, as shown in Figure 11.20.

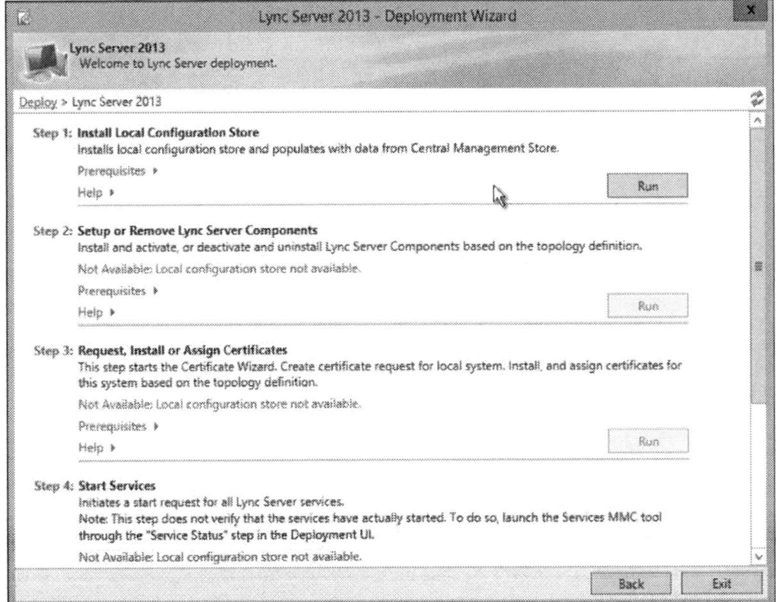

Figure 11.20 Final four steps

The first step is to install the local configuration store, which installs and configures the localRTC database and populates its configuration. When you click Run, you have the option of importing the configuration from the Central Management store or importing it from a file. Because we have already created the Central Management store, we will accept the default **Retrieve Directly from Central Management Store** and click **Next** and **Finish** to return to the default menu.

The next step that is run is Step 2: Setup or Lync Components. Step 2 installs things like speech files and is run by selecting **Run** and then clicking **Finish** when it completes.

Step 3: Request, Install or Assign Certificates launches the Certificate Wizard to allow you to enroll the computer account of the Lync server after you select **Run**, as shown in Figure 11.21.

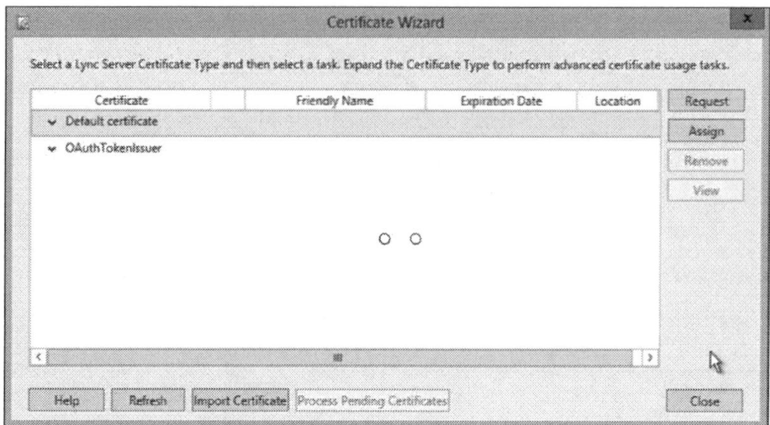

Figure 11.21 Certificate Wizard

To successfully request a new certificate, complete the following steps:

1. Ensure that **Default Certificate** is highlighted and click **Request**.
2. On the Certificate Request screen, click **Next**.
3. Ensure that the default **Send the Request Immediately to an Online Certification Authority** is selected, and click **Next**.
4. Under the Choose a Certification Authority screen, ensure that the default **Select a CA from the List Detected in Your Environment** is selected and that your certificate authority (CA) server is listed in the drop-down, and then click **Next**.
5. If you need to specify different credentials for the certificate enrollment process, you can by selecting **Specify Alternate Credentials for the Certification Authority** and then typing the username and password and clicking **Next**. If you do not need alternate credentials, you can just click **Next**.
6. If you created a specific certificate template, you can specify it on the next screen by selecting **Use Alternate Certificate Template for the Selected Certification Authority** and specifying the name in the Certificate Template name box and clicking **Next**; otherwise, you can just click **Next**.
7. Under the Name and Security Settings screen, provide a friendly name in the text box, such as Primary Lync Cert, and ensure the bit length is set to **2048** and click **Next**.
8. On the Organization Information screen, fill in your organization and organization unit in the text boxes provided, such as virtualguru.org and IT Department, and then click **Next**.
9. On the Geographical Information screen, select your county/region from the drop-down menu and specify your state/province and city/locality in the text boxes provided, and then click **Next**.

10. In the Subject Name/Subject Alternative Names screen, specify the subject name in the text box, which is usually the fully qualified domain name (FQDN) of the server itself; subject alternative names are the other names designating the host. The wizard should pick up the other A name records you created for the host in the AD and include them in Subject Alternative Name text box. Verify that the FQDN has been entered correctly for the subject name and that the alternative names are recognized and click **Next**.
11. On the SIP Domain setting on Subject Alternative Names screen, select your Configured SIP domains, as shown in Figure 11.22, and click **Next**.

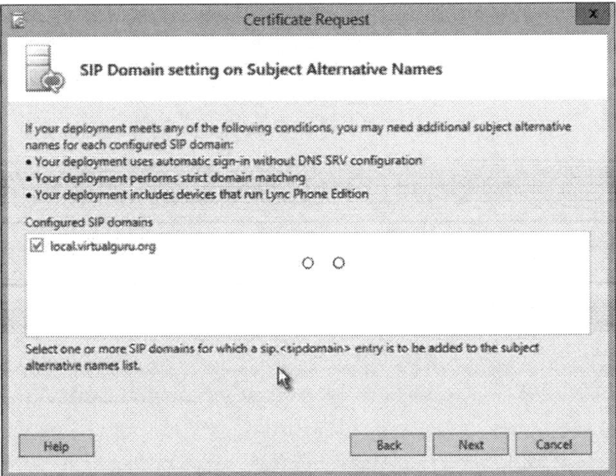

Figure 11.22 Selecting your configured SIP domain

12. If any alternative names were missed by the wizard, you can manually add them on the Configure Alternative Subject Names screen. Just type them into the text box and click **Add**. Once added, click **Next**.
13. Review the information on the Certificate Request Summary screen, and when satisfied that the information is correct, click **Next**.
14. Verify that the Request Certificate task completes successfully, and click **Next**.
15. Ensure that on the Online Certificate Request Status screen the default **Assign This Certificate to Lync Server Certificate Usages** is selected, and click **Finish**.
16. On the Certificate Wizard screen, ensure that **Default Certificate** is selected and click the **Assign** button on the right. Then click **Next**, **Next**, and **Finish** to finish assigning the requested certificate.

In addition to the default certificate, there is also an OAuthTokenIssuer that requires you to request and assign a certificate. You will need to repeat the process for the OAuthTokenIssuer, as well, but there is no need to change the values. Ensure that when you are finished, both the default certificate and OAuthTokenIssuer show check marks on the Certificate Wizard, as shown in Figure 11.23, and then click **Close**.

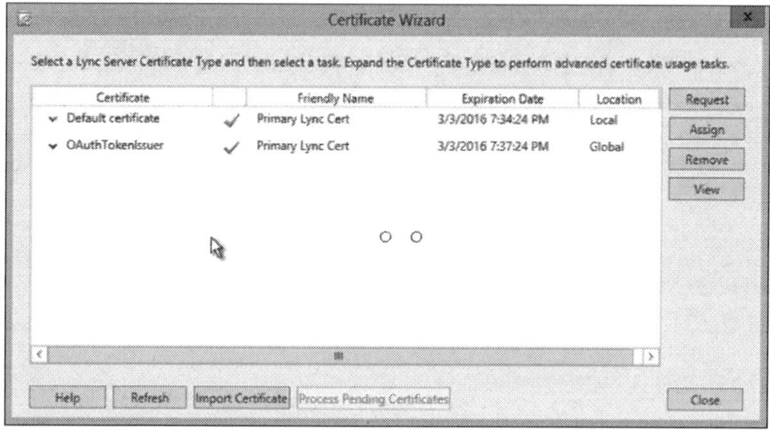

Figure 11.23 Ensuring that certificates are properly assigned

The final step to the installation of our Lync 2013 server is to run Step 4, which starts the services. To do this, select **Run**, and then click **Next** and then **Finish**. Be patient at this point because the services can take a few minutes to fully start. There is an optional step called Service Status (Optional). If you run this, it will fire up the Microsoft Management Console (MMC) and show you the current state of the services if you would like to double-check on how things are going.

Set Up Users and Test Lync

Although we have spent a good portion of this chapter reviewing how to properly install Lync in a small environment, most integration issues between View and Lync arise because of a misconfiguration in Lync rather than because of an issue with VMware View. Although we have a working Lync environment, we need to take it a step further and set up a few accounts, enable them for Lync, install Lync in our virtual desktops, and install the Microsoft Lync VDI plug-in on our physical devices. After we have completed these tasks, we should be able to see our Lync Client within the virtual desktop environment pair with our Microsoft VDI plug-in, enabling them send audio and video directly versus indirectly through the virtual desktop environment. To enable our testing, we will need to enable some users and install some clients.

To enable some users, we must log in to the Lync Control Panel. Earlier in the chapter, we mentioned that Lync uses Microsoft Silverlight. So, before logging in to the console, ensure that you have installed it. Once Silverlight is installed, you can log in to the console by running Lync Server Control Panel. When you click **Lync Server Control Panel**, it will prompt you to enter the administrator credentials of the Lync server to connect. On the AdminUIHost login screen, type the username and password and click **OK**.

When you log in, you are taken to the Lync Server 2013 home page. The home page contains links to common activities, useful checklists, and help links. There is a link to enable users for Lync server, but you can also select Users from the menu bar on the left, as shown on Figure 11.24.

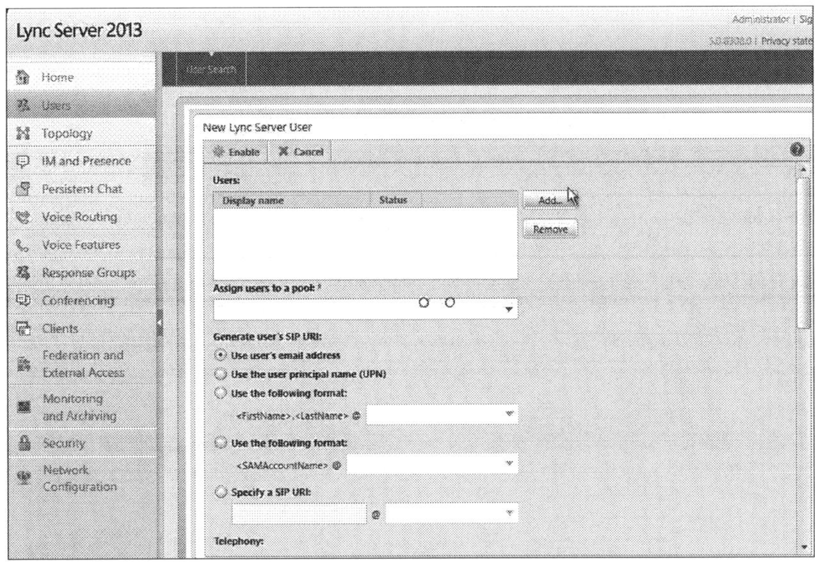

Figure 11.24 Selecting the users from the menu bar

From within Users, you can enable users. To enable users, you must first add the users. To add and enable users, follow these steps:

1. To enable a user, click the **Add** button on the right.
2. Type the beginning letters of the user or users and click the **Find** button.
3. Select the users or users and click **OK**, as shown in Figure 11.25.
4. Under Assign Users to Pool, click the drop-down menu and select your Lync Server 2013 pool.
5. Under Generate User's SIP URI, select **Use the User Principal Name**.

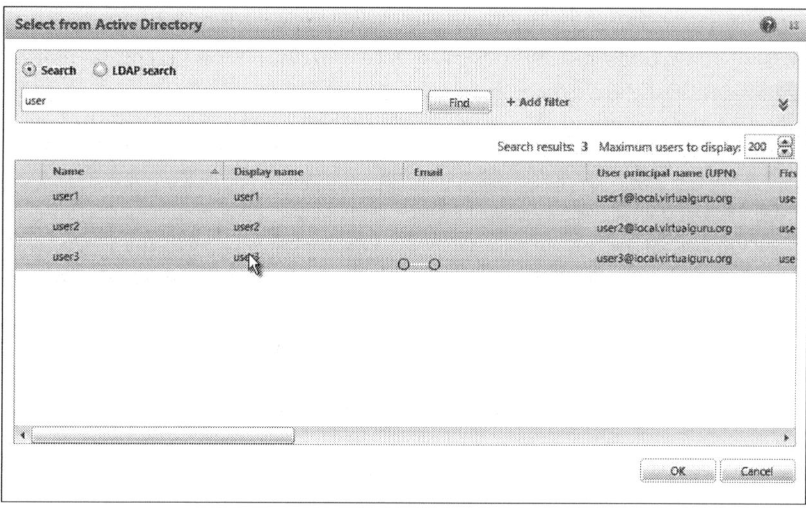

Figure 11.25 Selecting user(s) and clicking OK

6. Although there are other options we can select, we can enable the users at this point by clicking the blue **Enable** link under the New Lync Server User label.
7. Ensure that the users are now shown as enabled, as shown in Figure 11.26.

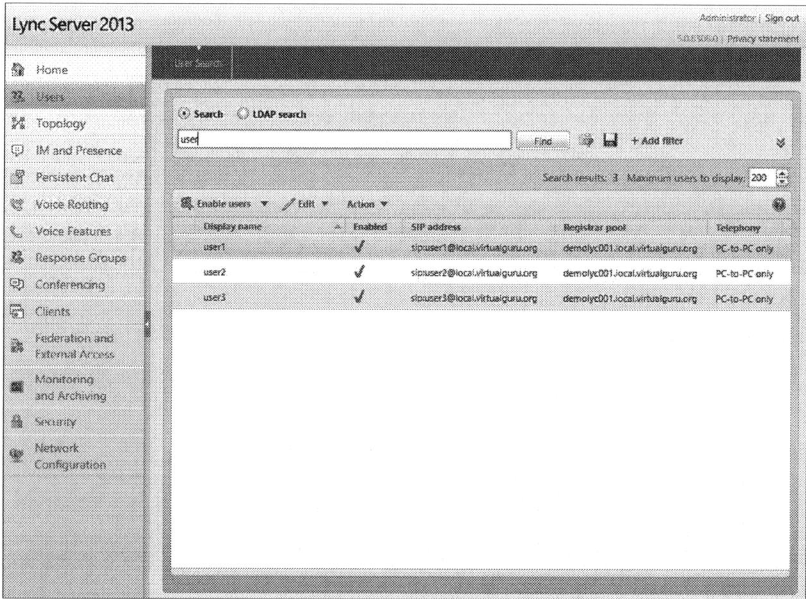

Figure 11.26 Users are now enabled

To allow media redirection, you must update the Lync policy to enable this option. This is done using commandlets through the Lync Server Management Shell. To complete the media redirection enablement, follow these steps:

1. Press the **Windows** button on your keyboard to bring up Tiles on your Windows Lync server.
2. Select **Lync Server Management Shell.**
3. To review the current policy, type the following in the Lync Server Management Shell window:

   ```
   Get-CsClientPolicy
   ```

4. Observe the value for `EnableMediaRedirection`; it should read `False`.
5. To enable media redirection, type the following:

   ```
   Set-CsClientPolicy EnableMediaRedirection $True
   ```

We are now ready to complete the client components to verify our configuration. From a configuration perspective, we have completed the setup of the Lync 2013 server and are setting up our VMware View environment with the Microsoft VDI plug-in.

View Desktops

We will need to install the Lync 2013 Client on our View desktop as the next step. Microsoft makes the latest version of Lync Client available for download, and installing the Lync 2013 Client is straightforward.

To ensure that the client components trust the Lync 2013 server, you need to ensure that the Lync server is trusted by the View desktops. You must first export the certificate and then import it to your View desktops. Ideally, you want to do this on the parent VM if you are using Composer-created View desktops.

On the Lync server, run the MMC. If you are new to Windows 2012, you can find the MMC by pressing the **Windows** key on the keyboard and the letter **F** to bring up find. Underneath the Find box, ensure that **Apps** is selected (not Files and Settings) and type **MMC**.

1. From the MMC menu bar, select **File, Add/Remove Snap In.**
2. Under Available Snap-Ins, select **Certificates** and click **Add.**
3. When prompted for what the snap-in will manage, select **Computer Account** and click **Next.**

4. On the Select Computer screen, ensure that the default **Local Computer: (The Computer This Console Is Running On)** is selected; click **Finish** and click **OK**.
5. Expand the Certificates (Local Computer) folder and the Personal and Certificates folder.

You should be able to see the certificate that was applied to the Lync 2013 server during the installation earlier in this chapter. To export the Lync server certificate, complete the following steps:

1. Select your Lync 2013 server certificate and right-click and select **All Tasks** and **Export**.
2. On the Welcome screen, click **Next**; do not export the private key and select **Next**.
3. Accept the default export file format and click **Next**.
4. Click **Browse** to determine a location to export the certificate to and provide a filename, and then click **Save**, **Next**, and then **Finish**.

You can use the process described here to import the certificate to the View desktops, but this time you will import the certificate to the trusted root authority folder:

1. From the File menu of the MMC bar, select **File**, **Add/Remove Snap In**.
2. Under Available Snap-Ins, select **Certificates** and click **Add**.
3. When prompted for what the snap-in will manage, select **Computer Account** and click **Next**.
4. On the Select Computer screen, ensure that the default **Local Computer: (The Computer This Console Is Running On)** is selected and click **Finish** and click **OK**.
5. Expand the Certificates (Local Computer), Trusted Root Certificates, and Certificates folders.
6. Select the **Certificates** folder and right-click and select **All Tasks**, **Import**.
7. On the Welcome screen, click **Next**. Browse for the file, select the location of the Lync 2013 certificate you exported, and then select **Open** and click **Next**.
8. On the Certificate Store screen, ensure that the default **Place All Certificates in the Following Store** is selected and that the Certificate Store box contains **Trusted Root Certificate Authorities**, and then click **Next**.
9. Click **Finish** to complete the process and import the certificate.

View Clients

On your physical endpoint, you will install the Lync VDI plug-in. If you are already running Office 2013, it is possible that Lync has been installed by default. Because we cannot run the Lync Client and the Lync VDI plug-in on the desktop, we need to uninstall Lync. We also do not need the Lync Client locally because we will be using Lync from our View desktop. Assuming it is installed, to uninstall Lync on the client, complete these steps:

1. Open **Control Panel**, **Programs**, and **Programs and Features**.
2. Select the **Microsoft Office Professional 2013** software, right-click, and select **Change**.
3. Leave the default set to **Add or Remove Features** and click **Continue**.
4. On the Installation Options screen, from the Microsoft Lync drop-down select **Not Available**, and then click **Continue**.
5. When complete, click **Close**.

After ensuring that the Lync Client is not installed, you must install the View Client as well as the Microsoft VDI plug-in. The plug-in is available from Microsoft for download. It comes in both 32-bit and 64-bit versions, but because PCoIP runs as a 32-bit process the 32-bit version should be used. Before installing it, you need to add the following registry keys on the client. (Replace the appropriate fields with your correct values and note that in this example the external and internal address are the same, whereas yours might not be.)

```
[HKEY_CURRENT_USER\SOFTWARE\Microsoft\Office\15.0\Lync] ConfigurationMode=
dword:00000001 ServerAddressInternal=[Fully Qualified Domain Name of your
Lync Server] ServerAddressExternal=[Fully Qualified Domain Name of your
Lync Server]
```

To install the Microsoft VDI plug-in, complete the following steps:

1. Download the plug-in from Microsoft.
2. Run Lyncvdi.exe.
3. Accept the license agreement and click **Continue**.
4. On the Choose the Installation You Want screen, select **Install Now**.
5. When the installation finishes, click **Close**.

Verifying the Plug-In

To verify your configuration, you must set up a few View desktops and clients as well as ensure that the clients have the necessary peripherals for making video calls. Microsoft publishes a list of webcams that are optimized for Lync, which you can find at http://technet.microsoft.com/en-us/lync/gg278173.aspx#webcams.

When you log in to a View desktop running the Microsoft Lync plug-in, the Lync Client detects that a plug-in exists and a pairing occurs between the Lync Client in the View desktop and the Microsoft VDI plug-in installed on the physical client. The pairing is indicated through an icon on the Lync Client. To verify that your configuration is working before attempting video calling, launch a View session from a client with the plug-in:

1. Log in to your View desktop.
2. Run Lync and verify whether you can sign in.
3. When Lync detects that the Microsoft VDI plug-in is available, you are prompted to sign in, as shown in Figure 11.27. Log in and ensure that you check the **Save My Password** check box to avoid additional prompts.

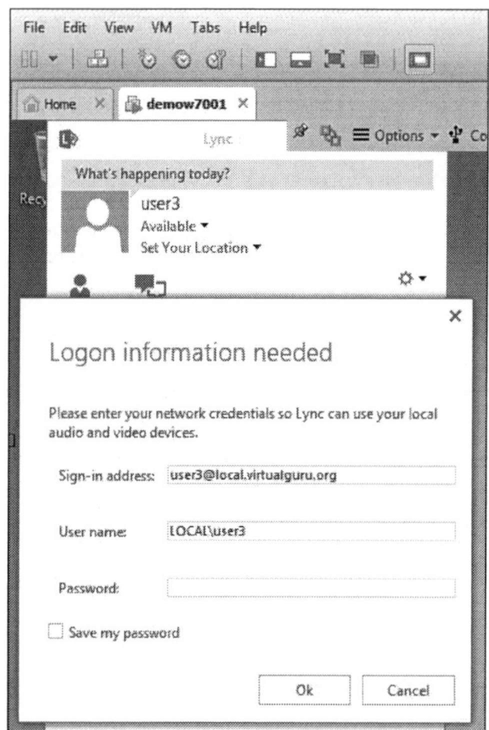

Figure 11.27 Login information needed

After you log in, the pairing takes place, and you will notice a successful pairing icon at the bottom right of the Lync Client and will get a notification that Lync is all set to use your local audio and video devices, as shown in Figure 11.28.

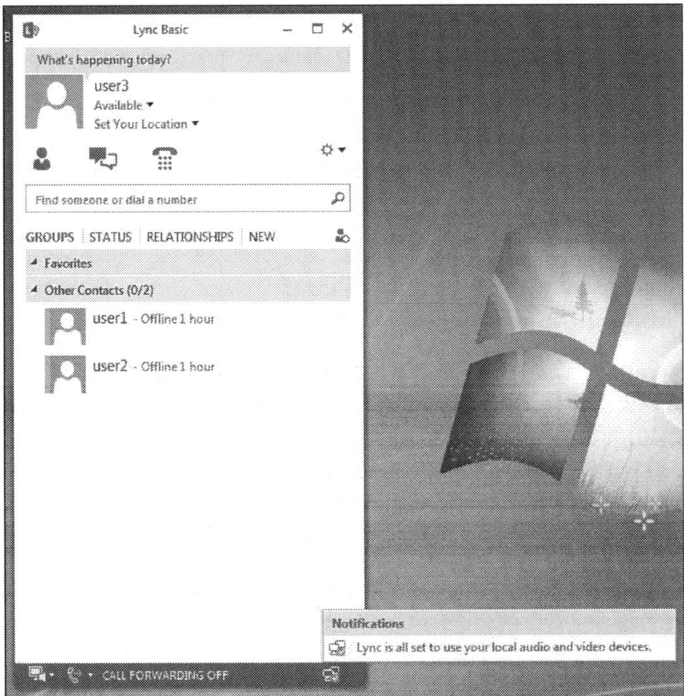

Figure 11.28 Successful pairing

Once this has occurred, you are ready to take advantage of the redirection afforded by this plug-in. Take some time to thoroughly test your configuration in the lab using the procedure in this chapter as your guide. In our testing, for example, we found that many of the default security settings on our Microsoft Windows 8 clients really wanted to block the installation of the Microsoft VDI plug-in limiting the options deploying this across a large number of desktops.

Summary

This chapter covered how to integrate the Microsoft VDI plug-in using Microsoft Lync Server 2013. The integration of this plug-in enables you to avoid many of the pitfalls of integrating voice and video conferencing within a VMware View environment. In addition, because the voice and video is redirected, the overhead of this activity is processed on the local client, optimizing your ability to scale your VMware View desktops. Because the traffic is controlled at the client side, it also allows you to configure QoS controls on the client network to prioritize this traffic to ensure robust performance.

There are some good use cases for voice/video as a feature of your virtual desktops. Consider, for example, this feature as an extension to a disaster recovery (DR) scenario where the DR desktops are provided by View. Integrated voice and video provides phone services in addition to a business suite of applications.

To be successful, ensure that you are comfortable with both Lync and View before starting the integration. In addition, you should apply QoS to prioritize VoIP traffic on your network before deploying Lync in production. When enabling webcams used with Lync, review what hardware has been optimized for Lync from Microsoft's website (www.microsoft.com/hardware/). After you have reviewed which webcams have been certified for Lync and selected an appropriate unit, standardize the hardware to avoid the number of user issues in production.

Chapter 12

Performance and Monitoring of VMware Horizon

This chapter describes the recommended approach to monitor your desktop and secure Workspace environment. In a successful deployment, you want to make sure that all components are running smoothly to provide the best user experience you can obtain from your infrastructure. There are a lot of solutions on the market to monitor performance of virtual infrastructure. We cover what we think are the top three on the market today. We also cover the key metrics we know are, in a virtualization deployment, what will break or make you. You have to keep in mind that no matter how "beefy" your servers are, user perception will most likely trump all of that. So, you must identify key indicators, provide statistics and facts to back up your claims, and ideally, provide your users a visual way to see for themselves that your environment is sound and stable.

After you've covered the reactive aspect of a desktop and secure Workspace project, on the other side, you want to be proactive. That's the main goal every IT administrator wants to achieve. Predicting the future is not possible, but being able to anticipate a problem before it happens is something that can be done with today's technology. The more proactive you are, the more you'll be able to respond to potential bottlenecks or resource utilization storms, before they happen.

This chapter covers different solutions that can help you get there and put the proper pieces in place to go from being reactive to being proactive. The chapter also covers what we think are the metrics, no matter what tool you use, that you should make sure to monitor in your virtual infrastructure.

Performance Monitoring Solutions

There are a lot of desktop monitoring solutions on the market today. Because we're talking about a virtual deployment, based on vSphere technologies, we focus on the solutions that are proven to work well in such an environment. The top three solutions we have evaluated and tested for a VMware View and VMware Workspace deployment are as follows:

- Xangati VDI dashboard
- Liquidware Labs UX
- VMware vCenter Operations Management (vCOps)

The Xangati virtual desktop infrastructure (VDI) dashboard leverages Xangati's patent-pending performance health engine to provide the end-user computing team with a live, to-the-second awareness of the performance health of all the moving parts within their VDI without requiring software agents.

Liquidware Labs Stratusphere UX is a comprehensive monitoring, performance validation, and diagnostics solution for organizations that support both virtual and mixed environments. Unlike physical desktops, virtual desktop workloads are supported by a shared infrastructure consisting of hosts, storage, networking, and a spectrum of applications and services.

The last one, vCenter Operations Manager, can analyze vSphere environmental statistics to provide a visual representation of the infrastructure's health, security risk, and efficiency. The vCenter Operations Management Suite, which is intended to help administrators build a hybrid cloud infrastructure based on VMware products, is also available as part of VMware's vCloud Suite.

As of this writing, the VMware vCenter Operations Management Suite is available in four editions:

- **Foundation:** Includes a limited version of vCenter Operations Manager and is included free with vSphere.
- **Standard:** Includes the full functionality of vCenter Operations Manager and vCenter CapacityIQ (which is no longer available as a separate product).
- **Advanced:** Offers additional configuration and compliance features. This edition includes vCenter Infrastructure Navigator and vCenter Chargeback Manager and a limited version of Configuration Manager.
- **Enterprise:** Allows for operating system and application-level monitoring and change and configuration management. It includes full versions of all products included in lower levels of the suite.

In this chapter, we cover the sections shown in Figure 12.1.

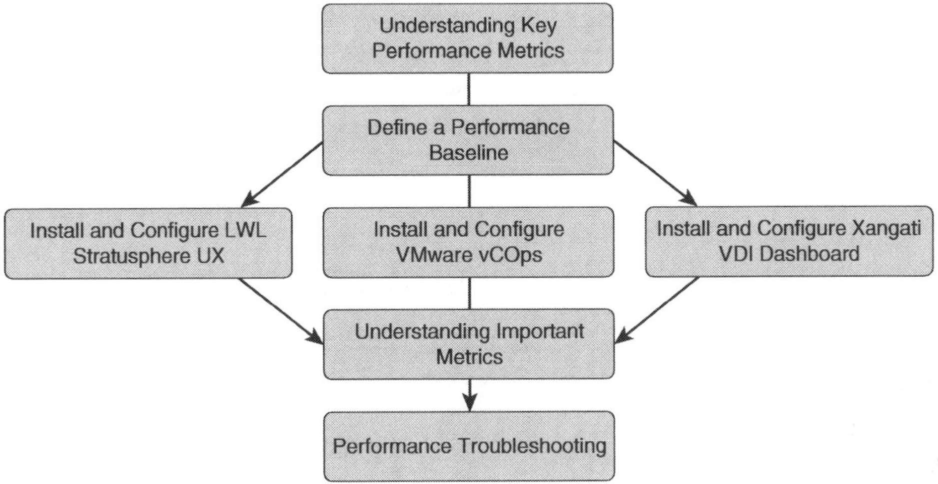

Figure 12.1 Performance monitoring workflow

Establishing a Performance Baseline

One of the most difficult things to do in any IT infrastructure is to establish what normal operations look like. The extremes are always easy to spot, of course, but the heavy demand that equates to normal business use is much more difficult to understand without good visibility. Establishing normal operations can be more complex in a virtual infrastructure, but no less important. If you are not sure what normal is, how can you properly identify what is problematic and needs to be investigated before it impacts your end users? This issue is critical in a virtual desktop environment because often much higher expectations are placed on performance. I had a conversation about this topic with a customer who had a mixture of older and newer physical desktops, and what we concluded is that users often do not report problems with physical desktops that are fixed with a reboot; they simply shut it off and on, and if the problem goes away, they consider it "fixed." Ask yourself how often the computer logs of a desktop are actually inspected for problems. When was the last time a system administrator looked at the application or system log of a Windows desktop?

With virtual desktops, however, these hiccups get a lot of visibility in the early stages of adoption, so you need high visibility on how everything is performing. This visibility must include the View desktops, management components, performance of the PC over IP (PCoIP) protocol on the local-area network (LAN) and wide-area network (WAN), and the hosts and storage of the vSphere environment. Monitoring all these pieces with traditional monitoring tools can quickly produce a lot of information that becomes difficult to correlate and understand. Traditional monitoring tools based on static thresholds generate alerts on utilization or monitor the Windows Event Viewer logs, but do not provide a complete picture of how the entire environment is performing.

Although a number of products from a variety of vendors monitor various aspects of the virtual infrastructure, VMware has developed vCenter Operations to bring this capability to VMware vSphere environments. It also has developed custom dashboards for monitoring the performance of a VMware View environment to extend the benefits to your virtual desktops. What is unique about vCenter Operations (vCOPs) is that you get near real-time (approximately 5 minutes by default), capacity and historical performance and problem-tracking information. The visibility extends to all components of your virtual infrastructure, down to the storage and its dependencies. Many third parties have also used the VMware application programming interfaces (APIs) to extend monitoring and alerting to their products, but vCenter Operations is tightly integrated with VMware View.

vCenter Operations Manager aggregates information that is collected by vCenter. For vCOPs, you need to ensure that you are running VMware vCenter Server 4.0 Update 2 or later at a minimum to be able to view storage system performance. Storage visibility closes a huge operational gap in running large virtual desktop environments. Often, you see symptoms of underperforming storage, such as delayed SCSI transactions in the Windows Event Viewer. However, it is difficult to identify what the cause is. Because many storage systems incorporate storage virtualization and distribute all writes across all spindles, it is difficult to pinpoint the source of the problem. It is rare now that a storage-area network (SAN) administrator dedicates certain drives to certain logical unit numbers (LUNs). This can make identifying storage bottlenecks extremely difficult because SAN performance reports average performance over time and across a large portion of the storage system.

vCenter Operations enables you to view specific performance characteristics of your datastores in relation to each other. VMware has extended vCenter Operations to aggregate information from both the View Connection Server and Composer to provide even greater visibility into your virtualization environment.

The benefits of vCenter Operations are many, but rather than go through them all, let's look at each in relationship to the VMware View environment to understand how they deliver value. The first thing you must do is install vCenter Operations and configure the adapter to turn on the performance and monitoring of the VMware View environment.

Xangati VDI Dashboard

The first one we'll look at is the solution from Xangati. We like this solution because of its simplicity to implement and for the live recording features.

You can download a few different versions of the solution. The version you want to download from Xangati website is the one called Xangati VDI dashboard, from www.xangati.com.

After downloading the appliance (it comes in the form of a ZIP archive), extract the file to a desktop or server that has the vSphere Client installed on it. You need the following resources to run the appliance:

- 1.5 GB of hard disk for the download of the archive
- 1.7 GB of additional hard disk space to extract the appliance
- Sizing recommendation for the appliance deployed on vSphere:
  - 138 GB (thick)/17 GB (thin)
  - 1 vCPU (2 GHz)
  - 4 GB

Once the appliance is unzipped, from the vSphere Client choose the host or clusters of host where you want to deploy the Xangati appliance, and from the File menu choose **Deploy OVF Template**. Figure 12.2 shows an example of deploying the template selection screen.

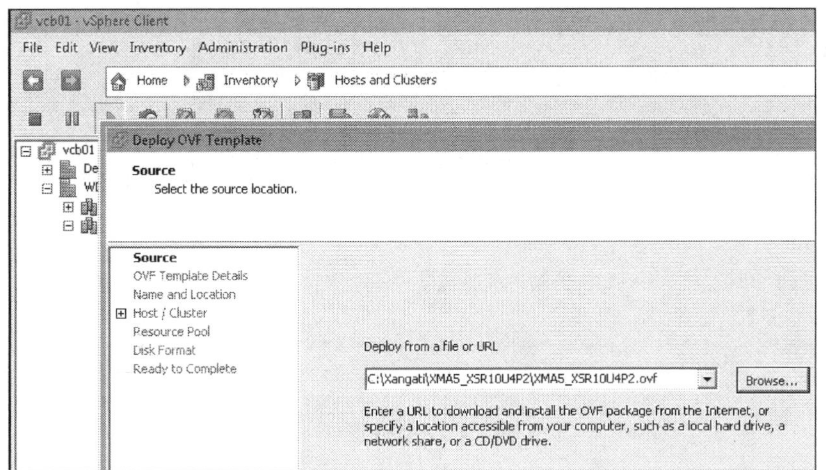

Figure 12.2 OVF deployment

After you've chosen the proper file, click **Next**. It will show you that the appliance is from Xangati and that it takes 3.9 GB of space thin provisioned but can grow to 320 GB. Ensure that proper disk planning was done before deploying this solution. Give the appliance a name, then click **Next**. The next screen asks you to choose on which host you want to run this solution. The next screen will ask you where you want to store the virtual machine (VM) files.

The disk format that Xangati chooses is thin provisioned. This is not something you can change by default. It might be possible to find custom scripts to have this changed during installation, but we did not ask Xangati; leaving the default is fine for the solution, again keeping in mind that the VM can expand up to 320 GB. On the Network Mapping screen, make sure that the Xangati eth0 is in a port group where you will be able to assign an IP address to it. The rest of the interfaces can be ignored during the initial installation. You can even remove the other network interfaces before you power on the VM.

When the appliance is fully deployed, power it on and let it do its initial boot; it will take a few minutes to complete. Open the console to the appliance and watch it boot. When the boot process is complete, a command prompt appears. At the prompt, log in with the user **xanuser** and the password **use.xangati**. You will then get a couple of window pop-ups to accept Java to run within the appliance. This is normal; the appliance comes with self-signed certificate, and when Java runs for the first time, you manually have to accept to run these. After accepting these, you will notice that the console resizes. You are now prompted to enter the administrative credentials to the GUI. Enter **admin** for the username and **admin** for the password. Figure 12.3 shows you what you should see in the console you've booted.

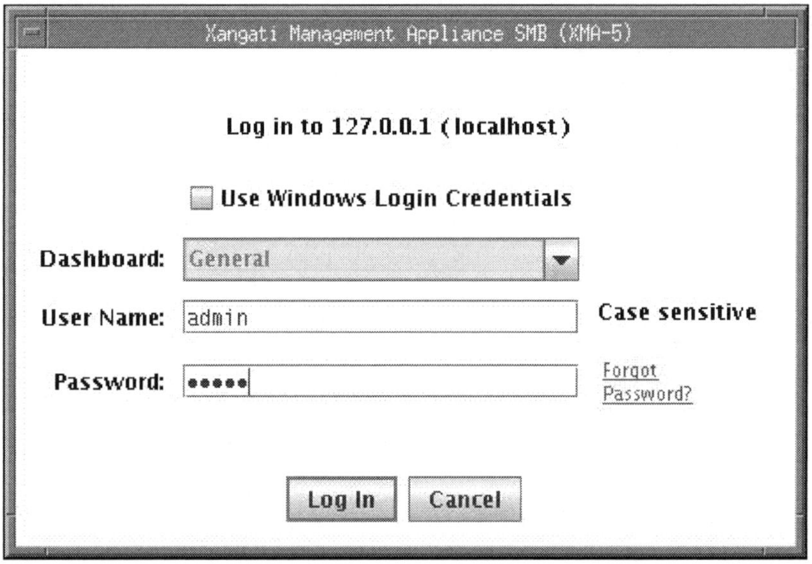

Figure 12.3 Xangati GUI login

The next screen asks you to accept the license agreement, and you then must enter an email address, identified by them as your Xangati ID. You need to retrieve information from the email later on, so make sure that you use an email address that is accessible to you during setup. (This is also the email used for their support site.)

The next screen asks you to enter the appliance name and the IP address. Again, make sure that eth0 is selected (it's the default choice, just validate), and fill in the network mask and the IP for your gateway. We will not configure an external IP address for our use-case scenario, so leave this field empty. The external IP address could be useful if you want the appliance to be reachable from the Web (for example, through a demilitarized zone [DMZ] or from a Network Address Translation [NAT] environment.) You also have the option to add another management network interface, which we will not do in this use-case. You might want to keep this information handy for future reference, though, because if a major network outage occurs in your environment on the network where the appliance will reside, you might want to configure a second interface, an out-of-band IP that you could reach in case the main interface is down. Figure 12.4 shows an example of what this information would look like.

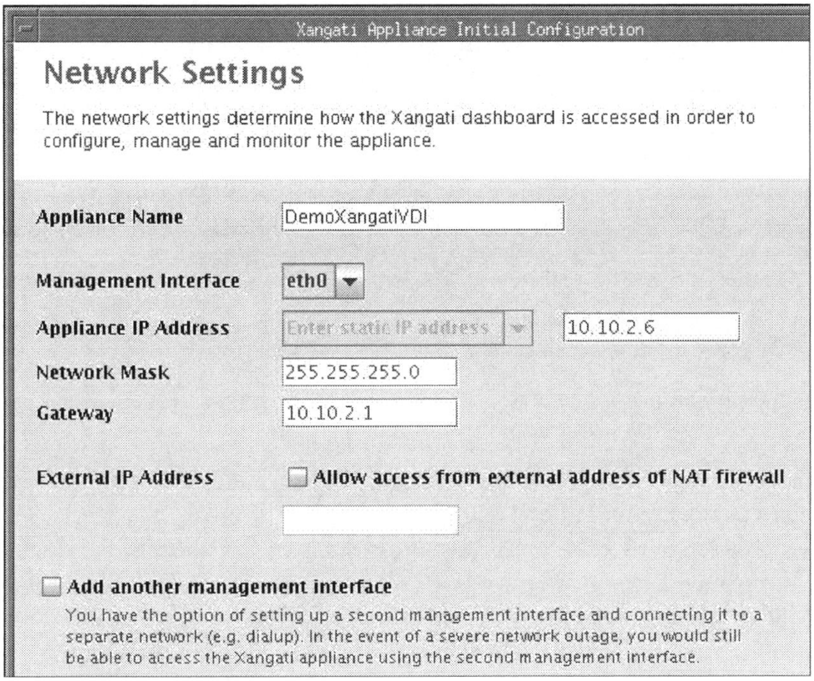

Figure 12.4 Network configuration

On the next screen, you can adjust the time for the appliance. We strongly recommend that you sync your appliance against the same Network Time Protocol (NTP) server that you have for your VMs and your View Connection Server. Data collection is all time based, and so having a reliable sync source is critical for valid reporting and troubleshooting.

The last configuration screen asks you for Domain Name System (DNS) information. Here again, we strongly recommend that you use the same DNS server that you use for your View environment. After all the information is entered, click **Finish**. This configuration takes a few minutes. When it completes, you are asked to reboot the appliance. If you don't touch anything, the appliance will reboot on its own after 60 seconds.

The rest of the configuration and future management of the appliance is done through a web browser, pointing to the IP address you configured in the previous steps. When you open your browser and point it to the IP address, you get a warning message about the untrusted certificate. Accept it, and you will then land on the main Xangati dashboard screen. Validate that your setup completed successfully; if so, you should have a login screen that looks similar to Figure 12.5.

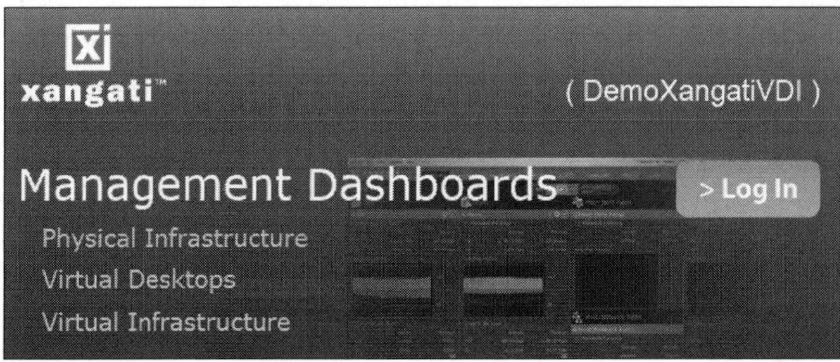

Figure 12.5 Xangati dashboards

Log in to the dashboard. Again, it's a Java-based interface, and so you must accept Java launch if you have limited execution of Java code from within your browser. When the application launches, you log in with the username **admin** and password **admin**. Because this is your first time opening the web interface, you are presented with a wizard that will ask you to change the password. As always, make sure that you use a strong password, following the golden three out of four rules (lowercase, uppercase, number, extended characters). Because this is an admin password for the appliance, we also recommend that you use a password that has a minimum of eight characters and does not refer to any known dictionary word (common sense, right?).

The next step is to specify vCenter connection information. We recommend entering an administrator user for vCenter. Although Xangati mentions that its appliance requires only read-only credentials to vCenter, we've seen issues where information was not flowing properly from vSphere to Xangati when using credentials that did not have enough privilege. You entail no security risk by providing such access to that user because Xangati only ever reads information from the infrastructure. If you have more than one vCenter, you will see on the next screen that the appliance can connect to multiple vCenters. (Remember that doing this will also generate more traffic between the vCenters and the Xangati appliance.) We recommend that whenever possible you keep one appliance to monitor one vCenter, unless there's a specific reason to monitor multiple instances.

The next step is to enter the IP address ranges where the vCenter and the View environment resides. Then, it will ask you to discover the ESXi hosts that are listed in vCenter. If it detects an environment where your hosts have multiple network interfaces, you will need to identify the various management addresses for your vSphere hosts. The next step is to identify the infrastructure data feeds. You have two options. You can either choose to collect network information from Xangati flow summarizers or use NetFlow. The tutorial video on the Xangati website provides details on how to install either solution. Xangati dashboards listen to the ESX/ESXi host they are deployed on and receive data from "flow summarizers" installed on your other hosts. The Xangati Flow Summarizer (XFS) listens to traffic on a vSwitch and then forwards that information to the dashboard for display. XFSs are deployed one per ESX host and support either standard or vSwitches. In this installation, we assume that you deployed the flow summarizer, so you will be able to skip the next screen where it asks you to deploy it within the Setup Wizard. You have completed the initial Setup Wizard. You can review everything on the Summary page and then click **Finish**.

When setup is complete and you log in to the Xangati appliance, you will notice that a lot of the screens are empty. This is normal; the appliance is now querying the various vCenter hosts (if you've set up more than one) and gathering data. Obtaining data should not take more than a minute or so.

You are now ready to create a custom dashboard. You can find Xangati tutorial videos that show the basics of the VI and VDI dashboard at https://www.youtube.com/watch?v=6ge1QUwWiA8.

Liquidware Labs Stratusphere UX

The second solution this chapter covers is Stratusphere UX. Like the first one, it is an easy-to-implement solution and comes in the form of an OVA download from the Liquidware Labs website. Liquidware Labs provides a 90-day free trial, so you can see how Statusphere UX performs and determine whether it gives you the key performance indicator (KPI) that your organization is looking for as part of your virtual desktop deployment. Similar to the Xangati appliance, Liquidware Labs Stratusphere Hub comes in the form of an OVF file. Log in to your vSphere Client and select **File, Deploy OVF Template**. The small difference with this configuration is that you install the file by pointing directly to a URL that Liquidware Labs will provide to you. The link will look something like Stratusphere Hub: http://download.liquidwarelabs.com/X.X.X/stratusphere_hub.ovf. We removed the version number, but from past experience using this solution, the link is pretty consistent.

This appliance also deploys thin provisioned, which we think is a good thing. However, similar to the previous solution, make sure that you plan proper storage capacity for this appliance; it will grow as time goes on and metrics are gathered from your environment. By default, the size of the disk is about 7 GB, and this will handle approximately 100 clients. The initial size can expand to a little over 14 GB (see Figure 12.6), but as explained later in this chapter, the size depends on your data-retention policy. You might need to add additional disks to the appliance to cover a longer cycle. Liquidware Labs has good sizing recommendations on its site. At the time of this writing, it has an Excel spreadsheet called LiquidwareLabs.Stratusphere.DatabaseDiskSizing where you can enter all the required information to get the proper-size disk for the appliance.

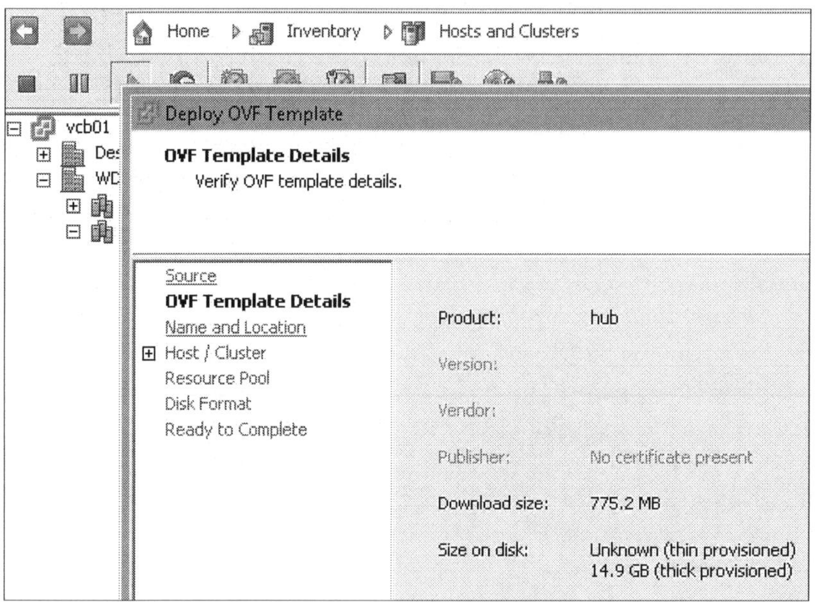

Figure 12.6 Stratusphere Hub deployment

They also give a couple of examples for sizing. They estimate that for about 1,000 clients, you need 65 GB of disk space, and for 500 clients, you need approximately 35 GB of disk space. So, make sure that you visit their site, download the spreadsheet, and plug in the numbers that make sense for you.

Follow the onscreen wizard, choosing the host and disk format. Review the Summary page and click **Finish**. Before booting the appliance, go back to the appliance settings and validate that you have chosen the right size for memory, CPU, and disk. For more information on right-sizing, based on the number of clients reporting back to the appliance, look at the *Stratusphere Sizing Guide*, available from the Liquidware Labs website. Once the appliance is deployed and the settings are properly configured, power it on. It will do its initial boot and will try to obtain an IP address from your Dynamic Host Configuration Protocol (DHCP) server. For now, don't worry about this; we will configure a static IP address and a fully qualified domain name (FQDN) for the appliance.

Log in to the console by pressing **Alt+F2** or **Enter**. The default username and password for the command-line interface (CLI) is **ssconsole** and **sspassword**. The CLI is pretty simple to use. You have two commands to start with. First, type **show system**. This will list the current system configuration for the appliance. Next, type **show management**. This will list the current management information for the appliance. Note that, in both cases, basic configuration information is missing; we will enter this information now. We recommend that you start by entering the IP address and Domain Name System (DNS) name for the appliance. Make sure that you have reserved a fixed IP address and have entered the DNS name in your DNS server before completing these steps. In the console, now type **set management IP *x.x.x.x***, where the *x*'s are replaced by your appliance's fixed IP address. Then type **set management netmask *x.x.x.x***, where the *x*'s are replaced by your organization netmask for that segment. Finally, type **set management default gateway *x.x.x.x***. You must commit those changes to the appliance. The Stratusphere Hub doesn't save the configuration information until you do a write to disk. Figure 12.7 shows a summary of all the commands mentioned so far.

```
set management ip
set management netmask
set management default gateway
LWL>show system
set system type hub
set system hostname localhost.localdomain
set system hub dns name 10.10.3.254
set system update client address on
set system mail relay
set system replay protection off
set system dhcp off
set system ondemand off
set system clear cache off
set system hardware check on
set system timezone America/New_York
set system time 201401261449
set system allow database connection
set system protocol 2
set system nonpersistent tracking on
set system user privacy off
set system machine privacy off
LWL>set management IP 10.138.38.14
LWL>set management netmask 255.255.255.0
LWL>set management default gateway 10.138.38.253
LWL>write_
```

Figure 12.7 Stratusphere Hub management configuration

The next step is to configure the FQDN of the appliance. You do this by entering the following two commands:

- Set system hub DNS name **FQDNofAppliance.domain.local**
- Set system hostname **FQDNofAppliance.domain.local**

Then, as before, you do a write to commit the changes. The last step we recommend you complete, before moving on to the web-based setup, is to configure the time synchronization of the appliance. You do this by looking at the default Network Time Protocol (NTP) information with the **show ntp** command. Then you can change the NTP server information by entering the **set NTP *server*** command and then finalizing with the **write** command.

Log in to the appliance from a browser using the default username and password **ssadmin** and **sspassword.** You will go through the initial Setup Wizard, accepting the end-user license agreement (EULA) and then entering your information. You should have a license key with you. So in the configuration screen, choose to enter your license information and paste the license in the box that appears. If you do not enter any license information, the appliance will still work with full functionality for five clients. Figure 12.8 shows an example of what this configuration should look like.

Registration Information

Please complete the information below to obtain techical support. Note that this information will be sen

* Your name: Stephane Asselin

* Your email: youremail@domain.com

* Your phone number: 111-111-1111

* Your company: YourCompanyName

* Company installed at: YourCompany

* License: Generate an evaluation license / I have a product license key

Paste your product license key here

You would enter your license information here

Figure 12.8 Liquidware Labs Stratusphere Hub configuration

After you have entered this information, you will be at the default administration screen. You can recheck your hub configuration information, the information we configured previously, by going to the Configuration tab. If any of the initial data is not accurate, you can correct it there. You have completed the initial configuration of the appliance. The next step is to configure the UX (User Experience) portion of the appliance. The main goal of Stratusphere UX is to be able to give you a normalized view of what your user experience should be, aggregating information from what you have, what you use, and what you might need to sustain a good environment.

You are now ready to move on to deploying the client software in your environment. You can download the client software from the web interface. Logged in as the administrator, go on the **Hub Administration**, **Connector ID Keys**, **Connector ID Key Software** tab (see Figure 12.9 for an example). When you are on that tab, you download the client software and install it on the client endpoint.

After the client is installed, the ConnectorID will make contact back to the appliance, establish a secure connection, exchange a certificate, and will start sending data to the appliance. You can validate the client is sending the right information on the Inventory tab under Machines (see Figure 12.10). Communication from the clients to the Stratusphere Hub upon installation happens fairly quickly; it should not take more than a few seconds to get the information listed. If you deploy this at scale, through ESD (electronic software distribution) software, it might take a little longer for the information to come back to the appliance.

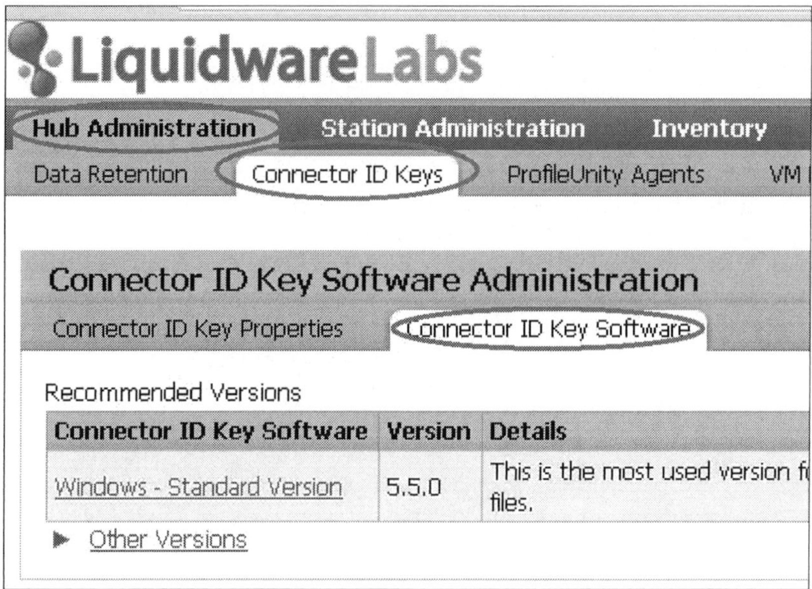

Figure 12.9 Client software installation

LiquidwareLabs

Hub Administration | Station Administration | Inventory | Event Log | Licensing | Confi

Machines | Users | Applications | Subnets

Machines

New

	Name	IP Address	Directory	Type	OS Version	Connector ID Key Version
	[illegible]	10.138.38.12	Local Directory	VMware	Microsoft Windows 7 Enterprise , Service Pack 1	Standard 64b 5.5.0-1

Figure 12.10 Client installation validation

Another important factor is that you want to be able to monitor the health of your hosts. Stratusphere provides functionality to connect to vCenter to obtain performance statistics such as CPU ready and memory swap. To configure the connection, go in the Hub administration, display the VM Directories tab, and configure your connection to your vCenter. Figure 12.11 shows an example of the configuration information.

To allow Stratusphere to initialize the information for your hosts, you also need to do an import. Click **Import from VM Directory**, and then click the **Import** button. Stratusphere will import the host definitions and the information about the VMs assigned to each virtual host.

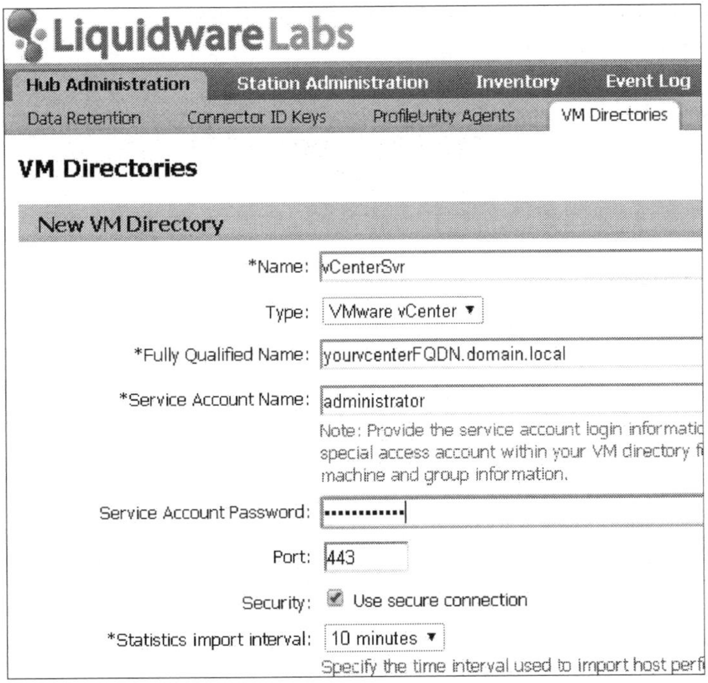

Figure 12.11 vCenter information configuration

Stratusphere UX Metrics

The first thing you want to do when you log in to the UX dashboard is to go look at the metrics. You want to make sure that you are okay with all the information listed there. Some information listed might not fit for your organization (for example, the login time). Figure 12.12 shows what the default values are. Every use case is different, and every organization will have guidelines and recommendations on what they consider to be a good/fair/poor user experience.

You will notice that you combine the actual value with the weight it holds on the overall picture of the health of the desktop. For some organizations, the time to launch an application will have more weight than the memory usage, for example. For others, as we often see in the healthcare sector, it's all about the login time. If a user cannot log in within 8 to 10 seconds, the user experience is poor. You need to play around with those values, adjusting them after your environment has been deployed for a few days, maybe even weeks; you will learn along the way the thresholds between a good/fair/poor user experience.

Machine Experience Indicators

Indicator	Weight (%)	Good			Fair		Poor	
Login Delay : Time it takes to login (sec.) ?	20	0	<=	15	<=	60	<=	un
Application Load Time : Avg. startup time for applications (sec.) ?	20	0	<=	10	<=	30	<=	un
CPU Queue Length : Length of CPU queue at inspection time ?	10	0	<=	3	<=	6	<=	un
Memory Usage : Memory (RAM) % usage during inspection interval ?	10	0	<=	75	<=	90	<=	un
Page File Usage : Page file % usage during inspection interval ?	10	0	<=	10	<=	30	<=	un
Page Faults : Avg. page faults per second during inspection interval ?	10	0	<=	20	<=	50	<=	un
Non-Responding Applications : Number of unresponsive applications at inspection time ?	20	0	<=	2	<=	3	<=	un

I/O Experience Indicators

Indicator	Weight (%)	Good			Fair		Poor	
Disk Load : Avg. disk IO per second ?	25	0	<=	25	<=	50	<=	un
Disk Queue Length : Avg. length of disk queue(s) ?	25	0	<=	1	<=	3	<=	un
Network Latency : Avg. network roundtrip time (ms) ?	25	0	<=	150	<=	300	<=	un
Failed Connections : Number of outgoing connection attempts that failed ?	25	0	<=	5	<=	15	<=	un

Figure 12.12 Stratusphere UX default values

You can even recalculate user experience based on previous data that you've gathered. Look at the bottom of that page (see Figure 12.13), and note that there is a field to adjust the data based on previous dates.

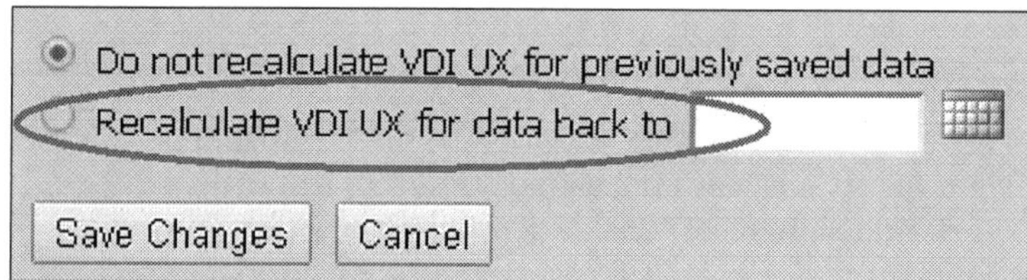

Figure 12.13 Recalculating user experience

Now, you can look at the various inspectors and see how your desktops are doing. There are multiple views within that section. To reach the various inspectors, click the Inspector tab and choose the live report you want to see, as shown in Figure 12.14. Depending on the report, you can choose to see it by machines, users, or applications, whichever makes sense for that inspector report.

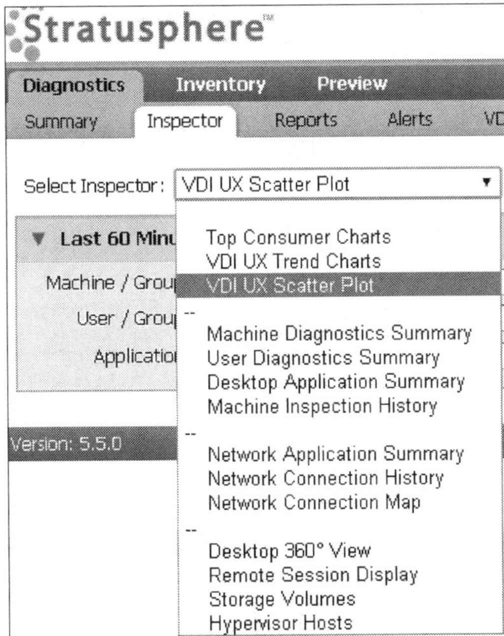

Figure 12.14 UX inspector reports

VMware vCenter Operations Manager

The last product we want to cover, which we found from our testing provides the most proactive monitoring solution, is vCOps. This solution is very good for monitoring virtual infrastructure and VMware Virtual Desktops. vCenter Operations Manager for View extends the functionality of vCenter Operations Manager Enterprise, and it enables IT administrators and help desk specialists to monitor and manage the health of the View VDI environments. vCenter Operations Manager for View is built on top of the vCenter Operations Manager Enterprise. Therefore, it includes the functionality of collecting performance data from monitored software and hardware resources in your enterprise and provides predictive analysis and real-time information about problems in your VDI. It presents data and analysis through alerts, in configurable dashboards, and predefined pages in the user interface.

VMware View–specific dashboards and resources are automatically configured when you install vCenter Operations Manager for View. These dashboards and resources, added as part of the vCenter Operations Manager for View installation and deployment, are preconfigured dashboards, resources, metrics, and alerts. As with vCenter Operations Manager Enterprise, you can customize your vCenter Operations Manager for View workspace. Depending on your access rights, you can add, delete, and arrange widgets on your dashboards, edit widget configuration options, and configure widget interactions.

vCenter Operations Manager for View incorporates the health ratings feature of vCenter Operations Manager Enterprise, which gives you a quick overview of the current state of a resource in your VDI environment. vCenter Operations Manager Enterprise uses an internally generated metric instead of the health badge used by vCenter Operations Manager Advanced. The vCenter Operations Manager Enterprise health score is calculated using resource metric anomalies and is best described as an indicator of how closely the resource is behaving to its "normal" observed behavior. If many resource metrics are outside their expected range, this is reflected in a lower health score.

vCenter Operations Manager for View is a solution built on top of the vCenter Operations Manager Enterprise platform, which enables you to monitor your VMware View environment.

The diagram in Figure 12.15 shows the relationship between vCenter Operations Manager Enterprise and the vCenter Operations Manager for View Adapter and their relationships with other vCenter Operations Manager for View VDI components.

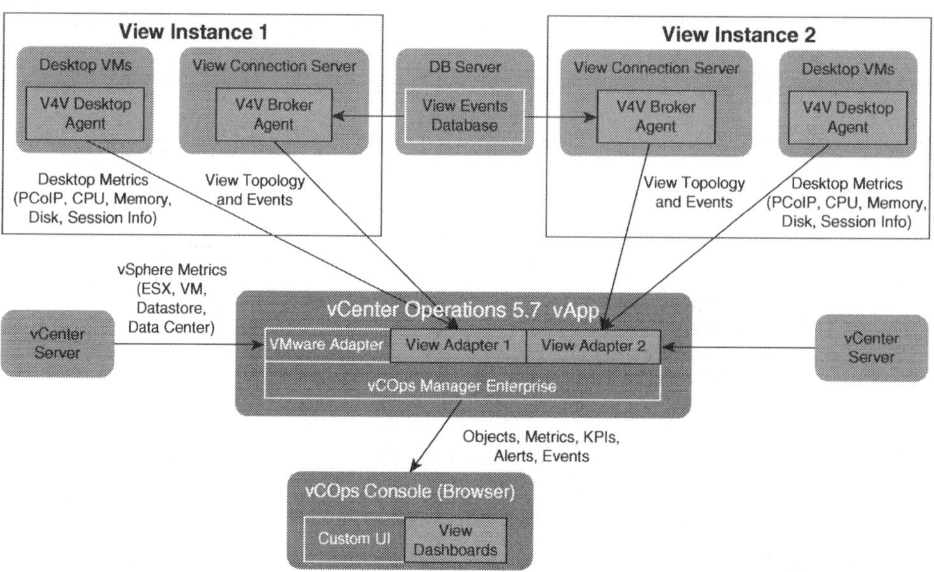

Figure 12.15 vCOps overview diagram

vCenter Operations for View uses the vCenter Operations Enterprise Version 5.7 platform to monitor a View environment. (View 5.0 or later is required.)

The two main components of the architecture are the vCenter Operations Manager VMs and the View Adapter. vCenter Operations Manager VMs are deployed as a vApp running on existing virtual infrastructure, and the View Adapter is installed as a separate installation step on the vApp (PAK file update). This combination of a single vCenter Operations

Manager vApp and a single vCenter Operations Manager for View Adapter is what constitutes a single vCenter Operations Manager for View *instance*.

The vCenter Operations Server pulls in the metrics from vCenter Server, while the View Adapter pulls in the metrics from the View desktops, View Connection Servers, and the View Events Database and feeds that information back to the vCenter Operations Server. The vCenter Operations Console presents all these metrics by connecting via a web browser. The View-specific information is displayed in a custom UI (https://<vcops-UI-VM-IP>/vcops-custom) based on vCenter Operations Manager Enterprise.

Figure 12.16 shows a logical presentation and the workflow of vCenter Operations Manager for View in a standard View infrastructure.

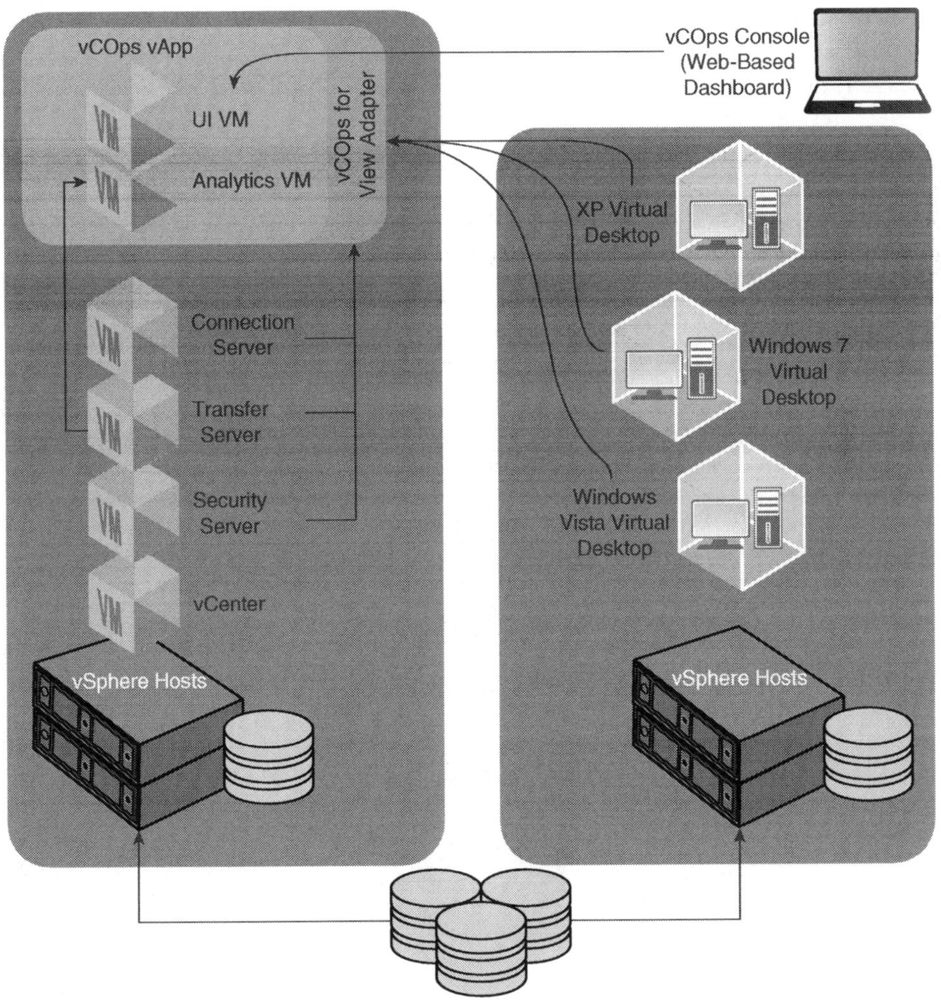

Figure 12.16 vCOps workflow

vApp Overview

The vCenter Operations Manager vApp consists of two VMs: the Analytics VM and the UI VM. The vCenter Operations Manager vApp is deployed in the View management block. The Analytics VM (by default) is provisioned with two vCPUs, 9 GB of memory, and 217 GB of storage space. The Analytics VM is responsible for collecting data from vCenter Server, vCenter Configuration Manager, and third-party data sources such as metrics, topology, and change events. The components within the Analytics VM are Capacity and Performance Analytics, Capacity Collector, File System Database, and Postgres DB.

The UI VM (by default) is provisioned with two vCPUs, 7 GB of memory, and 135 GB of storage space. The UI VM enables you to access the results of the analytics in the form of badges and scores using the web-based console. The applications in the UI VM are vSphere Web Application, Enterprise Web Application, and Administration Web Application. You can find more detailed information on the architecture and the individual components in the vApp in the *Deployment and Configuration Guide* for vCenter Operations Manager (https://www.vmware.com/pdf/vCOps-5-installation-guide.pdf).

vCOps for View Adapter

The vCOps for View Adapter is now integrated in the Analytics VM for the most part, and all you need to do is deploy the package to install the custom View dashboards in the environment. When the vCOps part is done, you still need to make sure that you deploy the broker agent on the View Connection Server and also make sure that your View desktops can talk correctly to the vCOps environment.

After you've downloaded that file, you must log in to your vCOps Admin environment and install the software through the update page by following these steps:

1. The URL for the Administration portal is https://<UI-VM>/admin/, where <UI-VM> is the IP address of the UI VM in the vCenter Operations Manager vApp.
2. On the Update tab, click **Browse** to locate the temporary folder, select the PAK file, and click **Open**, as shown in Figure 12.17.
3. Click **Update**, and click **OK** to confirm the update. The Administration user interface uploads the PAK file. The upload might take several minutes.
4. Read and accept the EULA, and click **OK**.

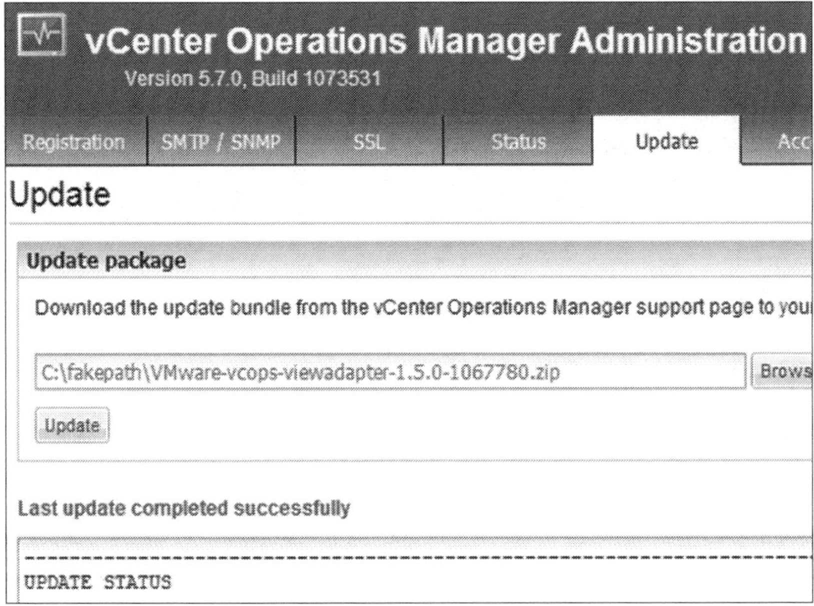

Figure 12.17 vCOps for View installation

5. Click **OK** to confirm and start the adapter installation process. The installation might take several minutes. Status information appears on the Update tab when the installation is finished.
6. Log in to the vCenter Operations Manager Custom user interface as an administrator. The URL format is https://<UI-VM>/vcops-custom/, where <UI-VM> is the IP address of the UI VM in the vCenter Operations Manager vApp.
7. Select **Admin, Support**.
8. On the Info tab, find the Adapters Info pane, and verify that the build number in the Adapter Version column for the V4V adapter matches the build number in the PAK file that you uploaded.

The vCenter Operations Manager for View Adapter is installed and ready for use.

NOTE The adapter installation process restarts the vCenter Operations Manager vApp. Data is not collected while the vApp is restarting.

The next step is to create an adapter instance to start collecting data. Log in to the vCOps custom dashboard with administrator privilege. Verify that the V4V adapter appears in the Adapter Info pane. Select **Admin**, **Support** on the vCenter Operations Manager menu. After you've confirmed that the V4V adapter is there, you need to create the adapter instance. To do this, follow these steps:

1. Select **Environment**, **Configuration**, **Adapter Instances**, as shown in Figure 12.18.

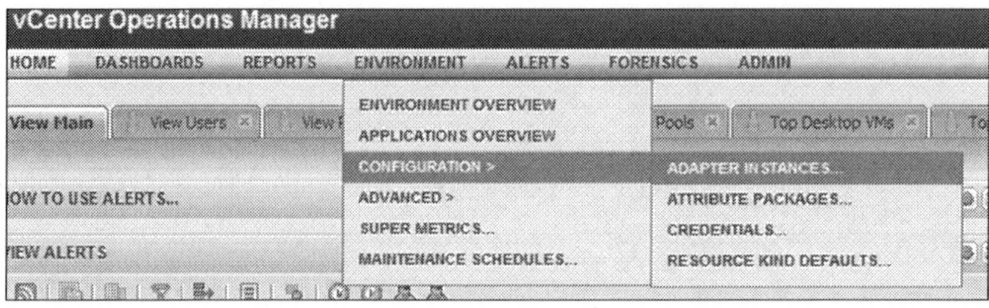

Figure 12.18 Adapter instance

2. From the Collector drop-down menu, select **vCenter Operations Server**.
3. From the Adapter Kind drop-down menu, select **V4V Adapter**, as shown in Figure 12.19.

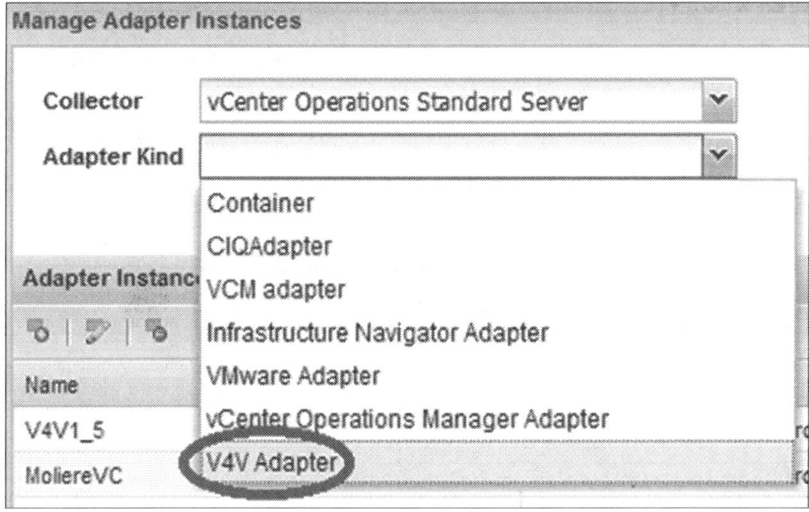

Figure 12.19 V4V adapter configuration

4. Click the **Add New Adapter Instance** icon shown in Figure 12.20.

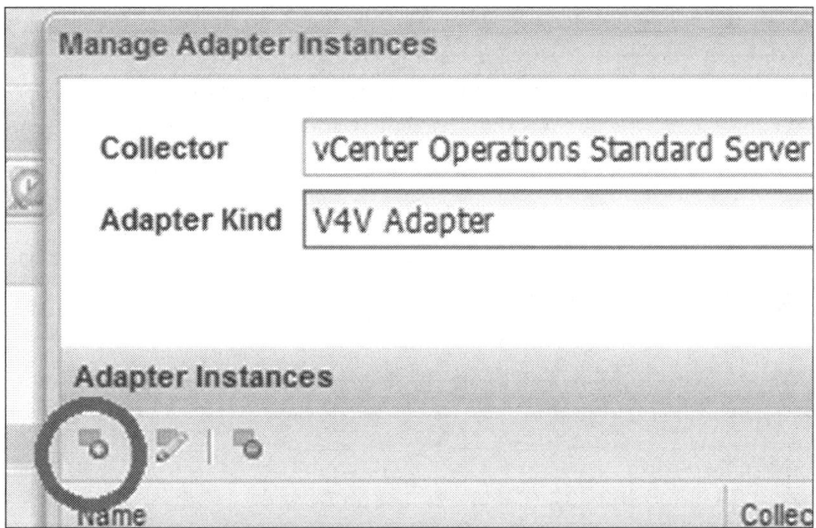

Figure 12.20 Adding a V4V instance

5. Type a name for the adapter instance.
6. From the Metric Set drop-down menu, select a set of metrics to be collected. Choose the Full set.
7. From the Credential drop-down, select the name of the credentials to use when the vCenter Operations Manager for View broker agent pairs with the adapter instance.

   When you create an adapter instance for the first time, the Credential drop-down is empty. You can click **Add** to create a server key password.
8. You must type the server key password in the broker agent configuration to allow pairing between the broker agent and the adapter. Pairing the broker agent with the adapter is an authentication step that ensures that the broker agent and the adapter know each other. Pairing must be finished to enable the broker agent and the desktop agents to communicate with the adapter.
9. Click OK to save the adapter instance.

Install the vCenter Operations Manager for View Broker Agent

You install the broker agent on one of the View Connection Servers in your View environment. The vCenter Operations Manager for View broker agent is a Windows service that carries out the connection between the vCenter Operations Manager for View adapter and the agent components on the View desktops. The broker agent collects the View inventory for the adapter, collects events from the database, and configures the desktop agents when used in View environments. You install the vCenter Operations Manager for View broker agent on one of the View Connection Server machines within a pod or a cluster. The broker agent is installed in the same folder as the View Connection Server. Only one broker agent must be installed in each View pod or cluster.

CAUTION Do not install the vCenter Operations Manager for View broker agent on View Security Server machines.

It is important to use a domain account with admin privileges to do this installation on the View Connection Server.

We are assuming here that we can install on a View Server, Version 5.2 or later. (This also means that you have a Windows 2008 R2 64-bit server running View.) If you have to use an older version of VMware View, refer to the vCOps for View installation guide.

1. Extract the broker agent installation file to a temporary folder on your View Connection Server. Look for this file on the VMware vCOps for View download page: VMware-v4vbrokeragent-x86_64-x.x.x-xxxxxx. (You will find the version number and build number in the name of the file.)
2. In the temporary folder, run the EXE file, accept the EULA, and click **Install**. (The installer does not provide configuration options.)
3. When the installation finishes, click **Finish**.

The vCenter Operations Manager for View Broker Agent configuration dialog box opens.

Configure the vCOps Manager for View Broker Agent

You configure the vCenter Operations Manager for View broker agent to connect to the vCenter Operations Manager for View Adapter, and to the database where View stores event data. You can also specify the desktop pools to monitor in vCenter Operations Manager. The vCenter Operations Manager for View Broker Configuration Wizard opens automatically at the end of the broker agent installation.

1. On the vCenter Operations Manager View Adapter page, type the IP address of the vCenter Operations Manager Analytics VM where the vCenter Operations Manager for View adapter runs, and type the port to use for the connection. (By default, port 3091 is used for communication with the adapter, but you can modify the port number depending on your network setup.)

2. You can check the IP address of the Analytics VM on the Status tab of the vCenter Operations Manager Administration portal.
3. Click **Pair** to pair the certificates of the broker agent with the adapter. You are prompted to type the server key that you specified when you configured the credentials for the adapter instance. Pairing the broker agent with the adapter is an authentication step that ensures that the broker agent and the adapter know each other. Pairing must be finished to enable the broker agent and the desktop agents to communicate with the adapter.
4. Click **Next**.
5. (Optional) If you have a previous version of vCenter Operations Manager for View, import the data collected by it.

NOTE You cannot import data at a later stage. If you choose to skip the data import, all data collected before the current installation will be lost.

6. Select **Migrate Data** from previous version check box, and click **Next**.
7. (Optional) Click **Browse** to locate the MetricBoundaryData.xml file, and then click **Next**.

vCenter Operations Manager uses the metric boundary data to determine the normal metric values in your environment. If you do not import the file, you might see abnormally high workload values until the new instance of View adapter calculates the normal values. The duration of the data-migration process depends on the size of the existing database and the topology of your environment.

1. If you have an Event Database set up in your View environment, type the credentials for the database in the Event DB text boxes, click **Validate** to verify the connection, and then click **Next**.
2. (Optional) To monitor specific View desktop pools in vCenter Operations Manager, check the **Specify Desktop Pools** check box, type the IDs of the pools in the text box, and click **Validate** to verify the connection. Use commas to separate multiple pool IDs.

NOTE If you do not specify pool IDs, vCenter Operations Manager for View monitors all desktop pools.

3. Review the summary of the broker agent configuration and click **Finish**.

4. The vCenter Operations Manager for View Broker Agent Settings dialog box appears to display the settings that you configured and the status of the broker agent service.
5. Verify that the service is running, and click **Close**.

The vCenter Operations Manager for View broker agent is installed and configured to run.

vCenter Operations for View: Adapter Tuning

In a VDI environment that manages a large number of remote sessions, you can modify a number of configuration settings. You can also monitor performance metrics to ensure proper functioning of the View Adapter. Ensure that data collection times are within an acceptable time range and are not exceeding collection intervals.

Data collection is divided into View topology collection, desktop metric collection, and View event collection. Each of these collection components runs on its own schedule independently of the others, and you can adjust their collection intervals separately. Monitoring collection performance is crucial when analyzing the scalability of a vCenter Operations Manager for View installation to ensure collection times for each component do not exceed collection intervals. Metrics built in to the View Adapter can be displayed in the vCenter Operations Manager console to monitor collection times and results. Refer to these collection times when you configure collection intervals.

Collection Intervals

By default, data is collected at 5-minute intervals. This interval is the standard for most vCenter Operations Manager metric adapters and should be the minimum configuration for all collection intervals. To improve scalability, you can increase collection intervals to accommodate the time required to collect data from more remote desktop sessions.

View Events Collection

View events are read and collected directly from the View Event Database. The interval used to collect View events is the same as that used to collect desktop metrics.

Event collection times are usually fast, and you should not need to change the collection interval even in large-scale environments. Use the View Events: Collection Time | Total (sec) metric to monitor how long collection is taking.

Monitoring View Adapter Performance

The View Adapter creates an application in vCenter Operations Manager for monitoring performance and behavior. This application contains View Collector resources that correspond to the desktop metrics, View topology, and View events collection components. Each View Collector resource has a number of metrics that you can use to monitor collection times, collection results, and other adapter behavior.

Monitoring collection times is the best way to judge the performance and scalability of vCenter Operations Manager for View. An additional PAK file is available that creates a dashboard that you can use to monitor adapter status and performance. Alternatively, you can view adapter performance by navigating to the View Adapter application listed on the Manager tab in the vCenter Operations Manager console.

vCenter Operations for View: Dashboards

Dashboards present performance data from monitored software and hardware resources in your enterprise and provide predictive analysis and real-time information about problems. Data and analysis are presented through alerts, in configurable dashboards, on predefined pages in the user interface. Depending on your access rights, you can add, delete, and arrange widgets on the dashboards, create new dashboards, and edit widgets and the configuration and interaction of widgets on your dashboards.

Each section of a dashboard is a widget. Each widget shows a specific type of data in a specific format. Each widget has a button bar at the top containing a number of icon buttons that perform actions on the selected data or control how the data is displayed.

Widgets include configuration options that you can edit to customize for your use. For example, you can select the metrics that the Alerts widget shows by editing its configuration. You can also configure widget interactions so that one widget, called a providing widget, provides information to another widget, called a receiving widget. For example, you can configure the Root Cause Ranking widget to receive data from the Tag Selector widget and the Health Status widget.

Main Dashboard

The View Main dashboard is used to visualize the end-to-end VDI environment, its underlying technology silos, and any alerts. The View Main dashboard is broken down into four sections:

- **VDI Environment Indicators:** Indicate the health of your VDI environment, broken down into categories such as overall VDI capacity used, connected and disconnected sessions, and so forth. This gives you a quick overview of how your overall VDI environment is behaving. vCenter Operations Manager for View presents information based on what it learns, what problematic behavior is normal, and what is outside of the metric ranges, based on previous behavior.

- **VDI Alerts:** The active alerts associated with VMware View–specific resources in your VDI environment display under VDI alerts. For example, for a particular client, you might see a certain percentage of packet loss, and you might want to find where that client is connecting from, such as from the Internet or intranet, and examine possible causes for the packet loss. You can double-click these icons to get more information and drill into each alert condition to troubleshoot the issue further.
- **VDI Health Tree:** Broken into six tiers, which represent the underlying technology silos supporting the VDI environment. Each tier is represented by an icon that you can double-click to drill down into for more information about that tier and its applications:
    - View Infrastructure
    - User Sessions
    - Network
    - Storage
    - View Clients
    - vSphere Infrastructure
- **VDI Tier Health:** Points the VI administrator to problem silos in the VDI environment, such as the storage tier. The VI administrator can examine the storage tiers in more detail by drilling into the datastores that are associated with the VMware View pools. If all the health indicators across the VDI Tier Health area are yellow or red, the health of the component data storage can affect the health of the entire tier, which the VI administrator can see by quickly reviewing these icons.

User Dashboard

The View Users dashboard is used to visualize and troubleshoot user-specific issues. For example, a VI administrator or help desk specialist would typically use this dashboard when a user calls the help desk/desktop specialist or IT operations teams or when there is a need to delve deeply into a specific user issue when troubleshooting other problems.

Top Session Dashboard

The View Top Sessions dashboard shows you a number of different metrics for pools or desktops, and which ones are exhibiting the longest times or have the worst performance.

The metrics displayed are as follows:

- Pool Capacity Used - Highest Last Month Average
- Pool Logon Times (sec) - Highest Last Hour Average

- Pool Reconnection Times (sec) - Highest Last Hour Average
- Pool PCoIP Latency (ms) - Highest Last Hour Average
- Desktop Logon Time (sec) - Highest Last Hour Average
- Desktop Reconnection Time (sec) - Highest Last Hour Average
- Desktop PCoIP Round Trip Latency - Highest Last Hour Average
- Desktop PCoIP Packet Loss (%) - Highest Last Hour Average
- Desktop PCoIP Throughput (Kbit/sec) - Highest Last Hour Average

Each of these widgets gives you the resources with the worst performance. For example, Desktop PCoIP Packet Loss gives you a ranking to get a quick view of how user desktops are performing in the area of PCoIP packet loss. You can drill down into a specific resource from this dashboard to the Details page for that resource. You can choose what types of metrics to display. You can choose from a number of configurations if you want to change what type of information is displayed and how it displays. Additional information is in the "Appendix" section of the vCOps for *View Integration Guide*.

Top Desktop VMs Dashboard

This dashboard is used to view the list of the top desktop VM consumers for a number of important indicator metrics. On this dashboard, you can quickly see which desktop VMs have the lowest health scores, the highest workloads, and which are using the most network bandwidth.

The View Top Desktop VMs dashboard shows you a number of different metrics for desktop VMs, and which ones are exhibiting the longest times or have the worst performance.

Each of these widgets shows you the resources with the worst performance. The View Top Desktop VMs dashboard collects similar information for the desktop VMs as the View Top Sessions dashboard. It collects metrics for CPU workload, critical alerts on the VMs, network workload, memory workload, and it averages those usage indexes over a selected period of time.

You can choose what types of metrics to display. You can choose from a number of configurations if you want to change what type of information is displayed and how it displays. Additional information is in the "Appendix" section of the vCOps for *View Integration Guide*.

View Pools Dashboard

The View Pools dashboard is used to assess the status of desktop VMs within View pools. To view statistics about the VMs and datastores contained in each View pool, select a configuration from the heat map in the upper left of the dashboard. You can use this dashboard to quickly identify and troubleshoot poorly performing VMs, VMs with high workload, or datastore capacity.

View Pool Statistics uses a heat map widget to show important information about the VMs and datastores used by View pools. Heat maps are an efficient way to show a large number of objects and quickly identify which objects may be experiencing problematic behavior. The View Pool Statistics heat map has a number of configurations showing the workload and health metrics for all desktops and datastores in View Pools. The VI administrator can select from among the following pool statistics configurations:

- VM Health
- VM Behavior
- VM Overall Workload
- VM CPU Workload
- VM Memory Workload
- VM Disk Workload
- VM Network Workload
- Datastore Health
- Datastore Overall Workload
- Datastore IO Workload
- Datastore Disk Space Available
- Datastore Demand
- Datastore Latency

You can choose what types of metrics to display. You can choose from a number of configurations if you want to change what type of information is displayed and how it displays. Additional information is in the "Appendix" section of the vCOps for *View Integration Guide*.

Desktop Sessions Dashboard

This dashboard is used to assess the PCoIP performance of VMware View clients connected to desktop VMs. To view PCoIP statistics related to View desktops and client network connections, select a configuration from the heat map in the upper left of the dashboard. Use this dashboard to quickly identify and troubleshoot poor View Client connection issues. You can quickly find issues such as increase in latency and other key measurements such as packet loss.

The View Desktop Sessions dashboard shows the following sections of metrics information:

- Active Desktop Statistics
- Object Metrics
- Alerts
- Object Tree

The Active Desktops Statistics heat map has a number of configurations showing health, workload, and PCoIP statistics for all currently connected user desktop sessions.

You can choose what types of metrics to display. You can choose from a number of configurations if you want to change what type of information is displayed and how it displays. Additional information is in the "Appendix" section of the vCOps for *View Integration Guide*.

View Adapter Status Dashboard

This dashboard is part of the standard View dashboards deployed with vCenter Operations Manager for View. You can use the View Adapter Status dashboard to monitor the performance of the View Adapter.

vCenter Operations for View: Alerting

vCenter Operations Manager generates an anomaly when a metric violates its threshold. If vCenter Operations Manager determines that the current combination of anomalies indicates a real problem, it generates an alert. An alert is a notification to inform you of an abnormal condition that might require attention.

An alert handler sends alert notifications. You can configure alert handler instances to send alert notifications as email messages or Simple Network Management Protocol (SNMP) traps or to save alert notifications in a log file. If you use EMC Smarts, you can configure an alert handler instance to send notifications to the SAMS Global Console. You can create an unlimited number of alert handler instances.

An alert handler instance sends alert notifications for all new, updated, and canceled alerts. If an attempt to send an alert notification fails, the handler continually retries the notification. After 5 minutes, if all alert notification attempts fail, the handler generates an administrative system alert and continues to retry the notification until it succeeds. Table 12.1 lists the common types of alerts and specifies the instances when they are sent.

Table 12.1 vCenter Operations for View: Alerting Handler Configuration

Attribute	Specification	Justification
SMTP Alert Handlers Enabled	Yes/No	SMTP alerts sent when thresholds met.
SNMP Alert Handlers Enabled	Yes/No	SNMP alerts sent when thresholds met.
Log File Alert Handler Enabled	Yes/No	Alerts written to log files.
SMTP Alert Handler Instance Names	TBD	Instance name(s) of alert handlers.
SMTP Alert – Host & Port	Host IP TBD – Port 25	SMTP host and port where alert will be sent.
SNMP Alert Handler Instance Names	TBD	Instance names(s) of alert handlers.
SNMP Alert – Host, Port & SNMP Community	TBD	SNMP community, host, and port where alert will be sent.
Log File Handler Instance Names	TBD	Instance name(s) of alert handlers.
Alert Output Folder	TBD	Type the log file path. The path must be on the vCenter Operations Manager Server. The complete path must be no longer than 50 characters. If the path is too long, vCenter Operations Manager cannot update the alert instance.
E-Mail Filtering Rule(s) Used	Yes/No	For vCenter Operations Manager vApp, edit the emailFilter.xml file on the second VM in the vApp. You can find additional information in the *vCenter Operations Administrator's Guide*.
E-Mail Template Definitions	Yes/No	For vCenter Operations Manager vApp, edit the emailFilter.xml file on the second VM in the vApp. You can find additional information in the *vCenter Operations Administrator's Guide*.
E-Mail Template Definition Name(s) & Associated Alerts Used with E-Mail Template	TBD	

Attribute	Specification	Justification
E-Mail Address used for sending SMTP Alerts	TBD	
File Reload Time for E-Mail Template Changes	30 Minutes (Default)	Number of minutes that vCenter Operations Manager waits before checking the emailFilter.xml file for changes. For vCenter Operations Manager vApp, edit the emailFilter.xml file on the second VM in the vApp. You can find additional information in the *vCenter Operations Administrator's Guide*.

vCenter Operations for View: Important Metrics

Table 12.2 provides a sampling of important metrics that should be reviewed in vCenter Operations for View to ensure a sound end-user experience.

Table 12.2 Sampling of Important Metrics in vCenter Operations for View

Resource	View Client
Metric	PCoIP | Round Trip Latency (ms).
Definition	Round-trip network latency between server and client.
Importance	Indicates a poor-quality connection between the View Client and desktop VM. May contribute to bad desktop responsiveness, slow screen refreshes, dropped connections.
Expected value	LAN connection should be less than 50 ms, WAN connections may exceed 200 ms. Values of over 250 ms may result in a poor user experience. Dynamic threshold breaches may indicate a problem with a View Client connection.
Resource	**View Client**
Metric	PCoIP | Receive Packet Loss Percent.
Definition	Percentage of received packets lost during the sampling period.
Importance	Packet loss can cause slower download and upload speeds, poor quality audio, pauses in streaming media, and so on.
Expected value	Value should be 0. Any value greater than 0 can cause degradation of the user experience.

Resource	**View Client**
Metric	PCoIP | Transmit Packet Loss Percent.
Definition	Percentage of transmitted packets lost during the sampling period.
Importance	Packet loss can cause slower download and upload speeds, poor quality audio, pauses in streaming media, and so on.
Expected value	Value should be 0. Any value greater than 0 can cause degradation of the user experience.
Resource	**View Client**
Metric	Network Interface|Packets Received Errors.
Definition	The number of inbound packets that contained errors preventing them from being deliverable to a higher-layer protocol.
Importance	
Expected value	Value should be 0.
Resource	**View Client**
Metric	Network Interface|Packets Sent Errors.
Definition	The number of packets that could not be transmitted because of errors.
Importance	
Expected value	Value should be 0.

Summary

Because a virtual desktop environment separates the relationship between desktops, the Windows operating system, and desktop applications, it is important to have accurate metrics that examine the real end-user experience. Few monitoring solutions aggregate all the information in a vSphere, View, and Workspace environment in a way that makes it simple to understand and enables you to react quickly when problems occur. No matter what solution you end up choosing, knowing the key metrics to observe and proactively monitor will ensure your deployment runs smoothly. vCenter Operations for View provides a comprehensive look at all the pieces, allowing you not only to see problem spots but also to plan for additional capacity and growth.

To make good use of this tool, you must ensure that, along with good visibility, you have defined roles and responsibilities within your IT organization for who supports what and at what level they support it. For example, it is quite common for server virtualization teams to be actively involved in architecting and deploying a VMware View environment because they already have a background in the underlying infrastructure. You want to take care, though, to ensure that the desktop support team is also trained on the management tools they will need to continue to support the desktop OS, applications, and end users. Having an end-to-end monitoring tool helps, but only if it is used in a way that complements both desktop and infrastructure support teams. Along with implementing vCenter Operations Manager, make sure that you carefully discuss how alerts flow and how issues are escalated when they occur.

I have seen virtual desktop deployments in which monitoring and support were not reviewed and discussed. When the desktops were virtualized and moved into the datacenter, the desktop team was not engaged early in the process. The desktop team felt that they did not have the necessary background or access to the tools to support the environment. The support load then fell to the server support team, who were not equipped to support end users. Along with integrating the tools, make sure that you integrate your teams to ensure that not only is the environment performing well but also that the support and service are provided.

Appendix A

A Design Questionnaire Worksheet

Session	Comments and Questions
EUC Strategy and Business/Technical Requirements Gathering	■ Does your company have a tactical or strategic EUC vision? ■ Does your company's IT and EUC vision align with the business goals of the company? ■ What are some of the pain points and challenges your IT group has, and how can a solid EUC vision and solution help? ■ Are your business units active stakeholders in IT projects? ■ Are you planning to build desktop or EUC as a service within your organization? ■ Are you building a service offering of "standard" desktops or aligning your service requirements based on specific business needs? ■ Are your requirements driven by the business? IT? Both? ■ Have you conducted an application rationalization and desktop assessment so as to better understand your user community and application needs? ■ Do you plan on having greater than 10,000 users? How does your strategy and design align for this type of growth?

Session	Comments and Questions
Design: User Community, Target Endpoint Devices, Peripherals, View Client Configurations, and Printing Support	■ Are you developing standards for supported endpoints? ■ Is BYOD part of your endpoint strategy? How does BYOD impact the rest of your design (network, security, and so on)? ■ Do you need to consider certain peripheral features if you are inside or outside the company? Do you restrict features as a "standard" and allow features on an approved exception basis?
Design: VMware View Desktop Design Considerations and Build Process Review	■ Do you have documented build processes for your image builds? ■ Are you using manual build processes or an automated desktop build process? ■ Do you have guidelines/operational procedures for updating or managing desktop base images?
Design: VMware View General Design	■ Are your design decisions tactical or strategic? ■ Do you have a standard set of design decisions, or are these driven by specific business unit needs?
Design: ESX Design Considerations, Tuning, and Optimization	■ Is the team responsible for VDI also responsible for vSphere? ■ Do you have a vSphere design specifically for VDI? ■ Do you think that the vSphere design and operating principles for VDI are *similar to* or *different from* server virtualization?
Design: Server Hardware	■ Is your hardware properly sized? ■ Do you plan for *oversubscription* of compute and storage resources for your VDI environment?
Design: vSphere Integration	■ Do you feel the vSphere design and operating principles for VDI are *similar to* or *different from* server virtualization?
Design: Application Integration and Distribution	■ Do you have an application virtualization strategy? ■ How do you plan to integrate applications into the desktop environment? ■ What level of integration do you plan on using with your existing electronic software distribution technology?
Design: Application Packaging Methodology Considerations	■ Do you have an application packaging team? ■ How does application virtualization play into the application packaging methodology in your organization? ■ Do you have UAT or application testing teams, testing plans, or other testing mechanisms for validating application packages?

Session	Comments and Questions
Design: Operational Support Policies/ Procedures	■ Do you think your organization can adapt to the operational changes needed for VDI, application virtualization, and EUC-based transformation? ■ Do you have any processes or procedures for image management? Change management? Incident management? ■ How do you plan on supporting VDI or other EUC service offerings? ■ Do you have SLAs for EUC services? How will they change with VDI? ■ Do you have a capacity management plan? ■ How do you plan to on-board new user communities onto VDI or application virtualization or other EUC services?
Design: Systems Monitoring and Management	■ Do you have a proactive monitoring strategy? ■ Does your monitoring strategy include capacity management? ■ How are you planning to monitor end-user experience and performance within the desktop?
Design: High Availability/ Clustering (VMware View-Focused)	■ What are the availability and resiliency requirements of your organization? ■ Do you have multiple datacenters? Are you considering an active/ active or active/passive design? ■ Does your design for active/active offer ideal application performance in *both* datacenters? Are your applications redundant, as well, and do they exist in both datacenters?
Design: Networking	■ Does your networking allow for VDI? ■ Do you have QoS/CoS/priority queuing? WAN optimization? ■ How are you measuring and monitoring network utilization and traffic patterns? ■ Are you planning to use multimedia within the desktop?
Design: Security	■ Are you applying physical desktop principles to your virtual desktops? ■ Are there any special requirements deemed necessary by your IT security teams? ■ Does your organization require forensic technology or data loss prevention within the virtual desktop? ■ What is your organization's data security policy, and how does it impact your EUC solution?

Session	Comments and Questions
Design: Directory Services and Group Policies	■ Do you have GPOs specific to your VDI environment? Have they been reviewed and adjusted to support VDI? ■ How are you planning to delineate virtual desktops from physical desktops and endpoints in AD?
Design: Storage	■ How are you sizing your storage and capturing the requirements needed for IOPS and other storage-related elements? ■ Does your storage design align with the needs of your organization? ■ Is your storage designed to scale out/scale up? ■ Are your desktop workloads sharing storage with other server workloads? ■ Is Persona management and home directories considered in your storage design? ■ Have you considered other storage alternatives (ILIO, SSD, stateless, tiered (auto/manual), and so on)?
Design: User and Application Data	■ Are your desktops close to your user data and applications? ■ Do the applications used in your organization have Persona and/or other dependent needs? ■ Can your applications operate in a persistent or nonpersistent desktop environment?
Design: User Profile/Persona Management	■ Does your organization require that desktop personalization settings be kept? ■ Do you need third-party Persona solutions (that is, the ability to move between XP and Windows 7)? ■ How are you measuring and capturing the needs of Persona to properly size the solution?
Design: Testing/ Validation	■ Do you have a testing/validation environment for testing changes and adjustments to your EUC solution? ■ Do you have a process or testing/validation area to capture performance statistics for new user communities?

Session	Comments and Questions
Design: Authentication and Access	■ Is BYOD a requirement? How does this impact your access methods (dirty VLAN for BYOD)? ■ Is two-factor authentication required? ■ Is there a VPN in use today? Will VPN be considered (SSL, IPsec, DTLS), or is remote access being replaced by other technologies? ■ Does the access method have enough capacity to handle the necessary user traffic?
Design: Backup/ Recovery	■ Do you have a plan to back up and routinely test recovery of key VDI and other EUC elements? ■ Are you backing up key data areas, including DBs, user and application data, and so on?
Design: Disaster Recovery and Business Continuity	■ How does VDI integrate into your DR strategy? ■ Are your applications also part of your DR strategy? ■ Where are desktops in the DR process? Before or after applications? ■ Does your architecture account for DR recovery in a third-party DR site? Alternate datacenter? ■ Is your DR equipment actively used in your production environment? Does it work at a full, operational, or degraded state in the event of DR? ■ Does other dependent infrastructure (network, storage, compute, and so on) account for a business continuity event (for example, snow day) and allow for proper and acceptable use?
Design: Performance Benchmarking and Scalability Testing	■ How do you plan to test your solution and dependent infrastructure at scale? ■ Do you have a scalability and functional testing strategy?
Design: ThinApp Operational Support Policies/Procedures	■ Have you considered the operational impact of ThinApp or application virtualization on your current support model? ■ Does your support and operational policies/procedures change because of application virtualization? ■ Is your staff ready to support a virtualized application?

Session	Comments and Questions
Design: Support and Training	■ Is your staff ready to support a virtualized application, virtual desktop, or other service offered in your EUC vision? ■ How does your support model integrate with EUC services? ■ How are issues classified and routed within your organization? ■ Do you have SLAs? How do they match up to issue severity and time to resolution?
Design: ThinApp Testing and Validation Process	■ How do you test applications? ■ Who owns testing and remediation? ■ Who owns testing plan development and application functionality validation?
Design: ThinApp Packaging Standards	■ Do you have packaging standards established for physical applications? How do they change for virtualized applications? ■ How do you determine which standards best suit your organization? ■ Do your application owners package the applications, or is this done by an application packaging team or other team?

Appendix B

VMware View Network Ports

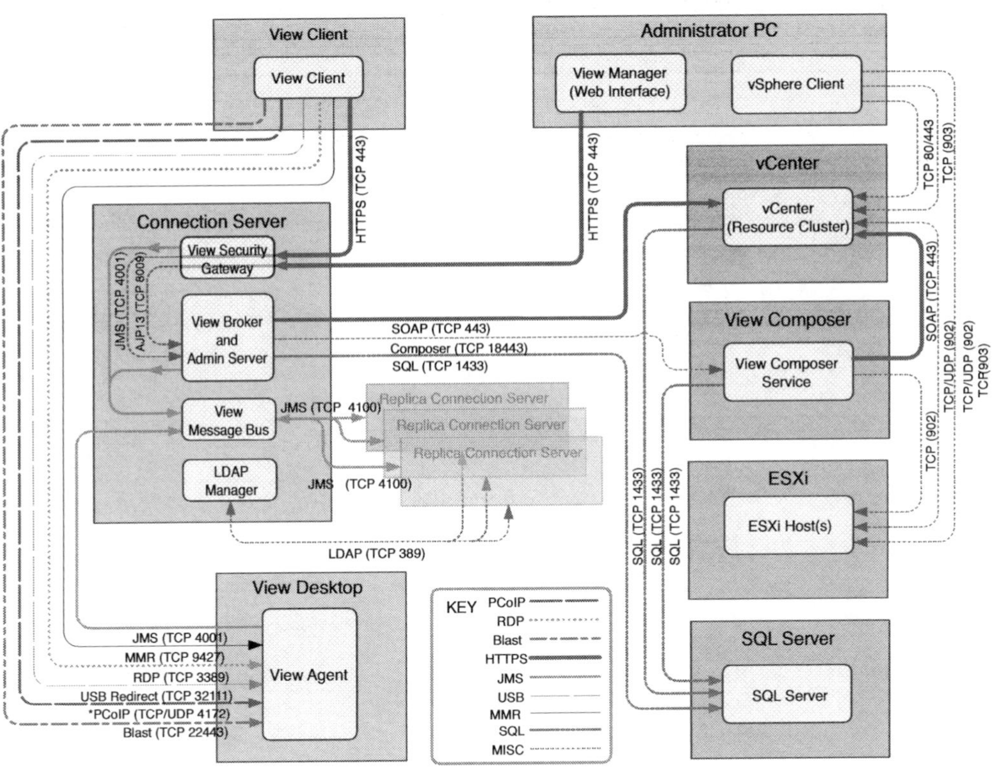

* PCoIP – TCP is only View Client > View Agent. UDP is both directions

All Port numbers are default port numbers and may differ per environment

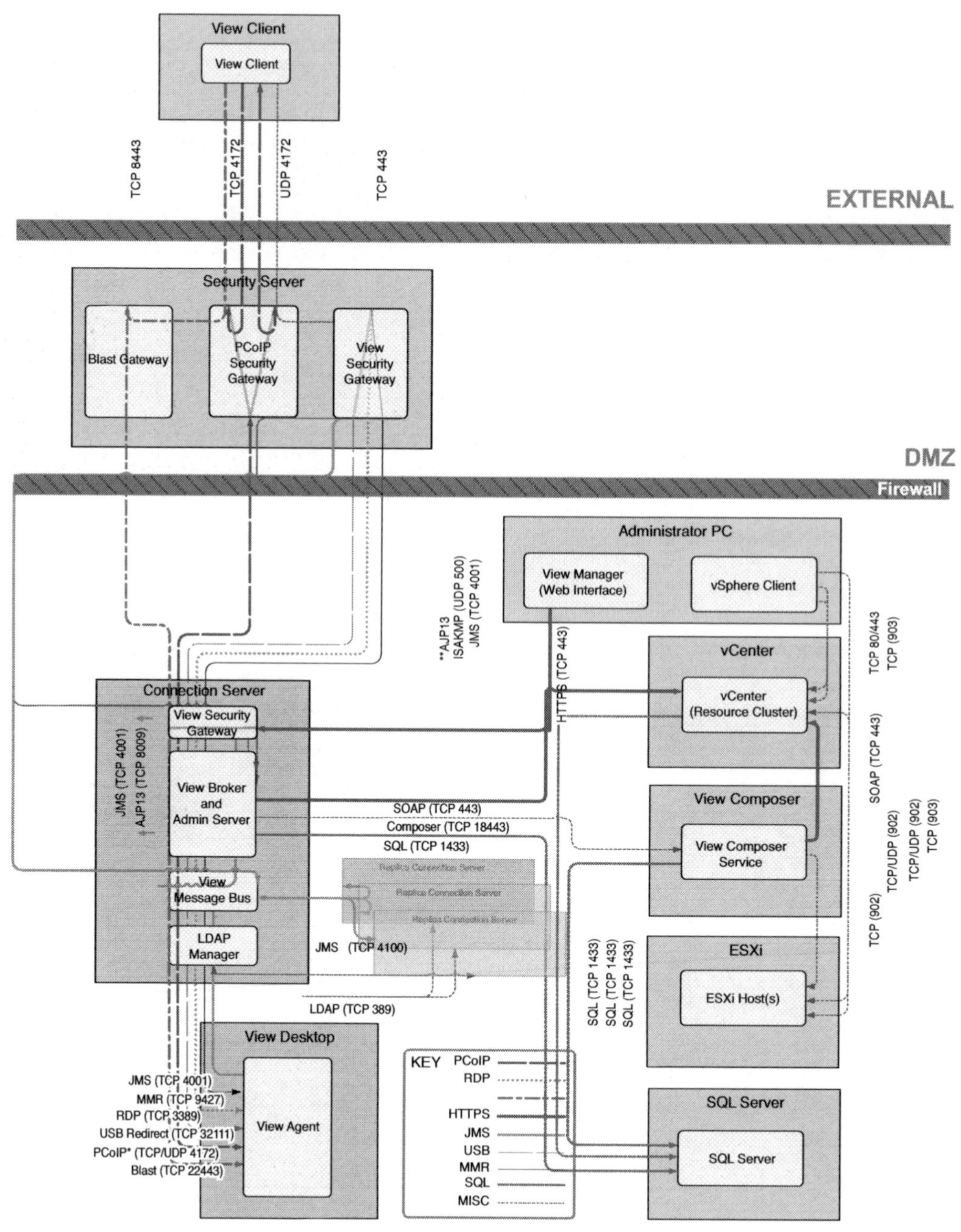

* PCoIP – TCP is only View Client > View Agent. UDP is both directions
**AJP13 – No IPSec = AJP13 over TCP 8009
IPSec, no NAT = AJP13 over ESP (Protocol 50)
IPSec, with NAT = AJP13 over ESP over UDP 4500

All Port numbers are default port numbers and may differ per environment

Index

Symbols

A

B

C

D

E

F

G

H

I

J

K

L

M

N

O

P

Q

R

S

T

U

V

W

X-Y-Z

vmware PRESS

VMware® Horizon Suite

Building End User Services

Paul O'Doherty
Stephane Asselin

FREE Online Edition

Safari Books Online

Your purchase of ***VMware Horizon Suite*** includes access to a free online edition for 45 days through the **Safari Books Online** subscription service. Nearly every VMware Press book is available online through **Safari Books Online**, along with thousands of books and videos from publishers such as Addison-Wesley Professional, Cisco Press, Exam Cram, IBM Press, O'Reilly Media, Prentice Hall, Que, and Sams.

Safari Books Online is a digital library providing searchable, on-demand access to thousands of technology, digital media, and professional development books and videos from leading publishers. With one monthly or yearly subscription price, you get unlimited access to learning tools and information on topics including mobile app and software development, tips and tricks on using your favorite gadgets, networking, project management, graphic design, and much more.

Activate your FREE Online Edition at informit.com/safarifree

STEP 1: Enter the coupon code: NQRKWWA.

STEP 2: New Safari users, complete the brief registration form. Safari subscribers, just log in.

If you have difficulty registering on Safari or accessing the online edition, please e-mail customer-service@safaribooksonline.com

Cisco Press

Made in the USA
Lexington, KY
23 January 2018